MONUMENTAL INSCRIPTIONS

IN

BARBADOS.

STOKVIS STUDIES IN
HISTORICAL CHRONOLOGY
AND THOUGHT
ISSN 0270-5338
Number 13

Monumental Inscriptions

Tombstones of the Island of Barbados

by Vere Langford Oliver

With a New Introduction by Michael Burgess

BORGO PRESS / WILDSIDE PRESS

www.wildsidepress.com

*   *   *   *   *   *   *

Copyright © 1989, 1995 by The Borgo Press

Library of Congress Cataloging-in-Publication Data

Oliver, Vere Langford.
    [Monumental inscriptions in the churches and churchyards of the island
of Barbados, British West Indies]
    Monumental inscriptions : tombstones of the island of Barbados /
[compiled] by Vere Langford Oliver ; introduction by Michael Burgess. —
New Borgo ed.
        p. cm. (Stokvis studies in historical chronology and thought, ISSN
0270-5338 ; no. 13)
    Originally published: The monumental inscriptions in the churches and
churchyards of the island of Barbados, British West Indies. 1st Borgo ed.
San Bernardino, Calif. : Borgo Press, 1989.
    Includes index.
    ISBN 0-89370-811-9 (cloth). — ISBN 0-89370-911-5 (pbk.)
    1. Barbados—Genealogy. 2. Epitaphs—Barbados. 3. Barbados—His-
tory—Sources. 4. Cemeteries—Barbados. I. Title. II. Series.
CS261.B3O44 1995   94-36625
929'.5'0972981—dc20   CIP

NEW BORGO EDITION

Preface.

THE following monumental inscriptions were copied by the Editor, during his visit to Barbados, in the winter of 1913-14.

They comprise all those in the churches and churchyards, but not those in dissenting chapels or modern cemeteries.

About 100 of the oldest Jewish inscriptions have been also included.

A few notes have been given, but the addition of many more would have delayed publication.

Every facility was afforded him by the Bishop and clergy, the former of whom, during a very long residence in the West Indies, has made an extensive collection of notes on the ecclesiastical history of his diocese, which his Lordship hopes, when he has leisure, to sort and print.

The Editor therefore, not wishing to encroach on Bishop Swaby's research work, confined his attention to the church memorials.

A collection of these, down to the year 1750, with a selection of those of a later period, was made by Capt. Lawrence Archer, when quartered in the Island, as he tells us, for a short period in 1857-8, and this appeared in his well-known quarto volume published in 1875.

Several of those inscriptions recorded by him are no longer to be seen, so that his collection is still invaluable, and in no way depreciated by the appearance of this present volume.

His MS., which he presented in 1860 to the British Museum (Add. MS. 23,608), should be consulted, as it contains many notes not in his book.

The churches throughout the Island are scrupulously clean and better attended to than most in England, the absence of glass windows and free current of wind keeping them very fresh and sweet. The churchyards are all walled in and well looked after.

The absence of frost has tended to preserve the marble slabs in the burial-grounds, but the prevalence of hurricanes and earthquakes has, on the other hand, helped to crack and destroy the tablets and slabs inside the buildings.

The well-executed armorial work on so many of the old blue marble slabs is evidence of English origin, but a certain number of the later plain marble tablets were cut locally.

Barbados, first settled about Feb. 1626-7, is the only island in the Caribbean Sea which has remained uninterruptedly in English possession. Its position so far to windward : its distance from any French naval base : and the great number of its fighting men, all conducing to its freedom from attack. It still enjoys a free elective House of Assembly presided over by its Speaker.

James Town, now called Hole Town, was founded in 1626-7 by Sir William Courteen's men, and Bridgetown in 1628 by the Earl of Carlisle's settlers. In 1629 Gov. Sir William Tufton created six parishes : Christ Church, St. Michael, St. James, St. Thomas, St. Peter, and St. Lucy.

In a deed of 1639 in the local Record Office I saw the signatures of the Council and Assembly, and it has been stated that there were then (as now) eleven parishes. In a deed of 25 Feb. 1640 Governour Henry Huncks "ordered ye church of St. George to pay 10,000 lbs. in May next 1641 to the parish of St. Michael, otherwise St. George to belong as formerly to St. Michael." In Lygon's "History," of which the first edition was issued in 1657 and the second in 1673, is an ancient map, probably by Captain John Swanne, who signed as surveyor in 1639 and several years later, on which are given the names of the settlers and four churches drawn, viz. : St. Peter's, St. James, St. Michael and Christ Church. Lygon describes how he himself superintended the cutting of " Church wayes " through the woods, using a compass in places. In 1645 many Royalists arrived after the battle of Naseby, and took a prominent part in affairs, until the colony submitted on good terms to Ayscue.

The first local Act is dated 1648, the earlier ones having been lost or burnt. The government continued to be proprietary under the Earls of Carlisle until the Restoration. By Act No. 18 of 1661 five precincts for courts were formed :—

    1. Christ Church and St. Philip.
    2. St. Michael, St. George and St. John.
    3. St. Thomas and St. James.
    4. St. Peter, All Saints and St. Lucy.
    5. St. Andrew Overhills and St. Joseph.

By another Act of that year it was ordered that registers were to be kept by the Minister, who was to send a certificate of the entries into the Secretary's office in March yearly, there to remain a record.

Marriage licences were always issued by the Governor, but I have never seen any record of them in the W.I., and the Colonial Secretaries have always stated that they had none.

A few years ago the Legislature ordered Transcripts of all parish registers to be made and deposited in the local Record Office, where there is also a complete general Index for the whole of the parishes.

The Hurricane of 1831 destroyed seven parish churches, viz., those of Christ Church, St. Philip, St. John, St. Joseph, St. Lucy, St. Peter and St. Thomas, also six chapels of ease.

In view of the inevitable recurrence of such disastrous visitations, it is the more essential to copy and print church memorials, serving as they do to remind us of many past worthies who did their share in building up the British Empire. *Quorum animabus propicietur deus.*

Oct. 1915.   V. L. OLIVER.

INTRODUCTION

A Monumental Work

Barbados's importance to American genealogists, and to researchers specializing in the pre-Revolutionary War history of Virginia and the Carolinas, has only truly been appreciated in the last two decades, with publication of a series of widely-distributed Barbados parish registers and other documents. Although discovered by the Portuguese in the sixteenth century (who named it for the fig trees which covered the island), Barbados was claimed and settled by the English as early as 1605, and certainly by 1627. The warm, gentle climate spurred the growth of huge sugar plantations, worked by slaves imported from Africa; and the island's relative isolation from the rest of the West Indies helped protect it from incursions by the French and Spanish warships. Exports of sugar and molasses kept money, colonists, and Blacks pouring into the New World.

These exports were shipped both to England, the mother county, and to the British colonies in North America, particularly the southern colonies, who sent back tobacco in return. With the active trade which soon developed, many of the farmers and workers (and slaves) who had originally immigrated to Barbados found themselves moving on to the broader vistas of mainland America. Thus, Barbados became almost a way-station for transportation to the Virginias and Carolinas, particularly in the period from 1650-1750; and the knowledgeable researcher can often find links between families recorded in Barbados records and their later cousins in the American South.

Oliver's transcription of Barbados church tombstones is little-known in the United States, having been privately published in England in an edition of only 200 copies. The Borgo Press edition is the first publication of these records in over sixty years, and we are proud to make this pioneering work available once again to American historians and genealogists.

—Michael Burgess
San Bernardino, California
July 15, 1989

MONUMENTAL INSCRIPTIONS

IN

BARBADOS.

ST. MICHAEL'S CATHEDRAL.

In the cross walk running from the south to the north porch are the following fifteen ledgers :—

1. Here lies the Body of | ROBERT HOOPER Esq. | late Attourney Generall | of this Island who | departed this life the 24 | of July 1700: aged fourty | three Years.

Almost certainly identical with Robert Hooper, son of Robert Hooper of L., gent., of Hart Hall, matric. 15 Oct. 1674, aged 16, perhaps bar.-at-law, Gray's Inn, 1684, as son of Robert of Sarum, Wilts, esq., deceased. (Foster.)

1700, July 26. Robt Hooper, Esq., in church.

1749, June 13. Reylond Hooper Esq^{ie}.

1754, Oct. 19. R. Hooper Esqr. (Burial Register.)

The pedigree of Tho. Hooper of Sarum was entered in the Visitation of Wilts Anno 1623. Robert his son was then dead s.p.

See his monument, No. 59.

---

2. The lettering is so sharp it must have been lately recut :—

UNDERNEATH THIS STONE ARE | DEPOSITED THE REMAINS | OF M^{RS} DOROTHY FRERE MOORE | WIFE OF EDWARD HENRY MOORE | AND DAUGHTER OF THE LATE | CHOLMELEY WILLOUGHBY ESQ. | SHE DEPARTED THIS LIFE | ON THE 6TH JULY 1819, AGED 32 YEARS | AND WAS PLACED BY THE SIDE OF | HER ELDEST SON FRANCIS HENRY | WHO DIED 15TH NOV. 1816, AGED 10 YEARS. (15 lines.)

1853, Dec. 27. At Westbourne-green, aged 60, Mary, relict of John Hodson, of the Audit Office, Somerset Ho., & niece of the l. Wm. Moore, Attorney Gen· of B. ("G.M.," 1854, p. 221.)

---

3. Sacred to the Memory | of JOHN HUMPLEBY Esquire | Who | In the 41st Year of his Age | Fell the Victim | of a Violent and Dreadful Malady. | He departed this transitory life | on the 28th of January 1814. (2 lines.)

The remainder is under a pew.

1814, Jan. 28. In Barbados, John Humbleby, esq. many years a respectable merchant in that island. ("G.M.," 408.)

---

4. Much cracked and cemented :—

THE | . . EPULCHR . | OF | . . . LIAM OXLEY | . . . . PTEMBER 1815.

1817, Dec. 2. Yesterday Miss Sarah, youngest dau. of Wm. Oxley Esq. of this town. ("Barbados Mercury.")

B

5. On a small square stone :—

.... OB KOPLEE (*sic*) ob | Augt 26th 1722 | Aged 56 | Years.

1722, Aug. 26. Mr Jacob Kopkee in Church. (Burial Register.)
Archer gives the age as 36 and the name Kopkee.

---

6. Nearly all obliterated :—

HERE LIES . . . BODY OF | CAPT. D . . . | DEPARTED THIS LIFE | (1 line
worn away) | . . . . BODY OF | (2 lines worn away | . . . . OF OCTOB^R |
1673.

Archer gives "Capt John Moody d. 1673," which may perhaps be this one.

The above six are up to the crossing in centre.

---

7. At the centre, nearly worn away :—

HEER LYES THE BODY | M. MARY MILLES, WIFE OF IOHN | MILLES . . . . |
CVSTEMES IN THIS ISLAND WHO | DEPA . . . . | SEPT . . . . | ABOVT.

Archer gives "Mary Miles, wife of John Miles . . . . d. . . . . 1695."
See gift of a silver bason by Mr. John Milles recorded in List of 1684.
1673, Aug. 25. Mary Mills. (Burial Register.)
1667, April 11. Mr John Mills & Mrs Mary Howard.

---

8. Of Lt Coll^o IOHN MERRING Efq | one of the Barons of her Matie |
Hono^{ble} Court of Excheco^r and | for Many years one of ye Com- | mifsion of y^e
Peace In this Ifland | of Barbados who Dyed ye 28 of | Auguft 1710 Aged about
49 | years.

1710, Aug. 28. Lt Coll^o Jno Merring, Esqr, in church. (Burial Register.)

---

9. CREST.—*Out of a coronet an animal's head over wreath and helmet.*
ARMS.—*Quarterly,* 1 *and* 4, *An inescutcheon between six mullets ;* 2 *and* 3,
A chevron between three escallops [CHAMBERLAINE]; *impaling: Between two
bendlets engrailed three covered cups* [BUTLER].

Here lyes interred the body | of the Honourable Colonel | EDWARD CHAM-
BERLAINE one of | His Majesties Councill of this | Ifland, who was borne in the |
County of Leicester in | England, who married MARY | ye daughter of EDWARD
BVTLER | of Stratfoold in ye County of | Bedford Esq. hee departed | this life y^e
23 of Iuly 1673 | Aged 50 years.

1673, July 24. Coll: Edwd Chamberlain in the Church.
1678, Aug. 19. Edw. Chamberlaine, Esq , in Ch.
1696, Dec. 1. Mrs Eliz. Chamberlaine.
1711-12, March 22. Mrs Tankerville Chamberlaine, Spinster, in ye Church.
(Burial Register.) See "Caribbeana," iii., 46.
A pedigree of Chamberlaine was recorded in the Visitation of Leicestershire,
1619, and of Butler or Boteler in that of Bedfordshire. There were several
Butlers merchants of this island. George, will dated 1676 (37, Hale); Jacob, will
dated 1669 (45, Penn); Jeffry, will proved 1662 (151, Laud). See the Registers
of St. Nich. Aćon., London.

10. A baron's coronet over Crest: *A bull's head.*

Here lieth the Body | of LORD CLARINA | who departed this life at Barbados | after an illness of six days.

(The remainder of the very lengthy inscription has been worn away by the passage of many feet.)

1810, Jan. . . At Barbadoes Nathaniel William Massy, Lord Clarina, Baron Clarina of Elm, a major-general in the army. His Lordship was born May 23, 1773 . . . . had been appointed to a command in the W.I., but was seized shortly after his arrival at Barbadoes with a malignant fever, which proved fatal after an illness of three days, etc. ("G.M.," 384. See also a long notice in the "Barbados Mercury," "Caribbeana," ii., 87.)

11. Very worn :—

Sacred | to the Memory of | JAMES BOWDEN ESQ^R | Merchant | of the City of LONDON | who died in this Island | on the 4 March 1821 | Aged . . . 1 Years.

1821, March 5. James Bowden. (Burial Register.)

I wrote first of all doubtfully 1 March 1824, whereas the correct date was 4 March 1821, thus proving how difficult it often is to distinguish between 1 and 4.

12. A brownish stone :—

. . . . RED | to the Memory of | ISABELLA | *Wife of* | . . . . Gen Charles |. Who died 25 Feb : 18 . . | Aged 32 Years.

13. In fine condition :—

CREST.—*An eagle (?) with wings raised over W. and H.* ARMS.—*On a chief a lion passant.* Archer gives the field as Ermine.

Here lyes Interr'd the Body of | MR WILLIAM GODMAN Merch^t | Son of the Revd MR HENRY GODMAN | of the KINGDOM of great BRITTAIN | who departed this life the firft | day of AUGUST 1710 Aged 37 years | and Resident in this | ISLAND 22 years.

1710, Aug. 2. Mr Wm Godman merch^t. (Burial Register.)

14. A very worn stone :—

Here lie the Remains | of | Samuel Larocque Bruce | . . . . Dr. 99 | in the Year of his Age | he died. | (About seven more lines illegible.)

1799, May 18. Samuel Laroque Bruce. (Burial Register.)

Son of the Hon. Joseph Osborne B., a Judge of Barbados, by Jane Barwick his wife, and brother of Barwick B., M.D.

15. Very large stone, the space left for arms being blank :—

Lieu: Coll° CHRISTº JACSON | Efq) lies here Vnderneath | Interred who Departed | this life the 9th Day of | January 169⅚ in | the 37th yeare of his Age.

1695-6, Jan. 10. Lt : Coll : Christopher Jackson.

1710, Oct. 18. Thomas Jackson Esqr, Provost Marshal.

1736, Aug. 2. Coll° Christ° Jacson. (Burial Register.)

Eliz. Jackson of B., wid. of Capt. John J. Will dated 5 May 1662. To be bur. in X^t Ch. near husband. Cousins Freres. Proved 21 March 1666 (38, Carr).

16. Proceeding from the centre down the central walk to the west porch. Helmet, no crest, mantling.

ARMS.—*Argent, on a chevron five horseshoes, points downwards.*

HERE LYETH Y^E BODY OF | MR EDWARD CRISP MARCH^T: OF THIS | PLACE
Y^E ELDEST SONN OF NICHO: | CRISP MARCH^T IN BRED STREET IN | LONDON IN Y^E
KINGDOM OF ENGLAND | HEE DEPARTED THIS LIFE Y^E 14TH OF | IENVARY 1678
AGED 50 YEARS | AS ALSO | THE BODY OF MR THOMAS YEATS WHO | DEPARTED
THIS LIFE UPON THE 2^D | DAY OF MARCH IN THE YEAR OF OUR | LORD 168½ | AS
ALSO | THE BODY OF M^{RS} MARY YEATS WIFE TO | THE ABOVE MENTIONED PERSONS
SHE | DEPARTED THIS LIFE THE 25TH DAY OF | AUGUST IN THE YEARE OF OUR
LORD 1682.

1678-9, Jan. 15. Mr Edward Crisp in Ch :
1679-80, March 7. Mr Jno Crisp in Church.
1680. March 25. Margrett ye D^a of M^r Jno & Sarah Crisp.
1680, Dec. 27. Mrs Sarah Crisp.
1681, Dec. 13. Mrs Jane Crisp in ye Ch :
1684, Dec. 12. The old Mr Jno Crisp in Ch :
Tho. Crispe from Barbados, merch^t, was of Eltham, co. Kent, in 1656.
The Hon. Sam. Crisp of Barbados was dead in England March 1695.
Major Joseph Crisp of St. Kitts buried his 1st wife, Sybella Jordan, sister-in-law
of Sir Fra. Morton of Nevis in St. Mildred, Bread Street, 5 May 1679. See the
Visitation of London and " History of the Crispe Family."
1681-2, March 3. Mr Tho : Yeats, in ye Ch.
1682, Aug. 26. Mrs Mary Yates (blot between Y. and a). (Burial Register.)
1656, Aug. 13. Tho. Yate of Bristol, merch^t, power of att^y to my brother
Richd Y., merch^t, now in Barbadoes. I am partner with Wm. Thomas, Esq., in
a plantation. (Deeds, vol. ii., 515.)
Mrs. Margaret Tovey of Nevis (will proved 1725) was sister of Robt Yate,
Esq., of Bristol.

---

17. *Omihi Curarum requies dilecta mearum* | *Fida*, *Parens*, *Conjux Spes
et Alumne Laris* | *Accipe Chara Comes noftri monvmenta dotoris* | *Hic tibi
perpetuo tempore vivet amor.* | *Exuviæ MARIÆ Vxoris ED: CHEARNLEY* |
2° Decembris Anno 1723.

1723, Dec. 3. Mrs Mary Chearnley wife of Capt Edward Chearnley, in the
Chancel.
1731, Aug. 22. Coll^o Edward Chearnley in the Chancel. (Burial Register.)

---

18. Alongside No. 17, its north edge being under a pew, and the surface
cracked and cemented. Shield with festoon encircling it.
ARMS.— *A cross moline charged with a mullet*, impaling, *In fess between two
barrulets wavy three lambs, and in chief two crosses potent, each ensigned with an
annulet.* No crest. Archer gives a third cross in base and bulls for lambs.

Here lyeth *Interr'd* the . . . . | of A[G]NIS WARD the [wife of] . . . . |
IOSEPH WARD *Merch* . . . | departed this Life the [12th] | . . . . *January 1713*
Aged . . . . | And three *M* . . . . | Here lyeth Interr . . . Bod . . . . | IAMES
P[EMB]E[RT]ON of this . . . . | *Merchant* . . . ho departed . . . . | the [29] . . y
of Iune 1736 and . . . . | . . . . 5th Year of his AGE.

The portions within brackets are from Archer.
1713, Jan. 23. Mrs Agnes ye wife of M^r: Joseph Ward Merch^t in Church.
1736, June 30. Mr James Pemberton. (Burial Register.)
His age on the stone was probably 35 or 55.
1781, June 2. At Putney, Tho. Ward, esq ; a B'es merchant. (" G.M.,"
294.)
1839, April 8. In Bernard-st., Henry T. Ward of B. (*Ibid.*, 553.)

---

19. A pew covers the left edge :—

..... our Children Sons of | .... AS and MARY WITHERS | ... ie Here Interred | .. e above mentioned MARY | .... THO^s WITHERS *Merch^t* who | .. ed this life *Feb^{ry}* the 15th 1735 | *Aged* 43 Years.

1735, Feb. 19. Mrs Mary Withers wife of Thomas Withers Esqre in the church. A Sermon. (Burial Register.)

20. Alongside No. 19. A pew covers the right edge :—

Here lieth Interr'd the .... | of ROBERT MOORE .... | who departed this L .... | the 8th day of September .... | in the 37th Year of hi ....

21. There are here three stones adjoining each other. This the south one of grey marble is almost entirely under the pew. The Inscription runs around in a border framewise. There are several of such stones in the Island, and they seem to have been in use during the period of 1670—90. The central oblong space is sometimes blank, more often it has a skull and cross bones, or a secondary inscription. In this case there are two thigh bones crossed.

.... TH THE BODY OF . VMPHRY BROCKDON MERCHANT | 1673 | .... years.

1666, March 29. Mr Humphrey Brockdon & Mrs Elizabeth Ford. (Parish Register.)

1672, Feb. 18. Mrs Eliz. Brockdon in church.

1673-4, Jan. 15. Mr Humphry Brockdon in ye Church.

22. Between Nos. 21 and 23 :—

Beneath this Stone are deposited | the Remains of the | Honble JOHN FRANK NICHOLLS | who departed this life | on the 16 of December 1807 | Aged twenty-five Years. See his tablet No. 120.

1807, Dec. 19. On Wednesday last, after an illness of only 4 days & a short residence in this Island (to which he had been lately appointed Solicitor-Gen.) John F. Nicholls, Esq. who has left a young widow far distant from her native home to lament her loss. ("Barbados Mercury.")

23. White marble, alongside No. 22, pews covering the right edge :—

(One line above). | .... IS PLACED .... | WILLIAM MARSHALL HA ... | CHAPEL IN THIS TO .... | TWO INFANT CHILDREN | (Seven lines.) | HIS MOTHER DIED JULY 29TH 18 .. | 67 YEARS | SISTER DIED SEPT^R 18 .. | 7 DAYS | THER INFANT DIED DEC. .. | 12 DAYS | BELOVED WIFE AND MOTHER | 1791 DIED MAY 25TH 183 . | MONTH AND TWO DAYS. | (4 lines.) | MARSHALL HARTE, | THE ABOVE INSCRIPTION | MEMBERS OF HIS FAMILY | JAN^{RY} 11 1851 | (8 lines.)

24. White marble :—

Here Lyes Interr'd | the Body of | EDWARD JORDAIN | Organeist | Obi Dec .... 28, 1722 | Al . o .... TH | IORD .... | .... faid .. | (Several more lines worn away.)

Archer gives " Elizabeth Jordan his widow d. 30 Sept. 1737 aged 65."

1722, Dec. 29. Mr Edward Jordan Organist of this Parish under the centre of the organ in Church. (Burial Register.)

25. White marble :—

Here lieth Interrd the Body .... | M: BERNARD HANNINGTON .... | who Departed this life the 14 | of July 1755 Aged 46 Years.

1755, July 14. Barnard Hannington. (Burial Register.)

John Hannington was at Eton 1770-7, s. of J. H. sugar maker from B'os, b. at Gloucester. Adm. sizar at St John's Coll., Camb., 2 May 1777, B.A. 1781, M.A. 1784, B.D. 1814. (Eton Lists in MSS.)

26. To the south, under the gallery and near the font, are 4 ledgers:—

Here lies Interr^d; the Body of | Mrs ELIZABETH CROUCH | who departed this life May | the 30th 1747 in the 52^d | Year of Her Age.

1747, May 30. Mrs Elizabeth Crouch in Church. (Burial Register.)

27. *JOHN INNISS* | died January 10th 1816, | Aged 40 Years.

White marble :—

28. CREST.—*A dove or martlet on helmet, Ermine a lion rampant, within a bordure engrailed Or.* MOTTO BELOW.—AUT CES .... JUS T .... C. Rossi.

Sacred | to the Memory | of | M^{RS} *JANE EDWARDS* | who departed this Life the | 11th April 1819. | Aged 63 Years.

29. HERE REST THE REMAINS OF | M^{RS} ELEANOR FARLEY, | THE LAMENTED WIFE | OF ISAAC FARLEY ESQ^R OF BERBICE. | (14 lines.) | OBIIT 11MO JUL: 1823, ÆTAT 30.

30 and 31. Two grey marble slabs in centre near the door with the inscriptions worn away.

32. To north of centre under the gallery :—

LIETH .. | .. BOVES .. | .... OD AND | (About 5 more lines undecipherable.)

33. Starting from the centre of nave, east towards chancel are the following: Nos. 33, 34, and 35 are adjoining. Blue marble, cracked :—

ALEXANDER SANDIFORD. No further inscription was ever on the stone.

34. Alongside No. 33, on a small stone :—

HELENA RICH NATA 25° | IVLII 1664 MORTUA 20 | NOVEMBRIS 1665 GVLIELMV^S | RICH NATVS 25° DECEMBRIS | 1666 MORTVVS 17° | SEPTEMBRIS 1667 | ROBERTVS RICH | NATVS 21 NOVEMBRIS | 1668 MORTVVS 17 SEPTEM | BRIS 1670 | FILIA ET FILII | ROBERTI & .... RICH* | VNA ET FRATERNE DORMIVNT.

1665, Nov. 17. Hellena the D^a of Mr Robert Rich, in Ch.

The inscription gives 20 Nov. It is impossible to say which date is the correct one.

1667, Sept. 19. W^m the son of Mr Robt Rich March^t in the church.

1670, Sept. 18. Robert the son of Mr Robert Rich in ye Ch. (Burial Register.)

Chas. Rich resided in B. for seven years, returned to England in 1656, and died 1658. His brother Robert Rich, sen., also of B., merchant, died Nov. 1679, bach. (166, King.) Their nephew Robert R., jun., married Helen, dau. of Dr. Thornborough, D.D., son of the Bishop of Worcester. Robert's brother Edward was of the same island.

Buried. 1679, Nov. 29. Robert Rich a Barbados Merchant. (St. Edmund, Lombard Street.)

* Cemented crack here and one line illegible.

85. On a small stone :—

M. D. OB. Y⁰ 1ˢᵀ OF | IANᵞ 17⁰⁰/₀₁.

1700-1, Jan. 2. Mʳˢ Mary Dowding. (Burial Register.)
The will of John Dowding of B. and L., mercht., was proved in 1745 (269, Seymer). Bro. Capt. Sam. D., decᵈ, brother Rev. Wᵐ D., sisters Rebecca Jones and Eliz. Parsons.

36. Pews cover the left edge in places :—
BENEATH THIS STONE | IS LAID | THE NATURAL BODY OF | . . . TTHEW COULTHURST ESQUIRE, | BORN SEPTEMBER 30ᵀᴴ A.D. 1757, | (8 lines). | ON JUNE 24ᵀᴴ A.D. 1833, | . . E RENDERED UP HIS SOUL TO GOD, | (5 lines) | AGED 76 YEARS. | THIS TRIBUTE TO THE M . . . . O . . . . | A REVERED UNCLE | IS OFFERED | BY HIS NIECE | (AND DAUGHTER IN AFFECTION) | GEORGIANA GIBBONS | (4 lines.)

1833, June 25. Mathew Coulthurst Age 76. (Burial Register.)
See the tablet No. 108.
1820, Oct. 12. Elizabeth, wife of Matthew Coulthurst esq. of the i. of B. ("G.M.," 478.)

37. Grey marble. Pews cover the left edge :—
. . . eth Interred yᵉ Body of yᵉ | . . e Francis Bond Esq. some | . . dent of his Majestyes Councill | . . . nd who was Borne in Bodmyn | . . . . y of Cornuall | in England on yᵉ | . . . of November 1636 and dyed | . . . d yᵉ 3 day of Auguſt 1699 | (3 Latin lines.)
Archer gives the coat of arms : *On a chevron three crescents*, but this is not on the slab.
1699, Aug. 6. The Honᵇˡᵉ Francis Bond Esq. late President. (Burial Register.)
His name does not appear in the pedigree of Bond of Earth and Holwood in the Visitation of Cornwall.

*39. In fine state and with very large and deep lettering. Pews cover the right edge of the north side. Jacobean shield and mantling in sunk circle. CREST.—*A talbot's head erased over W. and H.* ARMS.—*Three talbots' heads erased between nine crosses-crosslet* [HALL], impaling, *a fess wavy between three mullets* [? BLACKBORNE].
Here lyeth interr'd . . . . | Body of MARY *Da* . . . . | of CHARLES BUCKWO . . . | Esq₃ & *Wife* of HUGH . . . | Esq₃ who departed . . . . | life yᵉ 6ᵗʰ day of Octo . . . | 1711 Aged about 29 Ye . .
1711, Oct. 7. Mary yᵉ wife of Hugh Hall Esqʳ Churchwᵈⁿ in yᵉ Church. (Burial Register.)
1715, May 3. The Honᵇˡᵉ Charles Buckworth Esqʳ in Church.

40. Pews cover left edge, and there is a cemented crack in penultimate line :—
M.S. | . nder this ſtone | . . . ng a Glorious reſurrection | . . e Bodies of twoo wives of | . . . . Hoñ John Peers Eſq₃ | . . Hefter yᵉ Daughter of Sʳ Thomas | . . . . refordſhire who dyed Seṗ yᵉ | . . . . whom a young Son was interr'd | . . . . was Frances yᵉ Daughter | . . ellency Sʳ Jonathan Atkins who | d Aprill ye . ᵗʰ 1685 | . . . . on of Ioⁿ & Hefter ob. 2ᵈ Sept. 171 .
Richd. Peers was of B. as early as 1631, when he was appointed Dep. Govr. by his brother-in-law Capt. Henry Hawley. He owned a plantation of 600 a. called Lebanus or Rendezvous and made his will 18 Dec. 1659 (70, Laud). His eldest Son John, a M. of C., took up 1000 a. in Jamaica in 1673, and died at Streatham,

* No. 38, missing, is probably due to an error of mine in numbering. It cannot be conveniently rectified on account of throwing out cross references.

co. Surrey. Will dated 16 March 1688 (102, Ent). John inherited his father's manor of Liners Ockell in Herefordshire and Hester his 1st wife was evidently dau. of Sir Thos. .... of that county. Frances his 2d wife, dau. of Govr. Sir Jonathan Atkins was sister to the wife of Tho. Walrond.

Sir Jonathan Atkins was later Gov. of Guernsey, and died in 1702 in his 100th year ; bur. at Grimthorpe, Yorkshire. M.I. there.

Bur. 1678, Sept. Hester the wife of Jno Peerse Esq. buried ye 15th. (Christ Church Parish Register, Hotten, 494.)

Bur. 1678, Sept. 15. Elisabeth ye wife of John Peers, Esqre. (St Michael's. *Ibid.*, 429.)

1685, Aprill 5. Madam ffrances Pearce the wife of the Honble Jno Pearce Esqr in the Chancel. (Burial Register.)

---

41. Underneath this Stone | are depofited the Remai . . | of | MARY MYERS, | wife of | Captain CHRISTOPHER MY .... | of the 16th Regiment of Light Dra .... | who died November 29th, 18 .. | Aged 33 Years | Alfo of her niece | CATHARINE PALMER | who died December 3rd, 1 ... | Aged Nine Years. | Alfo of | Captain JAMES MYE .. | of the 15th Regiment of .... | who died December 15th 1 ... | Aged 26 Years | Alfo of | Captain TRYON BAYA ... | of the 13th Regiment of .... | who died January 11th, 180 . | Aged 26 Years. | And of | Lieutenant General | Sir WILLIAM MYERS, B .... | late | Commander of the Forces on this .... | who died July 29th, 1805. | Aged 53 Years.

See No. 111 for tablet to Mrs. Mary Myers.

1804, Nov. 30. Mary Myers.
1804, Dec. 16. Capt. James Myers.
1805, Jany 11. Capt. Tryan Byeard.
1805, July 30. Sir William Myers, Bart. (Burial Register.)
1805, July 29. At Barbados, Lieut.-gen. Sir William Myers, bart. of Inningham in Kings County, so created July 3, 1804, commander-in-chief of the Leeward Islands, which now devolves on Gen. Beckwith, governor of St. Vincents. He makes 14 out of 18 of his family who have died after their arrival in the W.I. Most fortunately his lady staid in England. (" G.M.," 881.)

See later, No. 97, for a separate monument erected to him.

---

42. Incised border. Pews cover left edge :—

LYETH Ye BODY | .... AN FULLER WI ....* | .... THE 14 OF | .... BY ANNO 1682.

I think this is the stone Archer gives as " JONATHAN EVILER (? Fuller), d. . . 1682." The " F " I mistook at first for an " E."

1682-3, Jan. 14. Mrs Jone ffuller, in ye Chancel. (Burial Register.)

---

43. Grey marble :—

Under this Stone lyeth .... | Seuerall of the Family .... | Collonel John Hallett.

[Here is a Jacobean shield with scrolls: Crest over H. worn away (? a demilion rampant). ARMS.—*On a bend three roundles*. Just below the shield is a wide cemented crack. Pews cover the right edge.]

1678 his fi . . | Chriftopher Hallett Aged Ten | The 4th of December 1678 his | Daughter Elizabeth Hallett A .... | Twenty Monthes | The 14 of May 1679 his .... | Capt Gregory Hallett who | Born at Lyme Regis in ye C .... | of Dorsett the 11th of May .... | †Also here lieth interred the bo . . | MARTIN

---

* Worn here.   † Different style of lettering from here onwards.

BENTLEY ESQUIRE SON of | MARTIN and his LADY MARY BENT . . . . | who departed this life the 17th Day | September Anno Domini 1724 a . . . . | being in the 36th Year of his Age | Here lyeth Inter'd the Body of MR IAMES . . . . | Mch^t who Dyed the . . . . August 1736 in the | . . . . his Age.

1678, Dec. 16.   Xtopher the son of Major John Hallett (bur.).
1679, May 15.   Mr Gregory Hallett, in the Church.
1724, Sept. 17.   Martin Bentley Esqr in the Chancel.
1736, Aug. 3.   Mr James Crowe in the Chancel.
1695-6, Feb. 16.   Mary the Lady Bentley.   (Bur. St James, Hole Town.)
1681, June 11.   Martin, s. of Martin Bentley.   (Bur. St Philip.)

Col. John Hallett, late of the town and p. of St. Michael in the I. of B., now in England. Will dated 16 Jan. 1698. Friends and relations at Lyme Regis. Grandsons Martin and John Bentley ; the late Sr Martyn B. their father ; dau. Christian Farmer, dau. Kath. Farmer. Wife Mary my coach and 4 horses, etc. My brother Richd H., dec^d. My eldest son John my est. of Bridye Farme in Dorsetshire and my two plantations in St Mich. and St John ; proved 1 Feb. 1698-9 (25, Pett). John, also of St Michael's, died in 1721, s.p.m. Will (7, Marlborough). Richard, his younger brother, owned the manor of Axmouth, mar. Meliora, dau. of the Hon. John Hothersall of B. and Giddy Hall, Essex, and died 1746, will (152, Potter), leaving issue, and his descendants sold the manor of Axmouth in 1890. In reply to a query of mine a very good account of this family is now appearing in " Somerset and Dorset Notes and Queries."

44. Cut on the north side of the Hallett stone is :—

. . . . ey Esq | Iames Crow Merch^t both underneath.

45. On a Jacobean shield with scrolls :—

CREST.—*A falchion erect over* H.   ARMS.—*Within a bordure engrailed Argent three birds* (? *doves*) *erased.*
A pew covers the left edge of 1st and 2nd lines.

. . . . E LIES THE HONORABLE COLLONELL | . . . . IAM SHARPE ESQ^R WHO DIED TH . .* | OF A . BILL ANNO DOMINI . . . . AND IN THE 53 | YEARE OF HIS AGE.

" 1683, Aprill 25. The Honble Coll: Wm Sharp, in the Church, under the Communion Table." (Burial Register.)

He was Judge of a Court and died intestate, aged 53. See account of his death in Besse's " Sufferings of the Quakers," II., 350. I was told that he gave the land on which the church stands. His son William was President in 1706 and 1714.

46. Adjoining No. 45 :—

HERE INTERRED Y^E BODY OF SVSAN | BARRETT, DAVGHTER OF RICH & MAR- | THA BARRETT, WHO DEPARTED THIS | LIFE Y^E 9TH OF APRILL ANNO DOM 1665.

Below on a plain incised shield :—

On a chevron three fishes hauriant in centre of chief a label of three points.

ALSO | THE BODY OF IOHN PEMELL SONNE | OF THOMAS : & SVSAN PEMELL WHO | DEPARTED THIS LIFE Y^E 9TH OF IVLY | *DOM 1665.

Sir Timothy Thornhill is stated to have married a Miss Barrett.
1665, Aprill 9.   Susanna the D^a of Mr Richd Barrett.
1665, July 10.   John the son of Mr Thomas Pennell in Ch.   (Burial Register.)

* Cemented crack.

47. Sixteen lines of this are covered up on the right for quite two-thirds of their length by a pew near the pulpit:—

Here lie t . . | Mary his . . . . | Edmund J . . . . | this Life 2 . . | and Mary . . . . | Sarah Eve . . . . |˙of Edmu . . | Mary is als . . | March 179 . . | William E . . . . | William a . . . . | died the . . . . | Rebecca . . . . | a Son of . . . . | Sarah is . . . . | 30th of Ju . . AND | HERE also lies ANN JORDAN, Aunt | of the above S . . . . and Grand Aunt | of the last men . . . . William, she died | the 2nd of December 1807, aged 82 Years. | Sincerely regretted by her Grand Nephew | William Eversley who in Gratitude for her | unbounded Affection to him and as a grate | ful Tribute to her Memory places this Stone | over HER who to the End of his Mothers | Life, to him for nearly 30 Years, and to his | eldest Son for Seven of those Years succefsive | fostered and adopted them as her Children.

1797, July 9.   William Husband of Eliz[a] Eversley.   (Burial Register.)
1801, Aug. 1.   Rebecca Eversley.
1821, Nov. 5.   T. D. Belfield, esq. of Mincing-lane, to Elizabeth Anne, dau. of W. Eversley, esq. of the i. of B.   (" G.M.," 468.)

48. In floor partly under pulpit floor is a blue marble ledger:—

SON OF PHILLIP ALLEN | MARCHANT HEE HAD BY DAMA- | RIS ALLEN HIS WIFE ONE DAVGHTER | TAMASIN ALLEN HE DEPARTED | THIS LIFE THE 12 DAY OF NOVE | MBER 1660* THE 36 YEAR[E] | . . . . GE.

There is a gap in the Burial Register July 1658 to Dec. 1660.

49. To the north of the above is a blue marble ledger, the first two lines partly covered by pew:—

Here Lie | JOH . . . . | (pew) | One of his Majeftys Council | In the Ifland of BABADO's, | Who died y[e] 5th of DECEMBER. 1715, | Aged 63 years, & Seven Months.

1715, Dec. 26.   The Hono[ble] Jn[o] Pilgrim Esq[r] in the Chancel.
The " 5th " of Dec. in the inscription should probably have been " 25th."
The will of John Pilgrim of the parish of Christ Church was sworn 3 Jan. 1715-16 at Pilgrim before Gov. Lowther.   He left his wife Eliz. his "coach & six "† and all residue to his son Joseph.   (80, Fox.)
Tho. Pilgrim, the Elder, formerly of Barbados, merchant, now of Putney, a Quaker, in his will dated 2 June 1716 says : "I forgive to the Ex'ors of my dear brother Councellor John Pilgrim £428."   (151, Fox.)
A house and land belonging to the Pilgrims was leased in 1704 for 21 years as a residence for the Governor.   The freehold was subsequently purchased, and the present Government House occupies the site.

50. In the passage close to the iron screen of the chancel.   A pew is fixed on part of the west end, and the lectern on the east end:—

(Pew) ˙. . . . D HIS LIFE | (pew) | THE FORTENTH | DAY OF FEBRVARIE IN THE YEARE OF | OUR LORD 168⅔ AND IN . . . . | AND FIFTIETH YEARE O . . . . GE.

1682-3, Feb. 14.   M[r] Jn[o] Grimwade in Ch.   (Burial Register.)

51. White marble, south of No. 50.   Half the inscription on the right to north is under a pew :—

Sac . . . . | to the Mem . . . . | HENRY JAMES L . . . . | Fourth Son . . | Sir WILLIAM L . . . . | of | Kirk Harle Nort . . . . | & | Ensign in the 4th or . . . | Died 23rd Dece . . . . | In the 20th Yea . . (Signed) C: Rossi.

1821, Dec. 23.   At B., aged 20, H. J. Loraine, esq. brother to Sir Charles L. bart. of Kirkharle, Northumberland, and Ensign in the 4th reg.   ("G.M.," 1822, 286.)

* The leg of stairs to pulpit stands here.
† The etiquette was for Members of Council to have six horses and those of the Assembly four to their coach.

52. South of No. 51. The inscription runs framewise in a border, and a pew covers the south-west portion. On the north side :—

The Body of Capt Jeremiah Egginton Merchant Borne.

At east end :—

In the County of Salop.

At south side :—

aged forty-feaven yea . .

1673, Oct. 23. Capt Jeremiah Egginton in Church.
1693, Sept. 10. Capt Jeremiah Egginton. (Burial Register.)
Egginton's Green in Bridgetown is shewn on Mayo's Map of 1722.
Wm. Chester of St. James's, Barbados, Esq. Will proved 1703. Sarah his widow married before 1696 John Eginton, Esq.

---

53. White marble south of No. 52, quite covered by pews.

WALL TABLETS.

54. On south-east wall of nave :—

In memory of | SUSAN wife of | joseph barker barrow; | born in this island, | July 23rd 1810, | died at peckham, january 24th, | 1871, | her remains are interred | in grave n° 11243, | at nunhead cemetery, | in the county of surrey, | england.

1772, April 4. John Barrow the s. of John Barrow merchant. (Burial Register.) See the M.I. to her husband No. 272.

George Barrow owned Mount Pleasant in St. Philips in 1790. Ann Thomasine (1765—1840), dau. of Wm. Clarke, overseer of the Thicket plantation by Thomasine his wife; married 1st, Nath. Barrow, brother of George, by whom she had a son Sam., who died at Codrington College, and a dau. Sarah Ann, who married Jonathan Higginson ; 2ndly, on 19 May 1790, General Robert Haynes. (Notes by the latter.)

---

55. Below No. 54 :—

Sacred to the Memory | of a good Christian, a gallant Soldier, and an honest Man | In Life beloved and in Death lamented. | Near this spot rest the mortal remains of Brevet Major | JOHN WYNNE FLETCHER. | (*Captain in the 4th King's Own Regiment of Foot | and Aide-de-Camp to Lt Genl Sir HENRY WARDE*.) | who departed this life | on the 24th of October 1824. | Aged 39 Years.   *C: Rossi, Barbados.*

1824, Oct. 24. At King's House, B., of inflammation of the lungs, after ten days severe suffering, Major John-Wynne Fletcher. His remains were next morning interred in St. Michael's Church . . . . &c. ("G.M.," 647.)

---

56. On the same wall. A tall narrow tablet surmounted by an obelisk, on which are a medallion of deceased and two figures :—

THIS MONUMENT | As a melancholy Tribute of Conjugal Affection is erected | To the Memory of | M^{RS} FRANCES ORDERSON, | who in the 31st Year of her Age | on the 20th *July*, 1810 | on her Pafsage to England (her native Country) | *DIED AT SEA* | and whose Body, during an awful Calm was | committed to the unfathomable deep. | (Thirteen lines follow).

Below three ships are carved in low relief.

1798, Sept. 10. Mr. Isaac Orderson, of B. to Miss Frances Toosey, niece of Philip Prior, esq. of Great Russell str. (" G.M.," 1148.)

1799, May 23. At B. Miss Toosey, late of Tavistock-st., Bedford-sq. (*Ibid.*, 621.)

1810, July 20. On her passage to England, for the recovery of her health, the wife of Mr. J. W. Orderson of the I. of B. (*Ibid.*, 190.)

---

57. Below No. 56. Above is a female mourning over an urn, with a cherub at each top corner:—

SACRED TO THE MEMORY | of MISS MARY TOOSEY | who departed this Life May 23d 1799 | universally lamented : | Aged 24 Years | (5 lines.) | ERECTED BY HER BROTHER WILLIAM TOOSEY AS A TRIBUTE OF HIS AFFECTION.

---

58. On the south wall, east corner :—

SACRED TO THE MEMORY OF | MARY KATHARINE, | THE BELOVED WIFE OF | JOSEPH H. BARROW ; | DIED 25TH OF SEPTEMBER 1859, | AGED 26 YEARS.

1822, Oct. 22. At Barbadoes, Lieut.-col. Amwyl, of the 4th reg. of foot, to Senhouse, dau. of J. Barrow, esq. of the above Island. (" G.M.," 560.)

1825, May 5. In Somerset-st., Portman-sq. aged 81, Frances, widow of T. H. Barrow esq. of Barbadoes. (*Ibid.*, 476.)

---

59. Above No. 58 is a boldly carved monument of white marble with cherubs' heads, curtain, and swags of flowers.

ARMS.—*On a fess three annulets between two moles*; impaling : *blank.* Archer gave the impaled coat as : *Per fess indented*, but that is no longer visible.

ROBERTUS HOOPER Armiger, Amicus | certus in re incerta, pius simul et | munificus notisq̨ amor Delicioeque | Vir haud vulgariter eruditus et egregio | Ingenii acumine ornatifsimus, nec non | multos in annos Iucolis hujusce Insulæ | beatis Regivs Attornatus Generalis | Obijt 24 die July AD:MDCC. | Siste, Lector, quid dixi ? | Non obijt, nec obire potest, sed vivet in ævum | Cum Christo in cælis, in terris ore virorum.

1700, July 26. Robt Hooper Esq. in church. (Burial Register.) See the floor-stone No. 1.

---

60. Between the first and second windows are six tablets and one brass :—

SACRED TO THE MEMORY OF | JOHN RANDALL PHILLIPS | OF LAMBERTS IN THIS ISLAND ESQ^R | HE DIED AT TORQUAY DEVON, | SEPT^R 9TH 1845, AGED 86. | ALSO OF ELIZABETH WENT, | WIFE OF THE ABOVE, | & DAUGHTER OF PHILLIP LOVELL ESQ^R | SHE DIED AT EDINBURGH, | JULY 20TH 1831, AGED 51. | (1 line.)

The present Colonial Treasurer, Mr. W. L. C. Phillips, is descended from J. R. Phillips, also Dr. Oliver Greenidge.

1803, Nov. 1. At B., P. Phillips, esq. to the eldest dau. of Mr. Sisum. (" G.M.," 1252.)

1828, Jan. 17. At Christ Church, Mary-le-bone, Geo. Geoffrey Wyatville, only s. of Jeffrey W. esq. of Windsor, to Ann Sisum, dau. of the l. Peter Philips esq. of B. (*Ibid.*, 80.)

1840, July 13. At the Hotwells, the wife of Abel Phillips, of B. (*Ibid.*, 328.)

1823, Aug. 6. At his house at Frenchay, aged 74, Philip Lovell, esq. formerly of B. (*Ibid.*, 190.)

See " W.I. Bookplates," No. 209, for that of his son Robert Lovell.

1844, March 22. At Streatham Common, aged 65, Mary-Anne, relict of Peter Phillips of B. (" G.M.," 552.)

1845, Oct. 9. At Torville, Torquay, aged 85, John Randall Phillips, of the I. of B. (" G.M.," 546.) See the M.I. to his 2d wife at Xt Ch.

61. Oblong brass :—

In Fond Remembrance of | JOHN ROUNDER WOOLCOTT, B.A. | who died in Dominica of fever, January 13th, 1887, aged 28 years. | this tablet is erected by his pupils of | HARRISON COLLEGE. | as a token of their affectionate esteem for one in whom | they have lost a valued and sympathetic friend as well | as an able and efficient master. | (1 line.)

62. In memory of | JOHN CUTTING PACKER, ESQre | late of this island, | who was born May 2nd 1777, died December 6th 1856, | aged 79 years | (2 lines) | also MARTHA, his beloved wife | who was born April 1st 1775, died May 18 1841, | aged 66 years. | (4 lines) | T. gaffin, regent st London.

63. Sacred to the Memory of lucy crichlow daughter of | john cobham esq. & Wife of henry crichlow esqr of this Island | Who died in the City of Bath in the Kingdom of England | on the 7th and was buried in the Abbey Church of that City | on the 14th Jany 1801, Aged 65 Years. | (27 lines.)

See the M.I. to her in Bath Abbey. " Caribbeana," i., 82.

64. Below 63 :—

Sacred to the memory of | CHARLOTTE | wife of | HENRY CRICHLOW, | who departed this life on the 10th of October 1839, | aged 39 :— in england | whither she had gone, in the hope that it might please | a merciful providence | to restore her to health, and spare her to | her afflicted husband and children | but he willed it otherwise ! | and her remains lie deposited thus far from | her native land, | in the vaults of the cemetery at kensall green, | near london, | where a tablet has been put up, | in commemoration of her, and her late father | THOMAS PIERREPOINT ESQr | who also died in england, on the 10th of | december, 1837, aged 66; | and | whose remains are likewise deposited | in the same vaults. T. bedford 256 oxford st, london.

1805, Nov. 26. Mr. Charles Kingston Pierrepont, brother of Thomas P. Esq. (" Caribbeana," i., 331.) See No. 216.

1837, Dec. 10. In Southampton-row, Bloomsbury, aged 62, Tho. Pierrepont, esq. l. of B. (" G.M.," 1838, 107.)

1839, Oct. 10. At St. John's-wood, aged 39, Charlotte, wife of Henry Crichlow of B. leaving 9 children. (Ibid., 546.)

Wm. Critchlow and family were of this parish in 1680.

65. In memory of | NORMAN J. D. CUMMINS, | for eight years | organist and choirmaster of this cathedral, | who died April 3rd 1887, aged 25 years. | (1 line.) | this tablet is erected | by his friends and the choristers of the cathedral | in fond remembrance | of his faithful and valued services. | (1 line.)

66. SACRED | TO THE MEMORY OF | BENJAMIN IFILL ESQUIRE, | WHO DIED | ON THE 21ST DAY OF SEPTEMBER 1835, AGED 60 YEARS. | (7 lines.)

See "Caribbeana," i., 32, for M.I. to his only dau. Susan, who died 18 April 1833, aged 28.

_____

67. Between the second window and south door are six tablets and one brass :—

INSCRIBED BY CONJUGAL AFFECTION | TO THE MEMORY OF | JOHN C. HILL | WHO DEPARTED THIS LIFE | MARCH 28TH 1838, | AGED 49 YEARS. | (14 lines.)

_____

68. SACRED TO THE MEMORY OF | MARIA JANE, | INFANT DAUGHTER OF | WILLIAM AND MARIA WARD | WHO DIED 6TH SEPTEMBER 1829, | AGED 9 MONTHS. | AND OF MARIA WARD, | MOTHER OF THE ABOVE, | WHO DIED 1ST NOVEMBER 1829, | AGED 28 YEARS. | THIS TRIBUTE IS HERE PLACED BY AN | AFFECTIONATE HUSBAND AND FATHER.   WOOD. BRISTOL.

_____

69. Brass :—

TO THE GLORY OF GOD | AND SACRED TO THE BELOVED MEMORY OF | JAMES PACKER, | WHO DIED AT BARBADOES ON 29TH JANUARY 1859, | AND OF HIS WIDOW | ELLEN DARLING, | WHO DIED AT EDINBURGH ON 15TH MAY 1900. | ERECTED 1902. | (3 lines.)

_____

70. Above are the Badge and Colours of the regiment.

Major JAMES CONNOLLY,	CAPT JOHN GORDON,
Lieut WILLM CLUTTERBUCK,	Lieut DUNCAN MCDOUGALL,
,, WILLIAM GRAY,	,, JOHN NORMAN,
,, JOHN ADAMS,	,, CHARLES GRANT,
,, THOMAS MASSIE,	,, ANDW RICHMOND,
Adjt JAMES SPENCER,	Asst Surgn JOHN PRENDEGAST.

Of the 2nd or Queen's Royal Regiment of Foot.

SACRED TO THE MEMORY OF THE ABOVENAMED OFFICERS, | WHO HAVING FAITHFULLY SERVED THEIR KING AND COUNTRY | IN VARIOUS PARTS OF THE WORLD, | FELL VICTIMS TO THIS FATAL CLIMATE, | IN THE YEARS OF OUR LORD 1816 AND 1817. | THIS MONUMENT IS ERECTED | AS A TESTIMONY OF AFFECTIONATE ESTEEM, | BY THEIR BROTHER OFFICERS.   J. KENDRICK, SCULPTOR, | LONDON.

1816, Dec. 18.   At B., aged 22, Lieut. Andrew Richmond, of h. M. 2d or Queen's own reg.   ("G.M.," 1817, 374.)

_____

71. In Loving Memory of | JOSEPH WATERMAN ROACH, BORN 3 JAN. 1827, DIED 5 FEBY 1899 | AND HIS SONS | JOSEPH DUDLEY ROACH BORN 4 JULY 1859, DIED 30 APRIL 1903, | NATHANIEL ALLAN ROACH . . 21 JULY 1860, . .   9 SEPT. 18 . 5,* | CLIFFORD AUBREY ROACH . . 7 FEBY 1863, . . 14 AUGT. 1885. | (3 lines).

_____

72. SACRED | TO THE MEMORY OF | CATHERINE ANN, | BELOVED WIFE OF | THOMAS ROACH FORD, | WHO FELL ASLEEP | 8TH NOVEMBER 1899. | (7 lines).

* The year is distinct, but an error has occurred in my MS.

73. Next the south door. Angel standing over an urn :—
GIBSON SCULPSIT ROMA.

Below is :—
FRANCESCÆ BOVELL | UXORI SUÆ | QUAM BENE MERENTI QUAM DILECTÆ | IMMATURA MORTE | SUBLATÆ | A.D. MDCCCXXIII | ET | ÆT XXII | HOC MONUMENTUM POSUIT | MŒRENS | GULIELMUS BOVELL.

See "Barbados Mercury" for many entries relating to the Bovells, and No. 317.

West of the south door there are one brass and four tablets as far as the next window.

74. Brass. Above is the Regimental Crest :—
IN MEMORY OF | Lᵀ COL. J. PIPER, MAJOR J. W. FLETCHER, CAPT. J. EDGELL. | LIEUTENANTS | W. BLAGROVE, J. DUTHY, F. ROBINSON, I. BEER, R. E. COTTON. | ENSIGNS | F. CLARKE, R. GAMBLE, H. M. SHIPTON, J. LORAINE. | QUARTER MASTERS | T. RICHARDS, B. DORAN, E. KELLY. | 21 Sᵍᵀˢ 1 Dᴿ 245 RANK AND FILE | 4ᵀᴴ THE KINGS OWN | WHO DIED WHEN THE REGIMENT WAS QUARTERED IN THE | WEST INDIES FROM 1ˢᵀ APRIL 1819, TO 10ᵀᴴ FEB. 1826. | ALSO IN MEMORY OF | Lᵀ COL. W. F. BLAKE LIEUT. T. E. LE BLANC. | SCHOOLMASTER | J. CUNNINGHAM | Sᵍᵀ INST. MUSKETRY J. PLATT SERGEANT T. MORGAN, | CORPORAL P. CALLAGHER, Lᴱ Cᴾᴸ J. MALLINS, | Lᴱ Cᴾᴸ F. B. BAKER, Lᴱ Cᴾᴸ J. LYDFORD | PRIVATES (24 named) | AND MARY, WIFE OF SERGEANT J. Mᶜ CABE, DIED AT BARBADOS. | Lᴱ Sᵍᵀ J. GREEN (and 5 privates) DIED AT TRINIDAD. | (8 privates) AND DR. W. WOOD | DIED AT JAMAICA. | WHEN THE 1ˢᵀ BATTᴺ 4ᵀᴴ THE KINGS OWN ROYAL REGᵀ WAS QUARTERED IN THE WEST INDIES, | FROM 20ᵀᴴ JAN. 1879, TO 26ᵀᴴ MAY 1882, HOC MONUMENTUM POSUERUNT COMMILITES | HAUD IMMEMORES | PRISTINÆ VIRUTIS.
1821, Dec. 12. At B., in his 39th year, Lieut.-col. John Piper, of the 4ᵗʰ or Kings Own Reg. (" G.M.," 1822, 188.)
See Capt. Charles James Edgill's vault, No. 350.

75. IN MEMORY OF | JOHN ELLIS Esqᴿ | M.A. F.S.A. | BARRISTER AT LAW | LATE OF THE | MIDDLE TEMPLE | LONDON | BORN 19ᵀᴴ JANʸ 1791 | DIED 24ᵀᴴ MAY 1825.
1825, May 24. At Kingston in B., whither he had been advised to go for the recovery of his health, John Ellis, of the Middle Temple, Esq. Barrister-at-Law, M.A., F.S.A. and Deputy Recorder of Huntingdon. He was son of John Ellis of the Stock Exchange. (" G.M.," 187.)
He was s. of John of Marylebone, esq., Xᵗ Ch., matric. 13 Ap. 1807, a. 19; of Peter House, Camb., B.A. 1816, M.A. 1819, bar.-at-l. Linc. Inn 1819, and of Mid. T. 1820, F.S.A., Dep. Recorder of Huntingdon. (Foster.)

76. Below No. 75 :—
This Marble | the tribute of LOVE & Gratitude | is confecrated by conjugal Affection | To the Memory of Mʳˢ HANNAH BROUGH | the beloved Wife of Mʳ CHARLES B . . . ., | She died the 31ˢᵗ day of January 1807, | Aged 30 Years. | (1 line).

77. Sacred to the Memory of | MARY ANN, | ELDEST DAUGHTER OF THE LATE | JOHN WILLOUGHBY, ESQᴿᴱ, OF HIGH STREET, | AND THE DEARLY BELOVED PARTNER OF THOMAS HALL, ESQᴿᴱ, | INSPECTOR GENERAL OF HOSPITALS; | WHO DEPARTED THIS LIFE ON 13ᵀᴴ MARCH 1859, | AFTER A BRIEF ILLNESS OF FOUR DAYS FROM MALIGNANT SORE THROAT, | IN THE 59ᵀᴴ YEAR OF HER AGE. | (10 lines; erected by her husband).

78. SACRED | TO THE MEMORY OF | MARY ELIZA | THE BELOVED WIFE OF EDMUND KNIGHT ESQ^{RE} | WHO DIED IN LONDON, 15TH JAN^Y 1854, | AGED 57 YEARS. | HER DEAR REMAINS ARE DEPOSITED | IN A VAULT IN HIGHGATE CEMETERY. | (6 lines).

79. There are five tablets beyond the first window :—

SACRED | TO THE MEMORY OF | ALFRED BARTRUM, ESQ. OF THE ISLAND OF MAURITIUS, | WHO DEPARTED THIS LIFE A.D. 1826. | ALSO TO THE MEMORY | OF MARY ABEL HIS WIFE; | ELDEST DAUGHTER OF ABEL CLINCKETT, ESQ. | OF THIS ISLAND, | WHO DIED APRIL 5TH 1830, AGED 32. | ALSO TO THE MEMORY | OF ELLEN PRINGLE THEIR ELDEST DAUGHTER, | WHO DEPARTED THIS LIFE JUNE 16TH 1834, | AGED 17 YEARS. | (5 lines).

80. WILLIAM CRANE ESQUIRE, | late Purser of H.M. Ship SAPPHIRE | Ob: December 10th 1833 | Aged 46.

81. A broken column supported by two cherubs, by Wood, Bristol:—

In Memory of | *CATHARINE SIMS SMITH* who died | the 23rd April 1800 aged 27 years. | (12 lines). | her afflicted Huſband | *WILLIAM SMITH Eſq^r* who departed | this life after a ſhort illneſs | the 27th Auguſt 1801 | aged 28 years.

82. Above No. 81.

Sacred | to the Memory | of | THOMAS M^CINTOSH ESQ^{RE}. | Who on the 15th. day of August | 1815, | And in the 72nd | Year of his Age, | Closed an Honourable | and Pious Life.   *C: Rossi.*

83. SACRED TO THE MEMORY OF | A FATHER AND DAUGHTER, | COLONEL S. T. POPHAM, | LATE QUARTER MASTER GENERAL TO THE ARMY | OF THIS COMMAND, | HE DIED ON THE 25TH. DECEMBER 1823, | AGED 50. | AND HONORA, | SHE FELL THE VICTIM OF FEVER | THREE YEARS BEFORE | ON THE 3^D OF DECEMBER, | AT THE EARLY AGE OF 17. | (6 lines).

1820, Dec. 3. At Collymore House, B., in her 17th year, Honora Alicia Lambart Popham, second dau. of Lieut.-col. S.T.P., Dep. Quarter Master Gen. of the Troops in that Colony. (1821, 186.)

84. On the south-west wall of nave are four tablets :—

Sacred to the Memory of HENRY NOBLE SHIPTON, | Senior Ensign of the Fourth or King's own Regiment of Foot, | and youngest Son of the Reverend JOHN SHIPTON, | Doctor in Divinity, Rector of Portishead near Bristol, Vicar of | Stanton Bury, in the County of Buckingham, and one of His Majesty's | Justices of the Peace for the County of Somerset, in England. | He was an active and valued Officer, | as well as a singularly amiable and excellent young Man: | who, escaping the dangers especially incident to his Profession, | particularly those of the siege of New Orleans, | and the ever memorable Battle of Waterloo, | was cut off, when on the Eve of Promotion, by the yellow Fever, | after only five days illness, whilst stationed with his Regiment | in this Island, on the fifth day of December 1821, | in the 26th year of his age, | to the very deep regret of his afflicted Parents, | who have caused this Tablet to be erected as a Token of | their affection for their beloved Son.

See also " G.M." for 1822, p. 188.

85. Medallion of head in profile :—

SACRED | TO THE MEMORY OF | JAMES BUTCHER | PHYSICIAN AND SUR-
GEON | WHO DEPARTED THIS LIFE MARCH 9TH 1856 | AGED 80 YEARS | (8 lines.)

---

86. Medallion of head and woman seated below :—

IN GRATEFUL REMEMBRANCE | OF JOHN BRATHWAITE Esqⁱ | OF THREE
HOUSES IN THE PARISH OF Sᵀ PHILIP, | MANY YEARS AGENT FOR THIS COLONY IN
GREAT BRITAIN, | WHOSE COMPREHENSIVE VIEWS | AND CONSUMMATE KNOWLEDGE OF
ITS VARIOUS INTERESTS | WERE ONLY TO BE EQUALLED BY | THE MASTERLY ADDRESS
WITH WHICH HE CONDUCTED AND | THE INFLEXIBLE PERSEVERANCE WITH |
WHICH HE PURSUED THEM. | THE LEGISLATURE OF BARBADOS ERECT THIS MONU-
MENT, | ANXIOUS | THAT POSTERITY SHOULD KNOW HOW HIGH HE STOOD | THROUGH
HIS DISTINGUISHED SERVICES IN | THE ESTIMATION OF HIS | COUNTRY. | HE WAS
BORN IN THIS ISLAND ON THE 25TH OF OCTOBER 1722, | AND DEPARTED THIS LIFE
IN GREAT BRITAIN | ON THE 21ST. OF SEPTEMBER 1800. | AT EPSOM IN THE COUNTY
OF SURRY | WHERE HIS REMAINS ARE INTERRED.

See his M.I. in Epsom Church, "Caribbeana," iii., 373. See under
St. Philip's.

---

87. Crest broken off, between two wings.

ARMS.—. . . . *a lion rampant, on a chief Ermine an anchor charged with a
coronet.* MOTTO.—IN CANOPO UT AD CANOPUM.

SACRED TO THE MEMORY OF | THOMAS LOUIS, ESQᴿᴱ | NATIVE OF DEVON,
ENGLAND, | AND SECOND SON OF THE LATE | ADMIRAL SIR THOMAS LOUIS, BART. |
IN 1813 HE SETTLED | IN THIS ISLAND AS A MERCHANT, | AND DIED THE 9TH OF
FEBRUARY 1862, | AGED 73 YEARS. | (11 lines ; erected by widow.)

H. CADE, BRISTOL.

---

88. On the north-west wall of nave are three tablets and one brass.

IN MEMORY OF | BENJAMIN THOMAS, | SON OF PETER AND MARY
EMLIN CHAPMAN, | BORN SEPTEMBER 29TH. 1857 ; | DIED MARCH 6TH 1859, |
AGED 17 MONTHS AND 5 DAYS. | (3 lines.)

---

89. Brass :—

TABLET OF INKY HUE | REMAIN | AND MARK THE SPOT | WHERE NOBLE DUST
IS SHRIN'D | FOR WELL THE POET'S STRAIN HATH SUNG, | AN HONEST MAN'S THE
NOBLEST WORK GOD : | THEN SAY, | BENEATH THIS CHURCHYARD'S MOUND | THE
BONES OF HENRY CHEEKS, | COMMINGLED WITH MUCH VALUED ROWES, |
ARE LAID | (5 lines.) | HE ATTAINED THE AGE OF | SEVENTY FIVE | THE 25TH OF
DECEMBER 1824 | (6 lines). J. SIM, LONDON.

---

90. Crest missing from nail. ARMS.—*Gules, three clarions Or, a crescent
for difference* (GREENFIELD) ; impaling : 1 and 4, *Vert, on a bend Or three mullets
Gules ; 2 and 3, Gules, a chevron Or, with a crescent for difference.*

Within | the Chancel of this Church | Lie the bodies of | *GENERAL
WILLIAM GRINFIELD* | Colonel of the 86th. Regt. of foot | and Commander
in chief | of the British Forces | *in the Carribbee Islands.* | And | of *EMMA
MARIA* his wife | Daughter of the Reverend *JOHN BROCAS* | *Dean of*

D

Killala in Ireland. | They fell victims to the yellow fever | He died on the 19th. November 1803 | having furvived her only three Days | Both were in the 59th Year of their Age.

1803, Oct. 19. At B., victim to the yellow fever, Gen. William Grinfield, commander of the troops in the Leeward Islands, who survived his lady only three days, and a very intimate female acquaintance of Mrs. G. By his will, his younger brother, a clergyman at Bristol, becomes entitled to all his fortune, except a legacy to the late Mrs. G's relations. ("G.M.," 1256.) A later notice in 1804, p. 179, enters into further details.

———

91. Above, on badge: "69 SOUTH LINCOLN." Below is: "WATERLOO, INDIA."

SACRED TO THE MEMORY OF | THE OFFICERS OF THE SERVICE COMPANIES | OF THE 69TH. REGIMENT, | WHO HAVE DIED DURING THE FOUR YEARS | THE REGIMENT HAS SERVED IN THE WEST INDIES, | FROM 1851, TO 1855, VIZ: | LIEUT. COLONEL J. W. L. PAXTON, | COMMANDING 69TH. REGIMENT, | WHO DIED AT TRINIDAD, OF YELLOW FEVER, | ON THE 24TH. OF AUGUST 1853 ; | CAPTAIN C. J. CARMICHAEL, | WHO JUST AFTER REACHING ENGLAND FROM BARBADOS, | DIED ON THE 2ND DECEMBER 1852, | LIEUTENANT H. C. STRICKLAND, | WHO DIED AT BARBADOS, OF YELLOW FEVER, | ON THE 14TH SEPTEMBER 1852 ; | AND SURGEON A. B. CLELAND, M.D. | WHO DIED AT TRINIDAD OF YELLOW FEVER, | ON THE 25TH. AUGUST 1853. | THIS TABLET IS ERECTED | BY THEIR BROTHER OFFICERS. | ALSO | LTS C. R. DORINGTON, AND H. T. ALLEN, WHO DIED | OF YELLOW FEVER, AT BARBADOES, ON THE 12TH. & | 15TH. AUGUST, 1855.

———

92. On the north wall of nave beginning from the west end :—

THIS MONUMENT | IS RAISED BY THEIR GRAND-CHILDREN, | AS A RESPECTFUL TRIBUTE | TO THE MEMORY OF | DOTTIN MAYCOCK, A.M. OXON. | BARRISTER AT LAW OF THE MIDDLE TEMPLE, | AND FORMERLY SOLICITOR GENERAL OF THIS ISLAND ; | DIED JULY 11TH, 1793, AGED 51 YEARS. | ALSO TO THE MEMORY OF | CATHARINE, HIS WIFE | WHO SURVIVED HIM MANY YEARS | DIED FEBRUARY 14TH 1849, AGED 85 YEARS.

Dottin Maycock, s. of John M. of I. of B., esq., St. John's Coll., matric. 31 Oct. 1760, aged 17, barr.-at-l., Mid. T., 1767.
See "Caribbeana," i., 30, for M.I. to Jas. Dottin Maycock.

———

93. Large grey marble monument built up from the floor :—

Ob. June 7, 1746 Æt: 57 | Here lies the Body of THOMAS HARRISON Efqr. | Who from a fmall and slender Beginning, | By the Arts of honest Industry, | Grew Rich, Belov'd and Honour'd | (10 lines.) | He was indeed difplaced from his Seat at the Council board, | In the Government Of Sir THOMAS ROBINSON, | But foon call'd forth by the Voice of the People, | To be the Affertor of their Rights and Liberties | In the General Afsembly. | (28 lines.)

1746, June 8. The honble Thomas Harrison Esq. in the new Chancel.
1755, April 26. John Harrison Esqr. (Burial Register.)

———

94. SACRED TO THE MEMORY OF | JOSEPH LOWE ESQUIRE, | (12 lines.) | HE DIED ON 31 MAY 1827. | AND HIS REMAINS ARE DEPOSITED IN A VAULT OF ST. ANDREWS CHURCHYARD, | THIS SIMPLE TRIBUTE OF GRATEFUL AFFECTION | IS ERECTED BY HIS DAUGHTER | SARAH SCOTT MAYCOCK. | (Married life 30 years, died at an advanced age & lost his only son.)

She was wife of the Hon. Dr. James Dottin Maycock, M.D., who died 18 June 1835, aged 48, and she died 8 May 1862, aged 75. ("Caribbeana," i., 28.)

95. THIS TABLET | IS ERECTED TO THE MEMORY OF | WILLIAM HAWKES-WORTH ESQR. | BY HIS AFFLICTED WIDOW | ELIZA ANN. | HE DEPARTED THIS LIFE | 29TH APRIL 1852 | AGED 67. | (7 lines.)

96. Near this place are deposited the remains of FRANCES | Daughter of R. GRAY, D.D. Lord Bishop of Bristol, and | ELIZABETH his Wife, who have erected this monument. | (3 lines.) | Born Novr 8th 1806. Died Feby 13th. 1827. | (1 line.)

97. CREST.—*A mermaid.* ARMS.—*An ancient ship with three masts, and on a canton Gules two swords debruised of a mural crown, a mullet in centre point of chief, and on a sinister canton the Badge of Ulster.* (See Burke's "Armory.")

Sacred to the Memory | of | Lieutenant General Sir WILLIAM MYERS, *Bart.* | Commander of the Forces on this Station | who departed this life | July 29th. A.D. 1805, | Ætatis 53. | (9 lines.)

R. BLORE. *Sculp. Piccadilly* LONDON.

See notice of him under No. 41.

98. Sacred to the Memory | of Mrs LÆTITIA AUSTIN, | (Wife of JOHN AUSTIN, ORDNANCE—SURGEON,) | (22 lines.) | This amiable and accomplished Woman arrived | from ENGLAND, in Septr 1801 ; and was removed | by a Fever, Novr the 19th following ; | (3 lines.)

99. To the east of the north door are eleven tablets :—

IN THE WESTERN PORCH OF THIS CATHEDRAL | ARE DEPOSITED THE REMAINS OF | BEZSIN KING REECE, | WHO DEPARTED THIS LIFE ON THE 23RD OF SEPTEMBER 1838, | AFTER A SHORT ILLNESS, AGED 73 YEARS. | (13 lines ; erected by his grandchildren.)

100. Shield of arms below : *Gules, three salmons;* impaling : *Or, a tiger passant guardant.* Nearly entirely defaced.

Above is an urn with a figure standing :—

In Memoriam | Honblis MICHAELIS KEANE Armigeri, | Nuper | Procuratoris Regii, et Conciliarii in Arcanis Domini Regis, | et diu | Insulæ Sancti Vincentii. | Incolæ. | Obiit Die Junii 11mo A.D. 1796, | Æt: 57 | Hibernicus Natu, | (7 lines.) | erected by his only son. W. Rogerson London Fecit.

Michael Keane, late of the I. of St. Vincent, now in Barbados, Esq.   Will proved 1799.   My son Hugh Perry K.   My mother Fra. K. of Ballylongford, co. Kerry.   My marr. sett. with my wife Esther (513, Howe).*

The son mar. in 1797 Susannah, youngest child of Sir Gillies Payne of St. Kitts, 2nd Bart.   She died 7 Oct. 1849, aged 81, at Netley, and he in 1821.

---

101. TO THE DEAR AND BELOVED MEMORY OF | BEZSIN REECE, | WHO (ON HIS VOYAGE TO ENGLAND | FROM THIS ISLAND | FOR THE BENEFIT OF HIS HEALTH | IN THE R.M.S. PACKET DEE) | DEPARTED THIS LIFE THE 22ND SEPT. 1842 | AFTER AN ILLNESS OF SEVERE SUFFERING | LEAVING A WIDOW AND EIGHT CHILDREN. | (15 lines.)

See No. 130.

---

102. SACRED | TO THE MEMORY OF | *SARAH CHRISTIAN,* | INFANT DAUGHTER OF | WILLIAM AND MARY WATSON, | WHO DIED OCT*. 26TH. 1834 | AGED 9 M. | *ALSO MARY WATSON,* | MOTHER OF THE ABOVE | WHO DIED MAY 17 1841 | AGED 28 YEARS. | (2 lines.)

---

103. Shield of arms carved :—

ARMS.—*Gules, on a chevron between three towers a pair of compasses;* impaling: *a cross between in 1st quarter a lion rampant, in 2nd quarter a donkey or sheep (?), in 3rd quarter a priest, in 4th an eagle displayed.*   CREST.—*A bier supported by two angels.*   MOTTO.—AUDI VIDE TACE.   SUPPORTERS.—*Two angels, the outer wing dropped.*

Below the tablet is :—

CREST.—*A dexter arm in armour, in the hand a cross pattée fitchée.*   ARMS.— *Argent, a chevron between three like crosses, all Gules;* impaling: *Azure, in bend a boar's head couped guttée de sang.*   MOTTO.—QUOD POTES ID TENTES.

SACRED TO THE MEMORY OF | THE HONORABLE JOHN ALLEYNE BECKLES, | FOR MANY YEARS PRESIDENT OF THIS ISLAND; | JUDGE OF THE COURT OF VICE ADMIRALTY, | AND PROVINCIAL GRAND-MASTER | OF THE FREE AND ACCEPTED MASONS OF BARBADOES. | HE DEPARTED THIS LIFE ON THE FOURTEENTH DAY OF JULY | ONE THOUSAND EIGHT HUNDRED AND FORTY | AGED SIXTY TWO YEARS. | (13 lines.)

See No. 307.

1677-8, Jan. 10.   Mr Thomas Beckles in Ch:

1679, Aug. 28.   Elisabeth ye dau. of Mr Robert & Susanna B. bapt.

1682, July 19.   Mr Robt B.   (Par. Regr.)

Henry B., s. of Tho. B. of B., gent., Queen's Coll., matric. 24 Oct. 1751, a. 19. (Foster.)

He mar. 1762 Miss Maxwell with £30,000, and was in 1768 Attorney-Gen. John Beckles was Judge of the Court of Vice-Admiralty 1807 and Attorney-Gen.   Edward Hyndman Beckles was Bishop of Sierra Leone 1860.

1840, July 14.   The Hon. John Alleyne B. senior m. of c. in B. & l. President of the island.   ("G.M.," 446.)

---

* See his bookplate impaling a different coat from that on the tablet.

104. CREST.—*A demi-lion rampant couped, in sinister paw a fleur-de-lis.* ARMS.—*Sable, a chevron Argent between three fleurs-de-lis.* MOTTO.—IN TE DOMINE SPERAVI.

IN LOVING MEMORY OF | SIR WILLIAM BRANDFORD GRIFFITH K.C.M.G. | LIEUᵗ GOVERNOR OF THE GOLD COAST COLONY | FROM 1879 TO 1885. | GOVERNOR AND COMMANDER-IN-CHIEF | FROM 1885 TO 1895. | BORN AT BARBADOES 11ᵀᴴ AUGUST 1824. DIED AT BARBADOES 18ᵀᴴ SEPT. 1897. | (3 lines; erected by his widow.)

1845, Sept. 13. In Upper Southwick-st. Hyde Park, Lucy-Cobham, wife of Dr. John Hennen, f. of Southampton & yst. dau. of the l. Tho. Howard Griffith, of the i. of B. ("G.M.," 543.)

———

105. Shield below :—

ARMS.—*Argent, a chevron between three hands couped Gules;* impaling: *Argent, on a chevron Sable between three lions passant guardant Or, as many arrows, all Or* [sic]. (Incorrect heraldry—metal on metal.)

JONAS MAYNARD *ESQᴿ.* | (4 lines.) | was gathered mature in Years and Honor, | on the 3ʳᵈ of Auguſt 1781, | Aged 86. | CHRISTIAN MERCY MAY-NARD | fourth Wife of JONAS MAYNARD *ESQᴿ* | (4 lines.) | reſigned a life of 52 Years, | on the 23ʳᵈ of March 1777, | (2 lines.)

Mary, sole dau. and heiress of Timothy Alleyne, and widow of Hooper and Ball, mar. Jonas Maynard. Reynold Alleyne mar. in 1744 Christian dau. of . . . . Forster. She remar. Jonas Maynard.
See "Caribbeana," i., 24, for M.I. to Wm. Maynard of this Island, who died 21 Nov. 1763, aged 58.
The Rev. Geo. Forster Maynard, M.A., Rector of St. Thomas, died in 1848, aged 58. He mar. a Miss Elcock and had a numerous family. A cousin, the Rev. Geo. Maynard, settled in Canada, and his descendants reside in Toronto. ("Harman Family History," 14.)

———

106. Female standing over urn :—

To | the Memory | of *THOMAS GRIFFITH Eſqʳ*, | and *JANE* his Wife; | (23 lines.) | They were tranſlated to their Reward ; | the former, | on the 4ᵗʰ of Auguſt, 1795, | in the 63ʳᵈ ; | the latter, | July the 11ᵗʰ 1796, | in the 59ᵗʰ Year, | of her Age.   W. PATY BRISTOL Fᵀ.

———

107. Gothic tablet :—

𝕿𝖍𝖎𝖘 𝕿𝖆𝖇𝖑𝖊𝖙 | 𝖜𝖆𝖘 𝖊𝖗𝖊𝖈𝖙𝖊𝖉 𝖙𝖔 𝖙𝖍𝖊 𝖒𝖊𝖒𝖔𝖗𝖞 𝖔𝖋 | 𝕵𝖔𝖘𝖊𝖕𝖍 𝕺𝖘𝖙𝖗𝖊𝖍𝖆𝖓 𝕰𝖘𝖖ʳ. | 𝖜𝖍𝖔 𝖉𝖎𝖊𝖉 𝕬𝖚𝖌𝖚𝖘𝖙 7𝖙𝖍 1809, | 𝖆𝖌𝖊𝖉 52 𝖞𝖊𝖆𝖗𝖘 | 𝖆𝖓𝖉 𝖔𝖋 | 𝕰𝖑𝖛𝖎𝖗𝖆 𝕺𝖘𝖙𝖗𝖊𝖍𝖆𝖓, | 𝖍𝖎𝖘 𝖂𝖎𝖉𝖔𝖜, | 𝖜𝖍𝖔 𝖉𝖎𝖊𝖉 𝕵𝖆𝖓𝖚𝖆𝖗𝖞 12𝖙𝖍 1848, | 𝖎𝖓 𝖙𝖍𝖊 87𝖙𝖍 𝖞𝖊𝖆𝖗 𝖔𝖋 𝖍𝖊𝖗 𝖆𝖌𝖊; | 𝖇𝖞 𝖙𝖍𝖊𝖎𝖗 𝖘𝖔𝖑𝖊 𝖘𝖚𝖗𝖛𝖎𝖛𝖎𝖓𝖌 𝖈𝖍𝖎𝖑𝖉𝖗𝖊𝖓, | 𝖙𝖍𝖊 𝕽𝖊𝖛ᵈ. 𝕵𝖔𝖘𝖊𝖕𝖍 𝕯𝖚𝖓𝖈𝖆𝖓 𝕺𝖘𝖙𝖗𝖊𝖍𝖆𝖓, | 𝖆𝖓𝖉 𝕷𝖚𝖈𝖗𝖊𝖙𝖎𝖆 𝕲𝖎𝖙𝖙𝖊𝖓𝖘, | (4 lines.)

———

108. SACRED TO THE MEMORY OF | MATTHEW COULTHURST, ESQ. | WHO DIED ON THE 24ᵀᴴ OF JUNE | 1833 | AGED 76 YEARS. | (1 line.)
See the floor-stone No. 36.

———

109. On the east wall of nave, north side, under the gallery, are five tablets :—

SACRED TO THE MEMORY OF | *MRS MARGERET ANN DUNN,* | WHO DEPARTED THIS LIFE | FEBY 19TH 1815, AGED 29 YEARS | AND WAS INTER'D FEBY 20TH THE | DAY ON WHICH HER HUSBAND | COMPLEATED HIS 28TH YEAR. | (9 lines.)

---

110. SACRED | TO THE MEMORY OF | DURBAN FREDERICK JENNINGS OLTON, | WHO DEPARTED THIS LIFE ON THE 3RD OF JULY 1861 | AGED 22 YEARS. | (7 lines.) | Erected by his mother ELIZ. ANN OLTON.

---

111. On an oval tablet :—

SACRED | to the Memory of | MARY MYERS, | Wife of CHRISTOPHER MYERS, | a Major in the 70th Regt. of Foot | Her remains are interred in the | Aifle of this Church | Obiit 29th of November A.D. | 1804.

See No. 41.

---

112. To the Memory of | SAMUEL the Son of THOMAS KING | of the City of Briftol | who died of a Decline | amidft the hofpitable attentions | of the Inhabitants of this Ifland | on the 24th March 1823 | aged 21 years.

---

113. SACRED | to the Memory | of | MRS ELIZABETH ANN | the beloved wife of BRYAN TAYLOR YOUNG ESQRE | and only sister of the Revd BRYAN TAYLOR NURSE, | of London | (4 lines.) | Obiit 19th April A.D. 1859.

---

114. On the north wall of chancel are a tablet and brass :—

CREST.—*An arm in armour couped.* ARMS.—*Two bars, in chief three escallops;* impaling: *Gules, a chevron between three demi-lions couped.*

In Memoriam | THOMAS CLARKE, M.A. CANTAB. | RECTOR OF ST MICHAEL'S PARISH | FROM NOVEMBER 1842 TO MARCH 1898 | APPOINTED FIRST DEAN OF BARBADOS MAY 1886, | BORN NOVEMBER 1810, DIED JANUARY 1900. | AND | HIS BELOVED WIFE JULIA | BORN APRIL 1816, DIED SEPTEMBER 1870. | (5 lines; erected by his children.) CATON, 491 OXFORD ST LONDON.

---

115. Brass :—

THIS ALTAR RAIL IS PRESENTED BY | MARIA E. FITZTHOMAS, | TO THE GLORY OF GOD AND LOVED MEMORY | OF HER BROTHER | WILLIAM VERSEPUY FITZTHOMAS | (SOLICITOR & J.P.) | HIS WIFE MARY WORRELL AND INFANT SON | (2 lines.)

---

116. Window, north of altar :—

TO THE GLORY OF GOD AND IN MEMORY OF ROWENA WIFE OF THE HON. JAMES LYNCH M.L.C. WHO DIED JULY 31ST 1885 THIS WINDOW IS ERECTED BY HER SON JAMES CHALLONER LYNCH.

---

117. Window, south of altar:—

TO THE GLORY OF GOD AND IN MEMORY OF THE HON. JAMES ALSOP LYNCH, M.L.C., WHO DIED DEC^R 24TH 1888 THIS WINDOW, etc., as above.

---

118. Circular window over altar:—

Arms of England and V.R. To the sinister side are the arms of the See, impaling: *Argent, on a mound Vert a bear, on a chief Gules a dove between two crosses pattée fitchée.* "W. H. B." St. Michael and the dragon.

---

119. On the south wall of the chancel is the bust of the Bishop in profile:—

IN MEMORY OF WILLIAM HART COLERIDGE D.D. THE FIRST BISHOP OF | THIS SEE, COMPRISING ALSO UNDER HIS JURISDICTION THE LEEWARD ISLANDS AND BRITISH GUIANA, | THIS MONUMENT IS ERECTED BY THOSE WHO WOULD THANKFULLY RECORD THE EXEMPLARY ZEAL | AND PIETY THE FIDELITY AND WISDOM WHICH MARKED HIS EPISCOPATE FROM ITS COMMENCEMENT | A.D. (1824) TO ITS CLOSE (1841) HIS MORTAL REMAINS LIE IN THEIR NATIVE SOIL THE FRUITS OF | HIS LABOURS ARE IN THESE LANDS, TO PROVOKE TO EMULATION AND ADVANCEMENT THOSE WHO | SURVIVE "TILL WE ALL COME IN THE UNITY OF THE FAITH AND OF THE KNOWLEDGE OF THE | GOD UNTO A PERFECT MAN, UNTO THE MEASURE OF THE STATURE OF THE FULNESS OF CHRIST."

To the dexter are the Crest and Arms of Coleridge; to the sinister the arms of the See: *In saltire a crozier and key, a crown in chief, and star in base.*

1825, Oct. 11. At St. Swithin's Church, Winchester, the Lord Bishop of Barbadoes (Dr. Coleridge) to Miss Sarah Eliz. Rennell, dau. of the Very Rev. Tho. R. Dean of Winchester. ("G.M.," 368.)

1827, June 13. At Barbadoes, Wm.-Rennell, infant son of the Lord Bishop and grandson of the Dean of Winchester. (*Ibid.*, 285.)

1849, Dec. 21. At his seat, Saltston, Ottery St. Mary, co. Devon, aged 60, the Right Rev. Wm. Hart Coleridge, D.D., etc. (*Ibid.*, 1850, 207.)

See pedigree in Vivian's "Visitation of Devon," p. 313.

---

120. On a tablet at west end of the south wall of nave, up the stairs to gallery:—

Near this Place are interred the Remains of the Honble JOHN FRANK NICHOLLS | late his Majesty's Solicitor General in this Island who departed this life the 16th | December 1807 Aged twenty five Years. | He was the Youngest Son of JOHN NICHOLLS, Esquire, many Years a distinguished member of the | English Parliament. He married FRANCES eldest Daughter of HENRY MOUNT Esquire in | the month of November 1806. He was called to the English Bar and being possessed of splendid talents | which had long been directed to the acquirement of professional knowledge much might have been | expected from the exercise of them. In the month of April 1807 He was appointed to the office of | Solicitor General and arrived at Barbadoes the later end of November following but unfortunately | survived only three weeks. | (7 lines; erected by widow.)

Signs of missing shield. See floor-stone No. 22.

---

121. In south gallery, on east wall of nave:—

SACRED | TO THE MEMORY OF | GEORGE BROWNE, ESQ^{RE} | (DIED) 30TH JULY 1860 | (7 lines; erected by his pupils.)

T. GAFFIN REGENT ST. LONDON.

---

122. **Sacred** | to the memory of | JN⁰ W. TYNES | Died 19th March 1857 | Aged 48 Years.

---

123.   South gallery, south wall.   Brass:—

To the Glory of God | and to the cherished memory of | JOHN SIMPSON POWELL | who died at Erdiston on the thirteenth August 1899, | in the Sixty ninth year of his age. | For the long period of thirty nine years (1860—1899) he had faithfully and efficiently filled the high and honourable position of Colonial Treasurer of this Island. | (4 lines.)

He mar. in 1862 Annie Bruce Murray, dau. of the Hon. Wm. Murray, head of the Colonial Bank.

See No. 417.

---

124. On west wall of nave, north corner, up the stairs to north gallery, is a wooden monument painted to represent marble:—

CREST.—*A griffin segreant holding an annulet.* ARMS.—*Per fess Argent and Azure three Annulets (2 and 1) counterchanged; impaling: Sable, a griffin segreant Or.*

VIRTUE alone makes all MEN | TRULY NOBLE | In MEMORY of THOMAS DUKE Esq. | TREASURER of this Island. | (16 lines.) | Ob: April 13 An. Dom. 1750 Æ. 53. | (2 lines.)

Humphry Duke, planter, was granted 60 acres in 1630. See Vivian's "Visitation of Devon," p. 311.

Wm. Duke was Clerk of the Assembly in 1756 and Henry his son matric. from Lincoln Coll. in 1760, aged 19.

There were several clergy of the name. See No. 154.

---

125.   North wall, up the stairs:—

IN MEMORY | OF | WALTER HERBERT LYNCH, | (ORGANIST) | WHO DIED 2ND. SEPTEMBER 1900, AGED 27 YEARS. | (6 lines.)

---

126.   East wall of nave, north gallery:—

IN HIS FAMILY VAULT WITHIN THE | CONSECRATED PRECINCTS OF THIS CATHEDRAL | REST THE MORTAL REMAINS OF | THE HONORABLE WILLIAM GILL, | WHO HAVING SERVED HIS COUNTRY FOR MORE THAN | THIRTY YEARS IN THE RESPECTIVE OFFICES OF AUDITOR | OF PUBLIC ACCOUNTS ADJUTANT GENERAL OF MILITIA | CHIEF BARON OF THEIR MAJESTIES COURT OF EXCHEQUER | MASTER IN THE HIGH AND HONORABLE COURT OF | CHANCERY AND TWICE PRESIDENT OVER THE COURT OF | GRAND SESSIONS | CONDUCTING FOR THIS LONG PERIOD (AS SENIOR PARTNER | OF THE FIRM) AN EXTENSIVE MERCANTILE ESTABLISHMENT | DIED ON THE 6TH JUNE 1846, IN THE 62ND YEAR OF HIS AGE. | (9 lines.)

1801. Lately. Geo. Gill, esq. of B., to Miss Catherine Wornum, of Wigmore-str. ("G.M.," 1052.)

127. THIS MONUMENT IS ERECTED | TO THE MEMORY OF MARIA ANNE, DAUGHTER OF | THOMAS DANIEL ESQᴿᴱ OF BERKELEY SQUARE, BRISTOL | AND OF HENBURY IN THE COUNTY OF GLOUCESTER, | AND WIFE OF THOMAS LEWIS ESQᴿᴱ OF Sᵀ PIERRE, | IN THE COUNTY OF MONMOUTH. | JOURNEYING FROM ENGLAND TO THIS ISLAND | FOR THE BENEFIT OF HER HEALTH, SHE DIED AT SEA | ON MONDAY THE 14ᵀᴴ DAY OF APRIL 1817, | IN THE 23ᴿᴰ YEAR OF HER AGE.

See account of the Daniel family in Cave's " History of Banking in Bristol."

In the west porch are two tablets and one ledger.

128. White marble tablet on west wall, south side:—

SACRED | To the Memory of | Serjeant Major | *ARCHIBALD JOHN- STON* | of the | Second or Queen's | Royal Regiment of foot | who | After having faithfully & honourably | served his *KING* and Country for the | space of 18 Years; with his Regiment | in the Campaigns, in Portugal, Spain | and France, under his Grace the | *DUKE OF WELLINGTON*, | discharging his duties with | advantage to the Service and | Credit to himself, Died after | a short illneſs at Sᵗ Ann's | Barracks Barbadoes on the | 14ᵗʰ September 1816 | Aged 36 Years. | This Stone is Erected as a tribute | of reſpect to his Memory, by the | Non-Commiſſioned Officers and | Privates of the Regiment.

W. D. Bartlett, Sculp: Barbadoes.

129. Tablet on west wall, north side:—

SACRED | To the Memory of the following Officers | of the 2ⁿᵈ (or Queens) Royal Regiment | Buried near this spot, | who after a Series of Meritorious Services | under his Grace the | *DUKE of WELLINGTON* | and in almoſt every Quarter of the Globe | fell together with many Old & valuable | Non-Commᵈ Officers & Soldiers early | Victims to a deſtructive fever raging in | Barbados A.D. 1816.

CAPTᴺ J. GORDON SENᴿ.	LIEVᵀ GRANT.
LIEVᵀ CLUTTERBUCK	LIEVᵀ ADJᵀ SPENCER
LIEVᵀ McDOUGALL	LIEVᵀ MASSIE
LIEVᵀ GRAY	ENSIGN RICHMOND
LIEVᵀ NORMAN	ASSᵀ SURGᴺ PRENDERGAST.

Brave Men | ye deſerved a brighter field, yet shall the | pale roſe shed its dews upon your untimely | grave, & memory cheriſh your contemplation | with no less dignity that ye fell before | an Almighty hand. | This Stone | is placed here | as a tribute of Regard to departed Merit by | Lᵗ Col. H. C. E. Vernon Graham | Commanding the Regᵗ. C. Ashmead, Sculp. Queens.

130. Ledger:—

Here lie the Remains of | .. EZSIN KING REECE | who departed this life on the | 23ʳᵈ day of September 1838 | Aged 73 Years.

See No. 101.

In the north porch there are no ledgers. In the south porch there are six.

131. Skull and hour-glass above in a circle:—

Here Lyes Interr'd yᵉ Body of | Mʳˢ DOROTHY SHEPHERD Wife of | Mʳ IAMES SHEPHERD Merchant | who departed this life on Wedneſday | the 7ᵗʰ of Iuly 1736 Aged 53 Years | 2 Months and 23 Days. | Here Lyes alſo

E

Interr'd yᵉ Body of | Mʳ IAMES SHEPHERD Merchant | Hufband of the above named | DOROTHY who departed this life | on Tuefday the 26ᵗʰ of May 1741 | Aged 48 Years 10 Months and | 25 Days.

Also the Body of The Honᵇˡᵉ JAMES SHEPHERD Son of the | abovenamed who departed this Life | the 7ᵗʰ day of June 1795 Aged 79 Years | *A Sincere Christian* | Also the Body of D. M. MURRAY Great Grandson of the | last named JAMES SHEPHERD, Who died 16ᵗʰ day May 1810 | Aged 5 Days.

See No. 167.

1736, July 8. Dorothy wife of Mʳ James Shepherd.

1741, May 27. Mʳ James Shepherd Merchᵗ. (Burial Register.)

Alex. Bruce, M.D., of Edinburgh, mar. 12 Jan. 1763 Dorothy, dau. of Jas. Shepherd, Chief Baron of the Court of Exchequer, and had an only dau. and heiress Keturah Shepherd Bruce, who mar. firstly, 24 June 1787, Lieut. Devenish, R.N., and 2ndly in Jan. 1798 Wm. Murray of the Customs, by whom she left a large family. ("Harman Family," p. 5.)

---

132. HEARE LYETH | ENTERRED Yᴱ BODY | OF ROBART FARRAR | SON OF THOMAS & | HANNAH FARRAK | WHO DEPARTED THIS | LIFE Yᴱ JJᵗʰ DAY OF | NOVEMBER 1695 | AGED 19 MONETHS.

1695, Nov. 12. Robert Farrar & children. (Burial Register.)

---

133. Small square floor-stone :—

Rob. Hoyle | 16 . 8.

1698, May 18. Mʳ [*blank*] Hoyle merchᵗ.

---

134. Inscription on a border framewise :—

Here lieth | the Bodie of Allan Lyde | Merch: who | Departed this . . . e the 17ᵗʰ of | January 1680.

In the centre, surmounted by an hour-glass and cross-bones, is this secondary inscription :—

And . . . . hear Lyeth | the Body of francis | ye Sonn of . . . . | . . . . and Jane his wife | who Departed this | . ife March . . . .

---

135. Small fragment :—

Elizᵗʰ Cole | 1698.

1698, May 11. Eliza Cole, a child. (Burial Register.)

---

136. Nearly obliterated :—

Vnder this Stone | expecting a glori | ous resurrection | lyeth interr'd the | Body of Cap . . . . | Christo B . adl* . . . . | who depᵈ this life | the 14ᵗʰ day of Augᵗ | 1683. | (1 line illegible.)

1685, Aug. 30. Capᵗ Christopher B . . . bury (? Bradbury).

---

137. Blue marble fragment :—

As also | GARET th . . . . | mentioned RI . . . . | sʜɪʀᴇ who dep . . . . | . ife the twenty | of *October* 1729 a . . . . | fifty 3 Year of . . . .

1729, Oct. 25. Mʳˢ Mary Wiltshire widᵒ in the Church, a sermon. (Burial Register.)

* " l " or " b."

In the way leading to the south gate are six ledgers.

138. About 13 lines, no name, mostly flaked away.

---

139. Traces of a shield above :—

Here lies the Body of THOMAZIN, | Daughter of Colonel THOMAS THORNHILL | & PHILIPPA his wife Daughter of IOHN DIVLES (?) | [crack here] Esq. who was firſt married to WARDALL | ANDREWS Esq. of this Iſland but afterward | to WILLIAM SAVAGE Esq. of *Bloxworth* in yᵉ | *County* of *Dorſet*, & then departed this life | the 27ᵗʰ day of *March* 1718.

1698, Sept. 22. Collᵒ Thomas Thornhill. (Burial Register.)
See St. George's parish, No. 825, and St. Thomas.
1718, March 29. Mʳˢ Thomasⁱⁿ Savage i'th Chancel. (Burial Register.)

---

140. Here lies Interrd the body of EDWARD | PEARCE *Obiit* the 19ᵗʰ Day of *Decemʳ 1725* | Æ. 23 Years.

1725, Dec. 19. Mʳ Edward Pearce. (Burial Register.)

---

141. Short inscription, name gone.

---

142. Here Lyes Interrd the | Body of ROB MILN Son to | DAVID MILN Merch .... | Barbados who died .... 1 .ᵗʰ | of March 1699 Aged .... | month & one day | Also the Body of | DAVID MILN 2 Son to the | above DAVID MILN who died | the 1 of .... 17 .. Aged | Seventeen months 2 days.

No burial of the name in March 1699.
1713, Nov. 23. Robert Miln a child in Church. (Burial Register.)

---

143. On a shield with mantling in sunk oval :—

CREST.—*A bird on W. and H.* ARMS.—*A chevron between three covered cups.*

Here Lyeth Interrd the Body of .... | SHAW Son of THOMAS | ELIZA-BETH SHAW who Departed | Ag .. | WILLIAM SHAW Son of Said | THOMAS & ELIZABETH SHAW | .... 1713 | Year of .... Age | Here lyeth A .. o the Body of | Mʳ THOMAS SHAWE Merch who | .... this life the .... 17 . 2 | In the 42 Year of his Age | Also yᵉ Body of Mʳˢ ELIZ: BOOTH Widow | who departed .... [12 Feb. 1721] | in the 67 Year of Her .... [crack here].

The date within brackets is given by Archer.
1713, Dec. 13. Wᵐ Shawe a child.
1728-9, Feb. 18. Mʳ Thomas Shawe. (Burial Register.)

---

144. In the paving to south of nave and east of porch are the following ledgers :—

Here lieth the Body of | IOHN FELTON Citizen | and Gouldſmith of | LONDON who Departed | this life the 14ᵗʰ of May | 1694 Aged 62 | years 9 Months.

1694, May yᵉ 5ᵗʰ. Mʳ John ffelton. (Burial Register.)

145. SACRED TO THE MEMORY | OF | *HENRY FOW .* E ESQ* |
FORMERLY A SEARCHER IN HIS | MAJESTYS CUSTOMS OF THE PORT | OF BRIDGE
TOWN IN THIS ISLAND | WHO DEPARTED THIS LIFE | DECEMBER 17 1788 AGED
62 YEARS | ALSO | *SARAH* RELICT OF | *HENRY FOWKE ESQ^RE* | WHO
DEPARTED THIS LIFE | NOVEMBER 14TH 1825 | AGED [*blank*] YEARS.

1788, Dec. 17th. Henry Fowke. (Burial Register.)

---

146. ARMS.—*A chevron.*

Here | Lyeth the Body of Edward fon of | Col° William Wanton | and Ruth
his Wife | Of Newport on Road Ifland | Who deceafed Feby ye 21st 172⁰⁄₁ | In
the 19th Year of his Age. | (11 lines, some of them flaked.)

1720-1, Feb. 22. Edward Wanton. (Burial Register.)
Edw. Wanton born, according to Austin, 11 April 1702, son of William and
Ruth (Bryant) Wanton of Newport. His father, a noted merchant, was Speaker
of the House of Deputies, Assistant Major for the Island, and in 1732 Governor
of the Colony.
See "Barbadian Notes," by G. Andrews Moriarty, Jun., A.M. of Newport,
R.I., in the "New Eng. Hist. and Gen. Regr." for Oct. 1913, vol. lxvii., pp. 360—
371.

---

147. Square tablet under the window :—

In Memory of | ELIZABETH FRASER | who died the 1st of | December
1792. | Aged 61 Years | 1 Month & 1 Day.

---

148. Much flaked :—

Here Lyeth Intered y^e | Body of John Wadwor^th | who Departed this Life
y^e | 10 Day of January . . 30 | Aged 4 . . . (flaked) | Here . . . . M^rs | Iane
W . . . . | of M^r . . . . | . . . . late | . . . . s . . | 169⁵⁄₆ | Aged 59 . . ars . . . . | . . . .

No burial Jan. 1730.
1695-6, March 11. Mrs Jane Wadsworth widow. (Burial Register.)

---

149. Surface flaking :—

Here rest entombed | the remains of Jos THORNE Pract. in Physic | Who
died Octr 30 1810 | In . . . . Year of his age. | (13 lines.)

---

150. . . . . ED | . . . . mory of M^r | A (?) Chase Son of I. A. Chase | & Sarah
his wife | who Depar . . . . life | . . . . | the 42 . . . . his Age.

---

151. . . . . | Body of Mary | Stephenfon wife | of Geo^e Stephenfon | Corp^l
i . . . . Royal | Brit . . | . . . .

---

152. . . . . D THE BO . . . . | BERT BLACK . . . . | 38 YEARS WHO . . . . | PARTED
THIS LIFE | MAY THE 10 167 .

(? Blackdon or Blackman.) Searched Burials unsuccessfully 1670—80.

* Crack.

153. Here l... In .... the Body | JOHN OWEN | Who Died Sepr 7th 1742 | Aged 29 Years.

1742, Sept. 8. Mr John Owen. (Burial Register.)

154. This sepulchre Belongs to the | REV^D IOHN DUKE | In which are deposited the Remains | of BULSTRODE WHITELOCK | Son of MAJOR | JOHN WHITELOCK | & MARY LEWIS his Wife | Who departed this life Augt 5th 1796 | Aged 3 Months .... Days.

1765, Sept. Rev. Mr. Duke, a planter at B. ("G.M.," 491.)
Rev. J. Duke went out 20 June 1783, John Duke on 31 Aug. 1779, and William Duke on 24 May 1758.
See No. 124.

---

155. The right half has been broken off and is missing :—

Here lyeth .... | of IN^O the .... | PILGRIM bor .... | ENGLAND ag .... | who deceafe .... | Septem .... | Allfoe the bo .... | the wife of IN .... | of HENRY & E .... | -MEW and bo .... | ENGLAND age .... | yeares who d .... | day of Octo^br A ....

---

156. Here lie the Remains of | Mrs ELIZABETH WHITE | who Departed this Life the | 15th. October 1818. | in the 64th Year of her Age.

---

157. Very deeply cut and a crack through the stone :—

Here lyeth the Body of | MR TIMOTHY PINDER | Who Departed this life | the 4th Day of October An^o Dom. 1723. | Aged 40 years | Allso Here Lyeth The Body of | Mr Thos Cheef Ma .... Who De : | Parted This Life The 6th Day | of FeBruary 1740 Aged 48 | Years.

1723, Oct. 6. Capt. Timothy Pindar.
1740, Feb. 17. Capt. Thomas Cheesman. (Burial Register.)
The Hon. Wm. Pinder, Chief Justice, died Dec. 1806.

---

158. Here lies the Body of | MARY the loving and beloved Wife of | MICHAEL M'NEMARA M.D. | She died February the 8th | 1757 | In the 34th Year of her Age | Here alfo are buried | MARGARET daughter of THOMAS | And | MARGARET ADAMS | Ob. October 14th | 1737 | Aged 3 Years 4 Months and 17 Days | THOMAS | Son of ditto ob. December 22^d | 1737 | Aged 1 Year 4 Months and 9 Days | JAMES ELLIOT | Son of ditto ob. Auguft the (30?) | 1740, | Aged 1 Year 3 Months 23 Days | And | MARGARET wife of THOMAS ADAMS | Ob. June the 30th | 1743 | Aged 38 Years 9 Months | and 15 Days.

1737, Oct. 14. Mary (sic) Da. of Mr Thos Adams.
1737, Dec. 22. Thomas son of Mr Thomas Adams.
1740, Aug. 31. James Elliott son of Mr Thos Adams.
1764, Sept. 3. Thomas Adams Esqr M.C. (Burial Register.)

---

159. White marble inscription, at present illegible; it requires scrubbing.

160. ELIZABETH JANE CAREW | Firſt Child of | WALTER and JANE CAREW | Died the 1ˢᵗ of October 1776 | Aged 8 Years and 27 days. | (12 lines.)

161. Small square :—

1876 | ARTHUR | C.

162. . . . . y of | . . . . y 2ᴰ of 10ʰᵉʳ | . . . . s Age | ᴇʟɪᴢ his wife who dyed | Xᴮᴱᴿ 1679 in yᵉ 59ᵗʰ yeare | of her ᴀɢᴇ | . . . . yᵉ body of ɪᴀᴄᴏʙ ʙʀᴀɴᴅᴛ their ſon | . . . . o died yᵉ 20ᵗʰ of ɪᴠɴᴇ 1700 in yᵉ 56ᵗʰ | yeare of his age.

1679, Dec. 6.   Mʳˢ Elizᵃ Brandt wido :
1700, June 21.   Mʳ Jacob Brandt.   (Burial Register.)

163. In corner of chancel and nave walls :—

Edouard Engren | A Native of Paris | Died 25ᵗʰ July 1819 | Aged 48 Years.

164. Upright stone against east wall of nave :—

Sacred | ᴛᴏ | The Memory of | JAMES W. KING, | Who died 15ᵗʰ May 1852 : Aged 57. | ᴀʟsᴏ | ᴇʟɪᴢᴀʙᴇᴛʜ ᴀᴜɢᴜsᴛᴀ, | *His Daughter* | The Wife of | JAMES GIRDWOOD, | Who died 17ᵗʰ January 1867, Aged 41.

165. Here Reſteth the Bodyes | of IVDITH and SVSANAH ELLICOTT | Daughters of THOMAS | and SVSANAH ELLICOTT. | IVDITH Departed this life yᵉ . . . . of | IVNE 1703 Aged 29 hours and | SVSAᴴ departed yᵉ 5ᵗʰ of Octᴬ 1704 | Aged twenty days.

1703, June 12.   Judith Ellacott.   (Burial Register.)

166. Inscription on a border framewise, touching south wall of chancel :—

Hᴇʀᴇ . . . . | . . ᴇ ʙᴏᴅʏ ᴏғ ʙᴇɴᴊᴀᴍᴇɴ ʟᴇ ɢᴀʏ ᴍᴇʀ | ᴄʜᴀɴᴛ ᴡʜᴏ | ᴅᴇᴘᴀʀᴛᴇᴅ ᴛʜɪs ʟɪғᴇ ᴛʜᴇ 7 ᴅᴀʏ ᴏғ | ɪᴠɴᴇ 1676 | ᴀɢᴇᴅ 27 . ᴇᴀʀs | In the centre is this secondary inscription :—ᴇʟɪᴢᴬ ᴛʜᴇ | ᴡɪғᴇ ᴏғ ɪᴏʜɴ | ʟᴇɢᴀʏ| ᴏʙᵀ 25ᵀᴴ sᴇᴘᴛᴇᴍʙᴇʀ 1677 | ᴀʟsᴏ ɪᴏʜɴ | ʟᴇ ɢᴀʏ. | (Hour-glass, skull, and cross-bones.) | ʜᴜsʙᴀɴᴅ ᴏғ ᴛʜᴇ | sᴀɪᴅ ᴇʟɪᴢᴬ ᴏʙᵀ | 14 ᴊᴠʟʏ 1685.

1676, June 8.   Ensigne Benjᵃ Legay.
1677, Sept. 25.   Elizᵃ the wife of Mʳ John Legay.
1685, July 15.   Mʳ John Legay.   (Burial Register.)
Jacob Le Gay.   Will proved 1721 (205, Buckm.).   Tho. Butler of Barbados and London, Merchant, mar. 1631 Kath., sister of Jacob Le Gay.

Returning now from the south porch, westwards, are the following ledgers :—

167. *JAMES SHEPHERD* Junʳ: | departed this life | November 1ˢᵗ: 1772 | Aged 30 Years | Thomas Harrison Shepherd Esqʳ | Son of the above | who departed this Life 9ᵗʰ Septʳ 1819 | Aged 48 Years and 10 Months.

See No. 131.

168. Mrs JANE DUFFEY | Departed this Life | November 9th 1757 | Aged 63 Years.

---

169. Here Lieth the Body of | IONES PARK who Departed | this Life 14th Day of Augst | 1749 | Aged 80 Years.

1750, Aug. 15. Jones Park. (Burial Register.)

---

170. Sacred | to the Memory of | ANN GASKIN WILLIAMS | Obiit . . . . December 1823. | . . . . Years. | (2 lines.)

---

171. Here Lyeth Interd ye Body | of My: D: of . . . . | Son of W^m M . . . . | Aged 13 Months | The . . . . Day . . . . ay 173 .

---

172. SACRED | TO THE MEMORY OF | EDWARD CHANNELL | LATE PURSER OF THE R.M.S. PACKET | THAMES | D. 11th JANUARY 1853, | AGED 33 YEARS. | (2 lines.)

1853, Jan. 11. At B., of yellow fever, aged 36, Edw. Channell, purser of R.M.S.P. Thames. ("G.M.," 329.)

---

173. Fragment; foot-stone of No. 178 :—

Capt JOHN | RAINSFORD | DEPARTED THIS | LIFE FEBRUA^{RY}. | Y^e III. 1710-11 | Made in Charlftown.

1710-11, Feb. 4. Captⁿ: John Randsford of N^w Eng^d. (Burial Register.)
Probably son of John Rainsford of Boston, ship-carpenter, who died 5 April 1698, and grandson of Edward of Boston. (G. A. Moriarty.)

---

174. ALSO | TO THE MEMORY OF | MARY HARRIET JAMES | THE BELOVED WIFE . . . . | WHO DIED . . . . | AGED . . . .

---

175. Here lyeth interred ye body | of SIMON COOPER Mafon who de | parted this life ye 2^d of Decemb^r 1694 | Aged 63 year's | Alfo MARY his wife who departed | this life the 26th of FEBRUARY 16⁹⁸/₉₉ | Aged 63 year's.

1694, Dec. 2. Mr Symon Cooper.
1698-9, Feb. 27. Mrs Mary Cooper. (Burial Register.)

---

176. Lyeth Interred the Body of | . . . . NCIS MOSE who departed | . . . . fe March the 4th 1773 | . . . . ged 38 Years.

1773, March 5. Francis Mose. (Burial Register.)

---

177. Underneath this Stone | Lie two Sons of SAMUEL | and MARY WOODIN | JOHN died Septr ye 10th 1747 | Aged 2 Years 6 Months | and 26 Days | SAMUEL died Septr ye 10th | 1748 Aged 6 Months and 23 | Days. | Here Lieth the Body of | Mary Ann Scott Wife of | Capt William Scott, | who departed this Life | November ye 23^d 1779.

178. Fragment of blue marble; ? formerly a headstone, now fixed flat. I chipped off cement from some words :—

Jac. mantling. CREST.—*A stag statant over W. and H.* ARMS.—*A cross, in first quarter a star of six points.*

Capt JOHN RAINSFORD OF Bofton in | NEW ENGLAND Ætatis Suæ XLIX & XI m°.

179. Here Lyeth Intered | of ANN MOORE wife | WILLIAM MOORE . h . . . | This Life the Eighteenth D . . | 1732 Aged 23 years.

1732, April 17. Ann wife of Mr Wm Moore. (Burial Register.)

180. Here lie the Remains of | ISABELLA, | the Wife | and | ELIZA and JOHN | Daughter and Son | of | ISAAC GITTENS.

181. To the Memory | of ADRIAN LERNOUET | LERNOUET ESQ who | departed this life | 1st Jvly 1703 aged 35 | Years & 2 Months.

No burial in 1703.

182. Inscription on border framewise :—
HEARE L . . . . ELIZ | (this cemented) . . . . GHTER OF THO | (end border missing.) | (Blank border.) | In the centre is this secondary inscription :—Here lyeth the . . . . | Of . . . z: wife Of | ffearcharson wh . | departed this ly. . | 18th of August 1681 A . . | 38 years. | Heere Lieth Bur . . . | ye Bodye of Kathari . . | Daughter OF Tho & | Eliz Fercharson Who | Departed This Life | May 31. 1666 | Also ye Body of ELIZ. | Goodall Mother of | Eliz Fercharson Who | . . parted this Life | 16 . 6 A . . . d . 4.

No burial May 1666 nor 1686.
1681, Aug. 19. Elizabeth the wife of Mr Tho: ffercharson. (Burial Register.)
Mary Fercharson mar. 15 Oct. 1726 Col. Robert Yeamans, Junr.

Many stones if cleaned would give better readings of doubtful lines.

183. Here lies the Body of | Katharine Weft Eldeft | Daughter of Edward & Ann | Weft died the 20th June 1779 | Aged 2 Years & 6 Months. | Alfo the Body of Elizabeth | Ann Weft Second Daughter | of the faid Edward & Ann | Weft died 20th Auguft 1779. | Aged 10 Months. | ALSO the Body of Edward | West Father of the above | mentioned children Died | 7th Iune 1780 | Aged 33 y^rs and 7 Months.

1779, June 21. Katharine Daug^r of Edward West.
1779, Aug. 21. Elizabeth Ann, Daug^r of Edwd West.
1780, July 8 (*sic*). Edward West. (Burial Register.)

184. In Memory | of | (2 lines illegible.) | . . . . 1807 | . . Years | ALSO | . . . . Child Elizabeth Goodson | . . . . August the . . . | Aged 19 Months | (5 more lines.)

185. In perfect condition :—

Hcre Lyeth Interred the Body | of Robert Draper Merchant | who Departed this life the xxii | of September MDCLXXXVII | about the xxx^th year of | his age.

1087, Sept. 25.   Mr Robert Draper.   (Burial Register.)

We are now at the south-west end of nave, where the passage is covered with two rows of ledgers up to the porch. I have taken the west row first. They are mostly of blue marble, and have probably been removed from the church or from vaults in the churchyard.

186. Blue marble, in perfect condition :—

Jac. mantling in sunk oval.   No crest.   ARMS.—*A chevron engrailed between three lions rampant.*

HERE LYETH THE BODY OF | ANN Y^E WIFE OF JAMES JONES | MERCHANT WHO DIED Y^E 3^D | OF OCT^BR 1731 AGED NEAR | 37 YEARS.

1731, Oct. 4.   Ann wife of Mr James Jones.   (Burial Register.)
The adjoining ledger has no inscription left.

---

187. Grey marble :—

HERE LYETH INTERRED Y^E BODY | OF MARGARET WIFE OF CAP_T | HERNY (*sic*) WHITE WHO DEPARTED | THIS LIFE Y^E 11TH OF APRILL | IN Y^E 29TH YEAR OF HER AGE | 1696.

1696, April 11.   Margaret y^e wife of Capt Henry White.   (Burial Register.)

---

188. Blue marble :—

Here lyeth the Body of | *JOHN BUCKLER* | Son of Andrew & Mary Buckler | who departed this Life | April 30th on thurſday 1752. | Aged 20 Years, 5 Months | and 20 Days.

1752, May 1.   John Buckler.   (Burial Register.)

---

189. Much flaked :—

Here lyeth Interred the Body | of MARTIN FRIDENBERG | who departed this Life ye 12 of Sep^t 1732 | Alſo the Body of MARY his wife | And of his Son Nicholas | Likewiſe three grand Sons of the above | Children of William & Ann Kelto | And another grand Child of the above | Daughter of Henry & Katharine Haughn | who . . . . ted this Life | the . . . . November 1748 | Aged one Year.

1732, Sept. 15.   Martin Fridenburg a Taylor.
1748, Nov. 19.   Anna Maria Daugh^r of Henry Haughn.   (Burial Register.)

---

190. Blue marble :—

To the Memory of | *Lieu^t & Adj^t* | JOHN DOLMAN | 86th *Reg^t*. | Died 8th Jan^y | 1828 | Aged 30 Years.

F

191. White marble and cracked:—

Here lies the Body | JAMES JEZZEPH | late Coachman to the Righ . . . . |
LORD COMBERMER . . | Governor of Barbados | and | Commander of the
Forces | in the Windward and Leeward Islands | who died November the 13ᵗʰ
1817 | Aged 50 Years. | (1 line.)

192. This stone has cement covering up the top:—

TUR . . . . | who departed . . . . | 31ˢᵗ October | In the 57 Year of his Age.

193. Blue marble:—

THE BVRIALL PLACE OF | Mʳ IOHN LEARY AND FAMILY. | Here Lies Interr'd
the body of Capᵗ | MATTHEW LEARY who Departed | this Life the 15ᵗʰ
October 1750 in the | 47ᵗʰ Year of his Age.

1750, Oct. 15.   Matthew Leary.   (Burial Register.)

194. Blue marble:—

This Tomb is erected | to the Sacred Memory of | CHARLES PADMORE
Eſqʳ of the Pariſh | of Saint James who departed this life | the 5ᵗʰ February
1794 Aged fifty Years. | And alſo for his dearly beloved Son | SAMUEL.

195. Blue marble:—

Here lie Interred the Body of | AGNES DOWNES HORDLE | *Wife of*
THOMAS HORDLE | died the 24ᵗʰ of July 1795 | Aged 26 Years. | *Alſo*
MARGARET HORDLE | *Daughter of the above* | died the 19ᵗʰ of July 1791 |
Aged 3 Years. | *Alſo* SARAH HORDLE | *Daughter of the above* | died the 30ᵗʰ
of Novʳ 1793, | Aged 16 Months.

Here we reach the porch, and return to the second row of ledgers touching
the west wall of nave, south end.

196. Blue marble. In corner of porch and west wall of nave:—

JOHN KIRTON | died September 14ᵗʰ 1797 | Aged 51 Years.

197. *SACRED* | to the Memory of | JOHN PILARO . T | THOMAS | who
departed this life | August the 9ᵗʰ 1804 | Aged 63 Years | and three Months. |
(8 lines.)

I could not find the burial entry.

198. Blue marble:—

Here Lyeth the Body of Mʳ | *William Jordan* Late of | This Town Merchant
Wʜᴏ | Departed this Life the 21ᵗʰ augᵗ | 1700 aged 56 yeares | Also *Mary* his
Daughter | Wʜᴏ Departed this Life the | 4ᵗʰ of Iune 1714 aged 16 yeares | one
Month and 26 Days.

1700, Sept. 7.   Wᵐ Jordan.
1714, June 7.   Mʳˢ Mary Jordan Spinstʳ.   (Burial Register.)
See No. 812.

199. In Memory of *SARAH REID* | who departed this life June the . . . . |
(All the rest flaked away. The adjoining stone has no inscription.)

----

200. White marble :—

𝔖𝔞𝔠𝔯𝔢𝔡 | to the memory of | 𝔊𝔯𝔞𝔠𝔢 | Wife of GEO. MACDERMOTT ESQ^RE |
Surgeon 4th (or the KINGS OWN) Reg^t. | Who departed this life | on the 22^d
Sept^r | 1822. | (2 Latin lines.)

----

201. Very much worn :—

Here lies the Remains of | JA . . . . SMITH | . . . . | . . . . the 6th October |
. . . . Year of her Age | HE . . Y WILSON departed | this life the 30th June
17 . . | In the . . . . Year of his Age.

----

202. Surface flaked :—

Here lyeth the Body of | Mrs SARAH . . NDFORD | who departed this
Life | the 5th day of Nov . . . . 1746 | Aged 43 Years.

1736, May 5. The honble John Sandford Esqr.
1746, Nov. 6. Mrs Sarah Sandford. (Burial Register.)

There are no ledgers in the way from the west porch to the west gate, nor to
the north side of the west wall of the nave.

In the way from the north porch into the churchyard there are nine ledgers,
as follows :—

203. Blue marble :—

HERE LYETH INTERRED | THE BODY OF EMLIN POLLARD | WHO DEPARTED
THIS LIFE | JUNE 21st 1712 AGED 78 YEARS | AND THE BODYES OF | IOHN POLLARD,
SAMUELL POLLARD | MARY POLLARD AND | IOHN POLLARD IUN^r CHILDREN | OF
DOCT^r IOHN POLLARD | ALSO MARY POLLA (cement) | OF THE S^d Dr IOHN
PO . . . . | WHO DEPARTED THIS L . . . . | MAY 26^tt (*sic*) 1733 AGED 45 YEARS.

1712, June 22. Mrs Emlin Pollard.
1733, May 27. Mrs Mary Pollard wife of Doct^r John Pollard, a Sermon.
(Burial Register.)
Dr. Tho. Pollard of Bridgetown had a son John at Eton 1761—71, matric. from
Queen's Coll., Oxford, 7 June 1771, aged 18 ; another son Walter at Eton 1761—
66, then at Harrow and Eman. Coll., Cambridge. See their correspondence
1771—88, Add. MS. 35,655, British Museum.

----

204. Blue marble, much worn, with inscription running around the border,
and skull and cross-bones in an oval in the centre :—

Here lyeth the Body | of Eli . . . . ore . . . . ton wife | Departed this Life the
xvii Day of | February 167 . | Aged about xv yeeres.

The foot of the stone is missing. I could not find entry in Burial Register.

----

205. 𝔥𝔢𝔯𝔢 𝔩𝔦𝔢𝔰 𝔦𝔫𝔱𝔢𝔯𝔯𝔢𝔡 𝔱𝔥𝔢 𝔅𝔬𝔡𝔶 | of PRUDENCE CHAUCER | Wife of
BENONY CHAUCER | who departed this Life | Dec^br the 20th 1795 Aged
67 Years.

206. This stone is illegible. It has been hacked to hold mortar, as though used upside down, before placed in its present position.

---

207. Blue marble :—

Here lieth John Son of James & | Mary Booth, he did (*sic*) 15th Septr 1749 | in the firſt Year of his Age. | Alſo Mary their Daughter died on | ye (*blank*) of April 1751 Aged (*blank*) Days.

1749, Sept. 15.   John Son of James Booth.
1750-1, March 21.   Mary Daughtr of James Boothe.   (Burial Register.)

---

208. This stone, if scrubbed, the inscription might be more legible :—

Here lies Interred the Body | of ANN WOOLFORD Wife of | THOMAS WOOLFORD | who Departed this life the . .th | December 1742 Aged 44 Years | Alſo her three Infants | ELIZTH ANN & ROBERT who died | Under two Years Old | Alſo WILLIAM JENKINS the | Brother of ANN WOOLFORD | who Departed this life the 26th | of Auguſt 1725 Aged 38 Years. | Alſo WALTER HYDE WOOLFORD | Son of THO. & DOROTHY WOOLFORD | who Departed this life | In . . . . Year . . . . Age | . . . . | . . sband | Children who died ye 24 of August 173 . | Aged | And also the Body of Rebecca | loving & beloved Wife of Tho. Woolford | . on of ye above who died ye 29 of Iune | . . . . the 19 year of her age.

1725, Oct. 19.   Mr William Jenkins.   (There was no burial in August 1725.)
1742, Dec. 28.   Mrs Ann Woolford wife of Mr Thomas Woolford.   (Burial Register.)

---

209. **Erected** | by the | Officers of the Mail Boat | to the memory of | JAMES JOHNSTON | who departed this life 16 July | **A.D.** 1821 | *aged 52 years.*

---

210. White marble :—

Sacred | to | the memory of | CHARLES OLIPHINT | *Native of Scotland* | who departed this life | the 16th of Sep. A.D. 1821 | aged 29 years.

---

211. White marble :—

Sacred to the Memory | *of* | THOMAS PAYNE | *and* | JANE NILES.

211A. **Sacred to Memory** | Here lieth the Remains | *of* | FRANCIS WATTS | who departed this life | the 6th October 1826 | Aged 44 Years.

---

212. SACRED | TO THE MEMORY OF | CHRISTIAN GAY EDGHILL | *WIFE OF SAMUEL EDGHILL* | Who d . . . . of August 1841 | Aged 61 YEARS. | (4 lines.)

---

213. Broken up blue marble ledger, just beyond No. 211. The three fragments do not fit together :—

. . . . y of Mar	. . . . ghter of	the ab . . . .
. . . MAS MORRIS de	. . . A . . . . Ob. 6th Febry	1764 Æ . . . .
8th day of Octobe		
. . . . 8 months.		

Nos. 214 to 256 are all flat stones laid down in the way around the church. They must have been brought from elsewhere. Commencing from the north porch.

214. On a loose fragment of very thick marble :—

Here lieth the body of .... | the daughter of THOMAS & ELEA .... | ... RRISON who departed this lif.... | .... mber the 9th 1712 Aged 2 Years & ....

1712, Nov. 1. Jane ye Da: of Mr Thos: & Mrs Ellenr: Harrison bo. Octobr: 30th. (Bapt.)
1712, Dec. 9. Jane Harrison, a child. (Bur.)

———

215. Sacred to the Memory | of Jofhua Hatton Efqr late | of Prefcot in Lancafhire | Ob. 22d Augst 1800 Æ. 38.

———

216. SACRED | TO THE MEMORY OF | THOMAS PIERREPONT SENIOR | WHO DIED 20TH APRIL 1846 | AGED 35 YEARS | AND | THOMAS PIERREPONT JUNIOR | WHO DIED 25TH MAY 1865 | AGED 31 YEARS.

See No. 64.

———

217. Here Lyeth the Body of | WILLIAM Son of MATTHIAS | and ELIZABETH HOLST | Died 29th December 1748 | Aged 7 Days. | Also the Body of ELIZABETH | the Wife to MATTHIAS HOLST | Died 27th June 1763 | Aged 18 Years 2 Months & 3 Days. | ALSO the Body | ELIZth DOVE Daughter to | the above and late Wife to Dr | WILLIAM GASKIN BANNIS | TER Died Jan. 22 1782 | Aged 26 Years.

———

218. This Stone covers the | Remains of five Children | of Mr THOMAS McINTOSH | and ANN his wife.

———

219. Grey marble, with circular bas-relief of woman and urn let in at top :—

Sacred to .... (flaked) | MARY ANN OUGHTERSON | Wife of | ARTHUR OUGHTERSON | Daughter of | IOHN AND WALKER SHEAFE | of this Island | Nat. Septbris 21mo 1774 | Nupt. Octbris 24to 1793 | Ob. Octbris 11mo 1802. | (5 Latin lines.)

———

220. THE | FAMILY BURIAL PLACE | of | SAMUEL TAYLOR | 1819.

———

221. White marble :—

Sub hoc marmore | Reponunt cineres | CLEMENTIS BOWCHER PRITCHARD | (7 lines.) | Vigefimo .. ii die A.D. 1772, | et | Anno ætatis svæ vigefimo fecundo | (8 lines, then ? 2 lines cemented.) | Cognatis et amic .... | ... carus | Qui .. | .. A.D. 1771, | Die Decembris vigefimo q .... | Ad Infulam Barbadienfe | Appulit | (fe)d febre correptus | flore ju .... | Occubuit | Die tertio Aprilis 1772, | .. um humanarum exitus.

1772, July 21. Clement Boucher Prichard Son in law to the Revd Thos Wharton. (Burial Register.)

———

222. On a fragment of blue marble. At top in border are an hour-glass, skull and cross-bones, an ornamental border on the other sides :—

HERE LYES Y^E BODY | OF GEORGE BADCOCK | OF BOSTON IN | NEW ENGLAND AGED | 21 YEARS & 2 M^O | DIED SEP^T THE 17 | 1714.

1714, Sept. 18. George Badcock mar^r.
This stone and the next one were not mentioned in Mr. Moriarty's recent article in the " New England Register."

223. On a blue marble fragment with ornamental border of swags of fruit on the left side and bottom, somewhat similar in style to the above. The right top edge cemented :—

Here lyeth th . . . . | Body of Natha . . . . | Son of Ioseph An | Mary Bryer of | Rhoad Iseland he | departed this life | february ye 17th 1718 | Aged 21st: years, | & 6 months.

No burial entry.

224. A very fine small blue marble :—

On a lozenge. Crest (? a fleur-de-lis, which may be a crest or only part of ornamentation) over W. and H. ARMS.—*Three eagles' heads erased*. The lozenge is set in a square with skull, wings and cross-bones at each angle.

HERE LYES INTER'D ye BODY | OF ELIZABETH YELLINGS DAU^r | OF JOHN & MARY YELLINGS | AGED ABOUT 8 YEARS WHO | DEC^D JAN^{ry} ye 30th 1717-18.

1717-18, Jan. 31. Eliz^a: Yellings, a child. (Burial Register.)

225. Blue marble :—

This Stone In Memory of ANTHONY Son of | NATHANIEL & MABELL WALROND wh° (*sic*) Departed this Life | July 10th 1757 Aged two Months. | And in Memory of | ANN Daughter of NATHANIEL & MABELL WALROND | who Departed this Life the 6th October 1758 | Aged three Months.

226. Blue marble :—

Jac. mantling in oval. CREST.—*A Paschal lamb over W. and H.* ARMS.— *Three chevronels.*

Here Lyeth Interrd the Body of | STEPHEN THOMAS Esq. | one of the BARONS of HIS Majes^ties | Court of Exchequer and for several | years a JUSTICE of the Peace in this | Island of Barbados who dyed | the 12TH day of October 1721 | Aged about 43 years. | ALSO the Body of *HANNAH DODSWORTH* | wife of *HENRY DODSWORTH* Esqr and | Relict of the abovesaid *STEPHEN THOMAS* | Esq. who dyed the (cement) . . y of | September 1723.

1721, Oct. 13. Capt Stephen Thomas in ye Chancel.
1723, 7^{ber} 11th. Mrs Hannah Dodsworth wife of Henry Dodsworth Esqr in ye Chancel. (Burial Register.)

227. Sacred | to the Memory of | WILLIAM HILL and DOROTHY his Wife | the former of whom | departed this Life on the 11th June 1800 (or 1806) | Aged 63 Years | And the latter | on the 10th November 1822 | Aged 80 Years.

228. **Sacred to the Memory** | *of* | HENRY MOSELEY | who departed this life | the 11th of January 1833 | Aged 47 Years | (4 lines.) | Here also lie the Remains of his four Infant Children | (2 lines; placed by Widow.)

---

229. Stone covered with patches of mortar which if chipped off the inscription might be legible :—

... ED .. Y BO .. | ... ARAH THOMA.. | EVEN.. | DEPARTED THIS .... | SEPTEMBER THE | . HIRD 1689.

1689, Sept. 24. A child of Mr Nathll Heywoods. (Burial Register.)
No burial 2 to 8 September.
This is the last of the ledgers along this passage way.

---

230. Close to the north wall of chancel are the following :—

Sacred to the Memory of | EDITHA the Wife of | JOHN L'ESPINASSE EsqRE | of Demerara who died in this Island | the 10th of June 1805 of a Decline | leaving her Husband to mourn the loſs | of an Amiable and affectionate Wife | after a Union of scarcely three years | their infant Daughter is also thus | deprived of the best of Friends | a tender and adoring Mother.

A slab to north is illegible.

---

231. **Sacred to the memory of** | JNO WM BONYUN | *who departed this life Jan. 27th A.D. 1821 aged 9 years.*

---

232. .... tered the | . ody of George Jonathan | . ſhby who died Sepbr 13th | . 793 Aged 27 Years. | Alſo the Bodies of Eliz | beth wife of Sergt John | Aſhby who died Decr 13th | . 793 Aged 32 Years.

No burial entry.

---

233. Blue marble ledger with inscription in border framewise :—

Here Lyeth the | Body of Edward B .... (cement) who Departed | this .... the | 17th Day .. (cement) ary ANNO DOMINI 1670 | Aged About | Forty ſeaven years.

1670, Jany 18. Mr Edward Body in the Church. (Burial Register.)

---

234. Touching a buttress :—

OUR LIT | SYDNEY | R. J. WORM | and | R. M. WORM | 1862.

---

235. Old slab much cemented :—

Als .... | C .... | Mo .. HE .... AIG .. | who D .... LIFE | 30 DAY OF JANz 169 . | AGED 37 YEARS.

---

236. **Sacred** | to the Memory of | DOROTHY EVANS HOLLIGAN | Wife of | *JAMES HOLLIGAN Senr* | who departed this Life | the 23rd of November 1823, | Aged 57 Years | AND | of Her Husband | JAMES HOLLIGAN ESQ^R | who departed this life on the | 27th Day of October 1834 in the | 69th YEAR OF HIS AGE. | Also | to the Memory of their Grandson | RICHARD SANDERSON | the second Son of | JAMES AND CAROLINE HOLLIGAN | who departed this life on the | 28th Day of Septr 1844 | Aged 17 Years. | And JAMES HOLLIGAN | Died 13th March 1860 | Aged 62 Years. | Also | HENRY HOLLIGAN | Died 12th November 1867 | Aged 37 Years. | [IN MEMORY OF B. HOLLIGAN | Son of Jam^s HOLLIGAN | Who Departed This Life Jan. 27, 1871 | Aged 37 Years.] | (Cut in the side.)

237. Family Burial Place | of | Lionel Parks.

238. **SACRED** | to | the **Memory of** | JOHN B. PRICE | Quarter Master | of the 35th Reg^t | who departed this life | the 27th of January 1827 | Aged 42 Years.

239. IN MEMORY | of Peleg ye Son of | Job Almy of Tivertown in y^e | County of Bristol & Province | of ye Massachusets Bay in | New-England Esqr and of | Bridget his Wife who died | Febr^y ye 18th 1734 & in ye 25 | year of his Age.

1734-5, Feb. 19. Capt Peley Almy.
Peleg born 25 Oct. 1709, son of Job Almy and his wife Bridget, dau. of Gov. Peleg and Mary (Coddington) Sanford of Newport, R.I. His grandfather Major Almy of Tivertown. See Essex Inst. Hist. Coll., vol. 49, pp. 172—6. (G. A. Moriarty in " New England Hist. and Gen. Reg.")

240. Shield with mantling in sunk oval. Blue marble. CREST.—*Out of a coronet a demi-eagle, wings displayed, over W. and H.* ARMS.—*A chevron between three eagles displayed.*

Here lyeth ye Body of ELIZABETH | the Wife of SAMUEL WADESON Esqr | who died ye 18th of June 1723 Ætatis 35 | Here lyes also the Bodies of | three Children of ye said SAMUEL | And ELIZABETH | Here lyes also the Body of the said | SAMUEL WADESON who died the 31st | Day of January 1739 Ætatis 44.

These are the arms of Wadesdon. (Burke's " Armory.")
1723, June 19. Mrs Elizabeth Wadeson wife of Mr Samuel Wadeson.
1739, Feb. 1. Mr Samuel Wadeson. (Burial Register.)

241. **To the memory of** | *M^RS LOUISA ANN NURSE* | Relict of | JAMES NURSE Esq. | who departed this life October 7 A.D. 1821 | aged 58 years.

242. Stone much cracked :—

To the Memory | *of* | THOMAS COB* | . . . . e of Bermuda | who died | August 9th . . . . | in the 48th year of his age.

* There are signs of another letter, perhaps a " B."

243. 𝕾𝖆𝖈𝖗𝖊𝖉 | to | the memory of | CONRADE MITCHLOR FRANK-LIN | of the Commiſſariat | who departed this life the 20ᵗʰ day of July | 𝕬.𝕯. 1821 | aged 43 years. | (9 lines.)

244. 𝕾𝖆𝖈𝖗𝖊𝖉 | to | the memory of | FRANCIS DAYRELL | Who departed this life the 20ᵗʰ day of december | 𝕬.𝕯. 1820 | aged 40 years.

245. On a fragment with mortar on it :—

Alexʳ & Elspe . . . . 6ᵗʰ Regiment | who Departed this life | 1790 Aged 4 Years.

246. Here rest the Ashes of | JOHN SMITH, | of *LIVERPOOL,* | in the County of *LANCASHIRE,* | who died November 4ᵗʰ 1822, | Aged 48 Years. | (11 lines.)

247. Here Lies Inter'd the Body of the Childrⁿ of | BENJAMIN & SUSAN-NAH PEMBERTON | BENJ who Departed this Life the 23 of | November 1739 Aged Eight Days. | BENJⁿ who Departed this Life the 21ˢᵗ of | of Augˢᵗ 1743 Aged Two Years Two | Months and Eleven Days. | FRANCES who Departed this Life the 7ᵗʰ of | Aug. 1743 Aged one Year one Month & Six Days | CATHERINE who Departed this life | the 6 of Octo: 1752 Aged Two Years | Three Months & Seven Days. | FRANCIS who Departed this Life Yᵉ 3ᵈ | of Oct. 1753 Aged one Year and Eight Months. | ANN who Departed this Life the 2ᵈ | of March 1754 Aged Three Months | PETER who Departed this Life the 28ᵗʰ | of July 1755 Aged Ten Years and Ten Months.

248. A small square stone :—

E. STRAGHAN 1884.

249. A small square stone :—

P. STRAUGHN 1904.

250. White marble, cracked and cemented :—

Sacred to the Memory of | ELIZABETH ASHBY, | The Infant Daughter of | JOHN & ELIZABETH ADAMSON ALLEN | *of this Town ;* | Who died September 24ᵗʰ (? 1822) | Aged 9ᵐˢ 20ᵈˢ. | Also | WILLIAM AR . . . ALLEN | . . . Son | . . April 5ᵗʰ 1865 | Aged 42 Years.

251. A small square stone :—

E. MᶜCOLLIN | 1889.

252. A crack runs through the surnames and year :—

SACRED | to the Memory of | . AMES WILLIAM HENRY B . . . ESFORD | Son of the late | Dʳ JOHN BERESFO . D | of Berbice | . ho departed this life on the 24ᵗʰ . . . . | In the 36ᵗʰ Year of His Ag . . | universally beloved and most . . . .

253. White marble :—

SACRED | to the Memory of | MARY R. EMERTON | who departed this life | *January 18th 1820 | Aged 56 years.*

254. Beneath this Stone | Lie the Remains | *of* | *MARIA SOPHIA* | Wife of JOHN LEANDER START* | . . . Daughter of JOHN RATCHFOR .* | . . arrousborough Nova SCOTI . | . . ho died of a Consumption | on the 17th day of Decr 1829 | *Aged 25 Years.* | (2 lines ; erected by husband.)

255. To north of chancel :—

Here rests the Body | of | THOMAS PERKINS. | who departed this life on the | 23rd day of April 1823. | Aged 48 Years.

255 A. *JOSEPH YOUNG Efq.* | Died 12th February 1744 | Aged 60.

1744, Feb. 12. The Houble Collo Joseph Young Esq. (Burial Register.)

256. White marble in corner of wall of north transept and chancel. Hour-glass, wings, skull and cross-bones in sunk circle. All in very perfect state :—

Here lies Interred the Body of | Mrs IANE RICHARDS Wife of Mr LATIMER RICHARDS | who Departed this life on Fryday the 2d of | October 1747 Aged 56 Years. | Here lies Interred also the Body of | Mrs JUDITH WOOD wife of Mr SAMSON WOOD | Mercht and Daughter of the above named | Mr LATIMER RICHARDS and IANE his wife | who Departed this life on Saturday the | 8th day of December 1750 Aged 24 Years, | 9 Months & 2 days.

1750, Dec. 9. Judith Wife of Samson Wood. (Burial Register.)
This completes the ledgers around the building.
The burial entry of Mrs. J. Richards I could not find.
Sarah, daughter of Cumberbatch Sober, married Samson Wood, Jr.

SOUTH-EAST QUARTER OF CHURCHYARD.

Commencing now in the churchyard proper, near the south porch and to the east of the path leading to it we have two fine armorial ledgers of blue marble.

257. On a shield with mantling in a sunk circle :—

CREST.—*A boar statant over W. and H.* ARMS.—*A pheon ;* impaling, *a lion rampant* (? *salient*).

Here lys the Body of ANN SIDNEY | wife to CAPT WM SIDNEY who dyed | the 17TH of Sept 1698. Aged 50 years. | Alfo ye body of CAPT WM SIDNEY | aforefd who dyed Octr ye 10TH 1701. | Aged 65 years. | (Then lower and in smaller lettering) | Died March 10th 1813 Mrs Elizabeth Willoughby | Aged 52 Years.

1701, Oct. 28. Capt. Wm Sydney. (Burial Register.)
I could not find his wife's burial.

* Mortar.

258. Touching it to the east. A Jacobean shield in sunk circle :—

CREST.—*A demi stag couped erect or, ? a hind, over W., no helmet.* ARMS.— *Ermine, a fess checky in base ? a lion passant* [WARREN]; impaling, *three chevronels.*

Here Lyes Interrd Susannah daughter of | Charles Tho . . . .* qʳ late wife of | Thomas Warren M . . chᵗ who departed | this life augˢᵗ yᵉ 19ᵗʰ 1730 aged 38 years.

1730, Aug. 20. Susannah wife of Thomas Warren Esqʳᵉ. (Burial Register.)
1735, Oct. 25. Robert Warren, Esq ; Clerk of the Assembly and Register of the Admiralty in B. ("G.M.," 681.)
1755, Nov. 24. Robert Warren Esqʳ. (Burial Register.)
The next vault to south has a flaked slab.

---

259. Blue marble :—

Here lyeth Interr'd the Body of | Mᴿ THOMAS BROWNE late of this | Iſland Merchᵗ Son of THOMAS & | ELIZABETH BROWNE who departed | this Life on the 15ᵗʰ day of February | in the Year of our LORD GOD 1725 | in the 31ˢᵗ Year of his Age. | He lived moſt dearly beloved & | dyed perticularly lamented by | SHELDON CHAMBERS of London | Merchᵗ to whom he approved | himſelf during yᵉ whole time of his | Trade yᵉ moſt deſervedly endeared | friend & as induſtrious gratefull & | faithfull a Correſpondent as ever | yᵉ Iſland bore.

1725-6, Feb. 16. Mʳ Thomas Browne Merchᵗ. (Burial Register.)

---

260. Blue marble :—

Here Lyeth the Body of | Mᴿˢ MARGARET SALMON | wife of Collᵒ IOSEPH SALMON | Eſqʳ who Departed this | Life yᵉ 27ᵗʰ of January 17¹¹⁄₁₂ | in the Sixty Sixth year | of her Age. | Also the Body of Collᵒ | IOSEPH SALMON Eſq who | Departed this Life yᵉ 18ᵗʰ day | of March 17¹⁵⁄₁₆ (*sic*) in the Sixty | Sixth year of his Age.

1711-12, Jan. 28. Madⁿ Margaret Salmon.
1715-16, March 19. The Honoᵇˡᵉ Collᵒ Joseph Salmon Esqʳ of yᵉ Life Guards. (Burial Register.)

---

261. Blue marble, touching No. 260 on its south side :—

Here lyeth the Body of WILLIAM MOORE | Merchᵗ Aged 69 or thereabouts, & near | this place lyeth the Bodys of MARY | MOORE and ROBERT MOORE, Children | to the ſaid WILLIAM MOORE.

---

262. This stone is next to the road and entrance gateway :—

Here lie the Bodies of | *ABEL COLLIER*, who died | Augˢᵗ 4ᵗʰ 1775, Aged 34 Years. | *SAMUEL COLLIER* | Sepʳ 12ᵗʰ 1786 Aged 50. | *JAMES K. COLLIER* | April 7ᵗʰ 1793 Aged 50. (*sic*) | & *JANE COLLIER* Janʸ 26ᵗʰ 1800 | Aged 67 all of this *Pariſh* | Sons & Daughters of *WILLIAM* | & *JANE COLLIER* of | *Sᵗ Andrews Pariſh* deceaſed | Alſo the Body of *WILLIAM* | Son of Aforeſaid *SAMᴸ COLLIER* | *ELIZᵀᴴ* his Wife died in 1777 | Mᴿˢ *JANE MILLER* | 1796 Aged 20 Years | . . . . of *JOSEPH* . . . . | . . . . & Great Grand . . . . | . . . . | . . . . | of afore . . | CO . .

* Flaked.

263. Head-stone, touching Collier's :—

Here lies the Body of | Capt Tho. TUDER Obijt | June the 11th 1726.

1726, June 12. Capt Thomas Tudor. (Burial Register.)

---

264. HERE LIES THE BODY OF SAMUEL, | SON OF SAMUEL AND ANN BOXILL, | BORN MARCH 14TH 1776 DIED AUGST 26th, 1782. | ALSO JOHN, SON OF THE ABOVE, | BORN FEB^{RY} 22ND 1780, DIED MARCH 15TH 1782. | ALSO SAMUEL, SON OF THE ABOVE | BORN DEC^R 17 1783 DIED DEC^R 20TH 1783 | ALSO ANN DAUGHTER OF THE ABOVE | BORN DEC^R 10TH 1789 DIED OCT^R 23RD 1793. | ALSO SAMUEL SON OF THE ABOVE | BORN MAY 15TH 1791 DIED OCT^R 19TH 1793 | ALSO THE BODY OF SAMUEL BOXILL, | FATHER OF THE ABOVE FIVE CHILDREN, | DIED SEPT^R 13TH 1816. AGED 64 YEARS.

---

265. Blue marble, with four armorial shields on it.

1. Above is a shield with these arms.—*A shake fork*; impaling, *three piles wavy issuing from the chief* [? PIKE].
It is followed by this inscription :—

Here Lie the Bodies of | JOHN CUNNINGHAM who Died ye 10th July 1679, Aged 41 years | ZEBULON his Son who died ye 13th of April 1679.

The 2nd shield is cut here. ARMS.—*A wolf's head erased* [BAYN OF SCOTLAND] ; impaling, *three piles as above.*

CHARLES y^e Son of LACHLAN BAYNE & ANN his Wife (Relict to y^e above^{sd} (*sic*) | JOHN CUNNINGHAM) born Febr^y 28 & died July 5th 1683. | ANN BAYNE (Daughter to JOHN PIKE) & widow to y^e f^{u} LACHLAN BAYNE | (who died at Deal March 5th 169$\frac{8}{9}$ in England) who died May 23, 1703 | MILBOROW Wife to ALEX^R son to LACHLAN BAYNE & ANN his Wife, | who died July [*blank*] 1704.

Here are the 3rd and 4th shields, alongside each other. No. 3 has arms.—*Quarterly, 1 and 4, a mullet in centre between three cinquefoils ; 2 and 3, a heart between three cinquefoils.* The 4th shield has the single coat of Bayn.

ANN Wife to CLAUDIUS HAMILTON & only Daughter to LACHLAN BAYNE | & ANN his Wife born Decr 5th 1685. & died Octo^r 22^d. 1705. | (4 English and 4 Latin lines follow.)

1679, July 11. Mr John Cuningham.
1679, Apr. 14. Zebulon the son of M^r Jno & Anne Cunningham.
1683, July 4. Charles the son of Mr Laghlin & Anne Banes.
1703, May 23. Mrs Ann Bains widow.
1704, July 10. Alex^r Cunningham Senr Esqr.
1705, Oct. 20 (*sic*). Mrs Ann Hambleton. (Burial Register.)

---

266. A ledger over vault surrounded by iron railing :—

In Memory of | MARY HORDLE | who died 30th Septr 1805, | Aged 8 Years | Also of | JOHN DAPWELL HORDLE | who died 20th Septr 1813 (?) | Aged 13 Years | Also of | ANN HORDLE | who died 14th July 1818, | Aged 13 Years | The Children of | THOMAS and MARY HORDLE | Also of | THOMAS HORDLE | who died November 26th 1830 | Aged 80 | And | HONOR HORDLE | Widow of the above who died | January 3^d 1860 | Aged 61. | (4 lines.)

Standing on above is a grey granite headstone :—

SACRED | TO THE MEMORY OF | ANNIE, | WIFE OF ROBERT ELDER, | died 22ND DECEMBER 1871, | AGED 43.

———

267. White marble upright stone set in large mausoleum :—

THE VAULT | OF | JAMES A. and BEZIN K. CURTIS | ERECTED October 1853.

———

268. . . . . e lyeth Interrd | MA . . | who dep . . . . life | (all the rest flaked away).

———

269. Here lyeth Interr'd the Body of | ANN REID who departed this Life | July yᶜ 24ᵗʰ 1743 Aged 48 Years | Alſo the Body of WILLIAM THOMAS | Son of the above ANN Relict of John Thomas | who departed this Life March 12ᵗʰ 1749 | in his paſsage from London to this Iſland | abᵈ the Ship Elizabeth Capᵗ Robert Manley | Aged 35 Years 1 Month & 26 Days | Here lies Interred the Body | of Mary Thomas Wife of Joʰ Thomas | Merchant, who departed this life | the 1ˢᵗ day of August | 1757 Aged 45 Years.

———

270. Loose oblong stone :—

Sacred to the memory | *of* | THE REVᴰ R. J. ROCK | Who departed this life | 28ᵗʰ Janʸ 1853 | Aged 42 Years | *HERE ALSO LIE THE REMAINS* | *OF HIS PARENTS* | SAMᴸ & ELIZABETH ROCK.

271. Two vaults side by side :—

Here lieth Interred the Body of | Mʳ WILLIAM WAYLES Merchᵗ | born at Dalton in Lancaſhire | who Departed this life the 28ᵗʰ | of May 1748 Aged 38 Years.

1748, May 28. Capᵗ: William Wayles. (Burial Register.)

———

The adjoining slab has only the remainder of the first and second lines left.

272. White marble tomb enclosed by iron railing :—

IN MEMORY OF | JOSEPH BARKER BARROW | *MERCHANT OF THIS ISLAND,* | BORN 9ᵀᴴ JULY 1804, | DIED 23ᴿᴰ APRIL 1875. | (Metal letters.)

See tablet to his wife, No. 54.

———

273. Tomb enclosed by iron railing. Inscription on tiles :—

In Memory | **of** | **Thomas Clarke Marshall** | **who Died Oct.** 10ᵗʰ 1879 | **Aged 55 years.**

———

274. Loose stone :—

SACRED | to the memory | *of* | FRANCIS READY | born 20ᵗʰ June | died | 26ᵗʰ October 1857. | Aged 4 Months.

———

275. Large altar-tomb. On the top slab is a Jacobean shield with mantling in sunk circle :—

CREST.—*A Tower over W. and H.* ARMS.—*On a chevron between three Towers a pair of compasses.* MOTTO.—LET BROTHERLY LOVE CONTINUE.

To the Memory of | ALEXANDER IRVINE Gent | The Founder of Free Mafonry | in Barbados | who lived Beloved and died | Lamented by all who knew him | the Brethren of Saint Michaels Lodge | of which he was the Firſt Maſter | have placed upon his Remains this Stone | to be a Monument of his Merit | and their Gratitude | He departed this life the 13ᵗʰ | day of November 1743 | in the 49ᵗʰ Year of his Age.

I could not find the burial entry.

———

276. Blue marble slab over stone vault, under a big tree :—

Here lieth the Body of | DAVID M.CLENAHAN Merchant | in Princeſs ANN County in Virginia | Aged about 38 Years who departed | this Life 30ᵗʰ day of October 1735 | the Son of NATHANIEL M.CLENAHAN | Merchant in Virginia | this Stone is [? was] order'd here by his | Loving Mother | ELIZABETH M.CLENAHAN.

1735, Oct. 31. Mʳ David McClennahan of Virginia. (Burial Register.)

———

277. A small headstone, decorated border :—

HERE | LIES th . (flaked) | BODY of | IOHN HARRIS | the SON of | HENRY HARRIS | *ESQ*ʳ & TABITHA his Wife | OF the COLLONY | OF RHODISLAND (*sic*) in | NEW ENGLAND | Who Departed | this Life May yᵉ 23ʳᵈ | A.D. 1753 Aged | 22 Years & 4 Days.

I could not find the burial entry.

———

278. Headstone at large curbed grave :—

H. WALROND | DIED 14 OCT. 1876 | AGED 39 | BY HIS AUNT | B. TROTMAN.

———

279. Sacred | to | the Memory of | RICHARD WILDEY Esqʳᵉ | who left this world | etc. ; (2 lines) Augᵗ 23ᵈ 1781 | Aged 42 Years | And | of | ELIZA-BETH his Widow | who departed this life | May 12ᵗʰ 1815 | (2 lines) | Aged near 73 Years | (4 lines.) | Their sole offspring & daughter | MARY SARAH LAKE ANTON | who passed from Death into Life | (2 lines.) | May 2ⁿᵈ 1849 | Aged 75 Years.

———

280. White marble slab over tomb, south of walk around chancel :—

Here lies the Body | Of | JOHN BRANDFORD Eſquire, | Who departed this Life | The Thirteenth Day of May | In the Year of our . ord (flaked) | One Thouſand ſeven Hundred and | Sixty-five | Aged Sixty-three Years | Depoſited In thiſ Vault Three Children | of HENRY CRICHLOWS by hiſ | Wife REBECCA; The Laſt Whoſe | Name Waſ JOHN, Died In 1769 Aged | 4 Monthſ | ALSO | Deposited in this Vault the Remains of | WILLIAM BRANDFORD Esq. | Surgeon Son of the above mentioned | IOHN BRAND-FORD : who | departed this life the 13ᵗʰ day of April 1782 | Aged 48 Years.

281. JOHN WRONG | departed this life | November the 14ᵗʰ 1845 | Aged 55 Years.

---

282. Granite upright enclosed by iron railing to " K. GILL " by his wife; no dates.

---

283. White marble slab, close to the east boundary wall of the churchyard :—

Here lies the Body of | FRANCIS SKEETE ESQᴿ | Eldeſt Son of | EDWARD & ELIZABETH SKEETE | who departed this Life | the 4ᵗʰ of May 1777 | in the 29ᵗʰ Year of his Age.

See " Caribbeana," i., 26, for M.I. to his sister Eliz. in Bath Abbey and other notes. He was at Eton 1760—68, and mar. 18 April 1776 Eliz. Hothersall.

---

284. East of chancel close to east boundary wall of churchyard :—

SACRED | to the memory of SARAH, wife of GILLIGAN MURRAY | who died July 30ᵗʰ 1817 Aged 30 Years | Their two infant Sons | IOHN HOLDER | and | HENRY HOLDER | (Erected by the husband and father.)

---

285. Here are three blue marble or slate headstones all in the same style, with decorated floral borders, and altar with figures at top :—

HERE LYES INTERR'D | THE BODY OF, | CAPᵀ GEORGE LEE, | OF BOSTON NEW ENGLAND | AGED 31 YEARS, WHO | DIED SEPTᴿ Yᵉ 17ᵗʰ 1737.

1737, Sep. 18. Capᵗ Thomas (*sic*) Lee of Boston. (Burial Register.)

---

286. A cherub's head and wings at top :—

HERE LYES INTER'D (*sic*) | THE BODY OF Mᴿ WILLIAM PICKMAN | MERCHᵀ FROM SALEM | IN NEW ENGLAND WHO | DEPARTED THIS LIFE Yᵉ | 10ᵗʰ DAY OF APRIL 1735 | AGED 24 YEARS & 6 Months (*sic*).

1735, Apr. 10. Mʳ William Pickman of Salem. (Burial Register.)
Wm. Pickman, son of Benj. and Abigail (Lindall) Pickman, was born at Salem 1 Oct. 1710. Through his mother descended from Nath. Veren of St. Andrew's, Barbados. (G. A. Moriarty.)

---

287. The third one is broken ; it has a skull and wings at the top:—

. . . . LYES INTER'D | . . . . E BODY OF | . . . . WATT | ERS OF | . . . . NEW ENGLAND | . . . . RTED THIS LIFE | . . . . 1741 | . . . . 5 YEARS. | (5 lines.)

1741, Aug. 20. Capᵗ John Walters (*sic*). (Burial Register.)

---

288. On a stone broken into three pieces :—

SACRED | . . . . *the Memory* | . . . . M WALROND | who died | Novʳ 30ᵗʰ 1832 | Aged 36 Years | and of his | son | . . . ASCOM.

On a fourth fragment :—

" who died | ˢᵗ August 1841 | Aged 2 Months."

---

289. Altar-tomb :—

𝕾𝖆𝖈𝖗𝖊𝖉 𝖙𝖔 𝖙𝖍𝖊 𝕸𝖊𝖒𝖔𝖗𝖞 | of | PATRICK NELSON LAMBLY | who departed this life | the 19ᵗʰ July 1834 | Aged 36 Years.

290. Headstone :—

SACRED | The | Family Burial Place | *of* | JOSEPH LEACOCK ESQ^ᴿ | Deputy Ordnance | Storekeeper | 1847.

1817, Aug. 28. On board the Hopewell, on his return to England, in his 35th year, Joseph Leacock esq. leaving a wife & six infant children. (" G.M.," 561.)

291. Headstone enclosed by iron railing :— ·

IN | MEMORY | OF | ANNE K. JONES, | DIED 1873 | (1 line.)

On shield : 26 | YEARS.

Below is : ALSO | F. BRANDON JONES, | DIED 8ᵀᴴ SEP. 1886 | AGED 37 YEARS.

292. Vault, with white marble top :—

WILLIAM WALROND | DIED 13ᵀᴴ NOVEMBER 1832. | CAROLINE FRANCIS (*sic*) WALROND | (HIS WIFE) | DIED FEBRUARY 1857 | CAROLINE FRANCIS BASCOM | DIED 19ᵀᴴ JULY 1851. | JOSEPH WILLIAM BASCOM | DIED 1ˢᵀ AUGUST 1841. | SARAH ELIZABETH MᶜCONNEY | DIED 17ᵀᴴ DECEMBER 1910. | *THIS STONE WAS PLACED HERE* | BY AGNES C. H. BASCOM.

The Bascoms own Baggatelle plantation in St. Thomas's, where there is an ancient " Great-house."

Wm. Walrond the younger (born 1796) and Frances Caroline Walcott (born 1799) were mar. 17 Sept. 1818 at St. Mich. Caroline Frances, their eldest dau., was born 27 Aug. and bapt. 17 Sept. 1819, mar. 31 March 1840 Joseph Strangham, 4th son of Dr. James Sarsfield Bascom. Wm. Walrond died of a very rapid decline 13 Nov. 1832, and was buried at the Cathedral. (Bascom papers.)

The adjoining tomb has no inscription. This completes the south-east quarter.

SOUTH-WEST QUARTER.

In the square nearer the church are three M.I. and a fourth grave without any inscription.

293. Peter Law . . . . June 1816 Aged . . . . (rest flaked away).

294. Headstone enclosed by iron railing :—

𝕾𝕬𝕮𝕽𝕰𝕯 | *TO THE MEMORY OF* | MEHITABEL RICHARDSON, | THE BELOVED MOTHER OF | JOHN MASON RICHARDSON, | DIED SEPTEMBER 18ᵀᴴ 1870, | AGED 82 YEARS | ALSO OF | JOHN MASON RICHARDSON, | WHO DIED 27 MAY 1885 | IN HIS 70ᵀᴴ YEAR.

295. Very much cracked :—

SACRED TO THE MEMORY | *of* | MARGARET CHASE NICHOLLS | (*Sister of THOMAS GRAINGER NICHOLLS*) | Who Departed this life 7th May 1823 | Aged 43 Years | Also | WILHELMINA ELEANOR | (beloved Wife of the above | THOMAS CHASE NICHOLLS) | who died 4th November 18 . 4 (crack) | Aged 41 Years | Also | ELIZABETH COLLYNS NICHOLLS | (Mother of the above | *THOMAS GRAINGER NICHOLLS*) | who died 25th January 1833 | Aged 83 Years | Also | THOMAS GRAINGER NICHOLLS | who died August 16th 1856 | Aged 69 Years.

1791. At the i. of B. the hon. Benj. Nicolls, chief judge of the Court of Common Pleas for the precinct of St Michael. ("G.M.," 586.)

---

296. Headstone to JOSEPH A. ARCHER. No dates.

---

297. On two broken pieces :—

Her . . . . he Remains | *of* | Sarah Ann Daughter of John and Susanna Cozier | and their Son John the former of whom departed this | life dec. 18th 1807 Aged 7 Months & 27 days and the latter | June 23rd 1812 Aged 16 Months & 28 days. | Also the above named Susanna who died | Febry 7th 1825 Aged 45 Years. | (Several lines of poetry.)

---

298. In the space further south are many vaults. Within railing :—

SA . . . . | to the memory . . . . | FRANCES MAYNARD | Relict of the Late RALPH WEEKES | of the Island of Barbados | Died Septr 19th 1833 | AGED 72 YEARS | also | FRANCES MAYNARD PAYNE | Born May 11th 1809 | Died Jan. 7th 1876 | AGED 76 YEARS. | (1 line.)

Ralph Weekes, s. of Nathl. W. of I. of B., esq., Trin. Coll., matric. 26 Nov. 1759, a. 18.
"Paynes" belonged to his nephew Dr. Nathaniel Week in 1808 (516, Loveday).

---

299. A large railed enclosure to the south has no stone.

---

300. Marble slab over vault in perfect preservation :—

Here Lyeth Interred ye Bodys | of 3 children of EDWARD | LASCELLES Merchant by | MARY his wife that is to say | FRANCIS MARY and DORO-THY. | ye said FRANCIS dyed ye 1st of | February 1698 aged 3 years | 7 Months 10 days. MARY dyed | the 29th of Ianuary 1700 aged | 21 Months 13 days. DOROTHY | dyed ye 6th of May 1701 aged 4 | Months 3 weeks in memory | of whom their Louing Father | Erected this Tomb.

1698, Feb. 2. A son of Mr Lascells.
1700-1, Jan. 30. Mary Lascells, a child. (Burial Register.)
The other burials I could not find.
He was later of Stoke Newington. Will dated 20 June 1726 (66, Farrant), leaving Mary his widow, 2 sons Edward and Thos., and 2 daus. Mary and Sarah. He was ancestor of Lord Harewood.

H

301. Cracked ledger :—

SACRED to the MEMORY | *of* | JOHN LUCIE SMITH ESQ^r LL.D. |
late an eminent Barrister and Member | *of the Court of Policy of* | *British
Guiana* | Died 10th April 1844 | *AGED 48 YEARS* | (11 lines; erected by
widow, 9 surviving children) | BENEATH REST ALSO THE MORTAL REMAINS |
of | WILLIAM SMITH ESQ^r | *Brother of the above likewise of British
Guiana* | He Died 6th March 1833.

John Lucie Smith, e Demerary, Indus Occid. 19 Feb. 1818. (Peacock's
" Leyden Graduates.")
1839, Feb. 20. At Blackheath, Anna, wife of John Lucie Smith, l. of
Demerara. (" G.M.," 442.)
1847, Ap. 18. At the Mead, Croydon, the residence of her brother-in-law,
Major Straith, Isabella McLaurin, fifth dau. of the l. John Lucie Smith, M.D.
(*sic*) of Roselle, Blackheath & f. of Demerara. (*Ibid.*, 677.)
1849, March 22. At Hinton House, Hants, aged 15, Ellen-Eliza, 2d dau. of
the l. John Lucie Smith, LL.D. of Blackheath & British Guiana. (*Ibid.*, 554.)
Sir Alfred Lucie Smith is the present Chief Justice of Trinidad.
Sir Wm. Fred. Haynes Smith, late Gov. of the Leeward Islands, born 1838,
was 4th son of John Lucie Smith.

---

302. A handsome altar-tomb. On top slab :—

Here Lyes Interred the Body of | Mr GEORGE OATES aged XLIII years | who
Departed this Life the XXI | day of Iune Anno | MDCXC | ALSO the Body of
Mrs HANNAH | the Wife of the Abovenamed M^r | GEORGE OATES who Departed
this life | the 27th day of December 1691 aged | 40 years.

At bottom :—

Here Lyes Interred the Body of | MARY (*sic*) OATES Daughter of GEORGE |
and HANNAH OATES aged 11 years | who Departed this life the V of | October
MDCLXXXIX.

1689, Oct. 6.   Mary Oats & children.
1690, June 22.   Mr George Oates.
1691, Dec. 27.   Mrs Hannah Oats.   (Burial Register.)

---

303. Close to south road wall :—

SACRED | TO THE MEMORY OF | EDWARD BRACE TERRILL | who
departed this life | 28th SEPTEMBER 1849 | Aged 62 Years.

---

304. On white marble panel on north face of tomb :—

Here lies the Remains of His | Excellency *WILLIAM SPRY* Efq^r | Captain
General Governor Chancellor | ordinary and Vice-Admiral of the | Iſland of
Barbados ; He dyed | the 3^d day of Septr. 1772 | Aged 43 Years.

1700, May 6.   Capt Lewis Spry.
1772, Sept. 4.   His Excellency William Spry.   (Burial Register.)
He arrived as Gov. 11 Feb. 1768.   His wife dau. of Tho. Pitt of Bocconic and
niece of the Earl of Chatham, died 3 Oct. 1769.   See his bookplate No. 236.
1847, Feb. 4. At Denton Hall, co. Linc. a. 74, Lady Welby, wife of Sir W.
Earle W. Bart.   She was Wilhelmina, dau. & sole h. of Wm. Spry, Gov. of B. ;
was m. in 1792, & had a numerous family.   (" G.M.," 331.)

The following four slabs are side by side north of Gov. Spry's :—

305. In Memory of Sarah the Wife | of Captn John Bell, of the Brig | Marquis Wellington, of Liverpool, | who departed this Life the 20th. | Day of Feb^{ry}. Anno Domini 1817, | Aged 38 Years. | (4 lines; erected by husband.)

306. Here lie interred | the remains of IOHN GIBSON, | Late of *Lancaster* who departed this Life | the . 3th (*crack*) September 1781, Aged 35 Years | And ELIZABETH his Daughter who died | the 5th January 1782 Aged 4 Years. | Also ANN GIBSON, Wife of the above | JOHN GIBSON. | departed this Life Auguſt 26th: 1796, | Aged 46.

307. Here Lyeth Interred the Body | of CAPT^N ROBERT BECKLES Merch^t: | who departed this life the 19th: day | of Ivly 1682 Aged 32 yeares. | As also SVSANNAH the wife of the | Aboveſaid ROBERT BECKLES Who | departed this life the 8th: day of | SEPTEMBER 1683 Aged 27 yeare (*sic*). | As also two of their Children. | Here also Lyeth Inter'd the Body | of MAD^M: ANN POVEY wife of WILLIAM | POVEY Esq and Mother to ye Above | ſaid SVSANNAH BECKLES who Dyed | the 22th day of FEBRVARY 1700 Aged | . . . . 7 yeares.

1677-8, Jan. 10. Mr Thomas Beckles in Ch.
1682, July 19. Mr Robt Beckles.
1683, Sep. 8. Mrs Susanna Beckles Wid^o.
1700-1, Feb. 23. Mrs Ann Povey. (Burial Register.)
In Add. MS. 11,411 are several letters from the three brothers Richard Povey, Sec. of Jamaica, Tho. Povey of Gray's Inn, and Wm. Povey, Provost Marshal of Barbados 1655-60. Mrs. Wm. Povey was also at Barbados in 1659.
Tho. Povey, gent., 2 s. of Justinian, one of the Auditors of the King's Exchequer, entered Gray's Inn 1 Nov. 1633.
See No. 103.

308. Above are the sun, moon, compasses, etc. :—

In memory of | Mr *JOHN LE MESSURIER* SMITH | late of this Parish | Cooper to His Majestys Ordnance | (4 lines) | who departed this life on the | 3rd of August 1802 | Aged 36 Years | (4 lines; placed by widow.)

309. SACRED | to the Memory of | AARON SOBER ROBINSON | who departed this life | October the 29th 1845 | Aged 64 Years | (4 lines; by widow.)

310. Granite headstone enclosed by an iron railing :—

SACRED | TO THE MEMORY OF | HONOR | WIFE OF ERNEST OLTON | DIED 23RD MAY 1875 | AGED 27 | (1 line.)

311. Headstone within iron railing adjoining No. 310 :—

IN LOVING MEMORY | OF | ELIZABETH ALLEYNE | WIFE OF | R. HART BONYUN, | DIED 7TH FEBRUARY 1894 | AGED 51. | ALSO OF | SUSAN DEBORAH | RELICT OF | JOHN W. BONYUN | DIED 8TH SEPTEMBER 1888 | AGED 87 | (1 line.)

312. Fragment of ancient slab, inscription in border framewise:—

.... yeth Ann Y⁰ | wife off Gab¹¹ Newman.

On another fragment is :—

.... ˢ 1680.

1680, May 13.   Anne the wife of Mʳ Gabriel Newman.   (Burial Register.)

———

313. Next south boundary wall :—

SACRED | to the memory of | ABRAHAM JACOB VAN IMBYZE |
VAN BATENBURG, | late | GOVERNOR GENERAL of BERBICE | &c. &c. &c. |
who died | in the Island BARBADOES, | 9ᵗʰ Octʳ 1806 | Ætatis Suæ | 55; | (4 lines.)
His affectionate Children | have caused this Tablet | to be placed over His |
REMAINS.

———

314. In large square enclosure :—

Died October 17ᵗʰ 1829 | ELIZABETH FRANCES | Daughter of |
GEORGE & SARAH BENSKIN | Aged 17 Months.

———

315. Large cemented enclosure railed in.   On iron plate :—

THE BURIAL PLACE | OF | THOMAS HERBERT'S FAMILY.

On a ledger to the south :—

In Memory | of | MARY HERBERT | died | 4th December 1787 | aged
34. | JANE MARTINDALE HERBERT | aged 63* died | 1 . th November
1831 | wife of | JOHN HERBERT | who died | 11th October 1842 | aged 76 |
THOMAS HERBERT | died | 14th May 1884 | aged 71 | SUSAN HERBERT |
died | 15th August 1901 | aged 89 | (2 lines.)

There are also two headstones :—

1st headstone: **In Memory** | of | JANE HERBERT | died | 14th January
1887 | aged 43 | (4 lines.)
2nd headstone: **In Memory** | of | THOMAS HERBERT | died | 15th
September 1886 | aged 49 | (3 lines.)

———

316. Here lie the Remains of | Mᴿˢ ANN SANSUM, | DAUGHTER of
Lᵀ Cᴏʟᴸ IOHN MORRIS, | late of the Provincials in | North-America, | (where he
bravely supported the Royal Cause, | and was an active and faithful Officer |
during the whole of the Revolution | in that Covntry) | and SARAH his Wife |
descended of the | Noble House of MONTROSE, | and WIFE of SAMUEL SANSUM |
of the Kingdom of England, | but late of the City of New-York, | Merchant. |
She departed this Life, | (in pure Christian Faith and Hope) | in the night | of
the 14ᵗʰ. of September 1803, | Aged 22 Years & 9 Months | (14 lines.)

Col. Morris is not mentioned by Sabine, unless identical with the Comptroller
of the Customs of South Carolina.

* Or 68.

We are now in line with the west porch passage way. There is a long row of eleven large cemented vaults or mausoleums.

317. Next the road:—

Erected | to the Memory of | JAMES BOVELL ESQ\^{RE} | Who died on the 12\th April 1816 | Aged 30 Years.

318. THE | *Family Vault of* | JAMES CUMMINS.

1838, Aug. 25. At St. James's, John Stuart, to Ann Smith, widow of Geo. C. of B. ("G.M.," 543.)

319. THE | *FAMILY SEPULCHRE* | OF | HENRY S. CUMMINS | 1810.

The next one has no stone for Inscription.

320. SACRED | To the Memory of | *FRANCES R. WEBSTER* | The Wife of | *ROWLAND WEBSTER* | who Departed this life on the | 1 day of September 1805 | in the 38\th year of her Age. ALSO | THOMAS DONOVAN | WHO DIED JAN\^Y 7\TH 1865 | AGED 59 YEARS | AND | MARTHA JANE | FRANCES DONOVAN | RELICT OF THE ABOVE | WHO DIED 25\TH JAN\^Y 1885 | AGED 69 YEARS.

321. WITHIN THIS VAULT IS LAID THE BODY OF | EMMA SOPHIA COLEBROOKE | THE WIFE OF | COLONEL SIR WIL\^M COLEBROOKE C.B. | WHO DEPARTED THIS LIFE | ON EASTER EVE THE 10 APRIL 1851 | AGED 42 YEARS. | IN MEMORY ALSO OF THEIR DAUGHTER | MARY HARRIET COLEBROOKE | WHO DIED AT SEA | ON THE 27 OF APRIL 1837 | AGED 12 YEARS | (1 line.)

1851, Ap. 19. At B., Emma-Sophia, the wife of Col. Sir Wm. Colebrooke, R.A. Gov. of the Windward Islands. Her body was interred in the cathedral burial ground. ("G.M.," 99.)

322. Here lies interred the Body | of | Doct\^r JOHN RAVEN, | Who departed this Life the 10\th Day of | September 1772 | Aged 65 Years.

323. SACRED | To the Memory of Cap\^t Valentine | Clarke who Departed this life the | 25\th of December 1803 Aged 73 Years.

324. *ABEL POYER* | died the 4\th July 1797 | Aged 43 Years | To perpetuate the Memory of | a most affectionate | and much beloved Husband | *SARAH POYER* | Inscribes this Marble.

The "History of Barbadoes," by John Poyer of Speight's Town, 4to, was published in 1808.

1850, May 27. In Russell-pl. Fitzroy-sq., a. 37, John Poyer Poyer, esq. of B. ("G.M.," 102.)

325. Here Lyeth the Body of M\^r | ARMEIAH MARSH and his two | Sons EDWARD and IOSEPH | and IOHN ADRIEN his son and | Daughter IOSEPH and REBECKAH (*sic*).

326. THE | FAMILY | SEPULCHRE | OF | THE HON^{BLE} JOHN STRAKER | WITHIN | LIE THE REMAINS OF | HIS DAUGHTER | FRANCES ALS | DIED | JUNE 26TH 1857 | AGED 68.

1814, March 6. In his 32d year, in the Duke of Kent packet, on his passage to Lisbon, Thomas James Straker, esq. of the I. of B. He was bred to the bar; but the care of a paternal estate & the Comptrollership of the Customs in that I. for which in 1807 he exchanged the Collectorship of St. Lucia, obliged him to relinquish the practice of the Law .... He married the eldest dau. of Dr. Valpy of Reading &c. ("G.M.," 414.)

———

327. On a slab touching and resting on the base of No. 317. The inscription is of 8 lines :—

Under this Memorial rest the . . . . | of a beloved Husband | . . . . Good . . . . | SAMUEL IOHN . . . . DAILE Esq. | . . . . | May 28th 17 . . | with . . . . | Affectionate.

The surname may be "Esdaile."

———

328. Touching path running south from the west porch. On the top:—

SACRED to the MEMORY of | EDWARD JAMES DUMMETT, M.D. | who departed this life | January 26th 1837 | Aged 60 Years.

On a square stone let into the west end :—

RICHARD HALL | A Youth | Of Merit and Genius | Obit 26 May 1782 : | Aged 16 Years and 5 Months.

———

329. On the top :—

B. BYNOE.

———

329A. Large earth enclosure within iron railings. On a headstone :—

In Loving Memory | of | JOHN M^CWILLIAM | DIED 7TH APRIL 1858, AGED 50 YEARS | MARTHA E. M^CWILLIAM | DIED 22ND MAY 1874, AGED 50 YEARS | ALSO JOHN M^CWILLIAM SON OF THE ABOVE | DIED 2ND MAY 1876, AGED 25 YEARS | (4 lines) | ALSO | JANE ALEXANDER, | AND | ARCHIE GIBBONS. | JAMES GIBBONS | DIED 4TH JULY 1903. | ROSA LUCOMB, | DIED 12TH MARCH 1909.

———

330. White marble loose stone within railing :—

In memory of | EDWARD R. RUSSELL. | Died 26th Jany. 1877 | Aged 34 Yrs.

———

331. To The Memory | of | ELIZABETH ANN | Wife of | MR RICH^D RUSSELL | Who Died Decr 22ND 1851 | Aged 27 Years 7 Months | Also | OF MARGARET | Second Wife | of the above | Who Died Mc^h 1st 1860 | Aged 30 Years.

———

332. Upright stone within railing. On west face :—

SACRED | TO THE MEMORY | of | P. R. FARNUM | AGED 78 YEARS | ALSO | P. R. FARNUM | AGED 32 YEARS. On south edge : P. J. FARNUM AGED 7 MONTHS. On north edge : LOUISA P. JOHNSON AGED 23 YEARS.

333. White marble slab :—

BENEATH THIS MARBLE | REST THE REMAINS OF | MARY CLARKE. | WIFE OF | JOHN WILLOUGHBY ESQUIRE, | WHO DEPARTED THIS LIFE | ON THE 21ST JANUARY 1847 | ALSO OF | JOHN WILLOUGHBY ESQUIRE, | WHO DIED ON THE 24TH OCTOBER | 1852 | (erected by a son.)

---

334. In oval, two skulls and foliage :—

Here lie intomb'd the bodies of | Elizabeth and Iohn Welsh Son and | Daughter of Thomas and Mary Welsh | Elizabeth was born ye: 4: of February | 1704 & dyed ye: 5th: of February 1704 | Iohn was born ye: 25th: of February | 1704 & dyed ye: 9th: of April 1708 | ALSO Mary the Wife of ye Said | Thomas Welsh Who departed this | Life the 14th day of May 1712 | aged 32 years.

1704-5, Feb. 7.   Eliza: Welsh a child.
1708, Ap. 10.   John Welch a child.
1712, May 15.   Mrs Mary Welch in Church.

---

335. Small loose stone :—

J. D. D. 1852.

---

336. SACRED TO THE MEMORY | of | SARAH E. SHANAHAN | Died Augt 9th 1843.

---

337. Headstone :—

Iebu L. J. Coppell | died 31st July | 1857 | Aged 4 Years.

---

338. White marble headstone, enclosed by railing :—

Sacred to the Memory | of | THOMAS W. SHILSTONE | MERCHANT OF THIS CITY, | WHO DEPARTED THIS LIFE | ON THE 16TH FEBRUARY 1870, | AGED 54 YEARS | (5 lines) | Also | THOMAS W. SHILSTONE JR | SON OF THE ABOVE, | WHO DEPARTED THIS LIFE | Decr 29th 1876 | Aged 35 Yrs | & 7 Months | CATHERINE ANN, | THE BELOVED WIFE OF | THOMAS W. SHILSTONE, | WHO DEPARTED THIS LIFE | On the 8th September 1883 | Aged 69 Years.

Several small headstones not noted.

339. In circle, the sun in centre, compasses above it :—

IN SACRED MEMORY | OF DEPARTED WORTH | THIS TABLET IS ERECTED | BY THE PAST MASTERS | WARDENS AND MEMBERS OF | THE SCOTIA LODGE | NO. 340 SCOTCH REGISTRY, | AS A MARK OF RESPECT | FOR THE DISTINGUISHED | TALENTS AND VIRTUES | IN THE CAUSE OF MASONRY, | AND IN REMEMBRANCE OF | OUR RESPECTED BROTHER THOMAS WATSON | PAST MASTER AND FOUNDER | OF THE ABOVE LODGE | WHO DEPARTED THIS LIFE | ON THE 2ND SEPTR 1854, | AGED 52 YEARS.

---

340. White marble:—

Beneath this Stone | lies interr'd the Body of | SARAH ELIZABETH DANIEL | Wife of | *JOHN THOMAS DANIEL* | of the Parish of Christ Church, | Who departed this Life | the 13th Day of August | 1826, | in the 33d Year of her Age | Also the Remains | of the said | IOHN THOMAS DANIEL | Who departed this Life | 27th of October 1828 | Aged 45 Years.

341. High altar-tomb in rails:—

SACRED | to the Memory of Mrs Mary O'Brien | Daughter of Mr John O'Brien late of | Hallifax Nova Scotia who departed this | Life 11th Day of December 1810 Aged 27 Years | also | JOSEPH FROST SENR | *Died in 1829* | *His Wife* | SARAH ELIZABETH WALCOT, | *Died in 1831* | *Their Daughter* | MARY HENRIETTA | *Died in 1854* | *Their Son* | JAMES | *Died 1879* | (3 lines.)

342. Headstone, inscription very faint:—

Here lies the Remains | of WILLIAM BAGGS GOODWIN | *Son of* IOHN .... ELIZABETH | *ANN GOODWIN* who departed | this life the 1 . of August 1795 | Aged Two Years | ALSO the Body of Mrs ELIZABETH ANN GOODWIN *Late Wife of* | *Mr IOHN GOODWIN* who | departed this life the 12th of | November 1795 Aged 54 Years | (6 lines.) | And Also SUSANNAH BAGGS | departed this life the 12th of | November 1792 Aged Thirty | Years and Six Days.

343. Large grey marble ledger set upright within railing:—

CŒLUM QUID QUÆRAMUS ULTRA | Under this Stone | are deposited the Remains of | HENRY FRAZER | who in the 45th year of his age | departed this life on the 14th April | 1828 | (10 lines) | Here also lie the bodies of | Frederick & Austin | infant Sons of the abovenamed | (by his beloved consort Maria Frazer | the former of whom departed this life | on the 11th Septr 1823 | (The remainder is buried.)

At the foot is a headstone of white marble.

344. In Memoriam | FREDERICK WILLOUGHBY FRASER | DIED 15 AUGUST 1881, | AGED 19 YEARS | ALSO | JAMES AUSTIN FRASER, M.D. | DIED 18 APRIL 1888 | AGED 31 YEARS.

345. Very long M.I. to JOHN AND LUCRETIA TURNEY, married life near 50 years. He died 20 May 1825 (or 3), Aged 73 or 78, and she Aug. 1829, Aged 71 or 74. Also Wm M. TURNEY died March 11, 1868, Aged 49.

346. SACRED | TO THE MEMORY OF | MRS ELIZA G. JOHNSON | Wife of | RICHARD JOHNSON Esqr | Who departed this life | on the 22d day of November 1836 | Aged 26 Years | Also of their Infant Son | SAMUEL DANIEL | Born 18th July 1831, | Died 18 August 1833 | Also of their elder Son | WALTER THOMAS JOHNSON | Born 2d Septr 1829, | Died 13th Janry 1849. | Also RICHARD PAYNE JOHNSON | who died Febry 1st 1851 aged 44 Years | (1 line.)

347. In memory of | RUTH JOHNSON | *wife of* | ANTHONY HOWARD | *Died Dec. 20 1852* | Aged 48 years | Also | ANTHONY HOWARD | *Died August 24 1872* | Aged 69 years.

348. White marble headstone adjoining No. 336 :—

In memory of | THOMAS ANTHONY | ELDEST SON OF | ANTHONY AND RUTH J. HOWARD | *Died March 20, 1853* | Aged 26 years.

349. Broken slab :—

IOHN GRASETT Died 5ᵗʰ Nov. 1786. | MARTHA | His Wife died August 25 1796.

Probably 1st son and heir and Ex'or of Mrs. Margaret Grasett of this parish, whose will he proved in 1745 (272, Seymer).

350. Broken white marble :—

Here lies the Remains | of | CAPᵀ CHAˢ JAMES EDGILL | of the 4ᵗʰ (King's Own) Reg. | who died at Sea | on the 4ᵗʰ day of June 1819 | Aged 39.

See the Regimental tablet No. 72.

351. In sunk circle a compass and square :—

SACRED | to the memory of | JOHN HAYNES ALKINS | who departed this Life | *March 24ᵗʰ. A.D. 1831,* | in the 35ᵗʰ year of his age | *On his passage from Liverpool to Barbadoes on* | *Board of the Brig Hannah and whose remains* | *are interred beneath this stone.* | *This tribute of affection is erected by his Son* | *George Alkins at present a resident of Philadelphia* | *U.S. of America* | (1 line.)

352. Small headstone on top of vault :—

IN | MEMORY | OF | FLEETWOOD THOMAS | HUGH WILSON, | CAPT. 8ᵀᴴ HUSSARS, | AUDITOR GENERAL OF BARBADOS | BORN JUNE 1817 | DIED 13ᵀᴴ SEPT. 1862 | (4 lines.)

353. Large vault enclosed by iron chains. On a white marble tablet on east face :—

ROBERT GORDON | Born Sep. 20 1858. | Died Sep. 22 1858, | aged 2 days | ROBERT | Born July 17, 1859, | Died Dec. 27, 1859 | aged 5 months & 10 days | sons of | *Robert & Elizabeth O'Neal.* | ELIZABETH GRAZETT CLINTON | Died July 8 1865 | aged 72 years.

At top is a grey granite upright stone :—

IN FOND | AND | LOVING REMEMBRANCE | OF | ROBERT WILLIAM O'NEALE | LATE | CONSUL FOR THE NETHERLANDS | AND | MERCHANT OF THIS CITY | BORN 16ᵀᴴ JUNE 1833 | DIED 15ᵀᴴ FEBʸ 1879 | (3 lines.)

354. Marble ledger, perfect, only one crack on corner :—

This Tomb is Erected to ye Memory of | MR CRISPUS GREEN and
GERTRUDE | his Wife who lyes here Interr'd | She Died June ye 7th: 1737
Aged 35 Years | He Died July ye 3^d: 1739 Aged 37 Years | they left Issue 1 Son
and 2 Daughters. | Here alfo lyes Interr'd the Body of | M^{RS} MARGARET
WALCOT Sifter to | the above-faid M^{RS} GERTRUDE GREEN | who Died
May y^e (*blank*) 1737 Aged (*blank*) Years | Like Wise ye Body of Marg^{tt} Daug |
ht^r. of ye above^{sd} Cris^s & Gert^e Who | Who (*sic*) Died Jan^{ny} 22th: 1740 Aged
8 yr^s.

    1737, May 27.   Mrs Margaret Walcott.
    1737, June 8.   Gertrude wife of Capt: Crispus Green.
    1739, July 4.   Capt Crispus Green.
    1740, Jan. 21.   Margaret Green a child.   (Burial Register.)

---

355. Sacred to the Memory of | M^{rs} ANN MARY MURROW | *Native of*
London ENGLAND | who departed this Life June 28th 1815 | Aged 63
(15 lines) | Beneath this Stone also lies the Body of | Mrs SARAH M^cDONALD |
of this Parish | who departed this Life August 29th 1817 | Aged 79.

---

356. A lofty mausoleum :—

(Two lines flaked) | of AGNES SAMPLE who | departed this life the 27th
Day | of Jan^{ry} 1810 Ag . . 60 Years. | Is Infcribed by an affectionate fon | Alfo
the Memory of (*sic*) | ELIZ^{TH} MAXMELL (*sic*) GITTENS | who died the 14th of
December | 1810 Aged 20 Years.

    Jas. Rich. Sample, o. s. of Richd. of St. Michael's, matric. in 1800 at Glasgow.

---

357. I.H.S. | SACRED | To the memory of JAMES COULSTEN ESQ^R |
Born at Drogheda in Ireland who | departed this life on the 5th day of May |
1822 aged 48 years (3 lines ; erected by his brother John Coulsten) | (12 lines.)

---

358. Mausoleum :—

The Family Vault of | BENJAMIN H. THORNE | in it are deposited |
the Remains of his Five | Infant Children.

On a ledger laid over entrance is :—

SACRED | To the Memory | of | . . . S ELIZ^{TH} JEMMETT Daughter |
. . . . EN J. HARRIS & SARAH JANE THORNE | who departed this life
June 30th 1812 | Aged 17 Months & 21 Days | Alfo Mafter JOHN THORNE |
Brother to the above who departed this life | April 17th 1813 Aged 15 Months &
7 Days.

---

359. Mausoleum :—

THE TOMB | *of* | WILLIAM GILL | In which was first Laid | his Infant
Son ROBERT | who died | March 11th 1817 | Aged 2 Years.

360. Mausoleum :—

SACRED | To the memory of | JOSEPH ALLEYNE PAYNE ESQ^R | who departed this life Oct^br 5th A.D. 1822 | aged 62 years | This Monument is erected by his | affectionate Daughters SARAH ANN | & JANE ALLEYNE HAYNES.

The latter mar. in Jan. 1816 Rich. Haynes of Newcastle, eldest son of Gen. Robert Haynes.

361. Mausoleum :—

In Memory | **of** | ALEXANDER KING Esq. | One of the Representatives of St Andrew's | in the General Assembly of Barbados, | and an exemplary Magistrate | of Bridge Town, | Who died the 11th of August 1826, | Aged 41 Years. | (8 lines; erected by widow.)

362. Mausoleum :—

THE FAMILY VAULT | OF | *WILLIAM BURNHAM* | Wherein lieth M^RS SARAH CARNOT | Wife of WILLIAM BURNHAM | Who departed this life on the | 23rd of August 1829 | Aged 18 years.

363. Fixed against the east end of the King mausoleum is a headstone :—

Beneath this Stone | rest the Remains of | EDWARD | Son of EDWARD (Quarter Master | of the 3rd West India Regiment) and | MARY BRICE | who departed this life the 27th August | 1818 | at the Age of Thirteen Months and | Four Days | (1 line.)

364. Headstone fixed against No. 360:—

Sacred | **to** | **the Memory of** | J. W. E. ELDER | Who departed this life | September 24th 1825 | Aged 44 Years.

365. Here lies the Body of | SAMUEL PERRY, | Who departed this Life | July 16th 1757 | Aged 60 Years | Alſo the Body of | SALVINA PERRY, | Wife of Henry Perry | And Daughter in law to the above | Samuel Perry; | Who departed this Life | May 15th 1761 | Aged 32 Years, 4 Months, | And 16 Days.

366. White marble panel in wall next road :—

NEAR THIS SPOT | LIE THE REMAINS OF | JACOB PERRY CLARKE ESQ | WHO DIED THE 21ST OF APRIL 1834 | AGED 69 YEARS.

367. On a cross :—

In Memory of | RICHARD GIBSON CODRINGTON | CHAPLAIN TO THE FORCES | BORN JAN. 28TH 1831 DIED MARCH 24TH 1877 | AGED 46 YEARS | (2 lines.)

368. Sacred to the memory of | NATH^L GREENIDGE | who departed this life after a long and painful illness | on the 20th June 1823 Aged 25 Years | Also | M^RS SARAH E. FARNUM | who departed this life Sepr 24th 1826 Aged 22 Years | (2 lines) | Also | her infant Son EDWIN who died Decr 16th | Aged 9 Months | (4 lines; placed by their Mother Eliz. G.)

There was a family of Greenidge in parish of Christ Church *circa* 1650.

Dr. Oliver Greenidge resides at Speights Town, and the Editor is indebted to him for assistance in searching for old graves on the plantations in that district.

369. Crest of Harman. Arms of Harman: *Quartering, Per pale Or and Azure a fess counterchanged.* (Cusack.)

In this Grave | are depofited the Remains of | SAMUEL HARMAN Efquire | One of his Majefty's Commiffioners for the Inveftigating | of Army Expenditure in the West Indies; | Who | (12 lines) | (died) on the [16th] day of March 1816 | in the fifty third year of his age | (7 lines; placed by son.)

He was born 8 Oct. 1764. Pedigree in "Antigua," ii., 62, and "Memoir of the Harmans." See "W.I. Bookplates," No. 54.

370. White marble headstone:—

THIS | Marble is erected by | *an affectionate Husband* | *in Memory of* | ANN WORRELL TORRES | who departed this life | March the 5, 1816, | *Aged* 42 | (2 lines.)

371. White marble slab at the south-west corner of churchyard: —

HENRIETTA MILLER | Died Oct'r 19th 1864 | Aged 85 Years.

372. On small square stone:—

The | Family Burial Place | *of* | SAMWEL (*sic*) PERRY OLTON | 1820.

On a larger stone :—

FAMILY SEPULCHRE OF | SAMUEL PERRY OLTON | within which lie the Remains of Several | of his Children | Thomas William departed this life | 30th Nov'r 1820 aged 3 Years. | Margaret A. 7th Sept'r 1824 | aged 10 Months | William 26th Feb'y 1829 aged 9 months | Samuel Perry 12th July 1831 Aged 12 Years | Wilhelmina 11th Nov'r 1831 Aged 7 Months | and | Albert 25th April 1838 Aged 8 Years. | *Also* | Will'm Henry Wilkey, Grandson of the above | S. P. Olton, 10th July 1839 Aged 11 Weeks | MARY CATHARINE MOORE | October 31st 1839 Aged 2 Years & 5 days | RICHARD THOMAS OLTON | died July 6th 1844 Aged 23 Years | Also | MARY L. OLTON Wife of S. P. OLTON | died July 26th 1848 Aged 54 Years | (3 lines.)

373. Headstone :—

Sacred | *To the Memory of* | JAMES GRIFFITH | *of Fishgard Pembroke-shire* | and late Commander of the | ship Berwick of London | (rest buried.)

374. Small flat stone :—

Sacred | to the Memory | of | MARY | Wife of | CHRISTOPHER T. DARBY | who died | November 8th 1820 | Aged 25 Years.

375. Sacred | to the Memory of | JOHN BLISS SOPER ESQ'RE | who departed this Life | the (*blank*)th day of July 1820, | In the (*blank*) Year of his Age.

376. Vault enclosed by railing :—

THE BURIAL PLACE | *of* | W. T. CODD.

---

377. . . . . s Sacred Repository lies | . . . . Remains of Master Roger | . mith Son of Roger and Alice | Smith of Pendleton near Man | chester in England. This most | promising and amiable young | man was early snatched from | his friends and relations in the | Fourteenth Year of his Age by | a most violent fever. During a | short residence in this Island | of scarce 22 Months, he had en | deared himself to all around | him and died as he lived highly | esteemed and regretted October | 23rd 1816.

---

378. SACRED | To the Memory of | GEORGE EDWARD DEAR | The Son of | JOHN & ELIZABETH DEAR | who Departed this life on the | 2 .st* day of September 1814 | Aged 23 Years and 3 Months.

---

379. Flat stone with remains of iron railing, also headstone :—

UNDER THIS STONE | REST THE DEAR REMAINS OF | JOHN | SECOND SON OF | HENRY & CHARLOTTE | COLLYMORE | WHO DIED | ON THE 11TH OCTOBER 1836 | AGED 11 YEARS.

On the headstone :—

THIS STONE IS ERECTED | AS A TRIBUTE OF FILIAL | LOVE AND ESTEEM | IN MEMORY OF | HENRY COLLYMORE | WHO DIED OCT. 14 1853, | AGED 58 YEARS | AND OF | CHARLOTTE | HIS WIDOW | WHO DIED SEPT. 30TH 1880 | AGED 80 YEARS.

---

380. Large slab near west wall by the road :—

In Memory of | ROBERT THOMAS CROMARTLE | *Son of* | ROBERT & MARTHA CROMARTLE | *of St Mary Rotherhithe* | *in the County of Surrey* | who died the 11th of November 1810 | Aged 16 Years | (several lines) | Here also lie interred | the Remains of | Captain ROBERT CROMARTLE | (of Ship RE . . . . L of LONDON) | who died on the 25 April 1822 | in the 52 Year of his Age.

---

381. Headstone against west wall :—

Beneath this Stone | deposited the Remains | of | THEOPHILUS D'OLIER Esq. | Merchant | of the | City of Dublin in Ireland. | who departed | this Life | on the 22nd Novr 18 . 9 (? 1809) | (3 lines.)

---

382. Headstone against west wall of road :—

Sacred | to the Memory of | *CAPTAIN DANIEL O'KEEFFE* | *of the Royal York Rangers* | *Deputy Afsistant Adjutant General* | who departed this life | on the 24th June 1819.

* Crack.

383. On two metal plates in headstone :—

J. W. DEANE | DIED 30ᵀᴴ JULY | 1871.
S. K. TODD | DIED 1ˢᵀ SEPTEMBER | 1872.

---

384. Large vault, white marble slab :—

IN MEMORIAM, | JAMES T. BROWNE. | *Died* | *February 26ᵗʰ 1857*. | *And his Wife* | MARY BROWNE, | *December 17ᵗʰ 1879.*

---

385. Ledger :—

SACRED *to the* Memory | of SAMUEL MORRISON who | departed this life the 6ᵗʰ Day | of February 1810 Aged 27 Years | this Memento of affectionate | regard is erected by his Widow | ANN CHRISTIAN MORRISON.

---

386. White marble slab :—

This Tablet Marks the interment of | Mʳˢ CHARLES MᶜALPIN | JOHN MᶜALPIN Her Son | JOHN and WILLIAM MᶜALPIN | INFANTS | ALSO OF | ISABELLA Sᵀ HILL | who died on the 1ˢᵗ March 1836 | Aged 5 Years 8 Months | ALSO | MARIAN MᶜALPIN | who departed this life | 26ᵗʰ SEPTˣ 1849 | Aged 28 Years.

387. Large square enclosure of earth, railed in ; on a headstone :—

IN MEMORIAM | ELEANOR BROWNE | DIED 4ᵀᴴ SEPTEMBER 1886 | JAMES BROWNE | DIED 13ᵀᴴ SEPTEMBER 1887 | (1 line.)

---

388. Headstone against west wall of road :—

(*Sic*) Memory of John Cock | a Native of Lancafter in England | who died 6ᵗʰ January 1807 | Aged 67 Years (5 lines) | Sacred alfo to the Memory of Richard Cock | Nephew of John Cock | who died 11ᵗʰ December 1807 | Aged 21 Years.

---

389. Headstone against west wall of road :—

Under this Stone | lie the remains of | REBECCA DUESBURY | and her Sister | ELIZABETH DUESBURY | REBECCA died Novʰʳ 10ᵗʰ 1803 | ELIZA-BETH died 14ᵗʰ Sepᵗʳ 1811.

---

390. Headstone against west wall of road :—

Here refteth the Remains of *JOHN IFMAN M.D.* | who departed this life | on the 11ᵗʰ Day of May 1799.

---

391. Headstone against west wall of road, which has been painted over :—

HRISTᵃ and | . . . . | vember 1770 Aged two.

392. In back row, a large vault :—

Sacred to the Memory of | Mr PAUL LIGHTBOURN | Native of BER-MUDA. | who departed this life Augst 19th | 1818 | Aged 31 Years | (3 lines) | JAMES FRANCIS LAWSON | *Died March 2nd 1853* | His Wife | ANNA MARIA LAWSON | *Died* .... (? *Oct^r*) *15th 1881* | (Cracked.)

393. Large mausoleum, pinnacles at four corners. On stone at cast end :—

THE | SEPULCHRE | OF | BRYAN TAYLOR YOUNG *ESQ^{RE}*.

394. Slab :—

HERE LIE THE REMAINS OF | LYNCH THOMAS ESQ^r | who died November 9th 1811. | Aged 58 Years | (7 lines; erected by widow ANN THOMAS.)

395. Vault enclosed by railing :—

SACRED | To the Memory of | JAMES BUTCHER M.D. | Died March 9th 1856 | Aged 80 Years.

396. Nineteenth-century slab to JOHN DIXON of Liverpool, etc., died 27 May 1815 ; almost illegible.

397. Sacred to the Memory | of | GEORGE CLARKE | and | FRANCES WILLIAMS | the former of whom departed this Life the | 20th July 1803 Aged 65 Years | and the latter August 17th 1819.

398. Cracked slab :—

Sacred to the Memory | of | SAMUEL TROT Esq. | Born Decr 16th 1776 | Died June 2^d 1819. | ELIZABETH BAMFIELD | departed this Life | July 3rd 1821 | Aged 67 Years.

Four headstones against west wall are covered with paint.

399. Small white marble tablet on west wall :—

THE | FAMILY | BURIAL PLACE | OF | C. H. ALLDER | 1855.

400. Here lies inter ... | IOHN MERCHA .. | IOHN and MARY MER-CHAN . | who departed this life the 7th Nov^r | 1810 Ætatis 1 Year and 7 Months | Also the Body of | SARAH MERCHANT Daughter of | IOHN and MARY MERCHANT | who departed this life | the 1 day of July 1811 Etatis 32 days | (4 lines.)

401. White marble square on two vaults :—

J. P. HENDY.

402. Headstone; at the top an urn and figure of woman:—

Here lies interred the Body | of RODERICK ELDER | who departed this Life | the 20th of January 1800 | Aged 38 Years.

_____

403. White marble slab:—

Sacred | To | the memory of | MERCY ANN INNISS | who departed this life | on the 23rd day of March 1820 A.D. | aged 4 years | ALSO OF | SARAH ANN INNISS | Who departed this Life | on the 7th July 1837 | *Aged 53 years.* | ET | ANN INNISS | Who died on the 19th day of October 1848 | Aged 21 years | WILLIAM who died in Berbice 7th July 1847, Aged 30 | SARAH JANE who died 6th Decr 1863 Aged 45. | WILLIAM INNISS Senior who died 15th Feby 1853 | Aged 76. He was the beloved | husband of Sarah Ann, and father of Mercy, Ann, | William and Sarah Jane.

See No. 27.

_____

404. Close to west wall:—

SACRED | To the Memory of | LOUISA MATILDA ANN | Infant Daughter Of | GEORGE PALMER | Who Departed This Life | On The 6th Of March 1848 | AGED 1 Year & 6 Months | (2 lines.)

_____

405. Small loose white marble:—

THE | FAMILY | BURIAL PLACE of | ALX^R (*sic*) SEALE | 1861.

_____

406. Two headstones within railing near west wall:—

IN MEMORY OF | NATHANIEL ALLAN, | BORN 21st JULY 1860, DIED 9th SEP^T 1885 | AND | CLIFFORD AUBREY | BORN 7th FEB. 1863, DIED 14th AUG. 1885 | SONS OF J. W. AND S. R. ROACH | (3 lines.)
SACRED | To the memory of | MARY LOWE ROACH | *relict of* | Nathaniel Roach Esqr | died Dec. 26 1856 | aged 62 years | (2 lines.)

On the railing : 1857 ROACH.

_____

407. *THIS MARBLE IS PLACED | BY | SAMUEL E. BRANCH* | Over the grave of his beloved Wife | SARAH HALL BRANCH | (3 lines) | She departed this life | on the 23^d of Octo^r 1841 | in the 28th Year of her age | (3 lines.)

_____

408. Adjoining it and against west wall:—

HERE LIES ALL THAT WAS MORTAL OF | SAMUEL EDMUND BRANCH, | ATTORNEY-AT-LAW | WHO FELL ASLEEP IN CHRIST | ON 25TH APRIL 1846, AGED 43 YEARS | ALSO OF | SAMUEL EDMUND BRANCH | HIS SON | WHO ENTERED INTO REST | ON 23 AUGUST 1852, AGED 15 YEARS.

? Father of the late Bishop and of Dr. W. J. Branch of St. Kitts. See M.I. of St. Peter's, Basseterre, St. Kitts.

_____

409. Headstone :—

PRUDENCE A. ARMSTRONG | died | Nov. 20, 1869 | aged 36 years |
(6 lines.)

410. Near west gate and in west wall is a small square stone :—
" W. Walrond."

411. Adjoining 410 :—

HERE Lies the Body of | Mrs MARY GI . . . | who Departed this Life |
May . . . . | Aged 72 Years.

412. Large vault enclosed by railing :—

THE | SEPULCHRE | OF | EDMUND KNIGHT.

413. Headstone :—

In Memory of | HENRY JEMOTT INCE | DIED 10TH DECR. 1910 | AGED
75 YEARS.

414. Headstone, compasses and square :—

In Memory of | *CRICHLOW JEMOTT* | *Died July 29th 1876* | *Aged 42
Years.*

415. Slab near west path :—

Sacred to the Memory of | GEORGE UMPHREY | who departed this life |
on the 19th June 1807 | Aged 38 Years | ELIZABETH ANN | His Wife | Died
Aug. 1827 | Aged 60 Years | Edward their SON | Died Aug. 16th 1875, | Aged
70 Years.

416. Headstone :—

C. J. | 1876.

417. White marble, shield shaped :—

Under this Marble | Reft | the Remains of | *JANE CARLETON
HOWELL* | Wife of | *CONRADE ADAMS HOWELL* | who departed this
life | on 16 September 1804 | Aged 64 Years | Alfo | the Eldeft & Youngeft |
of their Infant Sons | *THOMAS WALROND* | & *JOHN ROUS.*

Hinds Howell, 7 s. Conrad Adams Howell of Barbados, gent., Merton Coll.,
matric. 6 Nov. 1828, a. 19; B.A. 1834, M.A. 1860, held various curacies 1833—
55; Hon. Canon of Norwich 1856; Rector of Drayton, Norfolk, since 1855.

Conrad Goodridge Howell, 1 s. Hinds of Washfield, near Tiverton, Devon,
cler., Balliol Coll., matric. 17 Oct. 1855, a. 19, B.A. 1860; bar.-at-l., Linc. Inn,
1866. (Foster.)

See No. 123 for notes.

418. Under this ftone are depofited | the remains of two Infant | daughters of
HENRY THOMAS | & MARTHA CRANE | SARAH NATTALI departed |
this life December 2^d 1795 | Aged 21 Months 20 days | MARGARET ANN
departed | this life December 11th, 1795 | Aged 4 Months, 18 days.

419. SACRED | TO THE MEMORY OF | WILLIAM BASSELL WINTER |
OF THIS ISLAND ESQ^R | WHO DEPARTED THIS LIFE | THE 18th of DECEMBER 1808 |
AGED 72 YEARS.

K

420. Here under | are depofited the Remains of | THOMASIN-WILLIAMS DONOVAN | who departed this Life | on the 23ᵈ of March 1791 | Aged 32 Years | (15 lines) | erected by her husband Danˡ Donovan of this Parish goldsmith.

421. BARBADOS | Here lies the Body of William Henery Efq. | who departed this Life May 2ᴰ 1770 Aged | 50 Years 5 Months and 17 Days | Here lies the Body of Elizabeth Henery his | Wife who departed this Life 20ᵗʰ May 1791 | Aged 66 Years 1 Month and 16 Days | She was from her Marriage January 1 1741 | (3 lines) | Here lies too the Body of four of their | Grand Children Jofeph, Ifaac, Thomas, & | Eugene, fons of their only Son the prefent | William Henery of the Parifh of Saint | Jofeph in the Ifland aforefaid, who has raifed | this Vault and caused this ftone to be placed | on the top thereof in Remembrance of | his Parents and his Children.

422. Fixed against west wall of the west porch :—

𝕾𝖆𝖈𝖗𝖊𝖉 | TO THE | MEMORY OF | JOHN PARR, *Master Mariner*, formerly of | Liverpool in the County of Lancashire late | of H.M. Transport service, who departed this | life January 1ˢᵗ 1811, in the 41ˢᵗ year of his age | 𝕬𝖑𝖘𝖔 | MARY PARR, wife of the above JOHN PARR | and daughter of ABRAHAM & MARGARET | CUNARD, of Halifax N.S. who departed this | life January 4ᵗʰ 1811, in the 27ᵗʰ year of her age | 𝕬𝖑𝖘𝖔 | MARGARET ANN, infant daughter of the | above JOHN and MARY PARR, who died | January 19ᵗʰ, 1811, aged 7 months | The above Family, together with eight of the | Crew, fell victims to that dreadful malady | then committing its ravages in this Island | (8 lines.)

423. Against west porch, south wall :—

To the Memory of | BREVET MAJOR | EDWARD MICHAEL DE WEND | 4th Battalion 60th Regiment | Who died at | Garrison of Saint Ann's, Barbadoes, | The 9th day of May, | A.D. 1816.

We now come to a triangular portion to north of west walk, beginning at the west end.

424. White marble :—

Hereunder | lie the mouldering Remains of | JOHN CLEMENT Efqʳ | (9 lines) | He died on the 31ˢᵗ of July 1791 | When he had not, by 14 days, | Attained the 44ᵗʰ year of his age | Also | In memory of | R. ALBERT COX | who died July 17ᵗʰ 1875 | AGED 55 [or 35] YEARS | H. T. COX | died June 2ⁿᵈ 1893 | AGED 55 YEARS.

(The ages doubtful. They have been cut later by an inferior workman.)

425. Fragment :—

R. S. 1805.

426. Ledger :—

R. B.

427. SACRED | to the Memory of | M^RS ABIGAIL NEWLAND CLARKE | the relict of | CLEMENT CLARKE | who departed this Life | December 30th 1817 | Aged 52 Years.

428. Headstone :—

Sacred | *To the Memory of* | JOSEPH Eldest Son of WILLIAM and | MARGARET BOWMAN, of *West Derby*, | near *Liverpool*, who departed this Life | on the 11th of April 1845, Aged 21 Years | (11 lines.)

429. SACRED | to the Memory | of | ADJUTANT JOHN PLACKETT | Late of the 1st W.I. Reg^t | who departed this life the 18th day | of December 1822 | Aged 42 Years | Also | M^RS DOROTHY DESSE | Late Mother in law to the above | who departed this life the 23rd day | of July 1832 (?) | Aged 60 Years | ALSO | JOHN TIERNEY SON IN LAW | OF DOROTHY DESSE DIED 25th of March | 1836 AGED 28 YEARS.

430. SACRED | to the memory of | ROBERT MA^CCANN | Seaman late of HIS Majesty's ship Belvidera | who departed this life at Barbados on the | 19 day of May 1836 occasioned by a fall from | Aloft on the Previous day | AGED 27 YEARS | (13 lines.)

431. Mausoleum, white marble tablet :—

IN LOVING MEMORY | OF | JOHN FRANCIS TRIMINGHAM J^NR | BORN IN NEWFOUNDLAND JAN. 30TH 1839: DIED OCT. 6TH 1879 | AND | WARWICK GEORGE TRIMINGHAM, | BORN IN NEWFOUNDLAND OCT. 29TH 1843; DIED MAY 12TH 1896 | SONS OF | JOHN FRANCIS AND SARAH ANN TRIMING-HAM | (1 line.)

432. Fragment :—

Here lies interr'd the Body of | *BENJAMIN DUCK* | who departed this life | the 4th Day of December 1755 in the . . . . | Year of his Age.

433. Headstone :—

Here lie the Remains of | Lieutenant GEORGE RICKCORDS | late of | His Majesty's Ship *AMPHITRITE* | Son of WILLIAM and | JANE RICK-CORDS *of West Cliff* | *in the Co. of Kent ENGLAND* | who departed this Life | in the House of Dr ROBERTSON | in *BRIDGETOWN* | 13th Decr 1798 Aged 21 Years | (6 lines.)

434. Headstone :—

In Memory of | Lieu^t GEORGE ARMSTRONG | Late of H.M. R.W. India Rangers | who died 18th Octr 1811 Aged 34 Years | He left a disconsolate Widow | and Infant Daughter | (3 lines.)

435. Ledger :—

Underneath are interred the mortal remains of | Dep^ty Assist^t Commissary Genl GEORGE ACKROYD | Who fell a Victim to the Fever of the Climate on the 13th January 1821 | in the 47th Year of his Age.

436. Ledger :—

Underneath are interred the mortal remains of | Mrs JANE GRAHAM Wife of Mr M. E. GRAHAM | of the Engineer Department | Who fell a Victim to the Fever of the Climate | on the 31st October 1820.

437. In Memory of | *Lieutenant GEORGE PALMER*, | late of the 65th Regiment | and | attached to the | Quarter Master General Dep^t | in this Island | who on the 1st day of December 1820 | fell a Victim to a Malignant Fever | then raging in Barbados | in the 28th Year of his Age | (left widow and 4 infant sons) | (6 lines.)

438. 𝕾𝖆𝖈𝖗𝖊𝖉 | to | the memory of | JOHN BISSETT M^{c}KENZIE | *son of* | *L^t M^{c}KENZIE of* | *1^h 1st WI Reg^t* | who departed this life | the 10th day of july 𝖆.𝖉. 1821 | aged 13 months | (4 lines.)

439. In Memory of | THEODORE FORSTER, | who died 8th March 1808, | Also | SARAH ANN wife of the above | who died 1st September 1838 | (3 lines.)

440. 𝕾𝖆𝖈𝖗𝖊𝖉 𝖙𝖔 𝖙𝖍𝖊 𝕸𝖊𝖒𝖔𝖗𝖞 | of | EDM^D: BURMAN ROY^l: MIL^y: SURV^r: | AND DRAFTSMAN | who departed this life 11th November 1829 | Aged 43 Years | Also his Daughter Elizabeth | *who died 20th: Sept: 1824* | Aged 5 Weeks.

441. Flaked ledger :—

IOHN ROWE | . . . . his Life | . . . . Auguft 177 . | . . . . ears.

442. In Memory of | *MARY JOHANNA PHILLIPS*, | Died May 6th 1850, | Aged 27 | *WILLIAM WILSON PHILLIPS*, | Died September 1852, | Aged 26. | *MARY LORETTA PHILLIPS*, | Died October 24th 1856, | Aged 59 | (2 lines.)

443. White marble cross, within railing.   On east face :—

IN MEMORY OF | GEORGE WILKINSON M^{c}GLEAN, | BORN ON THE 26TH DAY OF MAY 1800. | DIED ON THE 22ND DAY OF JULY 1876 | (1 line.)

On south face :—

ALSO OF | GEORGE MILLS | SON OF | GEORGE WILKINSON M^{c}GLEAN | DIED 24TH OF MARCH 1862, AGED 24 YEARS.

On north face :—

ALSO OF | ROBERT ARNOTT | SON OF | GEORGE WILKINSON M^{c}GLEAN | DIED 26TH OF JULY 1863, AGED 30 YEARS.

444. Headstone, compass and square :—

WILLIAM E. CLARKE | AGED 64 YEARS | DIED 17TH JUNE | 1893.

445. Headstone, fixed against west wall of west porch :—

SACRED | TO THE MEMORY OF | ANN, THE BELOVED WIFE OF | JAMES SCOTT | MASTER OF THE BARQUE LAIDMANS | OF LIVERPOOL : | WHO DEPARTED THIS LIFE | ON THE 30TH DAY OF DECEMBER 1842 | IN THE 26 YEAR OF HER AGE | (8 lines.)

446. In the next block, ledger :—

SACRED to the Memory | of | RICHARD HOVELL JUNR | who died Jany 15th 1834, Aged 49 Years | also | RICHARD HOVELL SENR | Father of the above | who died Novr 4th 1834 aged 51 years | AND | ELIZABETH HOVELL | daughter of the above | who died august 8th 1844 aged 30 years | for many years a member of the Wesleyan Church | (1 line.)

447. Small headstone :—

SACRED | TO THE MEMORY OF | JOHN S. CRICK | WHO DEPARTED | THIS LIFE | DECR 26TH 1861 | AGED 52 YEARS.

448. Memorabilis | Here lies underneath this ſtone | Hoping for A GLORIOUS RESURRECTION | The body of MARY the wife off | MATTHEW BEST who Departed this | Life the 3d of March 1749 Aged 27 Years.

1749, March 4. Mary wife of Mathew Best. (Burial Register.)

449. Headstone :—

J. S. C. | 1861.

450. White marble upright, chains and corners broken :—

In affectionate Memory | of | RICHARD FRANCIS ROBERTS | DIED 22 MARCH 1884 | AGED 78 YEARS.

451. White marble tablet on vault :—

In Loving Memory | of J. N. TYNES | AND HIS WIFE | AUNT THOM | 1897.

452. White marble cross :—

SACRED | TO THE MEMORY | OF | SAMUEL GOWDEY | AGED 76 | DIED 6TH JULY 1875 | ALSO IN MEMORY OF | CRAGG GOWDEY | HIS BROTHER | WHO DEPARTED THIS LIFE | MAY 23RD 1890 | AGED 90 | (1 line.)

453. North of nave. Broken column within railing, painted brown :—

SACRED | TO THE MEMORY OF | BENJAMIN | CLAIRMONTE | WHO DEPARTED THIS LIFE | ON THE 12TH DAY OF | SEPTEMBER 1852 | AGED 17 YEARS | (1 line.)

454. Vault, nineteenth century, near cottage, inscription illegible.

455. Iron plate on railing :—

"THE BURIAL PLACE | OF | SAMUEL WHITNEYS | FAMILY."

---

456. White marble monument :—

SACRED TO THE MEMORY | OF | THOMAS PERKINS | WHO DEPARTED THIS LIFE | ON THE 7th AUGUST 1828 | AGED 46 YEARS.

---

457. SACRED | TO THE MEMORY OF | MARY FORTE MILLARD | DAUGHTER OF | JOHN & SARAH MILLARD | She Departed This Life (1 line) | OCTBR 6TH 1851 | AT THE EARLY AGE OF 20 YEARS | (5 lines.)

---

458. Next to 457 :—

SACRED TO THE MEMORY | OF MARY JANE | DAUGHTER OF JOHN ELLIOTT HEWETT | WHO DEPARTED THIS LIFE | 18TH MAY 1833 | AGED 23 YEARS | (4 lines) | ALSO | IN MEMORY OF THE ABOVE | JOHN ELLIOTT HEWETT | WHO DEPARTED THIS LIFE | JANUARY 10TH 1838, AGED 56 YEARS | ALSO | TO THE MEMORY OF | JOHN ELLIOTT HEWETT ESQR M.D. | SON OF THE ABOVE | WHO DEPARTED THIS LIFE | OCTR 8TH 1852 AGED 40 YEARS | (2 lines.)

---

459. SACRED | To The Memory | of | JOHN HENRY MARSHALL | Who Died July 2nd 1828 | Aged 33 Years | Also of | Catherine Clun (?) Marsh | granddaughter of | Henry and Matilda Marshall | who died Jany 15th 1857 | Aged 17 Years | And | Henry T. Marshall | died ... ch 16th 1860 [or 1866] | Aged 51 Years and | 6 Months | (cracked.)

---

460. Ledger, with cherubs, skull and crossbones at top :—

Here lyeth | interr'd the Body of | CLEMENTINA LOVE | Wife of | NATHANIEL LOVE | who departed this Life | the 25th day of October 1771 | in the 38th Year of her Age | Alſo | the Body of | NATHANIEL LOVE | who departed this Life | the 16th day of April 1784 | in the 49th Year of his Age.

---

461. Sacred to the Memory of | JOHN WATSON Eſq. | Who departed this life 31st July 1827 | also his beloved wife | MARY G. WATSON | Who departed this life 12th June 1837 | (3 lines; erected by Benjan L. W. the son.)

---

462. UNDER THIS STONE REST THE REMAINS | OF | THE REVERED PARENTS | THE BELOVED BRETHREN | OF WHOM WAS THE MUCH RESPECTED AND LAMENTED DR. HORSHAM | AND SISTER | (AMIABLE CONSORT OF DOCTOR CUTTING) | ALSO | THE CHILDREN AND WIFE | OF | WILLIAM HORSHAM | WHO ERECTS THIS TOMB TO THEIR MEMORY JUNE IV. | MDCCCI.

---

463. THE FAMILY VAULT OF | I. R. SAVEREY ESQr.

---

464. SACRED TO THE MEMORY | OF | JANE THE WIFE OF | DANIEL GROGAN | WHO DEPARTED THIS LIFE | ON THE 26TH SEPTEMBER | ANNO DOMINI 1841 | AGED 85 YEARS and 5 MONTHS.

465. Mausoleum, on iron plate :—
THE | BURIAL GROUND | OF | DANIEL GROGAN.

And at east end :—
SEPULCHRE | OF THE INNISS FAMILY 1842.

466. On iron plate on railing :—
FAMILY BURYING | PLACE OF | HENRY P. LEACH.

467. Ledger :—
JOHN R. HOMEYARD | Died April 10, 1861, | Aged 74 Years.

468. On iron plate on railing :—
THE BURIAL PLACE | OF | MARY E. NUTT.

469. There are five slabs side by side, with ladders on them* :—
Margaret Goodridge | died on the 13th of August | in the 44th year of her Age | and of Christ 1833 | (4 lines) | also | HUGH GOODRIDGE, M.D. | DIED 11 AUGUST 1846, AGED 60 | AND | ELIZA | HIS WIDOW | DIED 8 OCTOBER 1886 AGED 74.

470. THIS STONE IS PLACED | AS A DESERVED TRIBUTE OF FILIAL AFFECTION | OVER THE REMAINS OF | FRANCIS McCLURE MERCHANT | BY HIS SON SAMUEL McCLURE | HE DIED | SEPTEMBER XX A.D. MDCCCXI | IN THE LVII YEAR OF HIS AGE | (3 lines.)

471. SACRED | to .... | Memory | *Wife of* .... | who | departed this life | Augᵗ 27ᵗʰ | 1843 | AGED 33 YEARS | (flaked.)
At end is a small headstone to EDITH PRICHARD in Latin.

472. Erected by | DUDLEY P. COTTON | Sacred | to the memory of | DANIEL COTTON | of Boston Mass. U.S. | who departed this life | Sept. 28, 1842, | in the 26th year | of his age | MARY REBECCA | *Infant Daughter | of* | DUDLEY PAGE AND REBECCA JANE | COTTON | *Died February 3ʳᵈ 1855*, | Aged 7 Months & 9 Days.

473. SACRED | To the Memory of | ROBᵀ J. INCLEDON | who died Octr. 25, 1863 | AGED 40 YRS. | *Also* | MARY H. INCLEDON | THE BELOVED DAUGHTER OF THE ABOVE | WHO DIED JULY 10ᵀᴴ 1873, AGED 21 YRS. | (6 lines.)

* Workmen were in possession of this space, but I don't think I could have omitted the five inscriptions.

474. IN MEMORY | OF | ROBERT WOODROW BILTON | NATIVE OF GLASGOW, SCOTLAND; | WHO DEPARTED THIS LIFE | 13TH DECEMBER 1848 | IN HIS 20TH YEAR.

475. Headstone :—

SACRED TO THE MEMORY | OF | JOSEPH WILLIAM INNISS | BORN 24TH MAY 1814 | DIED 17TH JANUARY 1903 | AND OF HIS BELOVED WIFE | THOMASIN ANN | BORN 10TH OCTOBER 1834 | DIED 18TH JUNE 1899 | ALSO OF THEIR DAUGHTER | ROSE WALROND | DIED 20TH MARCH 1890 | AGED 19 YEARS.

476. The Family Burial Place | OF | EDWARD WILLIAM MILLS | RACHAEL WALCOTT MILLS | DIED 27TH JANUARY 1850 | AGED 49 YEARS | CAROLINE MILLS | DIED 27TH DECR 1900 | AGED 71 YEARS | EDWARD W. MILLS | DIED 4TH JULY 1901 | AGED 81 YEARS.

477. Close to north wall and road :—

SACRED TO THE MEMORY | OF | CHRISTIAN SKINNER | Widow | departed this life May 21st | 1847 | at the advanced age of | 83 Years | ALSO | MISS JANE LAMBERT SKINNER | SISTER TO THE ABOVE | Who Departed This Life | 23RD OF AUGUST 1851 | AGED 85 YEARS.

1852, July 16. In B. aged 87, Dorothy-Griffith, dau. of Wm. Rolloch, & widow of Isaac Skinner, of B., etc. (" G.M.," 655.)

478. Headstone within railing near cottage :—

SACRED | TO THE MEMORY OF | MARGARET, | BELOVED WIFE OF JOHN H. BRAITHWAITE | AND ELDEST DAUGHTER OF | SAMUEL WHITNEY | BORN 21 SEPT. 1810, DIED 22 JUNE 1875 | AGED 64 YEARS | (1 line) | ALSO OF | JOHN TROWBRIDGE | THIRD SON OF | F. A. R. AND ELLEN C. BRAITHWAITE | DIED 10TH MAY 1884 | AGED 3 WEEKS.

On a second headstone :—

IN LOVING MEMORY | OF | CLARA N. BRAITHWAITE | DIED 5TH MARCH 1894 | AND | OF OUR FATHER | JOHN H. BRAITHWAITE | DIED 12TH AUGUST 1894.

479. Enclosed by iron railing :—

IN MEMORIAM | SOPHIA MARY JULIA, | DAUGHTER OF GEORGE AND LEONORA WINTER | AND THE BELOVED WIFE OF JOHN PITCHER | BORN AT ST. JOHN'S, NEWFOUNDLAND | JANUARY 22ND 1836 | DIED AT ST. LEONARD'S IN THIS PARISH | DECEMBER 15TH 1859 | (many lines.)

480. Enclosed by iron railing :—

UNDERNEATH THIS MARBLE | ARE DEPOSITED THE REMAINS OF | MARIA FARRE JONES | ELDEST DAUGHTER OF | JOHN FORSTER DRAKE JONES, M.D. | AND ANNE ISABEL HIS WIFE | WHO DEPARTED THIS LIFE | ON THE 13TH OF APRIL 1832 | (10 lines ; died 4 days after arrival.)

481. On two small square stones on a vault :—

T. M. SALKELD
age 8 mos.
agst 14ᵗʰ 1851.

H. F. NAISH
DIED
SEPTᴿ 1ˢᵗ 1849
AGED 4 MONTHS.

---

482. ERECTED | BY | GEORGE WHITLA | of Barbados, | To the Memory of | WILLIAM JOHN WHITLA | Born at Belfast | died in Bridgetown | 6ᵗʰ October 1841, | Aged 23 years.

---

483. Here lieth the body of | George W. Patton M.D. Esqʳ | who died 7ᵗʰ Janʳʸ 1842 | three weeks after his arrival | from Tandragee Ireland | (10 lines ; erected by his children.)

---

484. HERE SLEEPS IN JESUS | REBECCA GITTENS | HAVERSAAT | WHO DIED JANUARY 29ᵀᴴ 1865 | AGED 80 YEARS.

---

485. Headstone adjoining 470 :—

TO THE MEMORY OF | FREDERICA | ELDEST DAUGHTER OF | GEO. FRED. HAVER-SAAT D.A.C.G. | AND REBECCA GITTENS | HIS WIFE | WHO WENT TO | THE BETTER LAND | OCT. 14 1865 | (4 lines.)

---

486. Broken slab, lying loose :—

Here lieth the body of . . . . | the daughter of THOMAS & ELEAN . . | . . RRISON who departed this life | . . cember the 9ᵗʰ 1712 Aged 2 Years & . . . .

· 1712, Dec. 9. Jane Harrison, a child. (Burial Register.)

---

487. IN | LOVING MEMORY | OF | JOˢ THOˢ NIGHTINGALE | BORN 25 JAN. 1815, | DIED 29 OCT. 1885.

---

488. Enclosed by iron railing : —

SACRED to the MEMORY | of | MARY ANN ARCHER | who died | July 21ˢᵗ 1842, Aged 70 Years | Also | To the Memory of | MARCUS BYRON McCLEAN | who died | August 10ᵗʰ 1870 | Aged 23 Years | Also | To the Memory of | MAUDE BYRON CHENERY MᶜCLEAN | Died 28ᵗʰ May 1871 | Aged 17 Days. | Also | WALLACE MᶜCLEAN | BORN JULY 24ᵀᴴ 1872, DIED JULY 24ᵀᴴ 1872 | Also | JULIAN WILKINSON MᶜCLEAN | Died 24ᵗʰ Febʸ 1876 | Aged 6 Years.

---

489. 𝕿𝖍𝖊 𝕭𝖚𝖗𝖎𝖆𝖑 𝕻𝖑𝖆𝖈𝖊 of | THOMAS HENRY REBITT.

---

490. TO THE MEMORY | OF | JOHN KEMP JUNᴿ | A Native of Glasgow | Who arrived in this Island | on | 17ᵗʰ Octʳ | and died of fever | on | 3ᵈ Novʳ | 1839 | AGED 20 YEARS. | Also | In Memory of | ROBERT GORDON | A Native of Port Patrick, Scot. | who died | on the 29ᵗʰ of May 1865 | Aged 33 Years.

L

491. Sacred | TO THE MEMORY | OF | M^{RS} HENRY BENTALL, | THE MOTHER OF | ALEXANDER STEWART ESQ^{RE} | COLLECTOR OF H. M. CUSTOMS | AT THE PORT | OF BRIDGETOWN, BARBADOS | WHO DEPARTED THIS LIFE | ON THE 25TH JUNE 1845, | IN THE 71ST YEAR OF | HER AGE. | Also | OF ALEXANDER STEWART ESQ^{RE} | SON OF THE ABOVE | COLLECTOR OF H. M. CUSTOMS | IN THIS ISLAND | WHO DIED ON BOARD THE STEAMER THAMES | ON HIS PASSAGE FROM ENGLAND | ON THE 27TH SEPT^R 1848, IN THE 47TH YEAR OF HIS AGE. | (2 lines ; left a widow.)

492. SACRED | TO THE MEMORY | OF | JOHN STEVENSON | DIED 25th Octr 1850 | AGED 31 YEARS.

493. Three headstones enclosed by iron railing :—

Sacred | TO THE MEMORY OF | JAMES ELDER | BORN IN SCOTLAND | FEB^Y 16TH 1823 | DIED FEB^Y 23RD 1867.

494. IN MEMORY OF | AUGUSTA MATILDA | WIFE OF | ROBERT ELDER | DIED 26TH MAY 1906 | AGED 46 YEARS.

495. SACRED | TO | THE MEMORY | OF | NATHANIEL THOMAS RAMSEY | WHO DIED 8TH JUNE 1847 | AGED 44 YEARS | ALSO | HIS MOTHER | ANN RAMSEY | DIED DEC. 25TH 1859 | AGED 76 YEARS.

496. IN MEMORY OF | MARIA ANN MARRIAGE | WIFE OF MR ADAM HARTHILL | SHE DIED OF YELLOW FEVER | 4TH NOVEMBER 1852, | IN THE 24TH YEAR OF HER AGE | AND OF | JOHN MARRIAGE | THEIR ONLY CHILD WHO DIED | AT RAMSGATE KENT | ON THE 13TH OF AUGUST 1853 | AGED ONE YEAR AND ELEVEN MONTHS.

497. Enclosed by iron railing :—

SACRED TO THE MEMORY OF | JOHN FREER | SON OF JOHN F. WHITFIELD OF CANADA | WHO DIED OCTOBER 19TH 1853 | AGED 17 YEARS | ALSO OF ANDREW CALVERT | ELDEST SON OF ANDREW CRICHTON LEE | OF EDINBURGH | WHO DIED DECEMBER 29TH 1853 | AGED 17 YEARS | THE ABOVE FELL VICTIMS TO THE YELLOW FEVER | AFTER A FEW MONTHS RESIDENCE IN THE ISLAND.

498. Near road wall, cracked :—

Sacred to the Memory of | THURBARNE PACKER, | Son of | . . . . & MARTHA PACKER | who departed this life | on the 19th November 1810 | Aged 2 Years & 1 Month | Also ELIZABETH | Daughter of | JOHN & MARTHA PACKER, | departed this life | on the 13th January 1812 | Aged 4 Years 5 Months & 20 Days.

499. Large mausoleum :—

The | Family Vault of | HENRY BECKLES GALL | built | Feby 1853.

500. Small headstone :—

Elizabeth A. Tancock | Died | 12ᵗʰ Decʳ 1860 | Aged 22 Months.

---

501. 𝕾𝖆𝖈𝖗𝖊𝖉 | to t𝖍𝖊 𝕸𝖊𝖒𝖔𝖗𝖕 of | Mᴿˢ E. P. BUCHANAN | who died
1ˢᵗ July 1887 | Aged 87 Years | (3 lines ; by children.)

---

502. 𝕾𝖆𝖈𝖗𝖊𝖉 | ᴛᴏ ᴛʜᴇ ᴍᴇᴍᴏʀʏ ᴏꜰ | MARTHA ELIZABETH | ᴛʜᴇ ʙᴇʟᴏᴠᴇᴅ
ᴡɪꜰᴇ ᴏꜰ | PETER CHAPMAN | ᴡʜᴏ ᴅɪᴇᴅ ᴛʜᴇ 17ᴛʜ ᴏꜰ ᴊᴜɴᴇ 1841 | ᴀɢᴇᴅ
20 ʏᴇᴀʀꜱ.

---

503. Headstone :—

SACRED | ᴛᴏ ᴛʜᴇ ᴍᴇᴍᴏʀʏ ᴏꜰ | Mᴿ ALEXANDER HUNTER
ENRIGHT | ᴏꜰ ᴋᴇɴᴛɪꜱʜ ᴛᴏᴡɴ, ɴᴇᴀʀ ʟᴏɴᴅᴏɴ | ᴡʜᴏ ᴅɪᴇᴅ ᴏɴ ᴛʜᴇ 16ᴛʜ | ᴏꜰ
ꜱᴇᴘᴛᴇᴍʙᴇʀ 1836, ɪɴ ᴛʜᴇ | ᴛᴡᴇɴᴛʏ ꜰɪꜰᴛʜ ʏᴇᴀʀ ᴏꜰ ʜɪꜱ ᴀɢᴇ | ʜᴇ ᴇxᴘɪʀᴇᴅ ᴏɴʟʏ
ꜰᴏᴜʀ ᴅᴀʏꜱ ᴀꜰᴛᴇʀ | ʟᴀɴᴅɪɴɢ ɪɴ ᴛʜɪꜱ ɪꜱʟᴀɴᴅ ʙᴇɪɴɢ ᴛᴏᴏ | ɪʟʟ ᴛᴏ ᴘʀᴏᴄᴇᴇᴅ ᴛᴏ
ᴊᴀᴍᴀɪᴄᴀ ᴡʜᴇʀᴇ ʜᴇ | ᴡᴀꜱ ɢᴏɪɴɢ ᴛᴏ ᴠɪꜱɪᴛ ʜɪꜱ ɢʀᴀɴᴅꜰᴀᴛʜᴇʀ ᴀʟᴇxᴀɴᴅᴇʀ ᴀɪᴋᴍᴀɴ
ꜱᴇɴʀ ᴇꜱQʀᴇ | ᴏꜰ ᴘʀᴏꜱᴘᴇᴄᴛ ᴘᴇɴ ɴᴇᴀʀ ᴋɪɴɢꜱᴛᴏɴ | ɪɴ ᴛʜᴀᴛ ɪꜱʟᴀɴᴅ. |

---

504. Headstone :—

A. H. E. 1836.

---

505. ꜱᴀᴄʀᴇᴅ ᴛᴏ ᴛʜᴇ ᴍᴇᴍᴏʀʏ ᴏꜰ | CATHARINE MARY | The Beloved
Wife of | JOHN MᶜSWINEY, ESQUIRE; | ꜱᴛɪᴘᴇɴᴅɪᴀʀʏ ᴍᴀɢɪꜱᴛʀᴀᴛᴇ ᴏꜰ |
ʙʀɪᴛɪꜱʜ ɢᴜɪᴀɴᴀ, | Who Departed This Life | ᴏᴄᴛᴏʙᴇʀ 27ᴛʜ 1850 | In The |
36ᴛʜ ʏᴇᴀʀ ᴏꜰ ʜɪꜱ ᴀɢᴇ.

---

506. ʙᴇɴᴇᴀᴛʜ | ᴀʀᴇ ᴅᴇᴘᴏꜱɪᴛᴇᴅ ᴛʜᴇ ʀᴇᴍᴀɪɴꜱ ᴏꜰ | ELLEN | ᴛʜᴇ ᴀꜰꜰᴇᴄ-
ᴛɪᴏɴᴀᴛᴇ ᴡɪꜰᴇ ᴏꜰ | C. C. DRAKE ESQ. DEMERARA | ᴅɪᴇᴅ 12ᴛʜ ꜰᴇʙʏ 1846 |
ᴀɢᴇᴅ 31.

---

507. SACRED | to the | MEMORY | of | WILLIAM A. ARCHER | who
departed this life December the 8ᵗʰ 1839 | Aged 29 Years | (4 lines.)

---

508. ERECTED | By | George Montgomery of Belfast, | Merchant | In
memory of his beloved son | GEORGE | Who died at Barbadoes | on the
13ᵗʰ October 1839 | Aged 23 Years.

---

509. ꜱᴀᴄʀᴇᴅ ᴛᴏ ᴛʜᴇ ᴍᴇᴍᴏʀʏ ᴏꜰ | ROBERT MATHER, | ᴍᴇʀᴄʜᴀɴᴛ ɪɴ
ɢʟᴀꜱɢᴏᴡ, | ᴡʜᴏ ᴅɪᴇᴅ ᴏꜰ ᴄᴏɴꜱᴜᴍᴘᴛɪᴏɴ ᴀᴛ ʜᴀꜱᴛɪɴɢꜱ | ᴏɴ ᴛʜᴇ 13 ᴏꜰ ɴᴏᴠᴇᴍʙᴇʀ
1838 | ᴀɢᴇᴅ 39.

---

510. ꜱᴀᴄʀᴇᴅ ᴛᴏ ᴛʜᴇ ᴍᴇᴍᴏʀʏ | of | WILLIAM CARTMELL | late of
Doncaster | but more recently of Liverpool | who repaired to this Island | for the
benefit of his health | and died the 15ᵗʰ May 1838 | Aged 32. | (5 lines.)

511. Headstone :—

WILLIAM BOWERS | died 14ᵀᴴ octʀ 1852 | aged 64 years.

512. Headstone :—

W. B. 1852.

513. Headstone :—

Frances Charlotte | daughter of | Chaˢ and Frances | Massiah | of Demerara | died 30ᵀᴴ sepᵀ | 1852 | aged 9 months.

514. SACRED | to the memory of | WILLIAM McQUEEN | a dutiful and affectionate son | who died october 23ᴿᴰ 1836 | in the 24ᵀᴴ year of his age | (3 lines ; by his father Jas. McQueen.)

515. Headstone :—

A. H. E. 1836.

516. sacred to the memory of | REBECCA ANNE | the most dear wife of charles thornton cunningham esqᴿᴱ | colonial secretary of this island | and the daughter of s. d. heap esqᴿᴱ | consul general of the united states of america | at tunis in africa | she died in giving birth to her first child | august 2ᴺᴰ 1837, aged 21 years.

1837, Aug. 2. At B., Rebecca Anne, wife of C. T. Cunningham, esq. Colonial Sec. (" G.M.," 551.)

517. Headstone :—

H. L. | died | june 1. 1853 | aged 80 years.

518. Headstone :—

ELIZᵀᴴ HUNTER 1851.

519. Sacred to the Memory | of | HENRY THOMAS TURTON | who departed this life | 16ᵗʰ day of Septᵇᵉʳ 1836 | Aged 49 Years.

520. Sacred to the Memory | of THOMAS CHENERY | who departed this life June 25ᵗʰ 1836, Aged 57 Years | Also | CHARLES CHENERY | who died April the 16ᵗʰ 1838 Aged 47 Years | likewise | ELIZABETH CHENERY | who died on the 15ᵗʰ April 1841 Aged 93 Years | And | William Chenery | who departed from this Life | October 4ᵗʰ 1845 | Aged 64 Years | being the second son of ELIZABETH CHENERY and brother | THOMAS and CHARLES CHENERY whose remains | are | herein interred.

521. Headstone with the lower part deeply sunk in the ground :—

Wᴹ FITZPATRICK Senʳ | departed this life | on the 21ˢᵗ of July 1835 Aged 67 Years | Also | . . . . FITZPATRICK.

522. **Sacred to the Memory** | of | SAMUEL BRANDFORD ARTHUR, | WHO DEPARTED THIS LIFE | ON THE 30ᵀᴴ DECEMBER 1868 | **And his Son** | JOSEPH INNISS ARTHUR | DIED 12ᵀᴴ SEP. 1910 | AGED 72.

---

523. Headstone enclosed by railing:—

SACRED | to the memory | OF THE | REV. THOMAS ROWE | who died | on the 22nd of June | 1870 | *Aged 60 years.*

---

524. **Sacred** | *to* | the Memory of | GEORGE CORSTORPHAN | late Merchant of Demerara | who died September 20ᵗʰ 1834. | Aged 28 Years | (Erected by brother.)

---

525. Headstone:—

IN MEMORY | OF | RICHARD C. BARNES | DIED 5º MARCH 1885 | AGED 60 YEARS.

On a second headstone:—

TO THE MEMORY | OF MARY, DIED | June 2ⁿᵈ 1875 | AGED 21 YEARS | Also | EMELINE—DIED | Sepᵗ 2ⁿᵈ 1867 | AGED 8 YEARS | *The Beloved Daughters* | *of* | *Richard C. Barnes.*

On a third stone a white marble cross:—

IN MEMORY | OF | RICHARD ALFRED BARNES | AGED 35 | WHO, ON THE 6ᵀᴴ JUNE 1897, LOST HIS LIFE | IN ATTEMPTING TO RESCUE | ERNEST HENRY JONES | FROM DROWNING AT BATHSHEBA | (3 lines.)

These three all in one curbed enclosure.

---

526. Headstone:—

REV. JOHN CROSBY | died May 26, 1833, | aged 29.

---

527. White marble headstone:—

In | **affectionate** | **remembrance of** | **Benjamin Powell Jones,** | **the second son of** | **Benjamin Jones, and Eleanor his wife,** | **of this Island** | **Died 14th September 1871, Aged 71 years** | (4 lines.)

---

528. On ledger enclosed by iron railing:—

Sacred | **to the Memory of** | MICHAEL OLTON | Who departed this life | 13ᵗʰ November 1830 | Aged 49 Years | and of his daughter | MARGARET ANN | Wife of Depʸ Assᵗ Comʸ Genˡ Swain | who died 10ᵗʰ March 1836 | Aged 31 Years | Also *His* "*SON*" | JOSIAH LLEWELYN OLTON | *Died 8ᵗʰ July 1854* | *Aged 44 Years.*

On a granite headstone, on above slab:—

IN MEMORY OF | ETHEL | WIFE OF WALTER T. BONYUN | DIED 8ᵀᴴ NOVʳ 1879 | AGED 28 YEARS | (2 lines) | ALSO | W. T. BONYUN | DIED 10ᵀᴴ NOV. 1903 | AGED 52 YRS. | (1 line.)

529. SACRED | TO THE MEMORY OF | MARY ANN | WIFE OF | JOHN MUNRO ESQUIRE | OF THIS ISLAND | SHE DEPARTED THIS LIFE | 24ᵀᴴ SEPTEMBER 1836 | AGED 27 YEARS.

530. (4 lines) | RICHARD SKINNER GRIFFITH ESQᴿ M.D. | WHO DEPARTED THIS LIFE | ON THE 15ᵀᴴ OF OCTOBER 1833 | AGED 26 YEARS.

531. SACRED | to the Memory of | ARABELLA HINDS | infant daughter of SAMᴸ S. FORTE, | who departed this life August 3ʳᵈ 1839 | Aged 17 Months | Also | . . . BETH (broken) WALCOTT FORTE | Died May 10ᵗʰ 1864 | Aged 50 Years.

532. Enclosed by iron railing :—

H. JONES | Died October 5ᵗʰ 1866 | Aged 68 Years | MARY JANE JONES | Died November 13ᵗʰ 1868 | Aged 67 Years | (4 lines.)

533. Large mausoleum :—

Sacred to the Memory of | Sarah Christian Hawkesworth | Wife of | William Hawkesworth | who departed this life | May 10ᵗʰ 1830 | Aged 41 Years.

534. Cross in curb and low railing :—

In Loving Memory of | Abel Clinckett Born 1775 Died 1854 | and Mary Judith Clinckett his wife | Born 1788 Died 1862 | (1 line.)

1851, Jan. 10. In Jamaica, the Rev. G. M. Clinckett, Incumbent of St. Matthews Claremont, yst. s. of Abel C. esq. of B. to Jane, yst. dau. of the l. Rev. Wm. Henry of Tooting, Surrey. ("G.M.," 545.)

535. Large mausoleum :—

Sacred | to the Memory of | Mᴿ JOHN MᶜOHLERY | WHO DEPARTED THIS LIFE | ON THE 3ᴿᴰ OF APRIL 1832 | AGED 19 YEARS.

536. On plate enclosed by iron railing :—

THE FAMILY | Burial Place | of EDWARD HENRY and | ROBERT ARTHUR MARSHALL.

537. On plate enclosed by iron railing :—

BURIAL PLACE | OF | W. H. & I. C. | ALLDER.

538. At the west end of No. 535 are three white marble tablets :—

SACRED | TO THE MEMORY OF | HENRY CUMMING | WHO DEPARTED THIS LIFE | ON THE 5ᵀᴴ OF DECEMBER 1839 | AGED 20 YEARS.

539. SACRED TO THE MEMORY OF | MICHAEL CAVAN ESQUIRE | WHO DIED THE 6TH JUNE 1832 | AGED 53 YEARS | A NATIVE OF SCOTLAND AND FOR | THIRTY YEARS A MERCHANT OF THIS ISLAND | (7 lines.)

1832, June 6. At B. a. 52, Michael Cavan, esq. many years a resident merchant. ("G.M.," 94.)

540. SACRED | TO THE MEMORY OF | DAVID MᶜOHLERY | WHO DEPARTED THIS LIFE | ON THE 6TH NOVEMBER | 1836, | AGED 27 YEARS.

541. SACRED | to | the memory of | MISS SARAH GRIFFITH | Who departed this | Life in the Faith | and Fear of | CHRIST | JULY 19th 1851 | AGED 75 YEARS.

542. SACRED | to the memory of | JOHN WEEKES JONES | who departed this life | January 7th 1852 | aged 30 years | (3 lines; placed by wife.)

543. SACRED | to the memory of | SARAH ANN | the beloved wife of | SAMUEL M. ALLEYNE. | who Died on the 13th of May 1850 | aged 61 years | (4 lines) | SAMUEL MAYNARD ALLEYNE | DIED | 13th May 1855. | aged 68 | (1 line.)

544. Sacred to the memory | of | ELIZABETH | Wife of GEORGE BROOMFIELD | Died 31st July 1839 | Aged 44 Years | ALSO | MRˢ EMILY STEVENSON | DAUGHTER OF THE ABOVE | DIED 24TH NOVᴿ 1847 | AGED 28 YEARS.

545. SACRED | to | the memory of | JOHN HENRY LAWRENCE | MASTER MARINER | Who departed this Life | JULY 9th 1852 | AGED 40 YEARS | (4 lines.)

546. IN MEMORY | of | HENRY CHEESMAN | Died 8th of Decbᴿ | 1844, | Aged 44 Years.

547. These three ledgers are in the walk :—

ANN GASKIN MAYERS | DEPARTED THIS LIFE | APRIL 20TH 1832, AGED 66 YEARS | AND | MARTHA ANN CRICHLOW | MAYERS | DEPARTED THIS LIFE | NOV. 14TH 1832 | AGED 75 YEARS | ALSO | THE BODY OF ISABELLA | .. WIS WIFE OF JOHN | LEWIS AND DAUGHTER | OF WILTSHIRE AND SARA | STANT(ON) WHO DEPARTED | THIS | LIFE THE 17TH OF APRIL 1811 | AGED 63 YEARS.

548. To | THE MEMORY OF | JANE | WIDOW OF | RICHARD FARMER ESQᴿᴱ | OF THIS ISLAND | SHE DEPARTED THIS LIFE | FEBRUARY 9TH 1832 | AGED 77 YEARS.

549. SACRED TO THE MEMORY OF | RICHARD MERRITE, | WHO DEPARTED THIS LIFE THE 10ᵀᴴ JUNE 1832 | AGED 72 YEARS | ALSO | JOHN RICHARD, SON OF | CHARLOTTE ELIZABETH AND JOHN C. ALLDER | WHO DEPARTED THIS LIFE THE 9ᵀᴴ JUNE 1833 | AGED 12 MONTHS | ALSO | CHARLOTTE ELIZABETH ALLDER, | WIFE OF JOHN C. ALLDER, | AND DAUGHTER TO RICHARD MERRITE | (3 lines) | (died) ON THE 15ᵀᴴ AUGUST 1833, | IN THE 25ᵀᴴ YEAR OF HER AGE.

550. Granite headstone :—

In Memory | of | SAMUEL THOMAS | YEARWOOD | BORN 22ᴺᴰ APRIL 1831 | DIED 24ᵀᴴ APRIL 1887.

551. Sacred to the Memory | OF | WILLIAM OCTAVIUS SIMMONS | BORN IN THE ISLAND OF SABA 28ᵀᴴ JAN. | 1854 | DIED IN THIS ISLAND 17ᵀᴴ APRIL 1874 | (8 lines.)

552. Headstone within curbed grave :—

Sacred to the Memory | OF | C. M. HAMMOND | MASTER OF AMERICAN BARQUE | *Montezuma* | WHO DEPARTED THIS LIFE | JULY 29ᵀᴴ 1874 | AGED 42 YEARS.

553. White marble fragment :—

E. N. C.   E. M. A.

554. Large mausoleum :—

SACRED | To the memory of | P. HARRIER | WHO DIED AUG. 18ᵀᴴ 1873 | (9 lines; by wife.)

555. Headstone in curbed grave :—

HOLLINGSWORTH.

556. Headstone over vault :—

(1 line) | SACRED | to the memory of | ELIZABETH NICOLLS | CRICK, | Died 26ᵗʰ Sep. 1836, | AGED 60 | SACRED | to the memory of | ELIZABETH MARTINDALE | ARMSTRONG, | Died 28ᵗʰ Sep. 1870, | AGED 39 | also | to the memory of | ELIZABETH LESLIE ARMSTRONG | Died August 18ᵗʰ 1877, Aged 75 Yrs. | *She was Daughter of the Former* | *and Mother of the latter.*

557. White marble upright :—

In Memory of | HENRY SACHEVERAL SMITH | ATWOOD | who departed this life | the 5ᵗʰ September 1832, | Aged 31 Years | (4 lines) | Here also lies his Infant Son JOHN, | died July 17ᵗʰ 1827 aged 3 Months | and his Niece Amelia Jane Atwood | 12ᵗʰ November 1831 aged 4 Months.

558. THOMAS WALTON | OBIT JULY 19, 1839 | ÆTAT 63 | (3 lines.)

559. Two white marble headstones in curbed grave :—

In Loving Memory | **of** | OUR FATHER | JAMES YOUNG EDGHILL | WHO WAS CALLED HENCE | 1ST OCT. 1897 | AGED 76 YEARS | (2 lines.)

On a second stone :—

CAROLINE EDGHILL | JOINED THE RANSOMED HOST | EASTER-EVE 1894.

560. Headstone :—

T. A. N.

561. IN MEMORY | OF | JOHN WASHINGTON YEARWOOD | who died on the 9th March 1853 | AGED 39 YEARS | (1 line.)

562. Beneath this Stone | rest the Remains of | LAURA | Daughter of BENJAMIN and ELIZABETH A. CHAPMAN | who departed this life July 30th 1817. | at the Age of 12 Years | (22 lines) | Also | To the Memory of | JAMES CHAPMAN, M.D. | who died December 3rd 1868 | Aged 61 Years.

563. Metal plate on headstone :—

MARGARET HARB . . . | SISNETT AGED | 79 YEARS | DIED APRIL 26.

564. Headstone :—

SACRED | to the memory | of | ELLEN T. MELVIN | who died Jany 17th | 1852 | aged 5 Years | 9 months.

565. Headstone :—

HERE | lie the remains of | CLEMENTINA | the beloved Wife of | CHAS E. Y. CROUCH | Who departed this life | Septr 25th 1863 | AGED 26 YEARS.

566. Headstone :—

SACRED | to the Memory of | WM JONES, | who departed this life | December 20th 1840 | AGED 51 YEARS.

567. Headstone :—

In Memory of | MARY BAILEY | Born 25 Dec. 1795 | DIED 16 SEP. 1874.

568. Headstone : -

ROBERT | Son of | JAS CARSTAIRS | DIED | 1ST DECR 1851 | AGED 12 YEARS.

M

569. Ledger :—

. . CRED | . . Memory of | JOSEPH OSTREHAN | who departed this Life | August 7ᵗʰ 1809 | Aged 52 Years.

570. On an iron plate fixed to railing :—

THE BURIAL PLACE | OF | WILLIAM J. KING's | FAMILY.

On a white marble headstone inside : —

SACRED | to the memory of | Wᴹ J. KING, M.D. | who departed this life | April 4ᵗʰ 1851. | ERECTED BY HIS WIFE ANN.

On another headstone inside :—

IN MEMORY OF | WILLIAM WILSON Junʀ | OF THE RETREAT, | NEAR WHITEHAVEN, CUMBERLAND | (several lines) | BUT DIED ON THE 23ʀᴰ OCTʀ 1839 | ONE MONTH AFTER HIS ARRIVAL | (several lines) | ALSO | THE REVᴰ JOS. HELLI-WELL | THE MUCH ESTEEMED PASTOR | OF THE CONGREGATIONAL CHURCH | WHITEHAVEN WHO DIED ON | THE 10ᵀʰ FEBʸ 1840 | (3 lines ; friend of Wilson.)

571. Headstone :—

Wᴹ Rᵀ PRICE | *Died* | JANʸ 10ᵗʰ 1840 | *Aged 22 Years.*

572. White marble headstone :—

To the Memory of | JOSEPHINE | BORN 1ˢᵀ NOVEMBER 1854 | DIED 18ᵀʰ APRIL 1913 | (1 line.)

573. In Loving Memory of | IDA | DAUGHTER OF S. W. KING | DIED 8ᵀʰ DEC. 1910 | AGED 21 YEARS | (1 line.)

574. G. DUNCAN GITTENS | "PRIEST" | DIED SEP. 3ʀᴰ 1893 | AGED 79 YEARS | RECTOR OF Sᵀ LUCYS | FOR 35 YEARS | MARY J. GITTENS | WIFE OF THE ABOVE | DIED FEB. 19ᵀʰ 1898 | AGED 79 YEARS.

As 2 s. of John of B., cler., matric. from Trin. Coll., Oxf., 30 Oct. 1834, a. 30.

575. Headstone over curbed grave :—

HENRIETTA SMITH | BORN JANʀʸ 15ᵀʰ 1812 | DIED OCTʀ 15ᵀʰ 1895.

576. FAMILY BURIAL PLACE | OF | JULIUS BRANKER.

577. White marble cross :—

In | loving Memory | of | ROBERT CHALLENOR, ESQUIRE | WHO DEPARTED THIS LIFE | ON THE 16ᵀʰ DAY OF JULY 1907 | AGED 65 YEARS.

578. H. 17ᵀʰ Novʀ 1870.

579. Headstone :—

In | Memory of | Joseph Jones Redman | who died june 28TH 1875 | aged 35 years.

580. B. INNISS.

581. Large mausoleum :—

H. G. PEIRCE.

582. White marble cross :—

In Loving Memory | JOHN SIMPSON HOWELL | died august 13TH 1899.

583. Red granite cross :—

In Loving Memory | of | JOHN MILNE | who died 24TH march 1883.

And on a grey granite headstone :—

In | Loving Memory | of | ALICE | beloved wife of | FRED DURANT | died 28TH of november 1897.

584. burial place | of | E. F. HUNTE.

585. sacred to the memory of | SARAH MASSIAH FIELD | the beloved wife of JAMES E. FIELD | who departed this life april 15TH 1887 | aged 42 years | also JAMES O. FIELD son of the above | who departed this life july 15TH 1890 | aged 16 years and 7 months | also to our dear father | JAMES E. FIELD | who departed this life sept. 7TH 1903 | aged 64 years | and our darling ADA H. FRENCH | this memorial tablet is erected | by JAMES E. FIELD ESQR | (3 lines; to his wife and son.)

586. White marble cross, tiled space. On west side :—

In Memoriam | JULIA, | the beloved wife of | the Revᴰ THOMAS CLARKE, | rector of sᵀ michaels, | born 25 april 1816, died 20 sep. 1870. | THOMAS CLARKE m.a. cantab : | rector of sᵀ michaels cathedral 1842—1898 | appointed first dean of barbados 1886 | born 25 nov. 1810, died 11 jan. 1900.

On north side :—

WAPLE, | eldest sister of the revᴰ thoˢ clarke | born 11 oct. 1805, died 3 sep. 1889.

On south side :—

ANNIE MILLICENT CLARKE | born 17 aug. 1876, died 2 oct. 1876 | PERCY WILMOTT CLARKE | born 19 dec. 1873, died 6 mar. 1877. | Wᴹ COLERIDGE CLARKE | son of dean clarke | born 27TH april 1841, died 17TH july 1907.

587. White marble cross :—

REV. ERNEST A. CUTTING, B.A. | Born 14th Oct. 1857 | Died 12th Feb. 1883 | (1 line.)

At foot of grave :—

In Loving Memory of | EMMELINE P. CUTTING | DIED 28TH FEBY 1895 | AGED 33 YEARS | (1 line.)

---

588. White marble, broken column :—

In | Loving Memory of | NORMAN J. D. CUMMINS | WHO DIED APRIL 3RD 1887 | AGED 25 YEARS | (2 lines.)

---

589. White marble cross :—

IN LOVING MEMORY OF A WEDDED LIFE | AND OF MARY WORRELL (*MAMIE*) AND HER INFANT, | THE WIFE AND SON OF W. VERSEPUY FITZTHOMAS, SOLICITOR AND J.P. | WHO ON THE MORNING OF THE 4TH AUGUST 1884, ENTERED INTO THEIR REST | (1 line) | In Memoriam | MY DEAR BROTHER W. VERSE-PUY FITZTHOMAS (*WILLIE*) SOLICITOR AND J.P. | BORN 5TH OCTOBER 1840, DIED 12TH FEBRUARY 1891 | (2 lines.)

---

590. Red granite slab :—

IN MEMORY OF | JULIA AMANDA | BELOVED WIFE OF | ALEXR A. COLE | DIED 29TH MAY 1909 | AGED 56 YEARS.

591. Near road wall :—

FAMILY BURIEL PLACE | OF | REGD E. BARROW.

---

592. IN | LOVING MEMORY OF | BESSIE | Wife of | JAMES D. LAMONT, | BORN 14TH JUNE 1850 | Died 15th Sept. 1889.

---

593. IN LOVING MEMORY OF | MY DEAR MOTHER | JUDITH SOMMER-VILLE. | DIED 15TH MARCH 1888 | AGED 61 YEARS ! (1 line.)

594. Headstone and cross :—

SACRED | TO THE MEMORY OF | JOHN A. BLACKMAN | *Obit Januy 20th 1882* | *Aged 52 Years* | (4 lines.)

---

595. Headstone :—

JAS CULPEPPER DRAYTON | DIED | 28 JUNE 1905 | AGED 74. | ELIZ: MELICENT BROWNE | DIED | 31 JULY 1911 | AGED 85.

596. Cross :—

E. C. T. | ELVIE | 1889.

At foot :—

RESTING IN HOPE | BENEATH | THIS TREE | MARY E. SKINNER | 1877 | AND | ELVIRA COX THORNE | ("ELVIE") | SEP. 1889 | TABLET & CROSS | PLACED BY THEIR | NIECE & SISTER | ELIZA S. THORNE.

597. In wall :—

WILHELMINA BASCOM | Died | 25 AUG. 1892 | AGED 75.

598. F. F. JONES | DIED 10 JUNE | 1874.

599. In wall :—

S. WALTER BABER | DIED | 7TH SEPT 1901 | AGED 56.

J. W. ATKINS | DIED | 25 JANUARY 1873 | AGED 37.

R. HAMPDEN PILE | DIED | 15TH JUNE 1911 | AGED 83.

(Above 3 over one grave.)

600. White marble headstone :—

In Sacred Memory of | NICHOLAS EVANS | DIED 12TH JUNE 1875 | FRANCIS HENRY WALROND | DIED 24TH OCTR 1880 | FRANCIS HENRY EVANS | DIED 1ST AUG. 1897 | SUSANNAH EVANS | DIED 10TH JANY 1901 | JOANNA WALROND EVANS | DIED 23RD OCT. 1901 | AGED 53 YEARS.

601. Wall :—

THE FAMILY | BURIAL PLACE | OF | R. J. WORM | 1890.

602. Wall :—

THE FAMILY | BURIAL PLACE | OF | I. W. CRONEY.

603. On two headstones :—

EDWARD WAITE DIED NOV. 1869 AGED 73 YRS.

SARAH WAITE DIED MAY 1873 AGED 70 YRS.

604. Headstone :—

SACRED | TO THE MEMORY OF | T. W. BELLAMY | WHO DEPARTED THIS LIFE | THE 10 OF SEPTEMBER 1855 | AGED 48 YEARS.

605. Cross :—

M. H. C. 1870.   S. R. M. 1854.

606. Ledger much flaked :—

To the Memory of | A beloved son | F. JACKMAN BOWEN | who departed this life | July 1. 1865 | Aged 19 Years | (4 lines) | sarah griffith | aged 81 | died 14 jan. 1891 | (1 line.)

607. 𝕾𝕬𝕮𝕽𝕰𝕯 | to the Memory of | ROBERT ELDER KERR | Assistant Surgeon | H.M.S. Atalanta | died Feby 4th | 1859 | Aged 26 Years | (2 lines) | *The Deceased was born at* | *Campbeltown Argyleshire.*

608. Loose headstone :—

Here lieth ye body | of Joseph Bvsbey Ivnio^r | who departed this | life ye 25th of Iuly 1700 | Aged 19 years and 11 | moneths.

Burial not found in 1700 or 1706.

Archer records the following 13 stones which have probably disappeared :—

609. Richard b . . . . died 1685.

610. Capt. christopher bradbury, died 14 Aug. 1685.

611. Dora Boelle, died Aug. 6, 1723.

612. Joseph Boulstrod, son of edward boulstrod, and mildred his wife Born 18 Feb. 1644, in the parish of Little St Bartholomew, London, died 1675.

613. henry carter, died 1753.

614. john frewen, died 1669 aged 44.

615. jonathan fuller died 1682.   (Fragment.)

616. garrett . . . . died Oct. 1729 aged 60.

617. Col. john hassitt. (Fragment.)   This is most likely Hallett.

618. Capt. John moody, died 1673.

619. edward pearce, died Dec. 19, 1725.

620. elizabeth dau. of . . . . smith, wife of . . . . d. 1680, aged 15 (*sic*).

621. john . . . . died 1715 aged 63.

PARISH REGISTER OF ST. MICHAEL.

BURIALS.*

1649-50	Feb. 17	Capt Edw. Ellis frō on board ship
1650	July 23	Mrs Byam in y^e church
,,	Oct. 3	Mr Morris the minister of St George
16$\frac{50}{51}$	Feb. 14	Lady Hincks in church
1651	April 19	Docto^r Ric^d Vines. Ch.

[Gap from 22 June 1655 to 25 Aug. 1656, from 28 June 1658 to Dec. 1660, and from 22 April 1663 to 15 Aug. 1664.]

166$\frac{4}{5}$	Mar. 23	Mr Geo. Brehoult of Lynn
1665	June 30	Capt Samuel Vinor in the C.
,,	Dec. 21	Jno Wadlow Esqr. Ch.
166$\frac{5}{6}$	Jan. 1	Eliz^a the wife of Ric^d Nubold Esq: dyed the 26th Decr 1665 and the next day buryed in Plantasion
1667	April 12	Mrs Jude the wife of Mr Nich^o Blake in Ch :
,,	Nov. 21	Eliza the daughter of Roger Lovell Esq.
1669	Dec. 1	Lieut. Genl Hen. Willoughby in the Church
1671	May 10	Mrs Bridgett the wife of Mr Nich^o Prideaux in Ch :
,,	June 26	Mr Edwd Pelham merch^t
1673	April 29	Coll^o Jno Redman†
1674	April 28	Mr Cornelius De Witt
,,	July 15	Monsr Henry Ant^o de la roche
1679	July 23	Sr Thomas Warner k.
,,	Aug. 8	Coll: Geo: Thornborough in Ch :
1680	Oct. 30	Mr Maurice Trant
,,	Dec. 27	Mr Gabriel Newman & Mrs Sarah Crisp
1681	June 21	Coll. Wm Beale in Ch :
1682	May 6	Hellenor Lynch fro^m Antigua
1690	Dec. 26	Mr Nathan^l Iiddon Attor: Genl in y^e Church
1691	May 25	Mr Roger Lovell
,,	Oct. 4	Mr John Netherway
1694	Oct. 12	Coll: John Berringer in Church
,,	Nov. 7	The Honble John Whetstone Dep^y Secretary of y^s Island
1700	Dec. 4	Coll^o Jno Johnson
1701	Aug. 9	Wm Beresford Esq. in Church
1702	May 2	Richard Bowles Esq.
170$\frac{2}{3}$	Mar. 6	Richd Forstall Esqre in Church
1703	June 27	Elizabth y^e wife of Wm Heysham Esqr in Church
170$\frac{3}{4}$	Mar. 10	The Honble Coll^o Wm Wheeler
17$\frac{11}{12}$	Mar. 22	James Cowse Esqr in y^e Chancell
1713	Aug. 11	Mad^m Judith Johnson widow of Coll^o John Johnson dec̃d
17$\frac{14}{15}$	Jan. 13	Mr Wm Pike of Antigua
1715	Aug. 9	Isaac Lenoir Esqr Sec^y of y^s Island
1723	Aug. 1	Honble Robert Vaughan Esqr in the Chancel
172$\frac{3}{4}$	Mar. 12	Susannah wife of Mr Rowland Tryon
172$\frac{6}{7}$	Feb. 27	Mr Richard Trant
1727	May 16	The hon^{ble} John Lenoir Esqre
1729	April 8	Coll^o John Whetstone
17$\frac{29}{30}$	Feb. 4	Coll^o Benjamin Bullard in the Church a Sermon
1730	Aug. 24	Coll^o Robert Harper Esqre

* These were jotted down at random, and they mostly do not relate to the principa landed families.

† See notes of this family in the New England Register, p. 367, by G. A. Moriarty, October 1913.

| 1731 | Sep. | 23 | Joseph Sherwood Esqr a Councillor at Law |

1731 Sep. 23 Joseph Sherwood Esqr a Councillor at Law
173$\frac{4}{1}$ Feb. 22 The Revd Mr Alex^r Le Hunt Rector of St Lucys in the New Chancel
1740 Oct. 7 His Excellency the honble Robert Byng Esq. in the new Chancel
1741 July 25 Coll^o Richard Forstall Esqr in the Church
1743 Oct. 26 Humphry Breadie a poor Scotchman aged 103 years
174$\frac{4}{1}$ Feb. 28 (A burial in the " old chancel ")
1747 Sep. 19 The honb^{le} Edward Legg Commodore Commander of his Majesty's ship the Captain in the Chancel
1752 Nov. 1 Robt Joycelin Esqr
1753 July 26 George Gascoigne Esqr
1759 Aug. 15 Cap^n William Ellery of Boston
 ,, Nov. 8 Thomas Tunckes Esqr in ye Church
1762 Jan. 12 Eliza Papon wife to Capt Papon went down to Martinico on ye Expedition
1764 Nov. 8 John Cargil Esqr Judge of Dominico
1766 Jan. 4 Thos Bedford Esqr
 ,, July 18 Anthony Lynch Esqr
1767 Sep. 17 John Carter Esqr
 ,, Sep. 22 The Hon^e Hamlet Fairchild
1769 May 17 The Honble Samuel Bedford Esqr

The marriages from their commencement in 1648 down to about 1668 were printed in the Diocesan Magazine, but they were so incorrectly transcribed that they are of little value.

On p. 379 of the 1st volume of St. Michael's Parish Register is a list of the plate of 25 Oct. 1688. One large chalice and cover and pair of flagons were the gift of Edwyn Stede, Lieut.-Gov., and a bason of Mr. John Milles.

Peregrine Tho. Hopson, b. 5 June 1696 ; Col. of 29 Reg. and 40 Reg., Maj.-Gen., Gov. of Nova Scotia 1752-5 ; d. in command of the troops at Guadaloupe 27 Feb. 1759, and was buried in the chancel of St. Michael's, Barbados, Monday, 19 March 1759. Will proved P.C.C. (" Notes and Queries," 11 Ser., viii., 443.)

Richard Harris, d. 11 Feb. 1735-6, aged 62. He was a good portrait painter from Southstoke near Bath, had resided in B. 30 years, and was buried at the S.E. end of St Michaels churchyard. (See the original " Caribbeana," vol. ii., pp. 124, 127, 128.)

1736, Aug. 4, Wed. Last Sat. was buried Mr Nich. Hope, attorney at law, a distant relative of Sir Jos. Jekyl, Master of the Rolls, leaving 2 young sons. (*Ibid.*, 166.)

The earliest church in Bridgetown formerly stood in the " old churchyard," where St. Mary's was erected in 1825. This is shewn on the accompanying plan, which is a reduced copy of the one drawn by Mayo in 1712—21 and engraved by Senex in 1722.

A great fire in 1666, which destroyed the town, may have included the church. Most of the houses were of wood (Lygon, p. 40), but by an Act of 1667 stone and brick were to be used.

The present cathedral, dedicated to St. Michael, is stated to have been built in 1665 on a new site half a mile away to the east of the town.

It was destroyed by the Hurricane of 1780, when, of eleven churches and three chapels, only those of St. Peter, St. Andrew, and All Saints were left standing. The church was rebuilt on the same site, and reopened in 1786. The great Hurricane of 1831 broke the roof and flooded the vaults, cracking many of the floor slabs, but the main structure did not suffer.

ST. LEONARD'S CHAPEL IN BRIDGETOWN.

622. Above the pulpit, on a brass :—

IN MEMORIAM | PERCY LAWRANCE GREAVES | AGED 10 YEARS | ELDEST SON OF THE REV^D | JOHN LAWRANCE | AND | EVELINA GREAVES | SUDDENLY CALLED AWAY | OCTOBER 4TH 1876 | (4 lines.)

---

623. On wall above pulpit north side of chancel arch. CREST.—? A hind's head erased :—

IN MEMORY OF | ANGUS FRASER | WHO DIED FROM AN ACCIDENT, 9TH OCT^R 1857, | AGED 3 YEARS AND 6 MONTHS | *HE WAS THE THIRD SON OF ROSE DEMPSTER FRASER, | AND HIS REMAINS WERE INTERRED | IN THE BURIAL PLACE OF THIS CHAPEL.*

---

624. North wall of chancel. Brass :—

(2 lines) | **Honourable William Parker Leacock, | Born in this Island January 21st 1838, | Died at his late residence "Maplewood" July 22nd 1912 | He was the eldest son of the | late Joseph Leacock by a second marriage** | (2 lines ; erected by widow.)

See No. 290 for note of his father's vault.

---

625. East window :—

IN LOVING MEMORY OF MY HUSBAND DUDLEY PAGE COTTON | WHO DIED JULY 30TH 1880 | R. J. C. 1884.

---

626. Marble tablet and brass on south wall of chancel :—

CREST.—*A lion rampant.* ARMS.—*A fess Gules between three lions rampant.* MOTTO.— PRINCIPIIS OBSTA. Bust of deceased in a square above the shield.

TO THE GLORY OF GOD | AND IN MEMORY OF | HENRY ALBERT THORNE | MAJOR OF THE WEST AFRICAN REGIMENT | AND FORMERLY OF 2ND WEST INDIA REGIMENT | SECOND SON OF HENRY EDWARD THORNE | AND EMMA LOUISE JANE HIS WIFE | (6 lines of service) | BORN 18 DECEMBER 1866 | DIED AT SIERRA LEONE 20 JULY 1903.

He is stated to have transcribed the M.I. of St. Michael's, but the MS. was not shewn me, though I offered to edit it for his family.

---

627. South wall of chancel :—

To the Glory of God and in memory of | Elliot Grasett Louis | son of Thomas Louis Esqr^e of this Island | and Grandson of Admiral Sir Thomas Louis Bart. | He was a constant worshipper in this Church from 1872 | a Member of the Committee and a Lay Reader | He went to England in 1893 where he died in Bristol on June 9th 1911 | Erected by his most sincere friend | J. Bonham Smith Esqr^e I.S.O. | Provost Marshal | (1 line.)

N

628. South side of chancel arch :—

In Memoriam | THE REV^D HAMBLE JAMES LEACOCK, | BORN IN
THE PARISH OF S^T LUCYS BARBADOS, | 4TH FEBRUARY 1794, | DIED AT FREETOWN
SIERRA LEONE | 20TH AUGUST 1856, | AGED 61 YEARS AND 6 MONTHS | (18 lines ;
first Minister of this chapel, then Missionary to West Africa.)

629. South wall of nave.   Brass :—

Sacred to | the Memory of | Bruce Inniss Austin | Son of |
Helen J. and James D. Austin | Born 21st May 1884 | Died
30th July 1885 | (3 lines ; erected by brothers and sisters.)

630. South wall of nave :—

IN MEMORY OF | JOHN HEYES | who died at Bath England | on the
21st December 1867 | aged 44 years.

631. North wall of nave.   Brass :—

TO THE GLORY OF GOD | AND IN MEMORY OF | THE REV. E. G.
SINCKLER | INCUMBENT OF S^T LEONARD'S | 1855—1881 | THE NORTH AISLE
OF THIS CHURCH | WAS ERECTED AND CONSECRATED | IN THE YEAR OF OUR
LORD 1883.

1854, Sept. 5.   At St. Pancras, Jas. W. Sinckler, M.D. of B. to Maria-Jane,
only dau. of the late Capt. Theophilus Patterson R.M.   (" G.M.," 618.)

632. North wall of nave.   Brass :—

IN | MEMORY | OF | THOMAS BOWEN M.D. | BORN 4TH MARCH 1837 |
DIED 27TH FEBRUARY 1906 | (10 lines.)

633. Brass below :—

IN LOVING MEMORY OF | FRANCIS GODING BOWEN, B.A., M.B., B.C.,
CANTAB : | M.R.C.S., L.R.C.P. LONDON | SECOND SON OF | THOMAS BOWEN,
M.D., | WHO DIED AT FORT JAMESON, NORTH EASTERN RHODESIA | ON 17TH
FEBRUARY 1905 | AGED 31 | (1 line.)

634. IN SACRED AND LOVING REMEMBRANCE OF | CHARLES EDWARD
YEARWOOD | SON OF W^M RICH^D AND JOHN* (NÉE DAVIDSON) YEARWOOD |
AND GRANDSON OF JOHN AND SUSANNAH (NÉE LYNCH) DAVIDSON | HE WAS BORN
27TH JUNE 1844, AND DIED 28TH DEC^R 1879 | ALSO IN MEMORY OF | MURIEL
OLIVE ROSE YEARWOOD | BORN 6TH SEPT^R 1871, DIED 27TH DEC^R 1872. |
AND MARY OLIVE YEARWOOD | BORN 16TH MARCH 1873, DIED 25TH NOV^R
1887. | AND JOHN DAVIDSON DALRYMPLE YEARWOOD | BORN
29TH MARCH 1874, DIED 26TH MAY 1876. | CHILDREN OF THE ABOVE | (2 lines.)

* There must be an error here.

635. IN SACRED AND LOVING REMEMBRANCE OF | JAMES MANNING, M.D. | SON OF JOHN AND ELIZABETH ANNE | (NÉE THURBARNE) MANNING | AND GRANDSON OF WILLIAM MANNING | HE WAS BORN AUGUST 1814, & DIED 24ᵀᴴ JUNE 1883 | (2 lines) | ALSO IN MEMORY OF | CHARLES MANNING | SON OF THE ABOVE | WHO WAS BORN & DIED SEPTᴿ 1845.

1825, Aug. At Kendal, T. J. Manning, esq. of B. to Anne-Cath-Rose, dau. of Fred. Nassau, esq. of St. Osyth Priory, Essex. (" G.M.," 270.)

Chas. Jas., o. s. of Jas. M. of St. Geo., Barbados, M.D. Queen's Coll. Oxf., matric. 20 Ap. 1866, a. 19. (Foster.)

The late Mrs. Graham Yearwood, who d. 2 Jan. 1915, aged 65, was a dau. of the above.

---

636. North wall of nave. Brass :—

In sacred and loving remembrance of | MARION CRAWFORD LOUIS | She died in England on the 21st February 1875 | in the 28th year of her age | (4 lines; erected by her husband Elliot Grasett Louis.)

---

637. Font :—

In memory of Emma Sophia Colebrooke deceased Easter Eve MDCCCLI.

The burial ground around the Church is very extensive. I have only copied a few inscriptions. I noticed stones to Berkeley, Blackwood, Bowen, Groney, Hinkson 1864, Laurie, Nurse 1862, Thorne 1865.

638. On a cross :—

In loving remembrance | of | JULIA SOPHIA | WIFE OF | WILLIAM ROBINSON | GOVERNOR IN CHIEF OF THE | WINDWARD ISLANDS | WHO DIED AT GOVERNMENT HOUSE | ON THE 10ᵀᴴ | AUGUST 1881 | AGED 42 | (3 lines.)

She was dau. of the Rev. R. Dampier of Rownhams, Southampton, and was m. in 1863 as his 1st wife. He was Gov. of Barbados 1885, Trinidad 1886—91, Hong Kong 1891—98, G.C.M.G. 1897, and d. early in 1914. His dau. is the wife of Mr. Aucher Warner, Solicitor General of Trinidad.

---

639. Cast iron obelisk with cherubs, etc. On the west face :—

Sacred | to the memory of | Benjamin Alleyne | died 21 December 1865 | aged 52 years | Also of | Georgeana | his beloved wife | died 29 July 1885 | aged 69 years.

---

640. Another tall obelisk. On the west face :—

In loving remembrance | of | JOHN ALLEYNE ESQ | Died in London 24ᵗʰ Novʳ 1875 | and was interred | in Kensal Green Cemetery | EDITH MAY | daughter of | JAMES AND FLORENCE HINKSON | died 14th November 1875.

On the east face :—

In Memory of | Sarah | Martindale Dean | (Sister of the late | Georgeana Alleyne) | died 12 Aug. 1893 | Aged 70 Yrs.

On the south face :—

ERECTED | TO THE REVERED MEMORY | OF | JOHN ALLEYNE | BORN 6 APRIL 1819 | DIED 28 JUNE 1869 | BY HIS WIDOW AND CHILDREN.

---

641. Obelisk within iron railing :—

EMILY WORRELL GRAHAM | ELDEST DAUGHTER OF THE LATE | COMMISSARY GENERAL | CHARLES GRAHAM | AND ANNE HIS WIFE | DIED OF FEVER IN THIS ISLAND | OCTOBER 11TH 1855, | AGED 21 YEARS | (3 lines ; by surviving brother and sister.)

This is the oldest stone in the burial-ground.

---

642. White marble headstone enclosed by iron railing :—

SACRED | To the Memory of | LIEUT J. T. COOKE. | 49TH REGIMENT | WHO DIED IN BARBADOS on the 10 of July 1859 | Aged 27 Years | (4 lines.)

---

643. Ledger enclosed by iron railing :—

IN MEMORY | of | THOMAS WILLIAMS ESQ. | Assistant Commissary General | to | Her Majesty's Forces | who died at Barbados on the | 7th day of October 1862 | Aged 40 Years | (4 lines.)

---

644. Sacred | TO THE MEMORY OF | SAMUEL BROCK ALDER | DEP. ASSIST COM. GENL | WHO DIED AT BARBADOS ON THE | 11TH JULY 1859, AGED 29 YEARS & 3 DAYS | (5 lines.)

ST. PAUL'S CHAPEL, BRIDGETOWN.

This is close to the old Barracks on the Savannah, and was much used by the officers. It was built in 1830—32.

645. On west wall of nave, south side :—

TO THE MEMORY OF | LIEUTENANT COLONEL | ORMSBY PHIBBS, | 88TH REGIMENT, | WHO DIED OF YELLOW FEVER | AT BARBADOES, | ON THE 17TH OF JANUARY 1848, | IN THE 42ND YEAR OF HIS AGE | (9 lines.)
See his vault No. 731.

---

646. On west wall of nave, north side :—

To | DEPUTY COMMISSARY GENERAL | JOHN BANNER PRICE, | WHO DIED OF YELLOW FEVER, | ON HIS PASSAGE | FROM Sᵀ KITTS TO BARBADOES, | ON THE 26ᵀᴴ DAY OF NOVEMBER, | ANNO DOMINI 1849, | AGED 54 YEARS | (11 lines.)

647. North wall of nave :—

SACRED TO THE MEMORY OF | MAJOR ROBERT NOBLE CROSSE. K.H. | 36ᵀᴴ REGIMENT, WHO DIED OF YELLOW FEVER | IN THE 50ᵀᴴ YEAR OF HIS AGE, ON THE | 13ᵀᴴ NOVEMBER 1838, ON BOARD H. M. SHIP HERCULES : | IN CARLISLE BAY BARBADOES : HAVING EMBARKED | WITH THE REGIMENT FOR NORTH AMERICA ON THE 10ᵀᴴ | (4 lines) | HE SERVED IN THE | 36ᵀᴴ REGIMENT FOR AN | UNINTERRUPTED PERIOD OF 33 YEARS, AND | WAS PRESENT WITH IT IN THE FOLLOWING | ACTIONS VIZ. BUENOS AYRES, ROLEIA, VIMIERA | CORUNNA, ALMEIDA, FLUSHING, FUENTES, D'ONOR | BOTH STORMINGS OF THE FORT OF SALAMANCA | THE ACTION OF SALAMANCA (WHERE HE WAS WOUNDED) | AND THE OPERATIONS BEFORE BURGOS.

1838, Nov. 13. At B., Major Robert Noble Crosse K.H. 36th reg. ("G.M.," 1839, 333.)

648. North wall of nave :—

SACRED | TO THE MEMORY OF | BRYAN PALMES, OF NABURN, | IN THE COUNTY OF YORK, | CAPTAIN IN THE 52ᴅ LIGHT INFANTRY, | WHO DIED HERE | ON THE 16ᵀᴴ DECᴿ 1839, | THE 28ᵀᴴ ANNIVERSARY | OF HIS BIRTH. | (5 lines.)

649. North wall of nave :—

SACRED TO THE MEMORY OF

CAPᵀˢ	LIEUᵀ
HONᴮᴸᴱ LE P. TRENCH	R. DE WINTON
B. PALMES,	ENSIGˢ
LIEUᵀ	E. GOUGH
V. A. SURTEES	J. ARCHDALL

PAYᴹˢᴿ J. WINTERBOTTOM & PENELOPE HIS WIFE | ALL OF WHOM FELL VICTIMS TO YELLOW FEVER | DURING THE TERM OF THE 52ᴺᴰ LIGHT INFANTRY'S | SERVICE IN THE WEST INDIES | BETWEEN NOVEMBER 1838, AND MARCH 1842 | (4 lines.)

650. North wall of nave :—

IN MEMORY OF | JOHN KING MACBREEDY | ASSISTANT COMMISSARY GENERAL | HE DIED 12ᵀᴴ MAY 1843 AGED 54 YEARS | (6 lines; com. of 41 years.)

651. On east wall of nave, north side, are 4 tablets :—

SACRED | TO THE MEMORY OF | JULIA WALLEY | INFANT DAUGHTER OF | GEORGE & K: A: T. WALLEY | A.D. 1840.

652. SACRED TO THE MEMORY OF | BREVET MAJOR WILLIAM KILLI-KELLY, | LATE OF THE 36TH REGIMENT: | WHO DIED AT SEA ON HIS PASSAGE HOME | FROM BARBADOES, ON THE 30TH MAY 1839, | IN THE 50TH YEAR OF HIS AGE | (8 lines; present at both captures of Guadaloupe.)

653. In loving memory of | KATHLEEN V. GARDINER | who died in Boston after a | short illness on June 5, 1893, | aged 24 years | (2 lines.)

654. On east wall of nave, north side, regimental badge:—

Sacred to the Memory | of | Cᴿ SERJᵀ E. PARSONS | and | SERJᵀ W. KENT, | of the 1st Battn 21st Fusiliers | who died at Barbados, | The former of Colonial Fever | on the 8th September 1860 | The latter of Yellow Fever | on the 15th September 1862 | (2 lines.)

655. North wall of chancel:—

(5 lines) | WILLIAM JOHN KING. M.D. | who fell asleep in Jesus, | on the 4th of April 1851 | aged 55 years | (9 lines.)

OUR CHARLIE | In Memory of | CHARLES LEWIS YOUNG, | only child of | CHARLES EDWIN YOUNG CROUCH | and MARY EDITH his wife. | Born Novbr 2nd 1866. | Died June 12th 1879 | (6 lines.)

656. IN MEMORY OF | HOWARD PLESTOW COX, | ENSIGN 21ST FUSILIERS; | SECOND SON OF G. H. RICHARDSON COX, ESQRE | OF SPONDON DERBYSHIRE; | WHO DIED AT BARBADOS, ON THE 31ST MAY, 1860, | IN THE 21ST YEAR OF HIS AGE | (3 lines.)

657. A brass:—

Our Violet | In Memoriam | Cordelia Violet Corbin | Died in Philadelphia Dec. 5, 1900 | Aged 17 years | (1 line.)

658. South wall of chancel:—

TO THE MEMORY OF | ANNIE, | THE FONDLY LOVED WIFE OF WILLIAM MURRAY JUNʳ | WHO | ON THE 5TH OF APRIL 1855 | (died) | (6 lines.)

659. WILLIAM RUTHERFORD HAYES, ESQ. | late Consul in Barbados, from the | UNITED STATES OF AMERICA, | who died at Hastings Village | the 13th of July 1852, | Aged 47 Years | (17 lines; worshipped here 17 years.)

660. East wall of nave, south side :—

𝕾𝕬𝕮𝕽𝕰𝕯 | to the memory of | JESSIE MARIA BONE MᶜNICOL | BORN | 24ᵀᴴ MAY 1819 | DIED | 26 NOV. 1892 | (Erected by children.)

———

661. South wall of nave. There are 6 tablets on this wall :—

𝕾𝕬𝕮𝕽𝕰𝕯 | TO THE MEMORY | of | LIEUᵀ J. A. NORIE, | ROYAL ARTILLERY | WHO DIED OF YELLOW FEVER | ON THE 13ᵀᴴ MARCH 1848, | AGED 22 YEARS | (2 lines.)

———

662. CREST.—A cross crosslet fitchy. MOTTO.—SPERO MELIORA.

SACRED | TO THE MEMORY OF | LIEUT. EUSTACE J. D. MOFFAT, | 46ᵀᴴ REGIMENT | LATE | DEPUTY ASSISTANT QUARTER MASTER GENERAL, | WHO DEPARTED THIS LIFE AT SEA | OFF Sᵀ LUCIA APRIL 2ᴺᴰ 1844, | IN THE 29ᵀᴴ YEAR OF HIS AGE | (8 lines.)

———

663. Royal Crown over F., and below on scroll :—

72ᴺᴰ DUKE OF ALBANY'S OWN HIGHLANDERS.

TO THE MEMORY OF | CAPTAINS | CHARLES MOYLAN, | DIED ON THE 25ᵀᴴ JANUARY 1849, AGED 39 YEARS; | JOHN THOMAS HOPE, | DIED ON THE 22ᴺᴰ NOVEMBER 1848, AGED 32 YEARS; | HENRY RICE, | DIED ON THE 28ᵀᴴ NOVEMBER 1848, AGED 27 YEARS; | QUARTER-MASTER JOHN LINDSAY, | DIED ON THE 21ˢᵀ NOVEMBER 1848, AGED 47 YEARS; | ASSISTANT-SURGEON MONTGOMERY IRWIN, | DIED ON THE 13ᵀᴴ OCTOBER 1848, AGED 29 YEARS; | WHO FELL VICTIMS TO THE YELLOW FEVER, | AT BARBADOS | (6 lines.)

1848, Nov. 22. At B. aged 32, Capt. John Tho. Hope, of the 72d Reg. eldest s. of the late Gen. Sir John H. ("G.M.," 222.)

———

664. Royal Crown   THE BERKSHIRE   LXVI.

SACRED TO THE MEMORY OF | CAPTAIN FRANCIS WILLIAM ASTLEY, | WHO DIED 13ᵀᴴ NOVEMBER 1848, AGED 23 YEARS 10 MONTHS | CAPTAIN HENRY JOHN TURNER, | WHO DIED 28ᵀᴴ JANUARY 1849, AGED 36 YEARS | LIEUT. HARDRESS ROBERT HOLMES, | WHO DIED 11ᵀᴴ SEPTEMBER 1848, AGED 25 YEARS | LIEUT. WILLIAM ROBERT PYNE, | WHO DIED 25ᵀᴴ OCTOBER 1848, AGED 21 YEARS 4 MONTHS | QUARTERMASTER MATHEW REILLY, | WHO DIED 17ᵀᴴ DECEMBER 1848, AGED 43 YEARS | PAYMASTER KENNETH TOLMIE ROSS, | WHO DIED 24ᵀᴴ NOVEMBER 1848, AGED 55 YEARS 6 MONTHS | LIEUT. AND ADJᵀ JAMES HAMILTON ROSS, | SON OF THE ABOVE, | WHO DIED 25ᵀᴴ NOVEMBER 1848, AGED 26 YEARS | ELIZABETH, WHO DIED 24ᵀᴴ NOVEMBER 1848, | AND MARIA, WHO DIED 23ᴿᴰ NOVEMBER 1848, AGED 17 YEARS; | WIFE AND DAUGHTER OF THE ABOVE KENNETH TOLMIE ROSS. | AND OF THE NON-COMMISSIONED OFFICERS AND PRIVATES | OF THE 66ᵀᴴ REGᵀ | WHO DIED OF YELLOW FEVER IN THIS ISLAND, | DURING THE EPIDEMIC OF 1848-9. | ALSO TO THE MEMORY OF | CAPTAIN JAMES HUNTER BLAIRBIRCH, OF THE SAME REGᵀ | WHO DIED JANUARY 22ᴺᴰ 1851, AGED 30 YEARS | (2 lines.)

1848, Nov. 13. At B., in his 24th year, Fra. Wm. Astley, Capt. of the 66th Reg. &c. ("G.M.," 222.)

———

665. SACRED TO THE MEMORY OF | LIEUTENANT COLONEL HENRY WILLIAMS, | COMMANDING THE ROYAL ARTILLERY IN THE WEST INDIES, | WHO DIED OF YELLOW FEVER | ON THE 10ᵀᴴ NOVᴿ 1852, AGED 60 YEARS | AND OF | LIEUTENANT JAMES THOMAS ORME, | *ACTING ADJUTANT ROYAL ARTILLERY,* | WHO FELL AMONG THE EARLIEST VICTIMS TO THE SAME EPIDEMIC IN THIS ISLAND | ON THE 10ᵀᴴ SEPTEMBER PREVIOUS, AGED 27 YEARS | (4 lines.)

1852, Nov. 10. At B. a. 60, Lᵗ Col. Henry Williams, commanding the R.A. in the W. I. ("G.M.," 1853, 216.)

---

666. Above is a lion couchant, its paw grasping a French "Eagle."

SACRED | TO THE MEMORY OF | LIEUᵀ COL: JOHN TYLER, K.H. | DEPUTY QUARTER MASTER GENERAL | IN THE WINDWARD AND LEEWARD COMMAND, | WHO DIED AT BARBADOS, JUNE 2ᴺᴰ 1842. | AGED 51 YEARS | (4 lines; erected by Lt.-Gen. Maister, etc.)

On either side are the following actions on flags :—

SALAMANCA,	ROLEIA, VIMIERA,
TORRES-VEDRAS, BUSACO,	OPORTO, TALAVERA,
REDINHA, CASANOVA,	CIUDAD-RODRIGO,
FOZ D'ARONZ, SABUGAL, BADAJOS,	FUENTE-GUINALDO,
FUENTES D'ONOR, EL. BODON,	PYRENEES,
ALDEA DE PONTE, VITTORIA,	LABASTIDE, ORTHES,
VIC BIGORRE,	QUATRE-BRAS,
TOULOUSE,	WATERLOO.

Below is his Crest :—

A demi-lion rampant guardant erased, in its paws a crescent.

ST. PAUL'S CHURCHYARD.

667. South side. Cast iron upright enclosed by iron railing :—

IN MEMORY | OF | ELIZABETH | THE BELOVED WIFE OF | THE REVᴰ G. T. BOWIN, | SHE FELL ASLEEP IN JESUS | FEB. 26. 1871.

---

668. White marble slab, recently smashed :—

SACRED | To the Memory of | JEMIMA | the beloved Wife of | .... EVA .. JOH .. | and of | .. ENRY JAMES | his Brother | who departed this life | .... the former | On the 1 Sepᵗ 1844 Aged 11 Years : | and the latter | On the 7 Jan. 1836 Aged 15 Years.

---

669. Headstone :—

S. E. TULL | *DIED 21ˢᵀ MARCH 1897,* | *AGED 68 YEARS,*

---

670. Loose white marble tablet against mausoleum :—

SACRED | TO THE MEMORY | *of* | JOSEPH VERFENSTEIN ESQ^R | ASSISTANT COMMISSARY GENERAL | TO HER MAJESTY'S FORCES FOR UPWARDS | OF FORTY YEARS, NATIVE OF TRIESTE | IN GERMANY, AND FOR THE LAST | TWENTY-SIX YEARS A RESIDENT | IN THE WEST INDIES, | WHO DEPARTED THIS LIFE OF YELLOW | FEVER ON THE 2ND DAY OF AUGUST | 1846, AGED 63 | (12 lines ; erected by Caroline Verfenstein, his sister.)

---

671. Slab on brick vault :—

SACRED TO THE MEMORY | *of* | MARK WILSON | Reporter of Vessels to the | Government in this Island | and formerly | Sergeant Major in the Royal | Artillery | Died on the 8th of April | 1857 | Aged 54 Years.

---

672. White marble headstone :—

SACRED To the MEMORY of | *JOHN PIPER Late Clerk* | *To the Roy^t Eng^r Dep^t* | *And Esteemed Husband of Mary* | *Died August 15th 1876* | *Aged 55 Years.*

---

673. Adjoining No. 659. Oblong slab of white marble stuck on end :—

SACRED TO THE MEMORY OF | JANE ANN REED | WHO DEPARTED THIS LIFE OCT^R 6TH 1844 | AGED 58 YEARS.

---

674. Slab over brick vault :—

To The Memory of | *James Sarjeant,* | *Who Died Decr 9th 1876* | *Aged 50 Years.*

---

675. Loose white marble :—

Sacred to the Memory | *of* | CAROLINE SOPHIA | Daughter of | Captain Charles Highmore Potts | of the 19th Regiment, | Who died at Saint Anns | on the 6th of July 1836 | Aged 8 Months.

---

676. White marble tablet at west end of mausoleum :—

SACRED to the MEMORY | *of* | NATHAN SMITH | who | departed this life | April the 20th 1846 | Aged 63 Years | and 4 months | (4 lines ; erected by nephew JAMES N. ROSBOTHAM.)

---

677. Flaking slab as step to south door of chancel :—

SACRED | (about 3 lines missing) | Ag . . . . | Also of *THOMAS* . . *OKELY* | who died the . . October | Aged 7 . . ths & . . . . | Children | QM . . . . G. | and . . . . his Wife | (3 lines.)

There is here a wire fence across from south-east corner of chancel.

---

678. Headstone :—

ADELAIDE MONTGOMERY | AMY | BORN | 8TH OCTOBER 1832 | DIED | 1ST APRIL 1900.

679. In the more westerly division :—

SACRED TO THE MEMORY OF | MARY F. BISHOP | the beloved wife of | JAMES BISHOP | who died 20th November 1857 | *Aged* 38 Years | (10 lines.)

680. SACRED | TO THE MEMORY OF | EDWARD T . . . . | The beloved Husband of | SARAH PHILLIPS | *who departed this life* | *February 27TH 1865* | AGED 48 YEARS | (2 lines) | He was for many years Foreman of | Carpenters in the Royal Engineers | Department.

681. SACRED | TO THE MEMORY OF | JULIA WALLEY | INFANT DAUGHTER OF | GEORGE & KAT. WALLEY | A.D. 1840.

682. SACRED | to the Memory of | JOSEPH MARIA | SON OF JOSEPH AND | MARY S. MARTINEZ | Who departed this life the | 17th of March 1838 | Aged 5 Years.

683. SACRED | TO THE MEMORY OF | MR RICHARD DILKES | A NATIVE OF ENGLAND | WHO DEPARTED THIS LIFE | MARCH 22ND 1834 | AGED 39 YEARS.

684. Headstone enclosed by iron railing :—

Sacred | TO THE MEMORY | OF | LIEUT E. BATTERSBY R.N. | OF | H.M.S. SATELLITE | WHO DEPARTED THIS LIFE | ON THE 3RD DAY OF OCTOBER | 1839 | AGED 33 YEARS | (5 lines.)

685. White marble slab :—

SACRED | TO THE MEMORY OF | JAMES THOMAS WILSON | only Child of Lt Col WILSON | of the 65th Regt | who died at St Anns | the 17th February 1834 | Aged 17 Months.

686. Headstone :—

Sacred | TO THE MEMORY | OF | *JOHN MACLEAR* | ASSISTANT SURGEON | OF | HER MAJESTY'S SLOOP | *ROVER* | WHO DEPARTED THIS LIFE | OF YELLOW FEVER | ON THE 30TH OCTOBER | 1841 | AGED 27 YEARS.

687. White marble slab enclosed by iron railing :—

BENEATH | THIS STONE LIE THE REMAINS OF | SARAH FRANCES, | THE WIFE OF ISRAEL BOWEN ; | WHO DEPARTED THIS LIFE | ON THE 27TH DAY OF MAY 1837 | AGED 33 YEARS | (8 lines.)

688. IN MEMORY OF | JESSE SARJENT | (1 line) | who died | (1 line) |
JANUARY 21ST 1842 | AGED 35 YEARS | (several lines; erected by Mary
Grayfoot, etc.)

---

689. IN MEMORY | of | KYFFIN HEYLAND | *formerly a Lieut. in the
25ᵗʰ Regt,* | late a Stipendiary Magistrate in | BRITISH GUIANA | and |
Third Son of | MAJOR ARTHUR ROWLEY HEYLAND | *who fell in the* | Battle of
Waterloo. Born March 25ᵗʰ 1808, | *Died &c.* | 24ᵗʰ March 1843.

---

690. White marble headstone enclosed by iron railing :—

𝕾acred to the 𝕸emory | OF | MARY THOMAS | the beloved Wife of |
JOHN F. BROWNE, | Who departed this life Octʳ 26ᵗʰ 1863 | AGED
32 YEARS | (3 lines; erected by husband and father) | (4 lines more.)

---

691. White marble headstone, broken across :—

SACRED | to the memory of | CAPTAIN GEORGE BEERE | Late
14 Foot | who died at Barbados | Janʸ 14 1840 | AGED 47 YEARS.

---

692. White marble headstone enclosed by iron railing :—

𝕾acred to the 𝕸emory | OF | CHARLES EUSTACE | the beloved Son
of | CHARLES AND ELEANOR PRAGER | Who departed this life Novʳ
12ᵗʰ 1865 | Aged Two Years and Three Months | (2 lines) | ALSO | To the
Memory of | LILLY OCTAVIO PRAGER | *Sister of the above* | Who died
21ˢᵗ October 1865 | *AGED 13 MONTHS* | (2 lines.)

---

693. Headstone :—

SACRED | TO THE MEMORY OF | ROBERT DUDMAN | SECOND OFFICER OF
R.M.S. SHIP | GREAT WESTERN | ELDEST SON OF CAPTN Rᴿ DUDMAN |
OF HYTHE NEAR SOUTHAMPTON | WHO | DIED ON THE 18ᵀᴴ NOVᴿ 1852 | AGED
22 YEARS.

---

694. Iron cross :—

𝕴n 𝕸emoriam | 𝕰liza 𝕸ells 𝕷awrence | a 𝕾tranger from 𝕭erbice |
𝕺b. 26th 𝕸ay 1870 | æt. 9 𝕸onths | (1 line.)

---

695. In the north-western division :—

SACRED to the MEMORY | of | JOHN THOMAS RUTHERFORD | who
departed this life | December 15ᵗʰ 1846, | In the 49ᵗʰ Year of his Age | (3 lines;
erected by adopted father John Lawless.)

---

696. 𝕾acred to the 𝕸emory | of | Wᴹ HENRY ROSKRUGE | *late
Master in the Mail Boat Service* | who departed this life | on the 25 September
1838 | Aged 20 Years.

697. Cross-shaped altar-tomb :—

IN MEMORY OF SAMSON MOORE FOR MANY YEARS SEXTON OF S^T PAULS CHAPEL | (3 lines) | DIED MARCH 22ND 1864.

---

698. White marble tablet in north boundary wall :—

SACRED | to the memory of | Three Infant Children of | SAMUEL HENRY and | ELIZA ANN His wife | CHARLOTTE ANN | Aged 3 Months | SARAH JANE | Aged 7 Months | JAMES WILLIAM | Aged 21 Days.

---

699. Altar-tomb :—

Sacred to the Memory | of | CAP^{TN} HORACE E. B. HUTCHINSON | of H.M. 76th Regiment of foot, | second Son of | LIEU^T GENERAL | SIR WILLIAM HUTCHINSON | K.C.H. | who died of fever at St Anns Barracks | on the 4th of January 1837 | after an illnefs of four days | Aged 29 Years | (4 lines.)

---

700. White marble in north boundary wall :—

SACRED | to the memory of | THOMAS CROFTON | died November 10th | 1860 | Aged 39 Years | Also | William, Son of the above born | April 7th 1849 died | same day.

---

701. White marble against north boundary wall :—

SACRED | TO THE MEMORY OF | DUGALD C. F. M^CNICOL | *Who Departed This Life* | November 14th 1866 | Also To MARY E. M^CNICOL, | *Who fell Asleep in Jesus* | *March* 25th 1874 | (2 lines.)

---

702. Ledger :—

A. COX.

---

703. Gothic stone against wall :—

JESSIE MARIA M^CNICOL | died April 1st | 1852 | Aged 11 months & 10 days | CONSTANCE-LESSALINE MAPP | Born May 15th 1875 | Died October 2nd 1875. | THEODORE C. G. MAPP. | Born May 31st 1876 | Died April 23rd 1878.

Above is :—

In | Memory of | OUR BELOVED MOTHER | JESSIE MARIA BONE M^CNICOL | BORN 24 May 1819, DIED 26 NOV^R 1892.

EAST OF CHANCEL.

704. Headstone in grave with six urns :—

IN | MEMORY *of* S. E. BAYNE | WHO *Died* MAY 16TH 1888 | AGED 44 Y^{RS}.

705. White marble ledger :—

𝕾𝖆𝖈𝖗𝖊𝖉 | To the memory of | LIEUTENANT COLONEL | HENRY WILLIAMS | Commanding the | ROYAL ARTILLERY | In the west Indies | Died of Yellow Fever | November 10th 1852 | Aged 60.

706. Metal lettering in granite ledger :—

IN LOVING MEMORY | OF | HENRY RICE | CAPTAIN 72ND HIGHLANDERS | SECOND SON OF | EDWARD ROYDS RICE ESQRE | OF DANE COURT KENT | DIED 28TH NOVEMBER 1848 | AGED 27 YEARS.

707. IN MEMORY | of | . . . HN THOMAS . . . . | CAPTAIN 72nd HIGHLA . . . . | Died | 2nd November 184 . | Aged 32 Years | (flaked ; ? 1848 next to several of that year.)

There was an epidemic in Oct.—Nov. 1848.

708. Cross-shaped altar-tomb :—

SACRED TO THE BELOVED MEMORY OF | CHARLES RICHARD DORING-TON, | LIEUTENANT OF HER MAJESTY'S 69TH REGIMENT | YOUNGEST SON OF JOHN EDWARD AND SUSAN DORINGTON, | OF LYPIATT PARK, IN THE COUNTY OF GLOUCESTER, | WHO DIED THE 12TH OF AUGUST 1855, AGED 21 | (5 lines ; placed by parents.)

His eldest brother, the late Sir John Edward Dorington, was created a Baronet in 1886.

709. White marble :—

BENEATH THIS SPOT REST | THE REMAINS OF | HOWARD PLESTOW COX | ENSIGN 21ST FUSILIERS | WHO DEPARTED THIS LIFE | ON THE 31ST MAY 1860 | IN HIS 21ST YEAR | (1 line.)

710. White marble :—

𝕾𝖆𝖈𝖗𝖊𝖉 | To the memory of | LIEUTENANT | JOHN THOMAS ORME | of the | ROYAL ARTILLERY | who died of Yellow Fever | on the 10th September 1852 | Aged 27 Years.

1852, Sept. 10. At B. of yellow fever, Lt. T. Orme, R.A. (" G.M.," 216.)

711. SACRED | to the memory | of | JAS HUNTER BLAIR BIRCH, | CAPTAIN 66TH REGT | Died | 22nd January 1851 | Aged 30 Years 4 Months.

1851, Jan. 22. At B., of fever, Capt. Jas. Hunter Blair Birch, 66th Reg. yst. s. of Lt. Gen. B., C.B. (" G.M.," 454.)

712. White marble headstone enclosed by iron railing :—

SACRED | *To the Memory of* | EUSTACE MALTRAVERS | The beloved Child of | WILLIAM & MARIA BRENDA GRASETT. | who died October 12 1851 | Ætat. 4 mo's. 16 d'ys | (17 lines.)

713. Small square of white marble set on vault :—

Sacred | to the Memory of | John Phillips | Shipwright | Died 4th February | 1860 | Aged 50 Years.

714. Headstone :—

Sacred to the Memory | *of* | MARGARET CLUNE | Wife to PATRICK CLUNE | Qr Master of the 52nd Regt | Who died on 12th Decr 1839 | Aged 32 Years.

715. Headstone :—

To the Memory | of | EUPHEMIA | Wife of | JOHN HUNTER | DIED 10th August 1852. | Aged 22 Years.

716. THIS TOMB | COVERS THE REMAINS OF | LT COL. JOHN TYLER | . . . . RS | DY QR MR GENERAL | *IN THIS COMMAND* | HE DIED 2ND JUNE 18 . . | AGED 51 YEARS | (2 lines.)

See the Regimental Tablet No. 666.

717. Loose grey marble :—

Sacred | to the memory | *of* | HARRIET EMMA LOUIS | *the beloved Child* | *of* | CAPTAIN *and* MRS PITCAIRN | 92ND HIGHLANDERS | WHO DIED OF CONVULSIONS | AT ST ANNS | ON FRIDAY THE 11TH JUNE 1811 (*sic*) | AGED 9 MONTHS AND 11 DAYS.

718. Altar-tomb.   At north edge, very indistinct :—

WILLIAM FISHER MENDS DEPUTY COMMISSARY GENERAL TO H.M. FORCES | BORN 19 JULY 1808 DIED 11 MAY 1860 IN CHRIST SHALL ALL BE MADE ALIVE.

On the south edge close to boundary wall :—

CHARLOTTE LOUISA DAUGHTER OF WILLIAM WALROND AND MARY SHEPHERD JACKSON | BORN 15 MARCH 1815 DIED 4 SEPTEMBER 1850 NOT LOST BUT GONE BEFORE.

The late Bishop of Antigua, Wm. Walrond Jackson, was b. in B. 9 Jan. 1811. Minister of St. Paul's in 1842.

719. White marble headstone at head of curbed grave :—

In Loving Memory of | JAMES H. G. GREENWICH | DIED 27TH FEBY 1894 | AGED 67 YRS | (3 lines.)

On a small ledger in centre of same grave:—

Sacred | TO THE MEMORY OF | MARTHA ANN | (wife of Mʳ Jaˢ H. G. Greenwich) *Who departed this life* | On the 31 of July 1864 | AGED 47 YEARS | (2 lines) | ALSO | To the Memory | *of her Sister* | *MISS SARAH ELIZᵀᴴ GOPPY* | Aged 51 Years | DIED IN 1846.

720. White marble slab on vault enclosed by iron railing:—

To the Memory of | MARY ROCHFORD REDWAR | BELOVED CHILD OF REVᴰ | HENRY RUSSELL & ELLEN REDWAR, | Who died on the 3ʳᵈ Novʳ 1852 | Aged 4 Years 9 Months & 7 Days | Also | To the Memory of the | REVᴰ HENRY RUSSELL REDWAR | 24 Years Minister of this Chapel | *Who fell asleep in Jesus on 15ᵗʰ February 1873* | Aged 59 Years.

721. Large white marble standing against mausoleum:—

Sacred | to | The Memory Of | THOMAS SHERIFF, | Born at Aghanloo in the County of | Londonderry Ireland, | on the 14ᵗʰ of Novʳ 1780, and for 46 Years, | a resident in this Island | Died 29ᵗʰ July 1846, | leaving a Widow to whom he had been | endeared by 38 Years of conjugal | affection and four Sons to | mourn his irreparable loss | ALSO | HENRIETTA SHERIFF | Granddaughter of the above Born 30ᵗʰ Aug. | 1816 | Died May 8ᵗʰ 1847 | Likewise | *of* | JANE SHERIFF | Relict of the above born | Scotland on the 6ᵗʰ December 1786 | *Died on the 2ⁿᵈ July 1854* | Aged 67 Years and 7 Months | ALSO | Chas. John Walker Sheriff | Died January 20ᵗʰ 1867 | Aged 56 Years | & | Chas. Eugene Douglas Sheriff | SOLICITOR | his Son. Died 16ᵗʰ Feby. 1888 | Aged 31 Years.

722. Slate slab enclosed by iron railing:—

To the Memory, | *of* | ELIZABETH ANNE WALKER | third daughter of | JAMES WALKER ESQᴿ | Colonial Secretary of this Island | Born | at Belmont in this neighbourhood, | 21ˢᵗ January 1845 | Died | at Government House | 21ˢᵗ Aug. 1859.

723. White marble headstone:—

(4 lines) | ELIZABETH FAULKNER | LIES BURIED HERE | SHE DIED | 9 JANUARY 1862 | AGED 70 YEARS.

724. Small ledger:—

MARY FOX | the only and beloved Child | of her Parents | Died July 31ˢᵗ 1845 | Aged One Year and Six Months | (1 line.)

725. Headstone, nearly all buried:—

To the Memory | *of* | JOHN WINTERBOTTOM | .. ASTER 52ⁿᵈ Regᵗ | .... May 1838.

726. Square stone pedestal enclosed by iron railing :—

CREST.—*A stork statant.*

SACRED | TO THE MEMORY OF | MAJOR ROBERT NOBLE CROSSE K.H. | 56ᵀᴴ REGIMENT | WHO DIED OF YELLOW FEVER ON THE | 13ᵀᴴ NOVEMBER 1838 | ON BOARD HER MAJESTY'S SHIP | HERCULES 74 | IN CARLISLE BAY BARBADOES | HE SERVED WITH THE REGIMENT FOR AN | UNINTERRUPTED PERIOD OF 33 YEARS | (7 lines; tablet erected in Cathedral.)
See No. 647.

727. Large grave enclosed by iron railing. On brass plate :—

THE FAMILY BURIAL PLACE | OF | CHARLES EDWIN YOUNG CROUCH | OF THE GROTTO | Sᵀ MICHAEL BARBADOS. W.I.

On white marble cross :—

OUR CHARLIE | BORN NOVᴿ 2 | 1866 | DIED | JUNE 12 | 1879 | (1 line.)

728. Small square white marble over vault :—

MARY RIVAROLA O'HALLORAN | INFANT DAUGHTER | OF | Bᵀ MAJOR H. D. O'HALLORAN | D.A.Q.M.G. | DIED 10ᵀᴴ AUGUST 1862 | AGED 16 MONTHS | (1 line.)

729. Oblong white marble on vault :—

SACRED TO THE MEMORY OF | Pay Master JOHN WINTERBOTTOM 52ᵈ Light Infantry | and of PENELOPE his Wife | also of Lieut. V. A. SURTEES and | Ensign E. GOUGH | All of whom fell Victims to an Epidemic | which attacked the Corps shortly after its arrival at Barbados | towards the latter end of 1838 | (4 lines.)

730. Headstone :—

SACRED TO THE MEMORY | of | THOMAS HONER WHEELER | STAFF SURGEON TO THE FORCES | Died 6ᵗʰ May 1848, | Aged 33 Years.

731. Vault. Small white marble square at west end :—

IN MEMORY OF | LIEUT. COLONEL | ORMSBY PHIBBS | 88ᵀᴴ REGᵀ | OR | CONNAUGHT RANGERS | WHO DIED | OF YELLOW FEVER | 17ᵀᴴ JANᵞ 1848.
See his tablet No. 645.

732. Flaked slab :—

To | the memory of | MONTGOMERY IRWIN | ASSISTANT SURGEON | 72ⁿᵈ HIGHLANDERS, | Died | 13ᵗʰ October 1848, | Aged 29 Years 8 Months.

733. SACRED | to | the memory of | WILLIAM Rᵀ PYNE | LIEUᵀ 66ᵀᴴ REGᵀ | DIED | OCTᴿ 25ᵀᴴ 1848 | AGED 24 YEARS 4 MONTHS.
1848, Oct. 25. At B. a. 21, Wm. Rob. Pyne, of 66th Foot, eldest s. of the Rev. Wm. P., R. of Pitney, Som. ("G.M.," 222.)

734. SACRED | to | the memory of | FRANCIS WILLIAM ASTLE | CAPTAIN 66TH REGIMENT | DIED | 13TH NOVR 1848 | AGED 23 YEARS 10 MONTHS.

735. SACRED | to | the memory of | JOHN LINDSAY | QUARTER MASTER | 72ND HIGHLANDERS | DIED | 21ST NOVR 1848 | AGED 38 YEARS.

736. SACRED | TO THE MEMORY | OF | LT COLONEL JOHN DOYLE O'BRIEN | DEPUTY, QR MR GENL | WHO DIED AT BARBADOS ON THE | 16TH DECR 1852 | OF YELLOW FEVER | AGED 45 YEARS.

737. Cross:—

I.H.S. | IN LOVING | MEMORY OF JOHN T. CHASE | WHO DEPARTED THIS LIFE | AUGUST XV 1882 AGED | 71 | ALSO TO THE | MEMORY OF MARY | C. CHASE THE | BELOVED WIFE | OF JOHN CHASE | WHO DEPARTED THIS | LIFE MAY XXIII 1877 | AGED 60 YEARS | (A later inscription on metal is rusted away.)

ST. MARY'S DISTRICT CHURCH, BRIDGETOWN.

The old parish church of St. Michael formerly stood here. It was pulled down and the monuments removed when the present Cathedral was built in the centre of the town. St. Mary's District Church was then built on the old site and consecrated in 1827 by the late Bishop Coleridge, the Rev. John Hothersall Pinder, M.A., being its first minister.

738. On the north wall of nave are five tablets :—

This Memorial of | CAROLINE THORNE | and her Christian Example of devoted | life, is erected by loving and thankful | Friends in Barbadoes and some neigh- | bouring Islands Born August 13th | A : D : 1810, she was called to Rest | December 2nd A.D. 1885, and lies near | her honoured husband Joseph Thorne | within the precincts of this Church | (1 line.)

739. Masonic emblem above:—

THIS TABLET IS ERECTED BY THE MEMBERS | OF THE ALBION LODGE 196 E.C. TO THE MEMORY | OF THEIR BELOVED BROTHER | THOMAS CLARKE MAR- SHALL | W.P.M. AND P.P.Z. OF THE SCOTIA AND ALBION | R.A. CHAPTERS P.E.C. OF THE STAR OF THE | WEST PRECEPTORY OF KNIGHTS TEMPLAR | AND PROVINCIAL PRIOR FOR THE W. I. | WHO DEPARTED THIS LIFE | ON THE 11TH OCTOBER 1879 | AGED 54 YEARS | HIS REMAINS ARE INTERRED IN THE | CATHEDRAL CEMETERY | (1 line.)

740. In Loving Memory of | John Montefiore, | a man of generous sympathies and | a respected Merchant of Barbadoes | (his native land) and London. He died | in this Parish deeply lamented on the | 26th day of Iune A.D. 1854 aged 60 years | (1 line) | Also | In Loving Memory of | Mary Elizabeth Montefiore | born in this Island and the devoted Wife | of the afore- named. Endeared to all who | knew her pious life, she fell asleep at | Streatham in England on the | 7th Day of March A.D. 1877 aged 78 years | (1 line.)

1854, June 26. Aged 60, John Montefiori, of B. ("G.M.," 314.)

P

741. IN CŒLO QUIES | SACRED TO THE MEMORY | OF | MARY ANN | THE BELOVED WIFE OF | THOMAS JOSHUA CUMMINS | WHO WAS BORN ON THE 12TH APRIL 1800, | MARRIED 26TH MAY 1819, | AND DIED 19TH MAY 1854 | (9 lines; by husband.)

742. In Memoriam | CATHERINE ANN SHILSTONE | DIED 8TH SEPTEMBER 1883 | AGED 69 YEARS | (6 lines; by children.)

743. On east wall close by :—

IN MEMORIAM | THOMAS WILLIAM SHILSTONE, | LATE MERCHANT OF THIS CITY, | DIED FEBRUARY 16TH 1870, | AGED 54 YEARS | (5 lines; by widow and children.)

744. Brass below No. 743 :—

In Loving Memory of | OUR DARLING SON | THEODORE MAXWELL SHILSTONE | WHO ENTERED INTO REST | 23RD DECEMBER 1909, | AGED 21 | (1 line.)

745. On the east wall of nave.   South side:—

SACRED | TO THE BELOVED MEMORY OF | BENJAMIN ALLEYNE, | WHO DEPARTED THIS LIFE DECEMBER 21ST 1865, | AGED 52 YEARS | (5 lines.)

On the south wall of nave :—

746. SACRED TO THE MEMORY OF | SARAH ELIZABETH ROBINSON | DAUGHTER OF AARON SOBER ROBINSON | AND MARY ROBINSON | WHO DEPARTED THIS LIFE 8TH SEPTR 1863, | AGED 32 YEARS | (10 lines; by mother) | ALSO THEIR SON | WILLIAM ROBINSON | WHO DIED 16TH DECEMBER 1863 | AGED 29 YEARS.

747. SACRED TO THE MEMORY OF | THE REV: WILLIAM MARSHALL HARTE, | (22 lines; clergyman of Church of England 50 years, and Minister of this chapel) | HE DEPARTED THIS LIFE ON THE 11TH OF JANUARY 1851, | AGED 74 YEARS | HIS REMAINS WERE DEPOSITED IN THE FAMILY BURIAL PLACE | IN THE CATHEDRAL.

Edward John, 2 s. Wm. Marshall Harte of St Lucia, B'os, cler. Q. Coll. Oxf., matric. 17 Oct. 1849, a. 21.

748. Medallion above, and on either side an angel :—

SACRED TO THE MEMORY | OF | JAMES BUTCHER M.D. | NATIVE OF THIS ISLAND | WHO HAVING GRADUATED AT EDINBURGH | RETURNED HERE IN 1804 | AND WAS ENGAGED IN PRACTICE UPWARDS OF 52 YEARS | AS PHYSICIAN AND SURGEON | HE DIED 9TH MARCH 1856, AGED EIGHTY | (7 lines) | HIS REMAINS ARE INTERRED AT THE CATHEDRAL | (2 lines.)

749. IN MEMORY | OF | SARAH ELIZABETH | THE BELOVED AND ONLY DAUGHTER OF | JAMES A. AND ROWENA LYNCH | BORN 17TH SEPTEMBER 1849 | DIED 22 APRIL 1872 | (1 line) | HER REMAINS ARE INTERRED AT ST LEONARDS CEMETERY.

750. West wall of nave :—

In Memory of | ELIZABETH THOMAS CRICK | who was killed by the late Hurricane | at the early age of eight years; | *also of her Mother* | MARTHA CRICK | who died in August 1828, | (2 lines ; by friend.)

---

751. Floorstone at south porch :—

In MEMORY *of* | William Brown, late shipwright | on the Ship Higginson, Capt Hall, of | Liverpool; who departed this life the | 1st March 1817, Aged 42 Years | (4 lines.)

---

752. Blue marble ledger at foot of stairs to gallery. The left top portion is missing :—

. . ALROND, who | . . . . this Life the 3^d of January . . 50 Aged 56 Years and 5 Months.

1750-1, Jan. 4. Anthony Waldron. (Burial Register.) His name does not appear in the Walrond pedigree.

---

753. Blue marble ledger at north porch, hour glass, skull and crossbones above, in perfect preservation :—

Here Lyeth HANNAH FOLLETT | daughter of IOHN FOLLETT & | SARAH his wife who departed | this Life the 5th of MAY 1681 In | the Fifth year of her Age | Here Lyeth also SARAH her | Mother who departed this | life the last day of MAY 1698 | in the Fourty Sixth year | of her Age.

1681, May 5. Hannah Hallett ye D^a of Jno & Sarah Hallett (*sic*).
1698, June 1. Mrs Sarah Follet. (Burial Register.)

ST. MARY'S CHURCHYARD.

The Sexton stated that many coloured people were buried here. Several modern inscriptions I did not take.

754. Old ledger, skull and wreaths above :—

Here Lyeth the Body of | ALEXANDER LAMPLEE | Who departed this Life the | . . February 1708 Aged | About 38 years.

1712-13, Jan. 18. Mrs Ruth ye wife of Mr Robert Lamplee, Merchant. (Burial Register.)

---

755. White marble slab over vault :—

Sacred to the Memory | OF | Master FREDERICK BARUH LOUSADA | who departed this life | 20th April 1816 | aged 13 Years.

The Lousadas, Portuguese Jews, were originally of this island, then flourished in Jamaica, whence they came to England. There are several stones to them in the Synagogue burial-ground.

---

756. Old ledger. The right-hand portion of 3rd to 6th lines is broken off :—

Here lieth the Body | of WILLIAM NUNES | who departed this Life the . . . . | Day of May one Thou . . . | Seven Hundred and Nin . . . . | Aged Sixty three Ye . .

1793, May 29. William Nunes, a free Mulatto. (Burial Register.)

757. Another old ledger adjoining :—

Here lieth the Body of | ANN NUNES Daughter of | WILLIAM NUNES who departed | this Life the 27ᵗʰ Day of Auguſt | one .... and Seven Hundred and | Ninety one Aged Nineteen Years.

1791, Aug. 28.   Ann Nunes, a Mulatto slave.   (Burial Register.)

---

758. Lower down, but very badly cut, is a mutilated inscription :—

ALSO | THE Body of Philenᴀh Nunes | Wife of Wᵐ Nunes Who | Depᴀʀted This Life 5ᵗʰ | of Sepᵗᵐ 1803 *Aged 77 Years.*

1803, Sept. 6.   Philenah (a free negro).   (Burial Register.)

There are enclosed tombs to Belgrave, Straker, Thomas, Cummins, and Da Costa families, the last named being "coloured," and now wealthy store-keepers.

---

759. Ledger adjoining No. 742 :—

To the memory of | Mʳ JOSEPH RACHEL who | Died the 15ᵗʰ Day of Octoʳ 1760 | Aged 50 Years.

---

760. White marble ledger, cracked :—

Beneath this Stone | Freed from this World | and all its cares | lay the remains | of Innocence & Youth | Untimely ſnatched, | A VICTIM | To the Pains ſhe bore in giving | Birth to a ſon the firſt and only | ſurviving Child. | of Mʳˢ RACHEL PHILLIPS | who departed this life | 14ᵗʰ of April 1799 | Aged 14 Years (*sic*) & 5 Months.

1799, April 15.   Rachael Phillips (a free Mulatto).   (Burial Register.)

---

761. White marble ledger :—

𝕾𝕬𝕮𝕽𝕰𝕯 | ᴛᴏ | 𝖙𝖍𝖊 𝕸𝖊𝖒𝖔𝖗𝖞 | ᴏꜰ | Mᴿˢ MARY OSTREHAN | who departed this life 27ᵗʰ June 1829. | aged 56 | (1 line.)

1829, June 27.   Mary Ostrehan, f. n.* (age) 58.   (Burial Register.)

---

762. White marble headstone north of churchyard :—

This Stone is here placed | to mark where the remains of | HARRIET HUSBANDS lie, | who died on the 10 of July 1844, | aged 63 years ; & also to show where | her son Sinclair Mackenzie & his | family are to be buried should | they die in Barbados.

1844, July 11.   Harriet Husbands, Bridgetown, 62 years.   **District of** St. Mary.   (Burial Register.)

---

763. The remains of | JAMES FAIRMAN ESQᴿ | Mʳˢ Mackenzies Father are also | deposited here.   He was Post Master | of this Island 33 years and died | on the 6ᵗʰ of Decʳ 1845 | aged 60 years.

1845, Dec. 7.   James Pairman.   Bridgetown.   63 ʏʳˢ.   (Burial Register.)

1845, Dec. 6.   At B. a. 63, Jas. Pairman, l. Postmaster of that i.   ("G.M.," 335.)

* Free negress.

Military Burial Ground.

This is close to Charles Fort at Nedhams Point, which commands the roadstead of Bridgetown. The earlier ground is covered with thick scrub which rendered exploration impossible, but I noticed a stone bearing the date of 1820 and one officer's grave .—

764. J. J. WARNEP, Esq. 1st Bat. 21st Fusiliers. d. 16 Sept. 1862.

———

The more modern ground appears to have been added about 1868, and is kept in good order. I noted the following names, but had not time to copy the inscriptions in full. There was an epidemic of yellow fever in 1881 which caused considerable mortality :—

765. Surgeon Major ESPINE WARD & his wife d. Aug. 1881.

766. Lt Col. R. BULLEN, R.E. d. 30 June 1883.

767. Col. DONALD ALEXANDER FRAZER, R.E. d. 5 Aug. 1881.

768. Col. SIDNEY BAYNTON FARRELL Commanding R.E. d. 7 Sept. 1879 a. 50.

769. Surgeon JAMES ROMAYNE, A.M.D. d. of yellow fever 10 Aug. 1881 a. 25.

770. Capt. E. LAWLESS d. 16 Aug. 1881 a. 42.

771. SEYMOUR BLANSHARD PEMBERTON Lieut. 2d W.I. Reg. d. 9 Oct. 1881 of yellow fever, a. 25.

772. HERBERT T. COUSINS, D.A.C.C. d. 8 Aug. 1881, a. 25.

773. T. E. LE BLANC. Lieut. 1st Bat. Kings Own R. Lanc. Reg. d. 28 July 1881 a. 26.

———

The Savannah of St. Ann.

Here was the old parade ground surrounded by the barracks. On an obelisk near the road :—

774. Near This Spot Rest the Remains of Fourteen Soldiers | And one Married Woman | of the 36th Regiment who were killed | by the destruction of the Barracks and Hospital during | The awful visitation of the hurricane | August 11th 1831. | (No names. 4 lines ; erected by the corps.)

———

775. On another obelisk are inscriptions on two white marble tablets :—

On the upper one :—

To the Memory | OF | THE UNDERNAMED OFFICERS AND SOLDIERS | OF | THE ROYAL YORK RANGERS | Who fell in Action in the Army commanded by Lieut. Gen. sir george beckwith, k.b. | at the Reduction of the French Colonies of martinique, the saintes, and guadaloupe | in 1809 and 1810 | Lieutenants john symons, p. g. copley, sam. gregg, robt. martineau | (and 47 names of non-com. officers and privates.)

On the lower one :—

𝕾𝕬𝕮𝕽𝕰𝕯 | TO THE | Memory of LIEUTENANT COLONEL PATRICK HEN-DERSON of the | YORK LIGHT INFANTRY VOLUNTEERS, | who expired at GUADELOUPE, as *MAJOR COMMANDING* the *ROYAL YORK RANGERS*, on | the 28th of August 1810 | (11 lines ; erected by Lieut.-Gen. Sir Geo. Beckwith.)

LEAR's, ST. MICHAEL'S PARISH.

776. Over the east gable of the great house :—

R. 1651 H. | JAN. 28 E. 1758.

Over the west gable is a shield of carved wood with festoons at sides. ARMS.—*Two bends and a canton.* Some charges have apparently been lost.

See my photo. Peter Lear of this estate was created a Baronet 2 July 1660, and died s.p. about 1684, when the title passed to his nephew Thomas.

---

777. Brick vault with ledger on the top and this inscription framewise :—

HERE LYETH INTERRED | THE BODY OF Mɪˢ ALCE LEAR WIFE OF THOMAS | LEAR WHO DEPARTED | THIS LIFE THE XXIIII DAY OF OCTOBER | ANNO DOM 1688.

A shield in a sunk oval is in the central space with mantling. ARMS.—. . . . *a fesse double embattled between three unicorns' heads couped.* CREST.—*A demi-unicorn rampant couped, in its paws a spear, over W. and H.*

BUSH HALL, ST. MICHAEL'S.

778. Marble slab lying in grass land :—

Here lyeth interr'd yᵉ Bodys | of RICHARD MORRIS & SARAH | his Wife | RICHARD MORRIS died May 19. 1694 | SARAH MORRIS died Jan. 10. 1709.

WELCHES, ST. MICHAEL'S.

779. Part of a blue marble ledger consisting of two fragments which fit together. Mr. Carrington informed me that it was brought from an old vault at Kingston :—

> . . . . . yeth Interr'd the Body of
> . . . . ᴛ Wife of ALEXᴿ SCOTT
> Departed this Life the 16
> . . . . ber . 720 Aged 24 Years.

Above on a Jacobean shield :—

CREST.—*A torch over W. and H.* ARMS.—*Three Catherine wheels, on a fess three lambs* (SCOTT) ; impaling, *Three unicorns' heads couped.*

1720, Oct. 17. Jane wife of Alexʳ Scott. (Burial Register.)

The christian name may have been Janet.

CHRIST CHURCH, OLD CHURCHYARD.

This ancient burial-ground is on a low rocky site surrounded on three sides by the sea, about a mile from Oistins Town. The parish church formerly stood here, though I saw no trace of its foundations, which may have been washed away by the sea. A new one was built more in the centre of the parish.

There are seven vaults.

780. Ledger. Quite perfect and sharply cut :—

Here lies the Body | Of JOHN KIRTON, M.D. | Who departed this Life | July 15th 1738 | Aged [blank] Years | (4 lines) | Here alſo lies | ANN his Wife | Who died | Auguſt 1st 1765 | Aged 65 Years | (13 lines) | This humble Monument | Is raised by the ſurviving Daughter | Of the aforeſaid JOHN and ANN KIRTON.

1765, Aug. 1. Ann Kirton. (Burial Register.)
See pedigree, *ante* I., 65.

781. Large deeply cut letters :—

HERE LYETH THE | BODY OF Mʀˢ MARY | ADDAMS Yᴱ WIFE OF | SAMVELL ADDAMS | WHO DECEASED | 15ᵀᴴ OF DECEMBER | 1672.

782. This vault has been joined on to No. 781 by about 2 feet of brickwork :—

HERE LYETH Yᴱ BODY | OF Mʀ SAMVELL ADDAMS | DECEASED | (No dates; quite perfect.)

1672, Dec. 15. Mary Adams. (Burial Register.)
The above three vaults adjoin each other.

783. A few yards away :—

HEAR LYES | WILLIAM RALSTON | ESQ | DEᴰ THE 26 OCTOBᴿ | ANᵒ DOM | 1659.

1659, Oct. 26. William Balston (*sic*). (Burial Register.)
1645, Oct. 16. William Balston.

784. A large lofty dome-topped tomb. Above the entrance, on a small oblong stone, dirty and flaked :—

J. W. GILES | DIED JUNE 14 185 . | AGED 56 YEARS.
Archer gives 1854.

785. A large flat vault. On a fine white marble slab. Above is a Jacobean shield. ARMS.—*A double-headed eagle displayed;* impaling, *A chevron between three roundles.* No crest :—

Here Lyes the Body of the Honble | Joseph Brown Esq : who departed | this Life June yᵉ 28 : 1728 | In yᵉ | 69 year of his Age.

Col. Joseph Brown b. 1665 had issue Joseph aged 25 in 1715, Wm., Jas., John & Damaris. (Archer, 379.)
1665, March 11. Sʳ James Browne Kᵗ & Barᵗ (Sᵗ John's Burial Register). See his will in " Caribbeana," iv., 49.

786. A large plain tomb some 7 feet high. At its west end is a classical front with inscription on an oblong of slate. Below this are three ovals of slate, perhaps designed for arms, but they are blank. Archer incorrectly stated there were inscriptions on them:—

QVOD RELIQVVM EST DOROTH- FRANCISC | ET JOANNÆ IARMAN FILIÆ DANIELIS | GILBERT MED- CONIVGIS HIC IACET IN | HVMATVM QVÆ OBIT 12° DIE IAN- | 1661 | IDEMQVE TVMVLVS PETRI VNA CVM | FRANC- RISLEY FILIOLO CONDIT CON | SECRATQVE ADIACENTES CINERES.

1661-2, Jan. 13.　Dorothy, wife of Daniel Gilbert.　(Burial Register.)

———

Archer also gave two more not now to be seen:—

787. ROBERT FARRER d. July 23, 1691.

788. Doctor JAMES HOLMES, d. Aug. 31, 1728.

———

CHRIST CHURCH.

This church, which stands on a hill overlooking Oistins, was rebuilt in 1835 after the hurricane of 1831.

In the centre walk of nave are five ledgers. Commencing from the west end:—

789. Blue marble slab:—

Here lyeth the Body of | JOHN CHASE Senior Efq | Ob: Feb: 9 1736. | Æt 31 Years 1 Month & 20 Days. | Alfo JOHN CHASE Junior Son | of JOHN & CHRISTIAN CHASE | Ob: April 11 1737. | Æt 10 Months & 9 Days.

Gap in Burial Register 25 May 1736 to 8 April 1750.

———

790. Blue marble :—

CREST.—*An elephant's head couped, collared, over wreath and helmet.*
ARMS.—*Within a bordure (? charged with roundles) a fess between four cotises.* (Archer gives *three barrulets wavy.*)

On an Inescutcheon : *Argent, three bulls' heads cabossed* (WALROND). The arms are apparently those of Elliot of Port Eliot, co. Cornwall. (Vivian, 147.)

Here lies the Body of | the Honble JAMES ELLIOT Efq : | Son of the Honble RICHARD ELLIOT Efq : | He Marryed ELIZABETH the Daughter of | the Honble THOMAS WALROND Efq. of this Ifland | He was Brave, Hofpitable, and Courteous. | of great Integrity in his Actions | and Confpicuous for his Judgment and | Vivacity in Converfation. | After his Merit had advanced him to the | Honour of being one of his Majeftys Councel | He was Snatched away from us, | the 14th of May, Anno Dom: 1724. | in the 34th year of his Age: | And died Lamented by all who knew him, | In Honour to his Memory His truly forrowfull | Widow has erected this Tomb.

1724, May 15.　James Elliot.　(Burial Register.)
Thos. Walrond, a Col. in the army, M. of C., was of this parish in 1679. See pedigree in A., iii., 180.

———

791. Blue marble :—

Here lies the Body | of | ELIZABETH EVERSLEY | Wife of WILLIAM EVERSLEY Esq. | She departed this *. ife the 6ᵗʰ Octʳ 1817* | aged 36 years five Months and two days | (12 lines.)

792. Blue marble :—

CREST.—*A sea-bird close, in its beak a ring over wreath and helmet.*
ARMS.—*. . . . on a bend three sea-birds close.*

Here lies the body of ELIZABETH | SEAWELL widdow of RICHARD | SEAWELL Esqʳ who died the 1ˢᵗ of | Septʳ 1728 aged 78 years.

1728, Sept. 2.   Elizabeth Seawell.   (Burial Register.)

793. Blue marble :—

CREST.—*Out of a ducal coronet a horse's head over wreath and helmet.*
ARMS.—*Per chevron argent and ermine two lions' heads erased.*

Here lies interred the Body of | REYNOLD ALLEYNE of *Mount Alleyne* | in the Parifh of Sᵀ JAMES Eſqʳ | who Departed this Life the | Thirtieth Day of June Anno Domini | 1749 Ætatis 49.

He was aged 21 on 23 Jan. 1720; 4th s. of Tho. A. of Mount A.; mar. the dau. and coheiress of Lawrence Price, and left two daus. and coheiresses : (1) Eliz., mar. John Newton of Newtons; he d. s.p., and left Mount A. to Sir John Gay A., Bart.; (2) Judith, d. spr. 11 July 1763, a. 36.   M.I. Bristol Cath. Gap in burials 1736—50.

794. In the chancel floor a stone ledger :—

Here lie the Remains | of | the REVᴰ ROBᵀ BOWCHER | Rector of this Parish 22 Years. | He died 25ᵗʰ Novʳ 1795 | †. ged 63 Years. | *In gratitude to his Memory* | †. . . . one is placed by | his Nephew : | ROBᵀ B. CLARKE.

1795, Nov. 26.   The Revᵈ Robert Bowcher, Rector of the Parish.   (Burial Register.)   Robert Bowcher, s. of Robert, of Isle of B'os, gent. Queen's Coll. matric. 4 Nov. 1752 aged 20.   (Foster.)   He went out 18 Jan. 1757. (Fothergill.)   Clement Bowcher went out 9 Oct. 1790, and was head master of Codrington College Grammar School Aug.—Oct. 1792.

In the church are seven tablets.

795. To left of communion rails.   White marble on black: REEVES.   BATH. ENGLAND.

Mitre.   Arms of See; impaling, *Argent, on a mount Vert in base an otter ppr., a chief Gules charged with a dove of the field, between two crosses pattée fitchée Or.*   (Coleridge.)

SACRED TO THE MEMORY OF | THE RIGHT REVEREND WILLIAM HART COLERIDGE D.D. | FIRST BISHOP OF BARBADOS, | WHO DEPARTED THIS LIFE AT SALSTON, OTTERY Sᵀ MARY, | IN THE COUNTY OF DEVON, GREAT BRITAIN; | 21ˢᵀ OF DECEMBER 1849, AGED 60 YEARS. | THIS TABLET IS ERECTED, | BY THE RECTOR AND PARISHIONERS OF THIS PARISH | IN GRATEFUL REMEMBRANCE OF THEIR LATE | EXEMPLARY AND ESTEEMED DIOCESAN.

* Cracked and cemented.   † Cemented.

Q

796. White marble on north wall of chancel :—

Sacred to the obsequies | *Of DOROTHY* | *Confort of the honorable* | *HENRY FRERE* | (26 lines.)

797. White and black marble tablet north wall of nave :—

THIS TABLET HAS BEEN ERECTED | IN TOKEN OF AFFECTIONATE REMEM-
BRANCE | BY A DEVOTED HUSBAND AND FATHER | JOHN RANDAL PHILLIPS
ESQ^{RE} | TO THE MEMORY OF | HIS WIFE MARY ANN COLE, | WHO DIED AT
LAMBERTS IN THE PARISH OF S^T LUCY | ON THE 12TH JULY, 1854, IN THE 27TH YEAR
OF HER AGE | AND CHILDREN | JOHN RANDAL, | BORN 19TH NOV^R 1849,
DIED 20TH JULY, 1850. | MARGARET ELIZABETH RANDAL, | BORN
3RD JULY, 1852, DIED 25TH SEP^R 1853, | MARGARET ELIZABETH
RANDAL, (*sic*) | BORN 17TH APRIL, 1853, DIED 28TH AUGUST 1854 | (1 line.)

BEDFORD 256 OXFORD STR^T LONDON.

See the M.I. to her husband in St. Michael's, No. 60.

798. Black marble north wall of nave :—

In memory of | RICHARD P. SHAW, | BORN NOVEMBER 3RD 1844, |
DIED OCTOBER 1ST 1875. | *THIS TABLET IS ERECTED BY HIS WIDOW,* |
MARIA | SHAW.

BROWNE & CO. BRISTOL, ENG^D.

799. White and black marble tablet to right or south of communion rails :—

In Loving Memory of | WILHELMINA | ANN STANTON
EVELYN, | BORN 19TH JUNE 1847, DIED 12TH JUNE 1884 | (14 lines ; erected by
brothers and sisters.)

800. South wall of nave :—

TO THE MEMORY OF | GEORGE SHARP, CLERK, M.A. | (CAIUS COLLEGE
CAMBRIDGE,) | OF MAXWELLS IN THIS ISLAND, | LATE INCUMBENT OF MERTHER,
CORNWALL, ENGLAND, | ONLY SON OF THE LATE WILLIAM SHARP ESQ^{RE} | AND
HENRIETTA PEARCE, HIS WIFE, | OF CLAYBURY IN THIS ISLAND, | BORN APRIL
7TH 1815. DIED AT TORQUAY NOV^R 29TH 1864 | (1 line) | ALSO | SARAH HENRIETTA,
ELDEST DAUGHTER OF | GEORGE SHARP, CLERK, AND SARAH HIS WIFE, | BORN AT
ROME, MARCH 26TH 1841, | DIED AT TORQUAY, DEC^R 1ST 1861, | (1 line) | ALSO |
ELIZABETH GEORGINA, | THIRD AND YOUNGEST DAUGHTER OF | GEORGE SHARP,
CLERK, AND SARAH HIS WIFE, | BORN AT CLAYBURY, MARCH 25TH 1845, | DIED
AT MAXWELLS, SEPT^R 21ST 1845 | (2 lines) | THIS TABLET IS ERECTED BY THE
AFFLICTED WIDOW, | AND BEREAVED MOTHER.

KING. BATH. ENGLAND.

801. On grey marble slab let into west wall of nave, evidently formerly a
floor-stone :—

Under this Stone | are the Remains of | M^{RS} ELIZABETH FARRELL |
who died | on the 18th day of June 1819 | in the 70th Year of her Age | (3 lines.)

1824, Dec. 30. At Lamplighters hall, John Richard Farrell, esq., of B.
("G.M." for 1825, p. 189.)

802. White marble on black tablet :—

IN MEMORY OF | REYNOLD ALLEYNE REDMAN, ESQ^{RE} | WHO
DEPARTED THIS LIFE ON THE 24TH MAY 1867 | AGED 48 YEARS | DURING THE
LATTER FIFTEEN OF WHICH | HE WAS THE EXCELLENT MANAGER | OF HANOVERS
ESTATE IN THIS PARISH | HIGHLY ESTEEMED BY ITS PROPRIETOR | AND ALL HIS
OTHER FRIENDS.

WOOD. BRISTOL ENG^D.

803. South aisle, east end, behind organ, white marble on black :—

SACRED TO THE MEMORY OF | SARAH ELIZABETH FITZPATRICK, |
WHO FELL A VICTIM TO EPIDEMIC CHOLERA, | JULY 20TH 1854, AGED 43 YEARS |
HER REMAINS REST IN AN ADJACENT VAULT WITH THOSE OF HER SON | JAMES
EVELYN FITZPATRICK AGED 11 YEARS | (11 lines ; survived his mother
10 hours ; erected by her husband Jas. Evelyn Fitzpatrick ; married life 26 years
and 10 months.)

On west gallery : REBUILT & ENLARGED MDCCCXXXVI.

804. On a very worn blue marble ledger in porch at west end :—

HERE lyeth Interr'd the . . ody of | SAMUELL GRYME | Son of
GEORGE GRYME Esq who | departed this Life the 28th July . . 28 | Aged
11 Years.

1728, July. Samuel Græme, a child. (Burial Register.)
1795, Mar. 6. Aged 65, Mrs. Margaret Græme, relict of Alex. G. esq.
of B., etc. (" G.M.," 260.)

805. Adjoining preceding is a white marble ledger with inscription nearly
obliterated :—

Here [lyeth interr'd ye Body] | of DOCTOR [JOHN DURANT, son of THO^S] |
DUR[ANT and MARY his wife who de-] | parted [this life ye 4th day of March
1726] | [aged 23 years 9 months & 12 days].

The portions in brackets from Archer.

806. Archer gives the following abbreviated inscription, now lost :—

ARMS.—*A fesse between three fleurs-de-lis* (the trick shews a chevron) ;
impaling, *on a bend wavy three swans statant.*
CREST.—*A dexter cubit arm grasping an imperial crown.*

BENJAMIN ASHEHURST, Gent. who departed this life Oct. 22, 1718, aged 60.
Also MAGDALEN, his wife died Feb. 21, 1715, aged 50. Also Capt JOHN
ASHEHURST died 27 Sept. 1729, aged 39 years 11 months & 16 days.

CHURCHYARD.

807. A large vault, now empty, which belonged to the Adams Castle estate ;
the property of the Walronds, then Elliotts. It has no inscription.

The following persons were once buried therein :—

1807 July 31 Mrs Thomasina Goddard.
1808 Feb. 22 Mary Anna Maria inf. dau. of the Hon. Tho. Chase.

1812   July   6   Dorcas Chase, another dau. of the Hon. Tho. Chase.
1812   Aug.   9   Hon. Tho. Chase.
1816   Sep. 25   Sam. Brewster Ames, an infant.
1816   Nov. 17   Sam. Brewster. Shot Ap. 15; brought from S¹ Philips.
1819   July   7   Thomasina Clarke and an elder sister.

Owing to mysterious movements of the coffins after the vault had been sealed up, they were all removed and buried elsewhere in the churchyard. See Aspinall's "West Indian Tales of Old," p. 224.

———

There are several large stone tombs without names.

808. Large vault :—

J. T. CHAPMAN | APRIL 1ST | 1852.

ANN ELIZABETH | WIFE OF | THOS. L. R. CHAPMAN | DIED 23 APRIL 1883 AGED 34.

———

809. Marble slab on stone tomb :—

SARAH TURPIN DIED 7 Oct. 1863 AGED 73.

REV. JOSEPH THOS. PIGOTT DIED 9TH AUGUST 1868 AGED 60.

———

810. White marble slab on six columns enclosed by railing :—

SACRED | TO THE MEMORY OF | JOHN JACOB GILGEOUS ESQRE | LATE PROPRIETOR | OF WINDSOR CASTLE ESTATE, | BRITISH GUIANA, | BORN AT BARBADOES, | 12TH SEPTEMBER 1781, | AND DEPARTED THIS LIFE | 4TH AUGUST 1841 | (9 lines; erected by widow and son.)

———

811. Tomb: "RICHARD KIRTON 1838."

812.   „   "EVELYN."

813.   „   "AMBROSE ATWELL died April 17th 1844."

814.   „   "R. REECE 1823."

815. Stone to " Waterman," with M.I.

———

816. Large tomb with grey marble slab at top :—

This Marble | is intended to perpetuate | the Memory of | JAMES REECE | Son of | ROBERT and SARAH REECE | who died | October the 25th 1811 | Aged 21 Days.

———

ADAMS CASTLE, PLANTATION.

817. There are two fragments of a thick blue marble slab lying in the yard, which fit together, and give eleven lines :—

> In obitum charissimi Patris Sui,
> Domini Roberti Hacket* Militis
> Qui ex hac vita migravit ultima die
> Calendarum Martis anno Domini 1679

> (Blank space here.)

> His jacet Reliquies Sac optima
> Nobilis et pruden[s candi . ta .] Sarcophago
> Quis [valeat] lachrymas [manentes sistere guttas]
> Quis cohibere potel t [vir pius ecce jacet]
> Te placant [nati] plor[ant charissima conjux]
> Mæfta domus pueri[luget et omnis inops]
> [Flere nefas] raptũ[in cœlesti sede beatum]

The words within brackets are from Archer, who also gives five more lines, now lost.

> Indigenus nobis qui Jove dignus erat
> Non decet elysium miseris implere querelis
> Hoc bona meus virtus, hoc pietasque dedit
> Virida perpetuum durabit fama per ævum
> Pensabit vitam gloria longa brevem.

1692, Nov. 23. Robert s. of Col. Robert Hacket. (Bur. St. John's.)
1678-9, March 3. Robert Hackett. (Burial Register.)
He was knighted at Whitehall 23 Nov. 1677. (Le Neve.)
Sir John Bawdon sent to Nevis " Mr Hacket brother to Sir Richard (*sic*) Hacket of B. & an excellent refiner." (Oldmixon, ii., 237.)
Sir John Yeamans, Bart., in his will 1671, names: My dau. Mrs Frances Hackett now wife of Robert H., Esq.
Wm., 1 s. Rob. Hackett of B'os, eq. aur. X^t Ch., matric. 27 May 1680, a. 17 ; subs. as of Merton Coll., d. 17 & bur. 19 Nov. 1708 in the outward chapel of Merton Coll. (Foster.)

HANNAY'S PLANTATION.

818. Archer recorded the following, but no trace of it is known by the present occupant of the estate :—

GEORGE INCE son of JOHN & MARGARET INCE buried March 9, 172. | 11 months old : and MARGARET, daughter of JOHN & MARGARET INCE, | buried July 13, 1734 . . 13 years, 2 months, and 21 days.

John Ince, P. of C. in 1803, was probably grandson of John and Margaret.

BANNATYNE PLANTATION.

819. Archer also noted two fragments here, part of a Latin inscription, to " Surgeon Carew " by his brother " Chr. Carew."

1680, April 23. John Carew (burial).
1662, July 24. Chr. C. gent. for 12,100 lbs of sugar sells 30 a. n^r Oistins Bay in X^t Ch. (vol. ii., p. 561).

---

* A crack has destroyed the second " t."

THE RIDGE PLANTATION.

820. I saw the remains of two stone vaults here, but without names. One belonged to the family of Wm. Trotman.

COVERLEY PLANTATION.

821. There is an empty tomb, but Sir Fred. Clarke, who resides here, assured me there was no name nor inscription.

NEAR MILITARY HOSPITAL.

822. A stone to Hugh Blair 4th Bat. d. 11 Aug. 1831. (Report on Historic Sites, p. 7.)

NAVY LAND.

823. Stone to Wm. Alfred & James sons of Peter Bayne Q^r M^r of the 4th Kings Own Reg. & of Eliza his wife; the former d. 1 July 1822 & the latter 12 Oct. 1825. (*Ibid.*)

SEARLES PLANTATION.

824. In a cane piece (at the back of a little hut occupied by a poor white woman who lives on the proceeds of one acre, part of an ancient charity) is a marble slab with the top broken off and lost. There is part of a shield with traces of Arms:—*A chevron, in base a martlet :—*

Here lyeth Interred ye Body | of CHARLES COLLINS Esqr | who Departed this life ye 3 | of July 1697 Aged 70th (*sic*) years.

There is a gap in the Burial Register 18 Oct. 1694 to 7 April 1700. He was a judge of Speights Bay in 1686. (Col. Cal., p. 180.)

ST. MATTHIAS DISTRICT CHURCH.

825. Brass in chancel :—

TO THE GLORY OF GOD | AND IN LOVING MEMORY OF | WILLIAM PHILLIPS CLARKE | WHO DIED 12TH DECEMBER 1895. | AT MONTE CARLO | PRINCIPALITY OF MONACO. | THIS EAST WINDOW WAS ERECTED BY HIS WIDOW. | R.I.P.

---

826. On brass rod of communion rail :—

FROM M. J. HARDING TO THE GLORY OF GOD AND IN LOVING MEMORY OF MY SISTER AGNES D. WALCOTT WHO DIED 29TH NOVEMBER 1893.

---

827. Brass lectern :—

FROM R. ROBINSON | TO THE GLORY OF GOD | AND | IN LOVING MEMORY OF | MY SISTER | S. E. HARDINGE | WHO DIED | 7TH FEBRUARY | 1892.

828. Oblong brass behind Vicar's seat south side of chancel arch :—

𝔉𝔯𝔬𝔪 𝔐. 𝔍. ℌ𝔞𝔯𝔡𝔦𝔫𝔤 | 𝔗𝔬 𝔱𝔥𝔢 𝔊𝔩𝔬𝔯𝔶 𝔬𝔣 𝔊𝔬𝔡 | & 𝔦𝔫 𝔩𝔬𝔟𝔦𝔫𝔤 𝔪𝔢𝔪𝔬𝔯𝔶 𝔬𝔣 𝔪𝔶 𝔰𝔦𝔰𝔱𝔢𝔯 | 𝔄𝔤𝔫𝔢𝔰 𝔇: 𝔚𝔞𝔩𝔠𝔬𝔱𝔱 | 𝔴𝔥𝔬 𝔡𝔦𝔢𝔡 29𝔱𝔥 𝔑𝔬𝔟𝔢𝔪𝔟𝔢𝔯 1893.

829. Brass. North wall of nave :—

IN | FOND & LOVING MEMORY OF | SARAH HENRY CRUMPTON | WIDOW & RELICT OF | THE LATE HENRY CRUMPTON | SECRETARY OF THE BARBADOS | MUTUAL LIFE ASSURANCE SOCIETY | BORN 21ST MARCH 1837 | DIED 26TH JUNE 1910 | (4 lines) | THIS TABLET IS PLACED | HERE AS A TRIBUTE OF FILIAL AFFECTION & | ESTEEM TO AN EVER DEVOTED & LOVING MOTHER | BY HER ELDEST SON ERNEST.

830. Brass, same wall :—

IN LOVING MEMORY OF | HENRY CROMPTON | FOR FORTY YEARS IN THE EMPLOY OF THE BARBADOS | MUTUAL LIFE ASSURANCE SOCIETY & FOR THIRTY TWO | YEARS SECRETARY OF THE SAME. | ALSO FOR MANY | YEARS LAY-REPRESENTATIVE IN THE DIOCESAN SYNOD | OF THIS ISLAND FOR ST MATTHIAS' DISTRICT | BORN 11TH NOVEMBER 1834 | DIED 1ST FEBRUARY 1895 | (4 lines) | THIS TABLET IS PLACED HERE BY HIS | ELDEST SON ERNEST.

ST. MATHIAS CHURCHYARD.

The Rev. John S. Hughes, the Vicar, told me that this monument formerly stood in the Savannah.

831. White marble tomb :—

At west end. Above is, in an oval, a painting of the steam frigate "H.M.S. DAUNTLESS 33 GUNS 330 MEN EDWARD PELLEW HALSTED CAPTAIN." A blue coiled rope surrounds it.

Below :—

AROUND THIS TOMB, | REST THE REMAINS OF | FIFTEEN OFFICERS | & THE CAPTAIN'S STEWARD | OF H.M. SCREW FRIGATE DAUNTLESS, | WHO, TOGETHER WITH THIRTY-EIGHT SEAMEN | TEN MARINES, & TEN BOYS, | BURIED IN THIS GARRISON ; | AND ONE OFFICER, THREE SEAMEN, | SIX MARINES, & ONE BOY, | COMMITTED TO THE DEEP ; | ALL PERISHED BY YELLOW FEVER, | WHICH BROKE OUT AT SEA, | ON LEAVING THE HARBOUR OF ST THOMAS, | ON THE 10TH OF NOVEMBER 1852.

At east end, a like oval. CREST.—*A lion rampant ;* and on garter : "DAUNTLESS."

THIS HALLOWED SPOT | WAS PURCHASED & ENCLOSED, | & THIS MONUMENT INSCRIBED | IN HONORED MEMORY | TO ALL WHO PERISHED, | BY THE LORDS COMMISSIONERS OF | THE ADMIRALTY, | THE CAPTAIN, & SURVIVING OFFICERS | OF THE SHIP, | & BY | THE SORROWING RELATIVES & FRIENDS | OF THOSE WHO REST BELOW, | THAT THEIR SACRED & BELOVED REMAINS | SHOULD AWAIT IN UNDISTURBED REPOSE | ·FOR THE COMING OF THAT GREAT DAY, | WHEN ALL GRAVES SHALL BE SUMMONED | TO GIVE UP THEIR DEAD.

Below this is a list of boys, which I have omitted.

South side of tomb:—

THIS ISLAND AT ONCE AFFORDED A GENEROUS REFUGE | & BY THE UNCEASING CARE OF ITS CIVIL MILITARY & MEDICAL AUTHORITIES, | THE SHIP WITH HER SURVIVING CREW RESTORED TO HEALTH, | WAS ENABLED TO SAIL HOMEWARDS ON | THE 21ST OF MARCH 1853. | COL. SIR WILLIAM M. G. COLEBROOKE C.B. K.H. GOVERNOR IN CHIEF | LIEUT. GEN. WILLIAM WOOD, C.B. COMMANDING THE TROOPS | THE THIRTY FOURTH REGIMENT, THE SIXTY-NINTH REGIMENT.

Below is a list of seamen, which I have omitted.

WILLIAM MUNRO ESQRE INSPECTOR GENERAL OF HOSPITALS | REVD WILLIAM W. JACKSON M.A. CHAPLAIN OF THE FORCES | WILLIAM DENNY ESQRE SURGEON 34TH REGIMENT | ALEXANDER B. CLELAND ESQRE M.D. SURGEON 69TH REGIMENT.

Below is a list of seamen, which I have omitted.

On the north face:—

ROSS MOORE FLOUD, FIRST LIEUTENANT,	ÆTAT 37,	OBIIT 28TH Nov. 1852.
CHARLES KENT, SECOND LIEUTENANT,	28,	2ND DEC.
ALFRED NEALE, THIRD LIEUTENANT,	25,	22ND Nov.
WILLIAM SIMPSON, LIEUTENANT,	23,	17TH Nov.
ALEXANDER LANGLANDS, CHIEF ENGINEER,	32,	22ND Nov.
ARTHUR C. COUPER (BURIED OFF THE PORT), MATE,	21,	17TH Nov.
HENRY I. NUTTALL, SECOND MASTER,	28,	23RD Nov.
EDWIN DEATH, CAPTAIN'S CLERK,	27,	6TH DEC.
GEORGE GORDON BUSHBY, MIDSHIPMAN,	20,	14TH DEC.
JOSEPH CRISPIN, MIDSHIPMAN,	15,	1ST DEC.
FLEETWOOD PELLEW HASWELL, MASTER'S ASSISTANT,	18,	14TH DEC.
CHARLES MARTIN, ASSISTANT ENGINEER,	28,	25TH Nov.
ST GEORGE G. S. DAVIS, ASSISTANT ENGINEER,	25,	2ND DEC.
JAMES T. HENWOOD, ASSISTANT ENGINEER,	21,	18TH Nov.
WALTER W. H. RICHARDS, ASSISTANT ENGINEER,	21,	24TH Nov.
WILLIAM WELMAN, CARPENTER,	40,	15TH DEC.
JAMES VENABLES, CAPTAIN'S STEWARD,	23,	12TH DEC.

Below is a list of marines, which I have omitted.

Around the tomb is a paved area of white marble with surnames of officers. An iron railing encloses it, and the whole is in very good order.

1852, Nov. 17. On board H.M.S. Dauntless, at B., Arthur C. Couper, 4th s. of Col. Sir Geo. C. Bart. ("G.M.," 216.)

1852, Nov. 22. At B. of yellow fever, aged 25, Lt. Alfred Neale, of H.M.S. Dauntless, s. of John Corbett Neale, of West-end House Wickwar. (*Ibid.*, 216.)

1852, Nov. 25. In the W.I. of yellow fever, Ross Moore Floud, senior Lt. of H.M. steam frigate Dauntless. He was the s. of the l. Tho. F. of Exeter, entered the Navy 1829, & gained his Lieutenancy in 1840 for his conduct at the battle of St Jean d'Acre. He had subsequently served in Hazard 18, Spartan 26, & as first of the Nimrod 20. The Dauntless (Capt. Halsted) has lost 16 of her officers & 60 of her crew by the same disease. (*Ibid.*, 216.)

1852, Dec. 2. At B. aged 26, St. George C. Sperling Davis, of H.M.'s s. Dauntless, only s. of the l. Comm. G. E. J. D. R.N. & grands. of the l. John Sperling of Dynes Hall, Essex. (*Ibid.*, 217.)

1852, Dec. 2. At B. aged 28, Cha. Kent, 2d Lt of H.M.S. Dauntless, 2d s. of the l. Cha. K. of Brickling Lodge, Norfolk. (*Ibid.*, 1853, p. 329.)

1852, Dec. 12. Drowned at B. aged 25, Tho. Pat. Rowlatt, chief officer of the R.M.S. Derwent. (*Ibid.*, 1853, 217.)

832. North side of churchyard:—

Under a jessamy tree is a brick vault with top stone slab, which has never had any inscription.

There are three tombs side by side at north-east corner.

833. On white marble let into the top slab :—

SACRED | to the memory | *of* | Thomas Salkeld Esq. | late master of | Hastings Grammar School | who departed this life | Oct* 12** 1852. | aged 25 years | His pupils, in whose memory | his name is embalmed | have placed this humble | tribute | of affection over his mortal | remains in testimony of | their high esteem | for his departed | worth | fama semper viret.

TAGGART   BARBADOS.

---

834. Sacred | to the memory of | William French, | who departed this life | Dec* 10** 1852 | Aged 24 | He was a native of Blaxham Oxfordshire | & master of the Highgate school | in this island | This tomb is placed over his remains | as a last tribute of respect | by his sorrowing widow.

---

835. To the memory of | Henry Williams Esq** B.A. | of Wadham College Oxford | & master of the | Hastings Grammar School | in this island | who departed this life | the 16** May 1853 | Aged 25 years.

As 6 son of Robert of Llangewny, co. Brecon, gent., he matric. from Wadham Coll. 26 June 1846, a. 18, B.A. 1850. (Foster.)

There is a group of five tombs close to the north wall of chancel :—

836. 𝔖𝔞𝔠𝔯𝔢𝔡 𝔱𝔬 𝔱𝔥𝔢 𝔪𝔢𝔪𝔬𝔯𝔶 | of | 𝕰𝕯𝖂𝕬𝕽𝕯 𝕷. 𝕯𝕴𝕾𝕻𝕰𝖄; | 3𝔯𝔡 𝔖𝔬𝔫 of | 𝕮𝕬𝕻𝕿𝕹 𝕳. 𝕬. 𝕿𝖀𝕽𝕹𝕰𝕽, 𝕽.𝕬. | 𝕯𝔢𝔭𝔞𝔯𝔱𝔢𝔡 𝔦𝔫 𝔭𝔢𝔞𝔠𝔢 20 𝕹𝔬𝔳* 1852 | 𝕬𝔤𝔢𝔡 4 𝖄𝔯* 6 𝕸* | (4 lines.)

---

837. Sacred to the memory | of | R. MATHILDA. S. Eldest daughter of | CAPT** H. A. TURNER, R.A. | Departed in peace 16** Nov. 1852 | Aged 7 Y** | 2 M* | (4 lines.)

---

838. 𝔖𝔞𝔠𝔯𝔢𝔡 𝔱𝔬 𝔱𝔥𝔢 𝔪𝔢𝔪𝔬𝔯𝔶 | of | FRED** MORSE, | 2** son of | CAPT** H. A. TURNER, R.A. | Departed in peace 1** Oct* 1852 | Aged 9 Y** 8 M* | (4 lines.)

---

839. White marble slab :—

FANNY KEMP | CLELAND, | THE CHERISHED WIFE OF | A. B. CLELAND M.D. | SURGEON TO H.M. 69** REGIMENT, | DIED OF FEVER, | AFTER FIVE DAYS ILLNESS, | SEPTEMBER 24** 1852, | AGED 34 YEARS | (11 lines.)

---

840. White marble let into top slab :—

IN MEMORY | OF | ANNE MARY HUTTON | WIFE OF | RICHARD HOLT HUTTON | & DAUGHTER OF | THE LATE | WILLIAM STANLEY ROSCOE. | She died from yellow fever | during a visit to Barbadoes, | on the 21** Dec; A.D. 1852, | Aged 31 Years | (2 lines.)

R

841. At east end of chancel wall :—

In Memory | of | Eliz Augusta | Youngest Daughter | of | Doctor Wilton George Turner | who died after a lingering illnefs of eight years | on the 5th of October 1853 | Aged 14 Years | (3 lines.)*

ST. GEORGE'S CHURCH.

There are fourteen slabs in the floor of the nave and one in the north porch.

842. On a white stone in the middle walk :—

Beneath this Stone | are depofited the Remains | of *JOSEPH JORDAN Efq^r* | of the Parifh of *Saint-George* | who departed this Life | on the 29th Day of March 1752 | Aged 63 Years | Alfo | of *ELIZABETH* his Wife | who departed this Life | Sepr 6th 1761, Aged 66 Years. | Likewife | of *EDWARD JORDAN* | Son of *Doctor JOSEPH JORDAN* | who departed this Life | Augt 15th 1780, Aged 19 Years. | And | of *WILLIAM WALKER JORDAN* | Brother to the above *EDWARD* | who departed this Life | Decr 31st 1781, Aged 23 Years | This Stone is placed | by *Doctor JOSEPH JORDAN* | (5 lines; to memory of his parents and children.)

See No. 198.

843. Grey stone, middle walk :—

Beneath this Stone lie the Remains | of | SAMUEL RAMSEY Senior, | who departed this Life July 29, 1813, | Aged 59 Years | (15 lines; placed by his son.)

844. Blue marble, under seats :—

Here Lyeth the Body | of Iane the wife of | Thomas Meell Chirurgeon | who Departed this Life y^e | 23th day of Iuly 1680 | Aged 29 years | And alfo of Iohn his Son | who was Buried the 17th | of Iuly 1678 aged about | two years & halfe.

845. Grey marble, under seats :—

Here lieth | The Body of Mary Berney, Relict | of Robert Berney Esqr | (15 lines) | Ob^t 17th July 1783 Ætat. 75 years.

846. Blue marble, in cross walk :—

ALEXANDER BRUCE | Doctor in Physick | Died Novr 3 |
Anno $\begin{cases} \text{Dom}^1 \ 1768 \\ \text{Ætatis } 37 \end{cases}$
Peculiar Blefsings bear y^e shortest Date !

3rd son of the Hon. James B. by Keturah French his wife. He graduated at Edinburgh.

847. Middle walk :—

Here lyeth Interred the Body of | Doctor *JOHN BATTYN* of yᵉ Pariſh | of Sʳ George, who departed this Life | *January* the 7ᵗʰ 1692. | Also the Body of WILLIAM REES | BATTYN, *Eſqʳ* | Grandſon to the above | mentioned Doctor Battyn who depart | -ed this Life the 14ᵗʰ of *August*, 1734, | Aged thirty Years | And also the Body of ELIZABETH yᵉ | Wife of EDWARD BRACE, *Eſqʳ* and | Daughter of the above mentioned Docʳ | *John Battyn*, ſhe departed this Life | the 26ᵗʰ day of *October*, 1736, | Aged, fifty ſeven Years.

See " Caribbeana," ii., 183.   Archer gives " Perce " for Brace.

———

848. Blue marble :—

Here lieth the Body | of KATHARINE, | Widow of The Hon. RICHARD WORSAM Eſqu* | late Member of HIS MAJESTY'S Council | of the Iſland of BARBADOS ; | who departed this Life Auguſt 25ᵗʰ 1769 | aged 52 Years | (4 lines) | Here alſo lie | JOHN, RICHARD-WORSAM, and CHARLOTTE | three Infant Children of | JOHN and CHARLES PRETTEJOHN ; | and Grand-children of the above KATHARINE WORSAM. | Here alſo lieth | CHARLOTTE, Wife of WILLIAM HUSTLER, Eſquire, | of ACKLAM-HALL, in the County of YORK ; | Daughter of | GEORGE and HENRIETTA-CONSTANTIA MEADE, | of PHILADELPHIA ; | and Grand-daughter of the above KATHARINE WORSAM, | who died 25ᵗʰ December, 1801 ; | aged 20 Years | Here alſo lieth | JOHN PRETTEJOHN, Eſquire, | (Son-in-law of the above KATHARINE WORSAM,) who departed this Life 29ᵗʰ June, 1803 ; | aged 72 Years | Here alſo lieth | LOUISA, the Infant daughter of Brigadier- | General | FREDERICK MAITLAND, and KATHARINE WORSAM MEADE | the Grand-daughter of the above KATHARINE WORSAM, | who departed this Life 27ᵗʰ September, 1803 ; | aged 8 Months.

1680, June 29. Jnᵒ Worsam Esq : Ch : (St. Michael's). See No. 861.

———

849. Blue marble, under seats :—

TO | the Memory of | The Revᵈ *JOHN CARTER* M.A. | who died | October the 21ˢᵗ 1796 | (5 lines ; placed by widow.)

1740, May 30. Revᵈ John Carter & Elizabeth Reynolds Alleyne (St. Michael). See monument later, No. 862.

———

850. Under seats :—

Beneath this Stone lie the Remains | of the Reverend *THOMAS FALCON* A.M. | Fellow of Queens College in Oxford | And Maſter of Codrington College | In this Iſland | He departed this Life February 4ᵗʰ 1762 | Aged 33 Years | (4 lines.)

Tho. Falcon, s. of Michael F. of Workington, Cumb. pleb. Q. Coll. matric. 31 Oct. 1745, a. 16 ; B.A. 1751, M.A. by decree of convocation 10 Feb. 1755, then of Cod. Coll. B. (Foster.)

———

851. Blue marble, under seats.   Hour glass, skull and crossbones, and festoon at top :—

Here lyeth Interred the Body of | MRS ELIZABETH IOHNSTOUN | who departed this life the 18ᵗʰ | of Iuly 1729, in the 69 Year of | her Age | Also | Are Deposited the Remains of | the Honᵇˡᵉ RICHARD SALTER, | Grand Son to the Above Lady, he | Departed this life the 6ᵗʰ Augᵗ 1776, | Aged 66 Years.

See the tablet to him later, No. 860.

* Cemented.

852. Blue marble, under seats:—

HENRY PETER KING Esqr | died (*blank*) aged | (*blank*) | This Stone was *Placed* Over | his Grave, as *order'd* | by his Grand-daughter | *SUSANNAH GOSLING, Widow* | in 1792.

853. Blue marble, under seats near pulpit:—

Here Lieth Interred the Body of | DRAX SHETTERDEN Esq Who | Departed this Life the 26th Day | of May 1699 in the 24th Year | of His Age.

A pew rests on his age.

Henry Drax, Esq., by his will dated 30 June 1682, gave his estate to his nephew Tho. Shetterden, eldest son of testator's sister Eliz., with remainder to Drax S., brother of Tho.

Eliz., 3rd dau. of Sir James Drax of this parish, mar. Tho. Shetterden of co. Herts (licence dated 25 Sept. 1666, he aged 31 and she 17). They had two sons, an elder Henry who, as heir to his uncle Col. Henry Drax, took that surname, and a younger Drax.

854. White marble, under seats. Jacobean shield in sunk oval:—

CREST.—*A swan, wings raised.*
ARMS.—*Gules, a chevron between three swans close.*

Here lies Interr'd the | Honble Col. *PAUL LYTE* | who Departed this Life | in the Year 1687 | Also | the Honble Coll. PAUL LYTE Esqr Son of the | above paul lyte. who departed this life in the | Year 1708 | Also | the body of Iane Iones, wife of the above | paul lyte, who departed this life the 13th | day of Octr 1755 aged 72 Years. | Also | the Honble IOHN LYTE Son of the | above paul lyte Esqr and Iane Iones | who departed this life the 17th day | of May 17 . 7 aged 61 years.

There was a family of Lyte of Lytes Cary whose pedigree was entered in the Visitation of co. Som., and whose arms were identical with the above. John Lyte, the Speaker of this Island, mar. a dau. and coheiress of Henry Peers.

? 1767. A pew rests on the date.

855. Blue marble, under seats:—

Underneath this Stone | are deposited the remains | of | TIMOTHY THORNHILL Esqr | who was born June 26th 1747 | and died April 25th 1813 | aged 65 Years.

1813, April 26. This day was buried by me in Church Timothy Thornhill Esqr of St Michaels husband to Mrs Elizabeth S. Thornhill. Anth^y H^y Thomas, A.B. She died at Jackmans in this parish Nov. following.

1813, April 27. Died on Sunday last and was buried on the following day at St. George's Church, Timothy T. Esq. a very respectable character, and a Captain in the Army. (Burial Register.)

856. North porch:—

On ye Northside of this tomb-stone | lyeth interred ye Body of | CHALES (*sic*) SAWYER ye S . . | ANN SAWYER who D . . . . this | life November ye 2, 1701 | Being in his 18th year.

857. Nave, south wall, beginning at east end. There are six white marble tablets and one brass. Marble of various colours :—

SACRED to the Memory | of the *Honble THOMAS APPLEWHAITE ESQ^r* | one of the *Honble* MEMBERS of his Majesties | Council, in this *Island, Lieut* GENERAL of the | Forces here, *Presid^t* of the Councils of War | Master GENERAL, of the *Ordnance,* and | *Colonel,* of the Windward | Regiment of Foot | He Died the 14 day of Iune | 1749 | Aged 59 Years | Also M^n *ELIZABETH APPLEWHAITE* Wife | of the above-mentioned *THO^S APPLEWHAITE* | Esqr. She Died the 11 April 1750 | Aged 59 Years.
(There are marks below where some decoration has been—possibly a shield.)
He was President. Tho. A. was a planter in 1672. Mr. John A. was buried at St. Michael 9 June 1672. (See "Caribbeana," ii., 187.)

858. SACRED | TO THE MEMORY OF | THE HONORABLE FORSTER CLARKE, | LATE MEMBER OF COUNCIL, COLONEL OF MILITIA, | AN EMINENT PLANTER, AND FOR MANY YEARS ONE OF THE | REPRESENTATIVES OF THE GENERAL ASSEMBLY OF THIS ISLAND | (7 lines) | HE DEPARTED THIS LIFE ON THE SECOND DAY OF JANUARY | IN THE YEAR OF OUR LORD ONE THOUSAND EIGHT HUNDRED AND FORTY ; | AGED 63 | (3 lines ; by widow and children.)

1850, Nov. 19. At B., Major Cha. Edw. Michel, 66th Reg. to Emily-Spooner, eldest dau. of Sir R. B. Clarke, K.C.B. Chief Justice of B. (" G.M." for 1851, 196.)

859. On brass below preceding :—

In Remembrance of GEORGE ELLIOTT CLARKE | Proprietor of Stepney Plantation who died at Frampost | East Grinstead, Sussex, England on the twenty second | of February 1877 | (erected by daughters.)

860. On a medallion is shewn the face of deceased :—

NOLLEKENS F^t ;

The Honble RICHARD SALTER, | many years a member of his Majesty's | Council of this Island an unbiass'd Senator, | an upright Magistrate, an honest man, | departed this life Augt 6th 1776, Aged 66. | His disconsolate widow Margaret daughter | of Ioseph & Sarah Salmon erected this | monument to the best of Husbands.

Below on a Chippendale shield are :—

CREST.—*A lion rampant.*
ARMS.—*Argent, on a chevron engrailed between three choughs as many crescents.*
On an inescutcheon : Quarterly, 1 and 4, *a saltire between four spears or fusils (?) ;* 2 and 3, *Argent, three salmon hauriant.*
See No. 260 and " W.I. Bookplates," No. 233.
He was son of the Hon. Timothy S., who was a M. of C. 1713 and 1723. Col. Richard S. commanded a Barbadian regiment in 1692 against Martinique.

861. SACRED TO THE MEMORY | OF JOHN PRETTEJOHN, ESQUIRE; | WHO WAS BORN THE 29TH OF OCTOBER 1731, AND DIED THE 29TH OF JUNE, 1803 | (many lines; erected by his widow Charlotte.)

CREST.—Broken off and missing.
ARMS.—*A lion passant between three mullets Or*; impaling, Quarterly, 1 and 4, *A lion passant between three pheons Sable*; 2 and 3, worn off.
MOTTO.—VINDICAT VIRT . S AST . A.   See No. 848, *ante.*

1801, Nov. 23.   John P. of B. to Miss Augusta Buckley.   ("G.M.," 1209.)
1803, July 29.   At Bath, the wife of John P. jun. of B. a dau.   (*Ibid.*, 787.)
1803, June 29.   At B. in his 73d year, John P.   (*Ibid.*, 882.)
1830, Aug. 16.   At Reading, in her 19th year, Charlotte, relict of John P. l. of B.   (*Ibid.*, 188.)
1840, April 8.   At Paston, co. Northampton, John P. of B. & Harehatch, Berks, to Laura, yst. dau. of Cha. Cole of Paston Hall.   (*Ibid.*, 536.)

———

862. A very fine white marble monument, with an urn at the top :—

On spade shield : *Per chevron Gules and Ermine, two talbots' heads erased* (facing to sinister) *in chief*; impaling, *Argent, a chevron Gules between three Catherine wheels.*

To | The Memory of | The Revd *JOHN CARTER* A.M. | (26 lines; near 50 years Rector, and for more than half that period Minister; erected by vestry) | died October the 21st 1796, Aged 90.

John Carter, s. of John C. of I. of B. esq. Q. Coll. matric. 14 May 1730, a. 18, but this does not agree with the date of birth as given by the M.I.

———

863. Sacred to the Memory of | Thos CARMICHAELL Esqre; Son of ARCHIBALD CARMICHAELL | & FRANCES his Wife, formerly FRANCES APPLEWHITE, WHO | departed this Life the 11th day of April 1789 aged 52 Years | (10 lines.)

———

864. On the west wall, north side of door :—

BARBADOS 1831 | A TRIBUTE OF FILIAL AFFECTION, TO THE MEMORY OF | SAMUEL AND MERCY DRAYTON.

1846, Dec. 26.   At St. John's Wood, Wm. Drayton, l. of B.   ("G.M.," 1847, p. 214.)

———

864 A. On the south side of door :—

Within this Sacred Enclosure | lie deposited the Remains of | *EDMUND KEYZAR* | Who resigned a life of 29 Years | on the 11th August 1795, | Together with those of his Consort | *ELIZABETH ANN KEYZAR* | Who departed this life | the 22nd July 1804 in the 33rd Year | of her Age.

———

865. On the north wall, commencing at the west end :—

IN MEMORY OF | GEORGE HALL, | TENTH AND YOUNGEST SON OF
WILLIAM HALL OF TULLEY | IN THE COUNTY OF DONEGALL, IRELAND, OF LOCUST
HALL ESTATE, IN THIS PARISH, | AND MANY YEARS A MERCHANT IN BRIDGETOWN |
WHO DEPARTED THIS LIFE ON THE 12ᵀᴴ OF SEPTᴿ 1810, | AGED THIRTY-FOUR
YEARS | AND WHOSE REMAINS LIE INTERRED WITHIN THESE WALLS ; | THIS STONE
IS ERECTED | BY HIS ONLY SURVIVING BROTHER ; | (11 lines.)

CREST.—*A stork statant, in its right foot a roundle.*
ARMS.—*Sable, a chevron Or between three cranes' heads erased, a border of the
second charged with eight trefoils of the first.*

(? Hall of Dunglass, Scotland.)

---

866. A large marble monument with the figure of Isabella and the pot of
basil ; above is an urn with medallions, on which are carved the faces of a man
and woman, all finely executed and signed " J. TYLEY Bristol " :—

To the Memory of HENRY TROTMAN Esq : | For many years a
representative of this Parish : | Who was universally esteemed | (etc., 3 lines) |
And to the Memory of ELIZABETH his Wife, | who was | (etc., 2 lines) |
This Monument is erected with filial affection | by THOMAS CLARK
TROTMAN, | ELIZABETH died Aug. 26ᵗʰ 1790 Aged 60 | HENRY
TROTMAN died Decʳ 8, 1804 Aged 68 | (1 line.)

1793, Sept. In Temple-pl. the Lady of Tho. Trotman, esq. lately arrived from
B. (" G.M.," 867.)
Tho. Clark T. d. 7 May 1826, a. 58. M.I. at Clifton. (" Caribbeana," ii.,
372.)

---

867. Over the porch on a decorated marble oval :—

Erected from the | Ruins of an unsparing Storm | In the year of Grace
1784 | By the spirited and unwearied Exertions of | HENRY TROTMAN
Church warden. | The applauding Parishioners in Zeal unshaken by the | wild
uproar of the Elements, rejoice to see their Church | with Dignity restored ; and
no longer remember with regret | the former House | (6 lines) | The Revᵈ
JOHN CARTER Rector.

---

868. A fine white marble oval, surmounted by an urn wreathed, and with a
shield of arms in the centre. ARMS :—*Argent, three battle-axes Sable* (Gibbes) ;
impaling, *Per chevron Gules and Ermine in chief two lions' heads erased Or*
(Alleyne) :—

Sacred to the memory OF CHRISTIAN GIBBS, | Consort of JOHN
GIBBS, | Daughter of the honourable REYNOLD ALLEYNE, | (34 lines) |
She dyed Feb. 22, 1780, aged 77 years.

---

869. SACRED | TO THE MEMORY OF | SARAH PAYNE, | THE AFFECTIONATE
AND BELOVED WIFE | OF WILLIAM BYNOE, | AND YOUNGEST DAUGHTER OF |
THE LATE JAMES CRAGG KELLMAN, | ALL OF THIS PARISH. | SHE DIED IN
LIVERPOOL | ON THE 25ᵀᴴ OF JUNE 1857 | AGED 28 YEARS | AND WAS INTERRED IN
THE CEMETERY | OF Sᵗ JAMES IN THAT TOWN | (6 lines ; by her husband.)

See her father's stone, No. 899.

870. This monument is a facsimile of the Gibbs one:—

ARMS.—*Two leopards' faces in pale, between as many flaunches Or.*
CREST.—This has been lost.

On a panel at the foot of the urn:—

M' FRERE | died 24ʰ May 1792 | Aged 50 Years.

Below this :—

In this monument are depofited the remains | of the honorable HENRY
FRERE | (22 lines; military officer, President of C.; lost his wife; left his
fortune to his niece, whom he had educated.)

See W.I. bookplates No. 188.   There is a large picture in the Church by Sir
Benjamin West which was given by Mr. Frere.

See the M.I. to Dorothy his wife at Christ Church.   By his will dated 19 May
and proved 10 Nov. 1792 (558, Fountain) he left his estate to his great-niece
Dorothy Jones, dau. of Rob. Burnet J., Atty.-Gen., by Eliz. Susanna, dau. of
Sam. Estwick, M.P., by Eliz. Frere, sister of testator.

----

871. On a small tablet:—

SACRED TO THE MEMORY OF | ANNE WILHELMINA, THE WIFE OF
CHARLES HENRY DARLING ESQᴿᴱ | (PRIVATE SECRETARY TO THE
GOVERNOR OF THIS ISLAND) | AND DAUGHTER OF ALLEN DALZELL ESQᴿᴱ OF
BUTTALLS IN THE PARISH OF Sᵀ GEORGE. | HER MORTAL REMAINS REST IN A
NEIGHBOURING ISLAND: | BUT THIS TABLET IS ERECTED IN THE CHURCH OF HER
NATIVE PARISH | (4 lines) | BORN 13ᵀᴴ JULY 1813, DIED 16ᵀᴴ OCTOBER 1837 |
SACRED ALSO TO THE MEMORY OF | CHARLES HENRY HAY DARLING, |
THE INFANT SON OF CHARLES HENRY DARLING ESQᴿᴱ | WHO DIED ON THE 18ᵀᴴ
NOVEMBER 1837, AGED 1 YEAR AND 9 MONTHS.

See the tablet to her in Clifton Church.   ("Caribbeana," ii., 373.)   She was
mar. in 1835.   He was eldest son of Maj.-Gen. Henry Cha. Darling, Lt.-Gov. of
Tobago, and was b. in 1809; became Gov. of several colonies, a K.C.B., and d. at
Cheltenham 25 Jan. 1870.   M.I. in the New Cemetery.   He mar. 2ndly in 1841
the eldest dau. of the Hon. Joshua Billings Nurse of B., who died 1848.
("D.N.B.")

----

872. On a small brass :—

IN MEMORY OF | JOHN PHILLIPS MASON | AND OF ANNA MATILDA
HIS WIFE | LATE OF BULKELEY IN THIS PARISH | (1 line; erected by their
children in 1906.)

----

873. A large white and grey marble monument with cherubs' heads and
mantling.   At the foot are :—

ARMS.—*A lion rampant, in its paw a staff raguly* ; impaling, 1, *Argent, an
inescutcheon ; 2, A chevron between three cocks.*
CREST.—*A lion's head erased.*

The HONOURABLE | HENRY PEERS Esqʳ | Obᵗ the 4ᵗʰ of September 1740 |
Ætaˢ 57 Years.

Son of the Hon. Capt. Geo. P. of St. Michael's.   He was M. of A. 1706 and
Speaker in 1727.   He had a s. Henry who d. v.p. and two daughters and
coheiresses who mar. Tobias Frere and John Lyte.

874. At the east end. A small tablet surmounted by a cross :—

In loving memory of | MARY LOUISE | only child of ALEXANDER and MARY ASHBY, | who died January 19th 1888, | aged 20 years | (4 lines.)

---

875. South-west wall of chancel :—

In affectionate remembrance of | ALEXANDER ASHBY | WHO DIED AT CASTLE-GRANT, IN THIS ISLAND | IN THE MONTH OF OCTOBER 1868, | AGED 56 YEARS, | AND WAS INTERRED NEAR THIS SPOT. | (2 lines) | **Also of** SARAH ELIZABETH ASHBY, | WIFE OF THE ABOVE, | WHO DIED IN LONDON, | THE 22ND DAY OF MAY 1874, | AND WAS INTERRED BESIDE HER HUSBAND | IN THE MONTH OF JULY 1874 | (2 lines.)

---

876. **In loving memory of** | ELIZABETH ALLEYNE AND MARIA PILGRIM, | WHO DIED WITHIN A FEW WEEKS OF EACH OTHER A.D. 1881. | **This tablet** IS PUT UP BY THEIR NEPHEWS AND NIECES | THE CHILDREN OF | WILLIAM AND ANNIE MURRAY | TO WHOM THEY SUPPLIED THE PLACE OF A MOTHER | (1 line.)

---

877. Ledger west of nave:—

Here lyeth the body of ALEXANDER | ANDERSON JUNR eldeft Son of | ALEXANDER ANDERSON ESQR | of the Parish | of St Peter All Saints | who departed this life the 17th Day | of Octobr 1730 Aged | 78 Years.

---

878. On a fragment of blue marble ledger, 18th century in style :—

. . . . Body of Cap | . . PSTER | . . . . this Life the | . . Years.

CHURCH-YARD.

879. SACRED TO THE MEMORY OF | THOMAS DRAKE BARKER ESQR | OF ANDREWS PLANTATION | IN THE PARISH OF ST. JOSEPH | WHO DEPARTED THIS LIFE JANUARY 15TH 1838 | AGED 69 YEARS | ALSO | REBECCA BARKER | WHO DEPARTED THIS LIFE SEPTEMBER 17, 1809 | AGED 29 YEARS | (3 lines; placed by children.)

1809, Sept. 11. Anthony Barker Col. of St Josephs Regt of Militia.

1809, Sept. 18. Mrs Barker wife of Thomas Barker Esqr of Pilgrim Estate Christ Church. (Burial Register.)

1822, Nov. Lately. At Bristol, Rev. W. S. Bradley, Preb. of Wells, & Vicar of Timberscombe, to Frances-Maria, dau. of I. A. Barker, esq. of B. ("G.M.," 464.)

---

880. South side of churchyard :—

To the Memory of | JOHN CUMMINS | Who departed this Life Jany 18th 1807 | Aged 60 Years | (3 lines; placed by widow ELIZABETH CUMMINS.)

This inestimable Woman whose remains are also | beneath this Stone died Jany 2d 1827 | Aged 74 Years | (11 lines.)

s

881. White marble, enclosed by railing south of chancel :—

Here Lieth Interred the Body of | The Honourable THOMAS APPLE-
WHAITE Esq | obiit Iune 14ᵗʰ 1749. | Ætatis 59. | Also Mᴿˢ ELIZABETH
APPLEWHAITE Wife of | the above mentioned THOMAS APPLE-
WHAITE | Esq. obiit the 11ᵗʰ of April 1750 | Ætatis 59 Years.

See his tablet No. 857.

---

882. Adjoining, also enclosed by railing :—

In Memory of | The Honourable JOHN FRERE Eſqʳ | who Died January
25ᵗʰ 1766. | Aged 60 Years | And of SUSANNA FRERE | who Died July
1ˢᵗ 1759 | Aged 46 Years.

See " W.I. Bookplates," No. 188. He was Lt.-Gen. and President. She was
dau. of Tho. Applewhaite, also President.

---

883. South of above. Broken and pieces lost :—

IN MEMORY OF | (7 lines) | Mᴿˢ DOROTHY FRERE | Daughter of |
RICHARD & MARY SCUDAMORE | OF KENT CHURCH COURT | IN HEREFORDSHIRE |
GREAT BRITAIN | AND | to the honourable | . . . . FRERE Eſqʳ; | . . OF
BARBADOS : | was born January, 26, 1734. | . . . . September 13, 1756. |
. . . d June 1, 1782. | . . . . daughters. | . . . . ously, | . . . . them all.

Her husband was the Hon. Henry Frere. See her tablet in Christ Church,
No. 796.

---

884. East of chancel. Skull and crossbones in oval :—

OMNIA VANITAS | GRACE ELLCOCK | Obᵗ December 17ᵗʰ 1774 |
An. nat 60 | (2 lines.)

Archer gives " Grant Ellcock " d. 11 Dec. I do not know which is right.

---

885. THIS STONE MARKS THE TOMB OF | THE HONORABLE FORSTER CLARKE |
OF THIS ISLAND | WHO DIED ON THE 2ᴺᴰ JANUARY 1840 | AGED SIXTY THREE
YEARS | AND OF HANNAH PRESCOD HIS WIFE | WHO DIED ON THE 25ᵀᴴ
FEBRUARY 1858 | AGED SEVENTY YEARS.

---

886. A large walled grave east of these two, no M.I., to Rev. Sisnett, a
former Rector. (Sexton.)

---

887. SACRED | TO THE MEMORY OF EDMUND DAYRELL Eſqʳ | who departed
this Life on the 16ᵀᴴ Septʳ 1789 | (3 lines ; relict) | (11 lines lower down.)

---

888. Close to north wall of chancel :—

Beneath this Stone | are deposited the Remains of | Elizabeth Jane Piggott, |
Daughter of Joseph Mosely | and Elizabeth Jane Piggott. | She departed this
life Febʸ 8ᵗʰ 1821 | Aged 19 Years.

889. This Stone is sacred to the memory | of | ANN TRUSLER | only Daughter & real comfort of | JACOB & MERCY TRUSLER | who left her Grey-headed Parents | June 15 1780 | Aged 23 Years | (3 lines) | Also her Father | Who Lived an Honest man | and died a good Christian | on the 3 of Decr 1785 aged 49 Ye^{ars} | (2 lines.)

890. Curbed grave :—

THE | FAMILY BURIAL PLACE | OF | J. C. COLLINS | (modern).

891. Here Lyes Interred the body | of Ann Sawyer wife of | Charles Sawyer who | departed this Life september | the 5th 1691 aged 30 years | And on her Right hand lyeth | Interred the body of hur (sic) | Brother Valentine Wilee who | died the 15th of novemb^r | 1691 aged 39 years | And on her left hand lyeth | the body of hur kinsman | Robert Wilee son of the above | named Valentine Wilee who | departed this life the 4th day | of May 1692 aged about 19 years | Also Here Lyes interred y^e | body of Elizabeth Sawyer daug | ter of ye Aboue menconed Ann | Sawyer aged 17 years who de | parted this Life ye 14 of May | 1697.

892. Vault enclosed by railing. White marble slab :—

SACRED | TO THE MEMORY OF | WILLIAM LUCIEN WARREN ESQ^E | WHO DIED JUNE 22ND 1854.

893. Headstone :—

SACRED | TO THE MEMORY OF | WILLIAM DEANE FREEMAN ESQ^R | M.B. T.C.D. SURGEON A.M.D. | WHO DIED AT BARBADOES | OF YELLOW FEVER WHILE IN | DISCHARGE OF HIS DUTIES ON | THE 5TH OF OCTOBER 1881 | AGED 24 YEARS | (3 lines.)

894. Skull and crossbones at top :—

Here Lyeth Interred the Body of Edward | Claypool Esqr who departed this life the 11th | of November 1692 and in the F . . . . and fifth | year of his Age. | And Also Alice Sarah and Elizabeth Claypo | ole the Daughters of the abovesaid Edward | Claypoole Esqr. | Alice departed this Life | luly the 16th 1679 Sarah the 21st of | November 1679 and Elizabeth the 18th of | December 1685.

895. On the top slab of a large tomb :—

Beneath this Stone | are deposited the Remains of | *JONATHAN BOYCE* | who at the age of 38 years | and after a short union of only six months | (31 lines ; died) March 11th 1832.

896. Here | lieth interred | the Body of | GEORGE HALL Esqr | who departed this life | the 2nd November 1742 | Aged 31 Years | Also | the Body of HANNAH SPOONER | Wife of | JOHN SPOONER Esqr | And | Daughter of the above | GEORGE HALL Esqr | who departed this life | the 15th May 1752 | Aged 20 Years.

Her husband was Attorney-Gen. of St. Chr. in 1727, and d. 1758. See pedigree, " Caribbeana," i., 2.

897. $\mathfrak{Sacred}$ | To the Memory of | ANTHONY GULSTON | who departed this life 19th September 1821 | Aged 44 years | (4 lines.)

---

898. Here lieth the Body of | SARAH BASCOM | who departed this life the | 30th of October 1777 Aged | 74 Years | Also the Body of SARAH wife | of GRIFFIN BASCOM | who departed this life 12th | of October 1798 Aged 52 years.

---

899. SACRED | TO THE MEMORY OF | JAMES CRAGG KELLMAN | WHO DEPARTED THIS LIFE | JANUARY 1ST 1852 | AGED 42 YEARS | ALSO | TO THE MEMORY OF | JOHN EYARE KELLMAN | YOUNGEST SON OF THE ABOVE | WHO DEPARTED THIS LIFE | SEPTEMBER 20TH 1866 | AGED 26 YEARS | (6 lines.)

See his daughter's stone, No. 869.

---

900. On a stone tomb :—

SUSAN FRANCES EVELYN | Died 30 August 1899 | Aged 78 years.

---

901. In Loving Memory of | E. T. GREGORY | died Sep. 14, 1894 Aged 59 years.

The clerk stated that the above was a plumber, related to the Rev. Mr. Bowen, and that his son the Rev. J. G. Gregory is now of St. Barnabas.

---

902. On a marble cross :—

LILIAN ISABEL DYDOGU (?) MARY, eldest child of | Colwyn & Lilian VULLIAMY | Born 25th of March 1898 | died 25th May 1894.

---

903. BELL. 1833.

---

904. On a stone slab enclosed by iron railing :—

UNDER THIS STONE | LIES THE BODY OF | RICHARD INNISS | WHO DEPARTED THIS LIFE | THE 17TH DAY OF NOVEMBER 1810 | AGED 59 YEARS.

---

905. On a stone vault :—

Sacred | to the memory of | ROBERT COLLYMORE Esquire | who served many Years in the Vestry | of this Parish | (6 lines) | He died at the advanced age of 80 years | on the 6th of May 1821 | (4 lines.)

1658-9, Feb. 10. Capt Robert Cullimore and Katherine Nichols. (St. John's.)

---

906. On a stone vault :—

SARAH ELIZABETH | RELICT OF WILLIAM HENRY HOWARD | AND MOTHER OF | ANTHONY HOWARD | OF GOLDEN RIDGE IN THIS PARISH | DIED JULY 4TH 1863 | AGED 81 YEARS.

907. On a marble slab on the south side of the sloping roof of a large stone sarcophagus :—

JAMES THOMAS WILLIAMS SEN^R | BORN 1ST MAY 1769, | DIED SEPTEMBER 4TH 1815 | MARGARET ELIZABETH WILLIAMS | BORN 25TH JANUARY 1779 | DIED MARCH 8TH 1836 | ELIZABETH ANN TROTMAN | BORN 20TH JUNE 1794 | DIED FEBRUARY 23RD 1831 | JAMES THOMAS WILLIAMS | BORN 16TH FEBRUARY 1797 | DIED SEPTEMBER 4TH 1821 | MARGARET SMITH WILLIAMS | BORN 31ST AUGUST 1799 | DIED NOVEMBER 15TH 1803 | JOHN HENRY CUTTING | BORN 21ST DECEMBER 1826 | DIED SEPTEMBER 30TH 1827 | SARAH MARGARET CUTTING | BORN 17TH AUGUST 1828 | DIED AUGUST 21, 1828 | HENRY TROTMAN | BORN 20TH AUGUST 1829 | DIED SEPTEMBER 3RD 1829.

At the east end :—

JAMES THOMAS WILLIAMS | Born February 16th 1797 | Died September 4th 1821 | IN MEMORY OF | SIMON LEE TROTMAN | OF LIVERPOOL | BORN 1801 | DIED 1862 | ELIZABETH P. W. TROTMAN | BORN 1811 | DIED 1895.

---

908. On a white marble cross enclosed by iron railing :—

EDWARD EVAN PARRIS | DIED JUNE 16, 1892 | AGED 48 YEARS | (1 line.)

---

909. Sacred to the memory of | FRANCIS BUTCHER Efq | who departed this life | the 8th of September 1777 | Aged 65 Years.

See Som. and Dorset N. and Q., V., 78, and Foster.

---

910. TO THE MEMORY OF | GEORGE WILLIAM BASCOM ESQ | BORN 16TH APRIL 1801 AND | DIED 29TH JULY 1831 | ALSO TO THE MEMORY OF | MARY CHRISTIAN BASCOM | THE BELOVED WIFE OF | THE ABOVE | BORN 4TH FEB^Y 1804 AND | DIED 18TH DEC^R 1857.

Edward Daniel, only s. of Edward B. of St. John's, B., gent., St. Mary Hall, matric. 26 Oct. 1837, a. 21 : B.A. 1841.

See No. 288 under Walrond.

---

911. North of nave :—

BENEATH THIS STONE ON THE | 17TH ANNIVERSARY OF HER MARRIAGE | WERE DEPOSITED THE EARTHLY REMAINS | OF SUSANNAH, THE BELOVED WIFE OF | JOSEPH TROTMAN ESQ^R A M. | AND DAUGHTER OF | THO^S W^M AND FRANCES BRADSHAW | WHO DEPARTED THIS LIFE IN CHILDBIRTH | ON THE 22ND OF APRIL 1852 | AGED 37 YEARS | (5 lines ; erected by husband and children.)

Henry Trotman, s. of Tho. Clarke T. of I. of B., gent., matric. from Q. Coll. Oxf. 16 Dec. 1812, a. 22.

John Warren T., 1 s. of Henry T. of St Geo., I. of B., gent., matric. from St Alban Hall, Oxf., 17 Oct. 1839, a. 18.

Joseph T., 2 s. of Tho. T. of B., esq., matric. from Worc. Coll., Oxf., 24 Oct. 1822, a. 18 ; B.A. 1827, M.A. 1829 ; bar.-at-l. Inner T. 1833.

912. Stone tomb:—

IN MEMORY | OF | LIEUTENANT COLONEL W. F. BLAKE | FIRST BATTALION OF THE KINGS OWN ROYAL LANCASHIRE REGIMENT | WHO DIED OF YELLOW FEVER AT GUN HILL BARBADOS | ON 6TH OCTOBER 1881 | AGED 46 YEARS.

Many of the stones in above list have been much broken, and are liable to be lost if not soon secured with cement.

———

Archer gives six other inscriptions now lost :—

913. The Hon. BURY FRERE . . . .

ARMS.—*Two leopards' heads affrontée Or, between two flaunches of the second.*

914. Mrs FRANCES JORDAN, wife of Mr THOMAS JORDAN, born 27 June 1757, d. 18 . .

915. . . . DURD LEWIS, Phys . . d. . . . . 1692 aged 40.

916. ARABELLA, wife of GEORGE PE . . . . (Very old fragment.)

917. . . . . MARY PARTRIDGE, wife of SAMUEL YARD PARTRIDGE . . . . JAMES GRASSELL. . . . .

918. The tomb of Dr SEDGWICK and his family.

———

ST. JAMES', HOLE TOWN.

On the floor of central walk of nave beginning at the west door.

919. Blue marble ledger. The right edge of last three lines has been cemented :—

Here Lyes Interr'd the Body of | Mr THOMAS KING | who departed this Life the 11TH | day of NOVEMBER, in the year | of our LORD 1722 and in . . . . | Sixtyeth year of . . . .

———

920. Blue marble ledger :—

Here Lyes the Body of | Mr EDWARD IORDAN, who Departed | this Life the 16th day of Febry 170½, | Aged 52 Years. | Here alſo Lyes the Body of | Mrs ANNE IORDAN Wife to Major | EDWARD IORDAN who Departed this | Life the 17th day of Auguſt 1726, | Aged 41 Years. | *Here under also lieth Interred the Body of Major | EDWARD IORDAN Son of the aforeſaid EDWARD IORDAN | Husband of the aforeſaid ANNE who departed this life | April the 16th Anno Salutis 1728 | Ætatis 47 years | Here also lieth Interred the Body of IOSEPH DOTIN | Esqr Son in Law to the ſaid Major EDWARD IORDAN | who departed this life March the 30th | Anno Salutis 1735 Ætatis 45 Years | Here alſo lieth Interred the Body of Mr EDWARD IORDAN DOTIN Son of the aforeſaid IOSEPH DOTIN by | his Wife ANNE Daughter of the above mentioned | Major EDWARD IORDAN and his Wife ANNE He departed | this life May the 21st Anno Salutis 1736 | Ætatis 11 Years | Thos HILL ſc. | Here alſo lyeth ANN Relict of the above Ios DOTIN Wife | to the Revd Mr Dudley Woodbridge to whose Memory the | Monument on the So Wall was erected with whom also | lyeth her Dater Ann Woodbridge who died Iuly 27th 1740 | Aged 29 Months.

* Lettering now smaller.

1736, May 21. Edward Jordan Dotin aged [*blank*], died of a malignant Fever.

1740, July 29. Ann Woodbridge aged 29 months, died of an Imposthume in her head. (Burial Register.)

1701, Sept. 1. Mr Edward Jordan & Mrs Ann Holder.

Rev. Dudley Woodbridge Inducted 21 April 1742.

See No. 934.

---

921. White marble ledger :—

Here lieth Interred the Body | of MARY PHILLIPS | who departed this Life the 9th July | 1763. Aged 61 Years | Here alfo lies Interred the Body | of MILLICENT Wife of SEPTUN MORGAN | who departed this Life the 9th Sept^r | 1768, Aged 22 Years.

---

922. White marble ledger :—

Here Lyeth Interr'd the Body of | the Revd Mr RICHARD SHIRE late | Rector of this *. . . ish who Died the | 17 *. . ctobe . . . . 17 Aged 34 Years.

1744, Aug. 29. Rev. Richd Shier Inducted.

Burial not recorded.

---

923. White marble at centre of walks (much worn) :—

Here lie the Remains | of | *GABRIEL LORD Esqre* | Who died October the . 1 (?) 1803 | Aged . . . Years | (4 lines.)

---

925. Blue marble ledger :—

To point out the Dust of | SAMUEL BARWICK | who in the 63^d Year of his Age Died | Commander in Chief of his | Native Country January ye 1st 1732 | WILLIAM his Eldest Son here | placeth this Stone Beneath which | the Ashes of SAMUEL the youngeft | Son reunites in one common Mafs | with those of his Father he Died | June 4th 1741 in the 39th Year of his | Age.

1732-3, Jan. 1. The Honble Samuel Barwick Esqr President, etc. (Burial Register.)

---

926. Grey marble in cross walk to north door (much worn) :—

Here lieth the Body of | Madam *MARY GLASGOW;* | Relict of the Reverend *John Glafgow;* | who died the 25th of June, 1734. | Aged 63 Years. | Alfo the Bodies of four Children ; | Sons & Daughters of *Edward & Judith Anne Henry* | *Eli* . . . . who died the 22^d Day of Decem^r 1738 (?) | Aged 2 Years | *John Gl* . . . . (? Glasgow) who died the 26th Day of J . . . . | Aged 10 Months. | . . . . who died the 26th Day of October 1. 4. | Aged 4 Years and 6 Months : | And *Thomas Henry* who died the 26 of Auguft | 1747 Aged 3 Years : | Alfo the Body of the faid *EDWARD HENRY* Efq^r. | who died the 14th Day of March 1756. | Aged 32 Years (? 32 or 52).

1734, June 26. Mary Glasgow aged 63 years died of a Leprosy. (Burial Register.)

* Cemented.

927. South porch. White marble ledger with a long inscription of forty-two lines (worn in places) :—

To the Memory | of DAME CHRISTIAN ALLEYNE, | the beloved Wife of *SIR* JOHN GAY ALLEYNE *BAR^T* | who | (6 lines) | (died) on the 2 day of . . . . of our Lord 1782 | (Married life 36 years.)

She was 4th dau. and coheiress of Joseph Dotin, and was mar. 19 Oct. 1746.

---

928. White marble font :—

" Dedit Richardus Walter to the church of St : Iames' Anno 1684.
The Hon. Richd. Walter, merchant and planter, was bur. here 17 Aug. 1700.

---

929. Bell :—

GOD BLESS KING WILLIAM 1696.

---

930. Brass under window in south porch :—

IN AFFECTIONATE MEMORY OF JOHN | BISHOP-CULPEPER LATE CAP^TN 14TH | LIGHT DRAGOONS OF EASY HALL IN THIS | ISLAND WHO DIED JAN^RY 3RD 1875. | Erected by HIS WIDOW.

---

931. Brass in floor of chancel :—

TO THE GLORY OF GOD AND IN LOVING MEMORY OF | CHARLES THOMAS ALLEYNE OF PORTERS IN THIS PARISH | THIS CHANCEL WAS ENLARGED AND BEAUTIFIED A.D. 1874.

Chas. T. A. was also of Litfield Place, Clifton. His son Mr. Forster McGeachy A., M.A., bar.-at-law, resided at Porters 1897—1908, and died 24 Nov. 1913, aged 68, in L. (Long obituary notice in " Times.") The family having lost money heavily, Porters estate was sold to Dr. Pilgrim.

---

932. On a brass plate inserted in wooden base of lectern :—

In memory of | HENRY ALLEYNE | Presented by M: R: A. | 1877.

933. On the south wall of nave are three monuments :—

CREST.—*A horse's head out of a ducal coronet.*
ARMS.—Quarterly, 1 and 4, *Per chevron Ermine and Gules, two lions' heads erased Or* (ALLEYNE) ; 2 and 3, *Sable, a hand issuing from sinister side couped, grasping three arrows, one in pale and two in saltire* (? LOWLE), *all Or* ; impaling, Quarterly of 4 : 1. *Argent, two bars doubly embattled Gules* (JAMES of Ightham, Kent) ; 2. *Argent, a chevron Sable between three millrinds transverse* (JAMES) ; 3. *Barry wary of six Argent and Azure, on a chief Or three swallows volant* (MORSKYN of Liege) ; 4. *Ermine, on a bend engrailed Azure three cinquefoils Or.* (See the confirmation of arms to the family of James by Wm. Camden 18 Nov. 1611 in the Visitation of Kent, A° 1619, edited by the late Dr. J. J. Howard.)
MOTTO.—JE CRAINS DIEU ET N'AI POINT D'AUTRE CRAINTE.

SACRED | TO THE MEMORY OF | THE HONOURABLE HENRY ALLEYNE | MEMBER OF HIS MAJESTY'S COUNCIL | IN THIS ISLAND | (YOUNGEST SON OF | THE HON^BLE JOHN FORSTER ALLEYNE | OF PORTERS, IN THIS PARISH,) | WHO WAS BORN ON THE 2ND JANUARY 1808, | AND PERISHED AT SEA, | BY THE BURNING OF | THE ROYAL MAIL STEAMER AMAZON, | OFF USHANT IN THE BAY OF BISCAY, | DURING THE NIGHT OF THE 3RD AND 4TH JANUARY 1852 | (13 lines ; erected by widow.)

            T. GAFFIN 63 REGENT S^T LONDON.

934. Large grey marble monument, white marble shield at top, then urn :—

Sacred to the Memory, | of ANN the beloved Wife | of the Revd Mr DUDLEY WOODBRIDGE. | (9 lines, and two verses of Bible at sides) | She Dyed | October 3. MDCCXXXIX. | Aged XXXVI.

On the shield are traces of arms. On sinister side are *two bendlets?*
1739, Oct. 3. Mrs Ann Woodbridge buried at St James. (St. Thomas Burial Register.) See No. 920.

———

935. Large black and white marble, surmounted by an urn :—

On shield below : 1 *and* 4, *Sable, on a bend cotised an alyrion displayed Or, a canton sin. of the second ;* 2 *and* 3, *Argent, two lions passant-guardant, Gules.*

W. PATY. BRISTOL. F^t.
(It has been recently repainted.)

This Memorial is consecrated by filial Gratitude | to the Memory of *EDWARD JORDAN*, who departed this life | October 23rd 1787, aged forty Seven Years | (3 lines) | And alſo to the Memory of *ANN JORDAN* his Wife, | (Daughter and Coheireſs of *JOSEPH DOTTIN* and *ANN JORDAN*,) | who died January 30th 1791, aged 69 Years | (2 lines) | Alſo to the Memory of *EDWARD JORDAN*, | Son of the above *EDWARD & ANN JORDAN*, he died | December 17th 1799, aged 58 Years.

———

936. On the north wall of nave are four tablets :—

At the top is an urn. At the bottom are these arms (recently painted) : *Gules, per chevron Ermine* and Gules two lions' heads erased.* On an inescutcheon : *Gules, two lions passant* [DOTTIN]. MOTTO.—APTISSIMA QUÆQUE. Crest of Alleyne.

To record the Virtues & perpetuate the Memory | of *Mercy* his dear beloved Conſort, | *William Gibbes Alleyne Eſq^r* as a Teſtimony of | Sincere Affection, has erected this | Monument. | After thirteen years of conſtant uninterrupted | Bliſs with a Partner, who by every Endearment, | ſweetned the Joys, alleviated the Cares, & | heightened the Pleaſures of the nuptial State ; to | his inexpreſſible Sorrow, and Concern She was | ſeperated from him on Thurſday | Aug^st 25th. 1774 Aged thirty years. | Her Deſcent from a Race of worthy Anceſtry | deriving her Lineage from the Honourable | *James Dotin*, who was Preſident of this Island | three different times, & being the Daughter of the | Honourable *Iohn Dotin*, a Gentleman who for a | ſeries of years, filled the moſt diſtinguiſhed civil, & | military Stations, in our Community, | Gave her that Conſequence among us, which is due | to Birth & Rank | (8 lines.)

———

937. On the west side of the north door. White marble medallion of head and shoulders, and on either side a large figure :—

SACRED | to the Revd FRANCIS FITCHATT M.A. | formerly Fellow of *St John's College Cambridge* | late Chaplain to the Houſe of Aſſembly | of this Iſland | and for 25 Years ſucceſſively Rector | of S^t. Josephs, this, and S^t. Peters Pariſh | who died December 5th. 1802 | in the 57th Year of his Age | (30 lines.)

———

* The *Ermine* has been painted *Gules.*

T

938. East of north door:—

Sacred to the Memory of | *DAMES* | *CHRISTIAN* and *JANE ABEL* | succefsively the Consorts | of *SIR JOHN-GAY ALLEYNE* Baronet; | Women in whose Praise | Encomium has to borrow no false Colouring | from Flattery ; | and of whom no Language | can describe the Lofs ! | with the *former* he lived *six* and *thirty* Years | of unspeakable Felicity | and but but little more than *fourteen*, | with the *latter* | In that short Period | She blefs'd him with the Birth | of *seven* lovely Infants ; | the eldest of which, | *JOHN-GAY-NEWTON-ALLEYNE*, | a Boy of Hopes commen- surate | to the fondest Wishes of a Father, | in *thirteen* Summers, | was too ripe for Immortality, | for longer Continuance upon Earth ! | The afflicting Intelligence of his Death | at Eton School | arrived but one Day late enough | to spare his expiring Mother, | such Pangs, as she was incapable of feeling | for her own Difsolution | but such, as the mournful Erecter of | this three-fold Monument | of the Instability of all human | Enjoyments | for the Sake of his surviving Children | and, in silent Resignation | to the Wisdom that ordains it, must labour to | endure !

The above M.I., written by the Rector, the Rev. Fra. Fitchatt, was contributed to the W.I. Com. Circular, vol. 27, p. 233, by the late Mr. Forster M. Alleyne.

939. *SACRED* | To the Memory of | the Honorable WILLIAM HOLDER | who died the 11th of August 1705, aged 48 Years | Mrs SUSANNAH HOLDER his Wife, | who died the 12th of March 1725 aged 57 Years | And of | WILLIAM HOLDER Esqr their Grandson | who died the 14th of August 1752, aged 31 Years | Who all were buried | at the Family Estate of Black Rock | in this Parish.

1705, Sept. 16th. Nathaniel Holder & Mrs Xtian Holder. (Par. Reg.) See later for the M.I. at Holder's plantation, No. 985.

CHURCHYARD, SOUTH-EAST SIDE.

940. Vault:—

In Loving Memory | of | GEORGE PAYNE | DIED MAY 1868 | AGED 42 | AND | CATHARINE HIS WIFE | DIED | JULY 17TH 1887 | AGED 60.

941. Headstone enclosed by iron railing:—

SACRED | TO THE MEMORY OF | ELIZA ANNE, | WIFE OF SAMUEL HENRY, | WHO DEPARTED THIS LIFE | ON 3RD JUNE 1853, | AGED 45 YEARS | ALSO OF THE ABOVE | SAMUEL HENRY, | WHO DEPARTED THIS LIFE | ON 26TH SEPTEMBER 1858 | AGED 76 YEARS.

942. White marble slab enclosed by railing:—

In Loving Memory | of | GEORGE LAURANCE | SECOND SON OF | JOSEPH R. AND REBECCA FRANCES KING | DIED OCT. 13TH 1881 | AGED 7 YEARS AND 7 MONTHS | (several lines.)

943. Cross over vault:—

JOHN BRATHWAITE MOE | PRIEST | 1881. See " Caribbeana," Vol. II., 81.

944. Headstone:—

IN MEMORY OF | S. E. A. DEAR | DIED 16TH DECR 1885.

945. Headstone within railing:—

FRANCES ANN LAWSON | Died | *26ᵗʰ June 1853* | *Aged 20 Years.*

---

946. White marble headstone within railing:—

IN MEMORIAM | LYTE. | ERECTED BY | HIS BELOVED WIFE | BESSIE.

---

947. Large vault, steps down to entrance :—

𝕾𝖆𝖈𝖗𝖊𝖉 | to the memory of | HAYNES GIBBS BAYLEY | WHO DIED THE 11ᵀᴴ JULY 1856 | AGED 54 YEARS.

---

948. Slab enclosed by railing :—

Here lie the Remains of | Sarah Frances Bayley | Daughter of Joseph Bayley | who died the 28ᵗʰ Sepʳ 1816 | Aged 22 Moˢ | Also the Remains of | Francis Bayley | Brother of the said Joseph Bayley | who died the 8ᵗʰ Decʳ 1816 | Aged 17 yrˢ | Francis G. Bayley erected this Tomb | to perpetuate the lov'd memory of his | Grand-daughter and Son.

---

949. On headstone adjoining:—

SACRED | TO THE MEMORY OF | JOSEPH BAYLEY | BORN MARCH 10ᵀᴴ 1791 DIED NOVEMBER 7ᵀᴴ 1865 | (5 lines) | ALSO | SUSAN | HIS BELOVED WIFE | BORN SEPT. 15ᵀᴴ 1793, DIED AUGUST 10ᵀᴴ 1862 | (2 lines.)

---

950. Ledger, white marble, level with the ground :—

HERE LIETH INTERD THE BODY OF COLᵒ | JOHN BEST ESQ. OF THE PARISH OF Sᵀ PETR | OF THIS ISLAND WHO DEPARTED THIS LIFE | THE 13 DAY OF NOVᵇʳ ANNO DOMINE 1750 IN | THE 46 YEAR OF HIS AGE.

See "Caribbeana," iv., 140. There is a gap in the Burial Register 1746-7 to 1751.

---

951. To the south of No. 911 the sexton unearthed the following ledger, which I saw later:—

Here lieth the Body of | LAWRENCE BOORE | Who departed this Life | December 4ᵗʰ | 1759 | Aged 42 Years.

1759, Dec. 5. Lawrence Boor. Aged 42 Yʳˢ. (Burial Register.)

---

952. Blue marble over vault, very large lettering :—

Here | Lye the Bodies of GABRIEL | RICHARD IOHN and GABRIEL | MARY and ELIZABETH FORD | alſo of | CHRISTOPHER FORD | who departed this Life | 14 May 1768 | aged 24 Years 6 months | Sons and Daughters of | Gabriel and Elizabeth Ford.

Lower in smaller lettering :—

HERE LIES THE BODY OF RICHARD FORD | WHO DIED NOVEMBER THE 29TH 1769 | AGED 26 YEARS | ALSO, HERE LIES THE BODY OF IONATHAN | FORD WHO DIED JULY THE 2 : 1772 AGED 20 YEARS | HERE LIES THE BODY OF ELIZABET | (inscription unfinished ; all perfect.)

1769, Nov. 30. Richard Ford. Aged 26 yrs. (Burial Register.)

---

953. West of nave, blue marble. Above are an hour-glass and skull :—

Here lyeth Interr'd the Body of | . . . *HILL Wife of ROBERT HILL | who departed this Life | the 10th day of *June* 1723 | Aged 26 *Years*.

---

954. Old ledger on vault :—

HERE LIES INTERD THE BODY OF | [RO]WLAND WILLY WHO DEPARTED | THE [2ND] OF JANUARY | [17]6[2] AGED 80 YEARS.

The portions within brackets are from Archer.

---

955. Cross :—

IN LOVING MEMORY OF | LAW GASKIN | WHO DIED MARCH 22 1867 | AGED 54 | AND HIS WIFE | MARGARET WILLIAMS | WHO DIED | MARCH 31, 1895 | AGED 81.

---

956. Grey marble over vault (perfect) :—

Here lieth Inter'd | The Body of | LYDIA LAWRANCE | Who departed this Life | The 11th of Auguſt | 1759 | Aged 27 Years.

---

957. White marble headstone, enclosed by railing :—

𝕾acred to 𝔐emory | of | JAMES HENRY SCANTLEBURY | WHO DEPARTED THIS LIFE DECEMBER 13TH 1861 | AGED 45 YEARS.

---

958. White marble headstone, enclosed by railing of older vault :—

IN MEMORY | OF | EDWARD DRAKES | OF "*TRY FAIR*," | WHO DEPARTED THIS LIFE | 27 APRIL 1884 | AGED 84 YEARS.

---

959. Old tomb adjoining :—No inscription.

---

960. High brick vault :—

THE BODY OF . . . . WOODWARD | WHO CHANGED . . . . IVNE.

---

961. Ledger :—

Beneath | this MARBLE | lie the mortal Remains of | Sir PHILIP GIBBES Barᵗ | who departed this Life | June 27th 1815. | Aged 85 | Years.

He was born 7 March 1730, and created a Baronet 30 May 1774. ("W.I. Bookplates," No. 189.)

* Stone scaled.

962. Old fragment :—

HEAR LYES THE | BODY OF DR IOHN | IAMES HARRISON | DEC^D IANR^Y 21TH 170⅔ | MARY HIS WIFE | (this line broken here) | 1711.

---

963. On a large vault, the inscription very worn :—

THOMAS LITTLETON | EDWARDI L . . . . Armigeri | Filiu . unicus, | D^{NI} ADAMI L . . . . Baronetti | Nepos | Optimæ indolis et Summæ Spei puer | Annis Septenis Nove os Menfes addiderat | immaturo abreptus fato, | Hic jacet | Adventum opperiens servatoris sui.

Sir Adam L. of Stoke Milburgh, co. Salop, was created a Baronet in 1642, and dying *circa* 1647, was succeeded by his eldest s. Sir Thos., who d. 1681 ; father of Sir Tho., Speaker, who d. s.p. in 1710. (Burke's Extinct Baronetage.)
Edward L. was agent for the Island in 1691. (Oldmixon, ii., 46.)

---

964. Touching No. 963 :—

CREST.—*An eagle displayed over helmet, with Jacobean mantling.*
ARMS.—*On a chief three eagles displayed.*

VNDER THIS PLACE LYETH BVRIED | Y^E BODY OF MAIJOR EDWARD HARRI^{SON} | LATE OF THIS PARRISH WHO WAS | BORNE AT BVRNENSON IN Y^E COVNTY | OF DARBY & DEPARTED THIS LIFE Y^E | 16 OF FEBRUARY 1669 BEING 63 YEARS OF | AGE.

Robert s. of R(obert) Harrison of B'os, gent., Merton Coll., matric. 23 Oct. 1705, a. 17.
Edward s. of R(obert) Harrison, same date, a. 16, adm. to Middle T. 1700.

---

965. Mausoleum :—

Here lies the Body of | *ANN* the Wife of | *IOHN COLLINS Efq^r* | who Departed this Life the 21st of | Novr 1763. Aged 67 Years. | Alfo Here lies the Body of | *ANN* the Wife of Colonel | *REYNOLD GIBBES*, and | Eldeft Daughter of the above | *IOHN* and *ANN COLLINS* | who Departed this Life the 17th of | June 1766 Aged 45 Years.

---

966. Adjoining No. 965 :—

HERE LYETH INTERRED THE BODY | OF MR IOSEPH GIBBES WHO DEPA- | RTED THIS LIFE Y^E 30TH OF SEPTEMBER | 1700 AGED 51 YEARES 5 MONTHES AND | 7 DAYS.

1700, Sept. 17. (11 bur. that day.) Mr Joseph Gibbes (of St Thomas's), Gout.

---

967. Large vault (rough lettering) :—

AVCO TRENT | DEPARTED | THIS LIFE | OCTOBER | 24th 1802 | AGED 62 years.

---

968. Stone, much flaked, several lines gone :—

OF | M^R . . . . HENRY ALLEYNE, | BY WHOM THIS TOMB IS ERECTED, | IN GRATEFUL REMEMBRANCE OF | HER FAITHFUL SERVICES | (1 line.)

969. Near road. Square walled enclosure containing seven vaults :—

Underneath this Stone are deposited | the Remains | of | M^{RS} ELIZ. HANNAH WILLING | Relict of | CHARLES WILLING ESQ^R | late of the City of Philadelphia | in the State of Pennsylvania | in North America | She was born the 12th of March 1739 | and | died the 12th of October 1795.

970. Underneath this Stone is depofited | the Body of M^{RS} MARY GIBBES | Relict of the late | Honble *THOMAS GIBBES* | She departed this Life December 24th | 1770 | In the forty fecond Year of her | Age.

1640, July 31. Capt. Tho. G. sells 50 a. (Vol. i. of Deeds, p. 738.) Several members of the family of Gibbes of Bristol settled in Barbados, but their exact relationship is difficult to define.

971. Here lie the Remains | of | Mrs MARGARET ELIZ. GIBBES | Late Wife of the | Revd Mr *HAYNES GIBBES* | She departed this Life the | 9th Day of March 1775 | In the fiftieth Year of her | Age.

Haynes Gibbes, s. of Joseph G. of B., gent., matric. from Exeter Coll., Oxf., 19 July 1735, a. 16; B.A. 1739.

972. HERE LIE THE REMAINS OF | THE HON^{BLE} JOHN FORSTER ALLEYNE | WHO DIED ON THE 29TH SEPT^R 1823 | AGED 63 YEARS | AND OF HIS BELOVED WIFE | ELIZ. GIBBES ALLEYNE | WHO DIED ON THE 12TH FEB^Y 1820 | AGED 55 YEARS | ALSO THOSE OF | MANY OF THEIR CHILDREN | WHO WERE PREVIOUSLY INTERRED | IN THE SAME GRAVE.

He was of Porters, and President in 1807.

973. To The Memory | of *SARAH GIBBES* | who departed this Life | June 24th 1783 | Aged 56 Years | .. Months and 16 Days | (16 lines.)

974. White marble ledger :—

𝕾𝖆𝖈𝖗𝖊𝖉 𝖙𝖔 𝖙𝖍𝖊 𝕸𝖊𝖒𝖔𝖗𝖞 | of | JOHN GAY ALLEYNE | WHO DEPARTED THIS LIFE ON THE | 4TH JULY 1885 | AGED 76 | (1 line.)

975. SACRED | TO THE MEMORY OF | MARY | FOURTH DAUGHTER OF | THE HON^{BLE} JOHN FORSTER ALLEYNE | AND ELIZABETH GIBBES ALLEYNE | OF PORTERS | IN THIS PARISH | WHO DEPARTED THIS LIFE | THE 6TH NOVEMBER 1835 | AGED 40 YEARS | (2 lines.)

976. Large tomb north of church :—
No inscription. ? Thornhill.

977. White marble north of nave :—
Long epitaph to a "dau." No name.

978. Headstone enclosed by railings :—

SACRED | TO THE MEMORY OF | JOHN FRANCIS HINKSON M.D. | *Died Sep* 17*th* 1869 | AGED 64 YEARS.

---

979. IN MEMORY OF | E. S. RICE | WHO DIED 19TH OF APRIL | 1883 | AGED 32 YEARS.

---

980. Marble ledger enclosed by railings :—

Above, Crest.—*A bear's head erased, muzzled, collared.*
On a spade shield are : ARMS.—*Sable, a fess humettée Argent.*

Sacred to the Memory of | BENJAMIN BOSTOCK ESQ^R | *Member of the Afsembly* | who Departed this Life the 28th of | June 1785 Aged 69 Years | (11 lines ; erected by his grandson Ben. Bostock, Esq.)

---

981. Here lyes the Body of | THOMAS FERCHARSON | Son to DOCTOR BOWDEN | FERCHARSON who Departed | this Life on Fryday the 4th day | of September 1724 Aged nine | months & six days | Here lyes the Body of | M^rn HONOUR FERCHARSON | Wife to DOCTOR BOWDEN | FERCHARSON who Departed | this life on Fryday the 28 day | of Iune 1728 Aged thirty two | years Eight months & ten days | Here lyes the Body of | THOMAS FERCHARSON | Son to DOCTOR BOWDEN | FERCHARSON who Departed | this life the 15th day of August | 1728 Aged tenn months | and Eighteen days.

---

982. Stone adjoining ; illegible, flaked off.

---

983. Archer gave two inscriptions no longer to be found :—

ELIZABETH wife of WILLIAM SPARKE Esq. and dau. of JOHN KELLOND of Pangsford in the county of Devon Esq. died Oct. 15, 1672 | Also JOANNES SPARKE.

ARMS.—*Chequy, a bend.*
CREST.—*Out of a mural crown a demi-fox issuant rampant.*

---

984. On a fragment :—

Boy of . . N . . GODWARD, who dep . . . . June 1670.

CHURCH PLATE.

On a large alms dish bearing the London hall-mark of a gothic "*F*" for the year 1683-4 :—

"In Vsum Eclesiæ S^tt Jacobi infulâ Barbados Jacobus Walwyn Armiger D: D:* xxv : x^bris 1684."

ARMS.—*A bend Ermine.*

* For "Donum Dedit."

On a flagon and large chalice marked with a gothic " 🜉 " for the year 1682-3:—

" To the Altar att St James's in Barbados | For the use of the Holy Communion | Devoted By the Honble Co^{ll} John Standfast."

A smaller flagon, which probably replaced an ancient one, has wreath and ribbon decoration around the inscription with the letter " f " for the year 1781-2.

John Stanfast of Bristol, now in Barbados. Will dated 20 Oct. 1680. My plantation called Mount Stanfast in the p. of St James of 400 acres & Fontable in the p. of St Michael of 270 acres. To the p. of St James 2 flagons of 2 quarts each one challis cup of 3 pints & 2 plates. Mr Charles Leard £10 a gown & cossacke. P. 1687 [P.C.C., 54, Foot.] He was Churchwarden 1679, a Colonel, M. of C. 1674, and his death announced 9 March 1681. His heir Col. Tho. Spiar, by his will of 1682, left to this church a pulpit cushion and a cloth of purple velvet, also a covering for the communion table. [P.C.C., 53, Foot.]

HOLDER'S PLANTATION.

985. In a cane piece north of the house. White marble slab:—

Here lieth Interred | the Bodies of the Honourable | *WILLIAM HOLDER Efq^r* | who departed this Life | on the 11th Auguft 1705 | Aged 48 Years. | And of | *Mrs SUSANNA HOLDER* | wife to the late | *WILLIAM HOLDER* | who departed this Life | on the 12th March 1725. | Aged 57 Years | Alfo the Body | of *WILLIAM HOLDER Efq^r* | Grand-fon to the above | *WILLIAM HOLDER* | who died 14th Augt 1752 | Aged 31. | *Mrs ELIZABETH HOLDER* | wife of the above *WILL^M HOLDER* | who died in ENGLAND June 19. 1783 | and was buried at *Hinton* | near *Bath* Somerfetfhire.

I could not find any entries in the Burial Register.

THORPE'S PLANTATION.

986. On a white marble slab over a vault :—

Here Lyeth ye Body of | ALICE THORPE Who Depa | rted this Life Nov^{br} 11th 1721 | Aged 91 years.

I could not find any entry in the Burial Register.

---

987. On the windmill here, cut on a stone lozenge, is :—

C . I . L . | 24 Oct^r | 1810.

PORTER'S PLANTATION.

On this estate, now the property and residence of Dr. Pilgrim, near the great house, is a small building used as a bath.

Fixed in the interior is a stone with this inscription, which Dr. Pilgrim copied for me on 7 Jan. 1914, when we attended a garden party here :—

987 A. Invito | Dudleio Woodbridge Arm^{gro} | (amante nihilominus munditia) | in Balnearium | Hoc Conclave | (aquā nimium inundant | abiit | VII Kal. Aps. MDCCXXXV | Thos. Hill. Inv^t.

ST. PETER'S, SPEIGHTS TOWN.

On the south wall of nave are five tablets :—

988. IN MEMORY OF | EDWARD PANTER, | INFANT SON | OF | JOHN LEACH PANTER & SARAH PANTER, | OF LONDON | WHO DIED | XIITH OF JANUARY MDCCCIV ; | AGED XII MONTHS.

989. Near this Place | are depofited the Remains of | ELIZABETH JENNETT SOBER | who died December the 26th A.D. 1795 | Aged 8 Months and 19 Days | (3 lines; erected by parents.)

990. Sacred to the Memory of | *SUSANNA ROLLOCK BRUCE,* | who at the early age of twenty Years | (16 lines) | died leaving a husband & infant | (no date.)

991. Sacred to the Memory of MICHAEL HOWARD who departed this life Auguft 29th A.D. 1816 Aged 36 Years | And of his two Sons MICHAEL SKEETE HOWARD and JOHN ROBERT HOWARD | The former died six days previous to his Father Aged 4 Years and 4 Months | The latter was taken from his sorrowing Mother ANN BELL HOWARD the 3rd of September following | Aged 2 Years and 9 Months | (4 lines.)

992. A Tribute of regard to the memory of | JOHN GAY GODING Junior Esquire, | who departed this life | the 18th of December 1845 | Aged 23 Years | (2 lines.)

993. On west wall of nave near font :—

In the Yard of this Church are entomb'd the Remains | of Mifs FRANCES E. HAWKESWORTH SPRINGER | (Daughter of THOMAS JOHNSON SPRINGER) and | HITTIBELLA his Wife) who died 31st October 1809 | Æt. 20 Months | (2 lines.)

994. Around white marble font :—

THE GEFT OF IOHN SOBER *Esqr* TO THE PARISH OF SAINT PETERS 1767.

Below, on the marble floor :—

TO THE GLORY OF GOD | AND IN MEMORY OF | JOHN SOBER, ESQ^{RE} | WHO DIED 1816 | THIS FONT IS RESTORED BY HIS GRAND-NEPHEW | COL. HARRISON WALKE JOHN TRENT-STOUGHTON, | *OF ASHTON HALL, 1891.*

John and Tho. Sober were of Barbados in 1638. The will of Robert was dated 1685. John of St. Peters, b. 1715, d. 1755, will (153, Cæsar), and his son John, b. 1739, was living 1772, and had three sons, Hope-Elletson, John and Abr. Cumberbatch. Several of the family were buried in the crypt of St. Paul's Cathedral. The will of Tho. Walke of Barbados, Esq., was proved in 1800 (826, Adderley). His niece Jennett mar. Samson Wood Sober, and their dau. Judith mar. 1818 Fra. Onslow Trent, Lieut. 14th Light Dragoons.

Col. Harrison Walke Trent mar. 1889 Rose, dau. of Wm. Plunkett, widow of Tho. Anthony Stoughton ; assumed the surname of Stoughton, and d. 1899.

995. At west wall of nave :—

To the Memory of | WARD HARRIS ESQ^R | Who died the 2nd of June 1761, | Aged 49 Years | (4 lines.)

996. Adjoining above is :—

Alſo to the Memory of | ELIZABETH HARRIS | Wife of the aforeſaid | WARD HARRIS ESQ^R | Who died the 13th of January 1791, | Aged 70 Years | (4 lines.)

---

997. On the north wall of the nave are five tablets. West of the door :—

In | Loving Memory of | ROBERT CHALLENOR ESQUIRE | WHO DEPARTED THIS LIFE | ON THE 16TH DAY OF JULY 1907, AGED 65 YEARS | (1 line) | **Also |** CAPTAIN R. R. CHALLENOR | THE LANCASHIRE FUSILIERS | ELDEST SON OF ABOVE | WHO WAS KILLED IN ACTION AT BOSCH BULT, | SOUTH AFRICA ; | ON THE 31ST DAY OF MARCH 1902, AGED 31 YEARS.

CREST.— *Lion passant holding broken spear.*
MOTTO.—DULCE ET DECORUM EST PRO PATRIA MORI.

---

998. Brass on north wall of nave :—

CREST.—*Out of a coronet a pelican vulning herself.*
MOTTO below.—GAUDET TENTAMINE VIRTUS.

SACRED TO THE MEMORY OF | ARCHIBALD JONES PILE C.M.G. | WHO DIED 2ND SEPTEMBER 1898 | AT GRENES S^T GEORGE, AGED 52 | AND IS BURIED IN THE VAULT | UNDER THE CHANCEL OF THIS CHURCH | SON OF NATHANIEL J. PILE. | A MEMBER OF THE HOUSE OF ASSEMBLY | FROM FEBRUARY 1872 AND SPEAKER FROM JULY 1883 | TO THE DATE OF HIS DEATH | HE WAS MEMBER OF THE EXECUTIVE COUNCIL | VICE PRESIDENT OF THE AGRICULTURAL SOCIETY | FIRST CHAIRMAN OF THE WATERWORKS DEPARTMENT | AND HELD OTHER PUBLIC APPOINTMENTS, IN ALL OF | WHICH HE TRIED TO DO HIS DUTY | HE WAS ALSO ATTORNEY FOR MANY ESTATES IN THIS ISLAND | (3 lines ; erected by widow and only son ; 4 lines follow.)

Brother of Mr. E. R. Pile of Warleigh. He was shot one evening while returning from Bridgetown.
Archibald Jones, 1 s. Nath. Jones Pile of B., esq., Exeter Coll., matric. 15 Oct. 1864, a. 18 ; B.A. 1867. Geo. Laurie, 1 s. Geo. Clarke Pile of B., gent., Exeter Coll., matric. 3 June 1876, a. 18 ; B.A. 1879. (Foster.)

---

999. North wall of nave :—

In affectionate remembrance | of | ROBERT CHALLENOR, SEN^R, | FOR 40 YEARS | A MERCHANT OF THIS TOWN, | BORN OCTOBER 12TH 1809 | DIED AUGUST 25TH 1876 | (1 line.)

1000. North wall of nave, to east of north door :—

SACRED TO THE MEMORY OF | THOMAS CHALLENOR ESQUIRE, | WHO DEPARTED THIS LIFE | THE 10TH OF MAY 1840, | AGED 64 YEARS | ALSO | TO THE MEMORY OF | MARGARET BEND | HIS WIFE | WHO DIED THE 9TH OCTOBER 1845 | AGED 64 YEARS | (3 lines ; erected by children.)

1001. North wall of nave. White marble oval to east of north door :—

SACRED | to the Memory of the Honourable William | Bishop, who for a Number of years was a Member of | Council and President of this his Majestys most ancient | and Loyal Island, and twice Commander in Chief of the same, | His eldest Son the Honourable Henry Bishop, Chief Judge of the | Precinct of Saint Michaels (which situation he was placed in by his | Parent) erects this Marble to him as a small but most sincere Token | of his Duty and Respect. He departed this Life in the City of | London on the 21 August in the Year of our Lord one | thousand eight hundred and one in the fiftieth Year | of his age generally lamented | Nil disperandum.

Wm. Bishop, s. of Henry B. and Eliz. his wife, was born in this parish, at Eton 1762—67, Fell. Com. of St. John's Coll., Cam., 3 Aug. 1767 ; student of the Middle Temple 2 Oct. 1767. The will of his son Henry was dated 29 July 1803.

1002. On a brass east wall of nave :—

In memory | of the | Venerable GEORGE MAY DALZELL FREDERICK, | Archdeacon of Barbados | and Rector for twenty years | of this Parish | Son of | GEORGE ONESIPHORUS FREDERICK of Bristol | and Margaret, (née Buchan) | who after a life of great | labour and usefulness | fell Asleep in Jesus | 8th of January 1897 | aged 66 years | (2 lines.)

1003. North wall of chancel :—

ARMS.—*Argent, a cross Gules between four piles.*
Crest and Motto of Pile, as in No. 998.

In Sacred | Memory of the | Honourable N. Jones Pile | of Warleigh & Haymans | Born July 29th 1803 Died May 19th 1876 | Member of His Majesty's | Honourable Board of Council | for twenty one years | (9 lines ; erected by widow.)

1003 A. White marble :—

SACRED | To The Memory | of | JANE HENDY | Who Died | July 7th 1830 | AGED 80 YEARS.

1004. On a tile in chancel floor :—

Sacred | to the Memory of | The Honble N. Jones Pile | by 3 children C. A. & M.

CHURCHYARD.

1004 A. Outside at west end of wall of nave :—

S. K. | 1787.

North of nave are two large slabs over vaults :—

1005. Here lies interr'd the Body of | *HETTABELLA HENDY* Wife of | *JAMES HENDY* and Daughter of | *JOHN & THOMASON HAWKESWORTH* | Departed this life 17th *November 1774.* | Aged 32 Years | Alſo | *HETTABELLA HENDY,* Daughter of | *JAMES & HETTABELLA HENDY* | Departed this life *Auguſt 23D 1777* | Aged 2 Years & 9 *Months.*

Geo. Gibbs b. 1779, m. 1802 Salvina, dau. & h. of Henry Hendy of B. (Burke's " Landed Gentry.")

1006. Adjoining preceding :—

Here lie interr'd the Remains | of *MARY* | Wife of *ROBERT EWING Efq.* | who departed this Life | the 28th of May 1776 | Aged 26 Years | Alfo two of their Children | *MARY* who died | the 23ʳᵈ of September 1774 | Aged one Year | And *ELIZABETH FORD* | the 24ᵗʰ of June 1776 | Aged 4 Years.

1007. A large high vault and a second lower one on north side of churchyard. The lower has :—

Sacred to the Memory | of | THOMAS GENT ARMSTRONG | who departed this Life | July the twenty first | one thousand eight hundred | and twelve | aged thirty one Years | and four Months.

1008. The higher one has a white marble slab on the top :—

Sacred to the Memory | of *Mifs* IOANNES BOVELL | who died on the 15ᵗʰ Day of *February* 1791 | Aged 39 Months. | Her afflicted Father JAMES BOVELL | has dedicated this Tomb to her | (3 lines.)

1009. SACRED | TO THE MEMORY OF | MARY E. FITZPATRICK, | WHO DEPARTED THIS LIFE | 1ˢᵀ NOVEMBER 1838, | AGED 29 YEARS.

1010. 𝕳ere | REST THE MORTAL REMAINS OF | MALINDA WALTER | *WHO DIED 30ᵀᴴ SEPT. 1846,* | Also of | THOMAS WALTER, | *WHO DIED 4ᵀᴴ JUNE 1851* | And of | ELIZABETH CHRISTIAN WALTER, | *WHO DIED 9ᵀᴴ NOVEMBER 1852* | (1 line.)

1011. A large vault covered with creepers at the east end of the nave :—

1012. On a buttress of the chancel :—

BUILT BY C. J. Greenidge 1876.

1013. On the east wall of chancel :—

J. W. A. & W. H. J.

1014. A broken white marble urn and part of slab lie in churchyard.

1015. SACRED | to the Memory of | JOSEPH JOHNSON | DIED A.D. 1853 | AGED 94 | (2 lines.)

1016 and 1017. Two large vaults north-east of churchyard covered by creepers.

1018. East of chancel :—

THIS STONE COVERS | THE REMAINS OF | .... STOREY, | DEPARTED THIS LIFE | .. ULY 1819, | .... 78 YEARS.

1819, July 20. William Storey. (Burial Register.)

1019. I.H.S. | Mrs ELIZABETH ORDERSON | who survived her husband | J. E. ORDERSON | 20 years of irreproachable widowhood | lies buried here | (4 lines.)

1020. There is a third stone between the above two, but without any inscription.

1021. On loose carved slab :—

SACRED | To the memory of | JOHN BISHOP ESQ^R | Who died on the 10th June 1790. | Aged 34 | (3 lines ; by widow.)

1022. Large vault :—

HERE | lies Interred the body of | . . . . . . *NER* who died the | . . . of June 1794 | (4 lines ; by only son and widow.)

Archer gives edmund skinner d. 1794, aged 50, and this is probably the stone.

1023. Large vault :—

sacred to the memory | of | miss elizabeth cadogan | who departed this life | July 5th 1842 | Aged 90 Years | ALSO | To the Memory of her Sister | Dorothy Cadogan, | who died Oct. 24th 1851, | Aged 85 Years.

1852, Dec. 25. At Brighton, Sarah, relict of Ward Cadogan, of B. & Brinkburn Priory, Northumberland. ("G.M.," 1853, p. 219.)

Tho. Cadogan was of St. Lucy's in 1679. (Burke's "Landed Gentry.")

1024. On a ledger near the south porch :—

. . re lies Interr'd the Body of | Mr ROBERT BELLGROVE late | of this Town Merchant who | Departed this Life the 25th day of | November 1741 Aged 51 Years | Also the Body of SAMUEL BELLGROVE | son of the said ROBERT who | Departed this Life the 7 day of Iune | 1736 | Also the Body of KATHERINE BELLGROVE | who Departed this Life the 17th day | of March 1743.

1025. On a broken ledger south of the tower :—

. . . . WADE | (many lines) | 18th Year of his Age | on the 12th Day of April 1761.

1026. A ledger :—

ELIZABETH . . . . KNIGHT | . . . . 1729 | Aged 20 Years | . . . . BOWLES to Jane Burch | departed this Life | (1 line illegible) | JAMES BURCH | . . 17 . . | . . . . 67 Years | . . . . S BURCH . . . | September 2 . 1749 | Aged 65 Years | . . . . KNIGHT late Merchant | (1 line illegible) | . . August 20, 1750 | Aged 64 Years.

1027. On a ledger :—

Here lies Interred | the Body of | ELIZABETH THOMAS | who departed this Life | the 6 Day of October 1771 | Aged 32 Years.

1028. (Several lines illegible) | . . . . erected by her sister MARY THOMAS.

CHURCH PLATE.

1029. A small alms dish of Jacobean design:—

CREST.—*A boar's head couped.*
ARMS.—*Per chevron Ermine and Azure, two boars' heads couped in chief,* impaling, *Azure, a lion passant between three ladders.*

On the back: A. S.

———

1030. On a paten, also of Jacobean design:—

ARMS.—*Argent, three talbots' heads.*
CREST.—*An arm in armour, in the hand a dagger.*

There is a large flagon like the one at St. James, but without inscription.

———

ST. PETER'S CEMETERY, PART OF WHICH WAS THE OLD QUAKER BURIAL GROUND.*

1031. Marble apparently:—

Sacred | to the Memory of | Benjamin Collynns M.D. | who departed this life | April 26th 1826 | Aged 68.

This tribute of grateful remembrance is paid by his affectionate wife:—

Generous cheerful and in friendship true
He calmly paid the debt to nature due
Blefs'd son of Genius whose capacious mind
Open'd to science, to no branch confined
He deign'd with skill'd botanic art to trace.
The many plants that does our Island grace
His Country's boast for Talents found so rare
Who knew him best will heave a sigh sincere.

He was a good Botanist, and assisted Dr. Maycock in the latter's " Flora Barbadensis." (" Desultory Sketches and Tales of Barbados," p. 181.)—ED.
The stone was in the Quaker's Ground.

———

1032. Marble monument:—

In | Memory of | Charlotte Caroline Baumgarten | Died 10 July 1891 | Aged 78 yrs. | wife of | Sir John Kelly Bart. | (4 lines.)

When Sir John Kelly came in for this title he was in the Police Force, Barbados.
The title does not appear in the Baronetage of 1883.—ED.

———

1033. To | the Memory of | MARY AMELIA | the beloved wife of | John T. Corbin | who departed this life | February 25th 1863 | Aged 42 years.

———

* Contributed by Mr. E. G. Sinckler of this parish, Police Magistrate.

1034. In Memoriam | Isaac Skinner | Died Novr 8 1868 | Aged 64 years. | John Seymour Sainsbury Skinner | Died Aug: 17th 1858 | Aged 19 years. | Frank Leslie Skinner | Died Oct. 17th, 1868 | Aged 5 Mo^s | Eleanor Clifford Skinner | Died Sep: 15th 1875 | Aged 1 month. | Children of Isaac Walrond and Eleanor Jane Skinner.

The present representative of this family is Allan O'Neal Skinner, J.P., merchant, of Speights Town. His sister Elise married the Hon. Henry Bishop Skeete of St. Lucy's.

————

1035. In Memory of | An affectionate and Exemplary Son | Henry Payne | Died July 16th 1876 | Aged 25 years | Erected by his Parents Revd W. M. & S. G. Payne.

Rev. Wm. Maynard Payne, deceased, was Rector of this Parish.

————

1036. Of thin iron, probably painted, but now rusty:—

In loving Memory of | Susan E. Eckel | Daughter of | Captain W. Oneal Grey | of Galway Ireland | Relict of Revd A. E. Eckel | of Strasbourg, Alsace. | Erected by her children. | She died 6 May 1894 | Aged 82 years.

The Rector of St. Lucy tells me Captain Grey was related to the Earl of Stamford, and that the Rev. E. A. Eckel was a German. His son the Rev. Theodore Eckel married a Miss Smith, sister of F. B. Smith, I.S.O., now the Provost Marshal of Barbados.

————

1037. Our Parents | In Memory of | Charles Corbin M.D. | Born March 19th 1815 | Died Sept: 18th 1873. | and | Mary E. Corbin | his wife | Born Jany: 13th 1816. | Died Aug. 8th 1872.

One of Dr. and Mrs. Corbin's sons Charles married a Miss Hinds, and I am told one of the Gibbons's (Kenrick?) married one of this Charles Corbin's daughters by Miss Hinds. The Hinds were wealthy Barbadians.

————

1038. Sacred | to the Memory of | James Corbin | who departed this life | February 24th 1856 | Aged 63 (? 68) years | This Marble is placed here by his widow and sons | in memento of their loss of a most affectionate husband | and of one of the most tender and best of Parents.

————

1039. In Memory of | William Archer S^r | who departed this life | June 7th 1862 | Aged 50 years | The deceased was a Member of the Ancient and Honorable | Fraternity | of Free and Accepted Masons | and was for many years a Merchant | of this Town | This sincere tribute of respect and affection is | dedicated by his sorrowing Widow and Children | to the Memory of a tender and loving | Husband and Father.

————

1040. Sacred | to the Memory of | Constance Louise | Daughter of | Joseph W. and Emma L. M. Agard | who died in the Island of Trinidad W.I. | January 30th 1867 | Aged 15 months : 4 days.

————

1041. Granite monument :—

Sacred | to the Memory of | Campbell Cave Greenidge | M.D.C.M. | who died 21ˢᵗ May 1907 | Aged 62 years.

Father of Dr. Oliver Greenidge, M.B.C.M. Edin., of this parish.

1042. Sacred | to the Memory of | B. S. Perkins | who died on 20ᵗʰ Sep: 1873 | in the 34ᵗʰ year of his age.

1043. In Memory of | Frances Elizabeth | the beloved wife of | Joseph C. Greenidge | of Swans Estate | in the Parish of Sᵗ Andrew | Died 12ᵗʰ May 1862 | Aged 28 years. | Also of his two infant children.

Related to the Skinner family, represented by Allan O'Neal Skinner, J.P. (his great-uncle, I am informed).

Archer gives six inscriptions, now lost :—

1044. JOHN BOVELL d. 10 May 1700, aged 28.

1045. Nearly all obliterated :—

DREIDUIZ .. 1710 .. 1713 .. 1716 .. 1718.

1046. MARY wife of ROBERT EWING 28 May 1770 ; also ELIZABETH FORD d. 24 June 1776.

1047. EDWARD LANG, Senior aged 50, and his granddau. KATHERINE LANG yᵉ dau. of his son JOSEPH d. 22 Jan. 1736.

1048. WILLIAM POOL SMITH d. 6 Dec. 1729 aged 30, also WILLIAM BEND d. 19 Dec. 1745 aged 56.

1049. WILLIAM WALKER a child d. 1752.

ALL SAINTS' CHAPEL, ST. PETER'S PARISH.

1050. On the floor of the nave.   Blue marble :—

Here lyeth Interred | the Body of Capᵗ ABELL GAY | who departed this life the 14ᵗʰ day | of Iune 1700 in th. 65ᵗʰ yeare | of his Age.

There is a crack through the penultimate line.   Archer omitted this inscription.

1051. At the cross way :—

Here lyeth interred yᵉ body of | the Honᵇˡᵉ Wᴹ SANDIFORD Esq. one of | yᵉ Iudges of this ifland born in Briftoll | dyed yᵉ 30ᵗʰ of Decᵐ 1668 Aged 80 years | Alfo Capᵗ HENRY SANDIFORD his Son | Aged 33 year's dyed yᵉ 7ᵗʰ of Sepᵗ 1685 | Alfo ELIZ: SANDIFORD his wɪᴅᴅow | Aged 82 year's dyed yᵉ 29ᵗʰ of Marᶜʰ 1701.

1052. Adjoining the preceding is another blue marble. Carved on it are an hour-glass, wings surrounded by a snake swallowing its tail, skull and wreaths :—

Here Lyeth Interr'd ye Body of | Mrs ELIZ: FORSTER who departed | this Life ye 18th day of *January* 1717 | In the 62^d Year of her *Age* | She was *Twice Married* | her Firſt Huſband was | *Coll.* WILL^M SANDIFORD Eſq | and her laſt *Cap^{tn}* J^Nº FORSTER Eſq^r.

Major Nathaniel Kingsland of B., planter, leased his plantation in Surinam in 1664 for five years to his nephew Wm. Sandiford. Col. Rob. Sandiford banished in 1662 from Surinam, and in 1668 from B. by Lord Willoughby, removed in 1670 to Carolina.

———

1053. North porch. A floor-stone :—

Crest and Arms of Gibbons.

In Memory of ROBERT GIBBONS Eſquire | Second Son to Sr WILLIAM GIBBONS Baronet. | He died July 13th 1744 | Aged 28 Years.

———

1054. North porch floor. Blue marble adjoining Rob. Gibbons :—

ARMS.—*Three talbots' heads erased.*
There are three large cracks across the stone.

HERE LYETH THE BODY OF | GILES HALL* .... OF THIS IS | LAND ESQ. BORNE IN Y . PA .. ſh | OF †. . . . STER IN THE COUNTY | OF GLOCESTER WHO DEPARTED | THIS MORTALL LIFE THE 26 DAY | OF IANVARY AN. DOM. 1686 | AGED 84 YEARES.

In 1679 he held 195 acres (Archer, 399).
A pedigree of Hall of High Meddow with the above arms was recorded in the Visitation of co. Glouc. in 1623, but there is no Giles given.

———

1055. West porch. Ledger lying loose on floor :—

HERE LYETH THE BODY | OF MR WILLIAM MORRISON | WHO DEPARTED THIS LIFE | THE 18 OF OCTOBER 1672 | Aged 60 years | ALSO HERE LYETH THE BODY | OF ELIZABETH NORVELL (?)‡ SHE | DECEASED 30TH DAY OF | NOVEMBER (crack) 1684 | AGED 14 Y . . . S.

Below are cut a skull and crossbones. Not given by Archer.

———

1056. On a small loose stone standing on above :—

HERE LYETH THE BODY OF | PHILIP GINKINS DECEASED | IN THE VIER (*sic*) OF OUR | LORD 166 .§ THE 9TH OF | IULIE.

See genealogical additions to the "History of Stockton-upon-Tees," by W. Downing Bruce *voce* Raisbick. (Archer.)

———

* Crack, indistinct, ? LATE.   + Whitminster.
‡ "NORV" is certain.   § Uncertain. Archer gives 1663.

1057. South wall :—

SACRED | TO THE MEMORY OF | SAMUEL JAMES FENTY, | DIED 9TH DECEMBER 1871 | AGED 50 YEARS.

1058. North wall :—

In loving remembrance | of | PERCY SINCLAIR, SON OF | J. T. SHUFFLER, | DIED 2 FEBRUARY, 1883, AGED 3 YEARS | (1 line.)

1059. North wall :—

In | Memory | of | The Honble | EDWARD PACKER Member of Council | of this Island, | Who died January 3rd 1858 | Aged 39 | (10 lines; erected by his wife.)

1060. North wall :—

Arnold Evans 2nd son of John and Dorothy Deane, died Feb. 19th 1902 aged 16 years 6 months.

1061. A large Gothic marble altar-tomb near the pulpit.

Around the base :—

ERECTED BY THEIR SON IN MEMORY OF JOSEPH LYDER BRIGGS | BORN 1792, DIED 1866. | AND OF ELIZABETH BRIGGS, BORN 1800, DIED 1859.

On a brass on step at the south side :—

SACRED TO THE MEMORY OF | SIR THOMAS GRAHAM BRIGGS, BART. | ONLY SON OF JOSEPH LYDER AND HIS WIFE ELIZABETH BRIGGS | WHO WAS BORN ON SEPTEMBER 30TH 1833 | AND WENT TO HIS REST OCTOBER 11. 1887 | (1 line.)

Joseph L. Briggs mar. in 1832 Eliz., dau. of Benj. Hinds, Treasurer of Barbados, and widow of John Abel Jackmann of Rockless. T. G. B., their only child, was sometime M. of C. of B. and Nevis; was created a Baronet in 1871; mar. 9 June 1857 Mary Jane, eldest dau. of Benj. Carlton Howell, Treasurer of B.   Lady B. survives and resides in L.   Two of her sisters inhabit the fine old family mansion at Farley Hill, which is now very bare and shorn of its ancient state.   It is a very large house standing in beautiful surroundings with extensive views over the district called Scotland.

1062. On the chancel wall, south side :—

In a sunk circle on gold ground: CREST.—*A pelican on its nest vulning itself.*

TO THE GLORY OF GOD | AND | IN LOVING MEMORY OF | AUGUSTUS BRIGGS, | BORN MAY 7TH 1813 | DIED MAY 17TH 1882, | FOR SOME TIME SPEAKER OF | THE HOUSE OF ASSEMBLY | AFTERWARDS PRESIDENT OF THE | LEGISLATIVE COUNCIL | OF THIS ISLAND, | THE ORGAN CHAMBER | OF THIS CHURCH HAS BEEN | ERECTED BY HIS CHILDREN.

1063. North wall of chancel, a small Gothic two-light window :—

In Memory of Joseph Lyder Briggs by Augustus Briggs.

1064. Eastward is another :—

In Memory of Joseph Lyder Briggs by B. Hinds.

1065. On the north side is a third :—

In Memory of Joseph Lyder Briggs by N. Fod .... ham.*

1066. Within the communion rail a fourth :—

" In Memory of . . . ." | (illegible.)

1067. On the east window :—

This window is erected | to the Glory of God | and in memory | of His Parents by | THOS GRAHAM BRIGGS 1867.

1068. On the south side is a window with inscription, but only the name of " Joseph Lyder Briggs " is legible.

1069. West window of the nave, a large three-light one :—

To the memory of Samuel Maxwell Hinds | Some time Speaker of the House of Assembly of this Island | This window is erected by his Widow.

1847, May 19. At Bath, aged 52, Sam. Maxwell Hinds, for several years Speaker of the House of Assembly, B. (" G.M.," 108.)

CHURCHYARD.

1070. On the north side is a blue marble, north of chancel :—

In Memory of ELIZABETH KENRICK, | Second Daughter of the Rev. Dr SCAWEN KENRICK | Sub Dean and Prebend. of Weftminfter | and great Neice to Sr WILLIAM GIBBONS Baronet. | She died Auguft 11th 1744, | Aged 16 Years. | with Her is Inter ... OBE .... †... RICK GIBBONS. | the Eldeft Son of IOHN GIBBONS Efq. | and Grandfon of the faid Sr WILLIAM GIBBONS. | He died September 16th 1746, | Aged 2 Years.

This stone must have been placed later than 1752, the year the baronetcy was conferred.

1071. Blue marble. Jacobean shield and mantling in sunk oval :—

CREST.—*A lion's jamb erased erect, holding a cross fitchée.*

ARMS.—*Argent, a lion rampant debruised of a bend charged with a cross pattée fitchée.* Badge of Ulster. On an inescutcheon: *Argent, three lions' heads erased.* (Archer says griffins' heads.)

In Memory of Dame FRANCES GIBBONS | Daughter of ROBERT HALL Efq. of th .‡ If land | and Wife of Sr WILLIAM GIBBONS Baronet | Speaker of the Affembly. | She was Mother of four Children | of which only one furvived Her. | She behaved in the different Relations of Wife & Mother | with the greateft Prudence and the moft tender Affection | And after prepareing herfelf through her whole Life | by an exemplary Courfe of Piety for her latter End | She felt the Approach of it with Chriftian† Refignation | and in joyfull hope of a bleffed Refurrection | died December 1. 1757 | Aged 64 Years.

* Foderingham. † Cracked. ‡ Flaked.

1072. Farther north and in same line is a third vault with very long inscription of fifty-eight lines on the top slab:—

Sacred | to the Memory of the Hon: Sr WILLIAM GIBBONS Baronet | who departed this Life the 11th day of April | in the year of our Lord 1760 | in the 67th year of his Age: | After having fucceffively filled | fome of the moft confiderable Offices in the Publick | civil and military, | with Honour to himfelf and with Advantage to his Country | For the Space of thirty and three years before his Death | He was conftantly elected a Reprefentative for the Parifh of St Peter | in the General Affembly : | and for the laft feventeen of thofe years | He was as conftantly elected Speaker of the Houfe | in that Affembly | He difdained ever to make his Seat the Occafion to promote | his private emolument | and fhew'd Himfelf fuperior to every Species of Reward | but the Applaufe of his Conftituents | In the year 1742 | He was by his Excellency Sr THOMAS ROBINSON Baronet | appointed Colonel of the Leeward Regiment of Foot | which Poft however | from an honeft diffatiffaction with the Profpect of Affairs | towards the Decline of that Gentlemans Adminiftration | he refigned | But, on a brighter View which open'd to this Ifland | with the Arrival of his Excellency Mr GRENVILLE | He foon returned with new Honours to the fame Command | And in the year 1753 | Having lately been created by his Majefty a Baronet | of the Kingdom of Great Britain | and by his many faithfull Services as well as by that Mark of Royall Favour | pointed out for greater Honours in this Community | He was by that difcerning Governour | made Lieutenant General of his Majefty's Forces in this Ifland | and Mafter General of the Ordnance | yet under fuch Preferments | He never once was known to Stoop | to any mean Complyances ; | He had a Soul too great to be employd | but for the Publick Good | At length ! | Declining in his Health, tho not depreffed in his Ardour | under another Adminiftration, in an inaufpicious Hour | He provok'd in high Difpleafure. | and | on the 28th day of March preceeding his Departure, | (to clofe indeed upon the fatal Period. | yet in one bright Moment of his patriot Flame) | He was by the offended Arm of Power | fuddenly difmiffed from all his Military Services | Unfortunate | in having liv'd fo long as to furvive | the Favour of his Chief | yet happy | in having liv'd poffeffed to the laft | of the Affection of his Country.

Crest of Gibbons at west end.   Arms with Inescutcheon at east end.

John G. of St. Mich., B., Esq.   Will dated 25 Dec. 1737.   I have settled my est. in G^t B. by deed and will.   My corpse to be sent home and buried in Bath Abbey.   My s. in l. the Rev. Scawen Kenrick, Prebend. of Westminster. My brother in l. the Rev. Stewart and my sister his wife, both in Virginia.   My brother Wm. G., Esq., Ex'or.   Sworn 19 Jan. 1737.

The burials of Bath Abbey for 1737 are defective.   A Mr. John Gibbons was buried 21 Oct. 1742, but that would be too late, unless the body were temporarily buried in St. Michael's and then subsequently removed to England.

The pedigree in Burke and Betham commences with Wm., the 1st Bart., who was probably s. of Wm., the brother of testator.   See several M.I. in previous volumes of " Caribbeana."

1073. White marble cross on tomb (near the other Gibbons' vaults) :—

WILLIAM BARTON GIBBONS. | BORN MARCH 1802. DIED 11TH AUGUST 1872.

1074. North of nave wall near the west end is an altar-tomb with steps leading up to the west end of it.   On which end are several initials now indistinct and doubtful, and the date 1688.   It is supposed to commemorate William Arnold and his companions, very early settlers.   Archer gives a drawing of it, but an incorrect one.   Arnold's mill still stands on the top of the hill.

1075. Ancient tomb, no inscription.

1076. Here lies the Body | of | JOSEPH WATERMAN | *who departed this life* | On Sunday the 25 August | 1763 | Aged 20 Years.

Archer gives the age as 26.

Archer records nine more inscriptions which I did not see, so they have been presumably covered up or destroyed:—

1077. Sarah Bell, dau. of Francis & Mary Bell ob. 23 Aug. 1736 | also, Francis Bell, Esq. ob. 6 April 1739, æt. 57 | also, Francis son of the above Francis & Mary ob. 16 Aug. 1747 æt. 14 | also, Sarah wife of Francis Bell ob. 14 Feb. 1747 æt. 35 | also, Hon. Francis Bell Esq. ob. . . 1760, æt. 56.

1078. . . . . Thomas Fox & his two wifes, Prudence & Rachel Fox, | two sons John & William, | two daus. Sarah & Esther. | also Thomas, Joseph, William and Mary, William being ye last, aged 27, dyed Sept. 14, 1754, Captain William Fox.

1079. Another "Hall" slab nearly obliterated, and apparently older than the former.

1080. Richard Haynes, | ob. 1768.

1081. No date, 17th century :—

Arms.—. . . . *three lions passant in pale.*
Crest.—*A dexter arm embowed brandishing a scimetar.*
Motto.—Signos sic sacra tuimur.

Mr Michael Mahon, of the Kingdom of Ireland, & Margaret his wife of Barbados, with several of their children & grandchildren & in memory of them this monument has been erected by Mr. James Mahon, son of the above Michael & Margaret Mahon.

1082. James Prat, son of Dr. Henry Prat & Dorothy his wife, ob. April 23, 1738, æt. 2 | also Henry Prat, s. of Dr. Henry Prat . . . also Dorothy Prat, wife of Dr. Henry Prat, ob. 19 Oct. 1749.

1083. Above are these arms.—*On a chevron between three ravens close a mullet.* Below are the same arms, impaling : *On a fess dancettée three stars wavy of six points, a dexter canton charged with a sun in splendour.*

Under this stone lyes the body of Katherine, late wife of John Rokeby, merchant, dau. & coheiress of Christopher Thompson, late of this parish gent. & Katherine his wife who departed this life yᵒ 15ᵗʰ of April 1666, in yᵉ 19ᵗʰ year of her age.

(Archer's notes 1 omit.)

1084. Here lyes ye body of Captain Edward Skeete, | born y^c 13 June 1639, | and died May 14, 1727, aged 88 years.

Capt. Fra. S. sold 70 acres in 1642, and was probably father of Edward. This family intermarried several times with the Alleynes. See the arms under St. Lucy's.—[ED.]

1085. On a very old stone :—

Timothy Roberts, ob. 13 October . . . . æt. 57.

MANGROVE PLANTATION.

1086. On a white marble slab surrounded by a circular wall close to the ruins of the Great House :—

Sacred to the Memory of | *JOHN BRATHWAITE SKEETE* Efq^r | who died 15th Novr 1794, | in the 43rd Year of his Age. | His remains at his own particular | defire were removed from | St *Peter's Church* | to this place.

In his will he names his wife Agnes, son John Brathwaite S., uncle John Brathwaite and brother-in-l. Wm. Harris. He mar. Agnes, sister of the Hon. Wm. Bishop, President, also of this parish. She d. 26 Sept. 1816.

ST. PHILIP'S CHURCH.

1087. West wall of nave, south side of door :—

In the Chancel | Are depofited the Remains | Of | *The Reverend THOMAS ALLINSON* | A Native of the County of *Cumberland* | And for more than Thirty Years a Refident in this Island | Four of which Period He paffed in the afsiduous difcharge | Of His Paftoral Duty as Rector of the Parifh of | *Saint Joseph* | And Eighteen as the Exemplary Minifter | *of this Parifh* | (21 lines) | He died Auguft 19th 1815 | In the 59th Year of his Age | (Erected by FRANCES ELIZABETH ALLINSON his widow.)

Crest, arms and motto broken off and lost.

1088. Same wall, north side :—

Parental affection confecrates this marble | to the memory of a beloved Child | *ELIZA GITTENS BRATHWAITE*[*] | Aged 22 Years. | Wife to *JOHN BRATHWAITE* Efq^r | (12 lines) | Obiit Novr 15th 1805.

1089. North wall of nave :—

To the Memory of | The Honourable *JOHN GITTENS* | (12 lines) | He quitted this fcene of Mortality | Feby 1768 | Aged 55 Years | (7 lines) | Erected by his son *JOSHUA GITTENS.*

His epitaph in the "G.M.," p. 239, describes him as Chief Judge of St Michaels, M. for St Philips parish, Col. of the Windward Reg. of horse & J.P., d. 25 Feb. 1768 aged 50.

John G. was a Quaker here in 1668. (Besse, II., 281.)

---

[*] Pronounced *Brathett.*

1090. North wall of nave :—

SACRED TO THE MEMORY OF | MARY THOMAS HUNTE | WHO DEPARTED
THIS LIFE NOV^R 10TH 1852 | IN THE TWENTIETH YEAR OF HER AGE | SHE WAS THE
ONLY AND BELOVED CHILD OF HER PARENTS | ALSO IN MEMORY OF | JAMES
THOMAS BROWN | A WORTHY FRIEND WHO DIED OCT^R 21ST 1852 | IN THE
TWENTY THIRD YEAR OF HIS AGE | HE WAS THE ONLY SON OF HIS MOTHER, AND |
A BROTHER OF TWO SISTERS | (3 lines.)

1091. SACRED | TO THE MEMORY OF | WOODROFFE SINCLAIR BYAR |
WHO DIED AT CLIFTON, NEAR BRISTOL, | JANUARY 10TH 1852 | AGED 42 YEARS |
(2 lines) | ALSO OF | HENRIETTA SHARP, | HIS BELOVED WIFE | WHO
DIED IN THIS ISLAND | MARCH 15TH 1852 | AGED 28 YEARS | THIS TABLET IS
ERECTED BY HIS | AFFECTIONATE BROTHER | JOHN E. KING.

1092. SACRED | TO THE MEMORY OF | JOHN RYCROFT BEST, | OF
BLACKMANS IN THE PARISH OF S^T JOSEPH, BARBADOES, | PRESIDENT OF THIS
ISLAND, | WHO PERISHED AT SEA ON THE 14TH OF JAN^Y 1852, | BY THE BURNING
OF THE ROYAL MAIL STEAMER "AMAZON" AGED 73. | ALSO TO THE MEMORIES OF
HIS SONS | JOHN RYCROFT BEST THE ELDEST, | OF THE BENGAL CIVIL
SERVICE, | WHO DIED AT CALCUTTA, ON THE 23RD DEC^R 1829, AGED 29 |
THOMAS CADOGAN BYAM BEST, the second | WHO DIED AT BLACKMANS
THE 8TH OF MAY 1838, AGED 33 | AND OF | ABEL WILLIAM DOTTIN BEST,
FOURTH AND YOUNGEST, | CAPTAIN IN HER MAJESTY'S 80TH REG^T WHO WAS KILLED
IN ACTION | 22ND DEC^R 1845, AT FEROZESHAH IN THE EAST INDIES AGED 29 | IN
DUTIFUL AND AFFECTIONATE REMEMBRANCE OF HIS FATHER | THIS TABLET IS
ERECTED BY CHARLES HENRY BEST | THIRD AND ONLY SURVIVING SON.

His widow Cath. Henriette, yst. dau. of Richard Count De Vins, d. 1855;
M.I. at Leckhampton, co. Glouc. Her father's will was dated 1799 and proved
1808 (100 Ely).

Tho. Best, son of John B. of B., of Magd. Coll., Oxf., matric. 24 Jan. 1801,
aged 18; killed Lord Camelford in a duel, and died Sept. 1829, aged 48. He
may have been younger brother of John.

1093. CREST.—*A dove, from its beak* DEO GRATIAS. MOTTO.—VÆ VICTIS.

SACRED TO THE MEMORY OF | EDWARD HOOPER SENHOUSE | A
POST CAPTAIN IN THE ROYAL NAVY, | AND FOR MANY YEARS PROVOST MARSHAL
OF THIS ISLAND ; | WHO DIED ON THE 22ND MAY 1863 | AGED 75 YEARS | (6 lines;
erected by widow.)

He mar. in 1815 Eliz. Bishop, dau. of John Spooner. ("Caribbeana," I., xiii.)
He designed Christ Church.

1094. On east wall of nave, near pulpit, on north side :—

IN MEMORY OF | NATHAN YOUNG | FOR MANY YEARS | A PRACTITIONER
OF MEDICINE IN THIS PARISH ; | HE DIED IN 1754, AGED 54 YEARS | AND OF HIS
SON | NATHAN LEWIS YOUNG | FOR MANY YEARS ALSO | A PRACTITIONER
OF MEDICINE IN THIS PARISH ; | HE DIED 28TH FEBRUARY 1771, AGED 37 YEARS |
AND OF HIS WIFE MARY YOUNG, | WHO DIED 10TH MARCH 1809, AGED
74 YEARS | AND OF THEIR SON LEWIS YOUNG, | WHO WAS HIGHLY ESTEEMED
FOR HIS PROBITY | AND VALUED FOR THE ZEAL AND KNOWLEDGE | HE DISPLAYED
IN HIS PRACTICE | OF THE MEDICAL PROFESSION FOR 30 YEARS | IN THIS PARISH
ALSO | HE DIED 5TH APRIL 1817, AGED 52 YEARS | AND OF HIS WIFE ELIZABETH

YOUNG, | who died 25ᵀᴴ february 1816, aged 42 years | and also of | ASTLEY ANN COOPER YOUNG | who died 6ᵀᴴ december 1858, aged 18 months | and of MARIANNE CHARLOTTE YOUNG | who died 6ᵀᴴ december 1858, aged 68 years | the child and wife of NATHAN LEWIS YOUNG | by whom this tablet is erected 1863.

On brass below :—

In Memoriam Nathan Lewis Young M.D. | died at St Leonards on Sea England | July X. M.DCCCLXVI Aged LXXI Years.

———

1095. On a triangular tablet at west end of south wall of nave:—

In Memory of | NATHANIEL SIMS WEEKES Esqr: | Native of this Island | who died at the Cove of Cork | on the 12ᵗʰ of December 1800, | and was there Inter'd, | Aged 60 Years.

Probably father of Dr. Nath. Weekes of this parish, whose will was dated 1808. (516, Loveday.)

———

1096. HUGH FRASER MACPHERSON, | of inverness | died at sea 20ᵀᴴ april 1852, | and rests in this churchyard | (1 line.)

———

1097. AFFECTION | dedicates this little tablet to the memory | of a beloved wife | MARGARET ANN GITTENS, | (5 lines) | born april 1ˢᵀ 1821, died august 3ᴿᴰ 1854 | to the memory also of a dear child | HERBERT CALLENDER GITTENS, | the last pledge of mutual affection, | born april 17ᵀᴴ 1852, died september 8ᵀᴴ 1855.

———

1098. sacred to the memory of | ROBERT PILGRIM TOPPIN, ESQUIRE, | who died january 15ᵀᴴ 1839, aged 36 years | (1 line) | also of, | MEHETABLE MORRIS TOPPIN, | mother of the above; | who died at clifton, near bristol, | december 18ᵀᴴ 1840, | aged 61 years.

Major Miles Toppin was of St. John's parish, *circa* 1680—90.

———

1099. On a brass to north side of reredos :—

to the glory of god and in loving memory of GEORGE HENRY ALLEYNE born august 9ᵀᴴ 1821, died december 16ᵀᴴ 1884 | (dedicated by his widow.)

The window was also placed to his memory.

———

CHURCHYARD.

1100. On the north side is a blue marble under a large cotton tree :—

Hic Sepvlta jacet | Margarita Noke vxor | Richardi Noke nvper | Hvjvs Insvlae Secr- | etarii & Filia Gvlielmi | Bytton ex antiqva Fam- | ilia de Bytton de D- | vffy; in cvjvs optime | Merentis Memoriam | trist . . . Dolensque | Conjvx Hoc posvit | OBiit xxiiii ivly 1677.

1677, Aug. 11. Margaret, wife of Richard Noake Esq. (Burial Register.)

"1. Richard Noke of London Gent: eldest son now going to live in Barbados ætatis an: 45: Nov: 2: 1666." (Visitations of Berkshire, Harl. Soc. Pub., p. 251.)

"3. Charles Noke obijt sine prole, buried in Barbadoes 166⅘."

1101. Jacobean shield in sunk circle :—

ARMS.—. . . . *three roundles, a chief embattled.*

Here lyeth interred y⁵ body of William | Goodall of Hampshire in y⁵ Kingdom of | England Esqʳ, who departed this life y⁵ 8ᵗʰ | of November 1690 in y⁵ 70ᵗʰ year of his | age and Jane his wife who dyed y⁵ 19ᵗʰ of | September 1670, in y⁵ 29ᵗʰ year of her age | and also their two daughters Millesaint | & Ann, who dyed in their Infancy | This ſtone was laid by ther (sic) surviving | daughters viz | Jane y⁵ wife of Edward Wintour of Londᵒ | merchᵗ & Millesaint y⁵ wife of Capᵗ | David Ramsay of Barbados | In testimony of their duty to y⁵ pious | memory of their deceased Parents.

1690, Nov. 9. William Goodall Esq.
There are several Ramsay entries in the Registers.

———

1102. Under this stone were interr'd the bodie(s of) Elliot Saer & Iane his wife. | He died the 27 of March 1756 aged 66 . . e died the 21ˢᵗ of April 1761 Aged 6 . | (3 lines.)

———

1103. White marble slab. Jacobean shield in a sunk circle :—

ARMS.—*Argent, a saltire engrailed.** On an inescutcheon : *Argent, a St. George's cross ;* impaling, *Argent, three lions rampant, ducally crowned.*
No crest.

Here lye the Bodies of | ROBERT BISHOP Eſqʳ who departed | this life Septʳ 16ᵗʰ 1715 Æ. 35 Years | And | MARY FORBES Relict of ROBERT BISHOP | Eſqʳ who departed this life | May 26ᵗʰ 1734 Æ. 48 Years | And | MARY MORRIS Daughter of ROBERT | and MARY BISHOP, who departed | this life May 25ᵗʰ 1743 | Æ. 33 Years.

1734, May 27. . . . . wife of Col : Will Forbes.
1743, May 27 (*sic*). . . . ., wife of Jasper Morris. (Burial Register.)

———

1104. Blue marble :—

Here Lyeth Interrd y⁵ Body of | JOHN BAKER who departed | this life the 23ᵈ day of Iuly 1716 | Aged 53 years | And his three Children.

———

1105. White marble :—

SACRED | To the memory of | CONNOR JOSEPH O'BRYEN | eldest son of | JAMES POWER O'BRYEN | Ireland who died | April 9ᵗʰ 1861 | Aged 41 Years | (4 lines.)

———

1106. IN MEMORY OF. | NATHAN LEWIS YOUNG, | WHO DIED 28ᵀᴴ FEBRUARY 1771, | AGED 37 YEARS | AND OF HIS WIFE MARY | WHO DIED 10ᵀᴴ MARCH 1809, | AGED 74 YEARS | ALSO OF THEIR SON LEWIS | WHO DIED 5ᵀᴴ APRIL 1817 | AGED 52 YEARS | AND OF HIS WIFE MARY ELIZABETH | WHO DIED 25ᵀᴴ FEBRUARY 1814 | AGED 42 YEARS | ALSO OF ASTLEY ANN COOPER THE | INFANT DAUGHTER OF NATHAN LEWIS | AND MAIANNE CHARLOTTE YOUNG | WHO DIED 26ᵀᴴ OCTOBER 1820 | AGED 14 MONTHS.

* Archer gives "indented."

1107. Large vault, six feet high :—

RICHARD BAYNE | obᵗ sepᵗ 3 | 1767.

1108. Similar vault, six feet high :—

WILLIAM COX | obᵗ febʸ 6 | 1766.

1109. At north-west corner of churchyard are these two blue marble slabs side by side. At the top is a Jacobean shield with mantling in sunk circle :—

CREST.—*A man in armour holding in dexter hand a battle-axe across shoulder over W. and H.*
ARMS.—*Argent, three battle-axes.*

Near this Place lyes the Body of | IAMES AYNSWORTH Efq. | Who Departed this life | the Seventh Day of May 1723. | Ætᵃ 56 years.

Gap in Burial Register 1720—23.

Then comes a Jacobean shield with mantling in circle :—

W. and H. No crest. ARMS.—*Three mascles.*

And here lyes the Body of | *ELIZABETH AYNSWORTH* | (*Wife* of the abovesaid *JAMES AYNSWORTH Efq*) | who departed this Life the Eighteenth | Day of September Anno Domini MDCCXXIII | in the LV Year of her Age.

1110. A Jacobean shield and mantling in circle :—

CREST.—*Out of a coronet a lion sejant over W. and H.*
ARMS.—*Argent, between three griffins segreant, a bar indented.*

Here lyeth the Body of | JOHN HOLDER Efqʳ | who departed this Life the 22ᵈ day of March | Anno Domini MDCCXXIV | Ætaᵃ XXXI years.

1111. Two stones under a willow tree :—

Here Lieth the Body of | ROBERT HAYNES who | Departed this Life the 9ᵗʰ | Day of October 1727 in | the 70ᵗʰ Year of his Age.

.1727, Oct. 10. Robert Hanes. (Burial Register.)

1112. To the worthy Memory of | ROBERT BOWCHER ESQᴿ who was | born Sepᵇʳ the 3ᵈ 1707 and died march 7ᵗʰ 1739 | his disconsolate widow Elizᵃ Bowcher as the | last Instance of her love and Gratitude has | caused this monument to be erected.

1113. Large vault :—

To THE MEMORY OF | WILLIAM FRANCIS CARTER | WHO DIED JUNE 5ᵀᴴ 1858 | AGED 30 YEARS | (several lines; erected by widow, etc.)

1114. Sacred to the Memory of | *JOHN ARCHER Efq^r* | who died October 30th 1786 | And of ANN his Wife who departed | this life May 8th 1794 | Both Aged 50 Years | (4 lines) | Here is alſo Intered the Remains of | *M^{RS} MILLICENT WHITE* | Siſter to the above *ANN ARCHER* | 1798.

1115. Sacred to the Memory | of | NATHANIEL ROACH ESQ^R | of | White River Plantation | who departed this Life | May the 6th 1819 | In the 24th Year of his Age | *This Marble* | *is erected by his affectionate Wife* | *HARRIOT ROACH* | ALSO | In Memory of | JANE ROACH | Mother of the above Nathaniel Roach | who departed this life 14th December 1837 | Aged 63 Years.

1116. Aberdeen granite :—

SACRED TO THE MEMORY | OF | JAMES SAMUEL CLARKE | WHO DIED ON | 18TH DECEMBER 1875 | AGED 51 YEARS.

At foot of above, enclosed by railing :—

Sacred | to the memory of | ANNE ISABEL | WIFE OF | JAMES SAMUEL CLARKE | BORN 11TH DECEMBER 1834 | DIED 7 JANUARY 1884 | AND | ANNIE HELEN LOUISE | THEIR DAUGHTER | BORN 5TH DECEMBER 1871 | DIED 24 DECEMBER 1875.

J. S. C. was a planter, and father of the present Attorney-Gen. the Hon. C. P. Clarke, and of the Speaker, Sir F. J. Clarke, K.C.M.G.

1117. South of walk to the Tower :—

SACRED | to the memory | *of* | ELIZABETH ANN | the beloved wife of | EMANUEL JOHN COCK HUTCHINSON | who departed this life the 11th day of | October 1847 Aged | 64 Years | (2 lines.)

1118. *SACRED* | To the memory of | KATE ANNIE | daughter of JOHN ALLEYNE and | ANNE WALROND DEAN | who died 8th October 1848 | Aged 1 Year and 11 Months | Also of | ANNE WALROND DEAN | Mother of the above who departed this life | February 3^d 1852 Aged 30 Years.

1119. Aberdeen granite to George Henry Deane, died 26 March 1864, aged 50 (s. of J. A. D.).

1120. Two very large vaults without names.

1121. Grey granite east of chancel :—

HERE LIE THE BODIES | OF | JAMES THOMAS BROWN | WHO DEPARTED THIS LIFE OCTOBER 21ST 1852 | IN THE 23RD YEAR OF HIS AGE | HE WAS THE ONLY SON OF HIS MOTHER | AND A LOVING BROTHER TO HIS SISTERS | ALSO | MARY JANE HARDING | AUNT OF THE ABOVE YOUTH | WHO DIED DECEMBER 11TH 1847 | IN THE 42ND YEAR OF HER AGE | (erected by IAMES HUNTE.)

1122. North side. White marble :—

In Loving Memory | **of** | REV^D E. LISLE SMITH | RECTOR OF THIS PARISH | FROM 1892 TO 1901 | DIED 24TH APRIL 1903 | AGED 68 | (2 lines.)

1123. On a large vault to the north of churchyard :—

TOMB | OF THE | LORD FAMILY | LONG BAY CASTLE. | TABLET | ERECTED BY | L^T COL. F. C. TROLLOPE | LATE GRENADIER GUARDS.

1844, Nov. 5. In Jermyn-st. Sam. Hall Lord, of Long Bay Castle, B. father of Mrs Haywood, of the Willows, near Birmingham. ("G.M.," 104.)

The local tradition is that the Lords acquired wealth from wrecking ships. Their fine house close to the sea is unoccupied ; it contains some good plaster work, the rooms and passages being very lofty and spacious. See "Caribbeana," IV.

1124. Near the east path to rectory. Large vault surmounted by a Sheraton white marble urn :—

MOTTO.—NON OMNIS MORIAR.
CREST.—*A greyhound couchant.*
ARMS.—*Gules, on a chevron [Argent] three crosses-crosslet fitchy [Sable]* (BRATHWAITE).

There is no inscription, and the Rector did not know whose tomb it was.

1125. Within iron railing is a large enclosure containing seven ledgers, on each of which is fixed a lead plate with the inscription :—

(1). Bessie Brathwaite Obit 25th Novr 1859 Aged 24 years.

(2). Henrietta D. Brathwaite Obit 1st April 1870 Aged 27.

(3). Mary E. Brathwaite Obit 15th Augst 1869 Aged 38 y^{rs}.

(4). Sacred to the memory of James Butcher Brathwaite Died Sep. 19th 1877 Aged 39 y^{rs}.

(5). Christopher Moe Brathwaite Died Sep. 6th 1877 Aged 77 years.

(6). Mary Jane Brathwaite Died 13th Feby 1875 Aged 70 years.

(7). Caroline Brathwaite Died 18 February 1875 Aged 38 y^{rs}.

The Rector said he had heard that several of the above died of leprosy.

1126. Sacred | to the Memories of the children of | William Senhouse Esquire | & Elizabeth-Ward his wife | Humphrey Senhouse | Died November 10th 1780 aged one month | Sarah-Ward Senhouse | died December 2nd 1785 Aged 1 year | James-Lowther Senhouse | died March 31st 1794 aged 21 years | (6 lines) | Also Joseph Senhouse | died Augst 17th 1797 aged 14 years | Also Edward Hooper Senhouse Cap. R.N. | Died May 22nd 1863 | Aged 76 years.

1127. Sacred to the Memory | of | THOMAS PIGGOTT Son of | THOMAS PIGGOTT and | SARAH his Wife who died July 20th | 1801 Aged 40 Years.

1128. Large tomb :—

R. & F. Hunte 1823.

1129. Large tomb :—

I. SIMMONS 1828.

I was told that he came from Scotland, and was in the Customs, and his descendants about two years ago acquired his Scotch property. The family is now called Simmons-Anderson.

See " Caribbeana," I., 66, for pedigree of Simmons.

1839, June 20. At Hellingby, Sussex, James, 2d s. of James Baber, of Leelands, to Mary Anne, dau. of H. P. Simmons, of B. (" G.M.," 196.)

1130. Ledger :—

Sacred to the Memory of | TEMPERANCE CARTER, Wife of | TIMOTHY CARTER | died Sunday 21st June 1789 . . 37 | (13 lines.)

1131. SACRED TO THE MEMORY OF | CHRISTIAN ROSE DIED DECEMBER 5, 1818, 50TH YEAR OF HER AGE | (Stone inscribed by her dau. Jane Ann Gittens.)

1132. SACRED TO THE MEMORY OF WILLIAM HARRISON DIED APRIL 16TH 1845 IN HIS 42ND YEAR.

1133. Sacred to the Memory of | NATHANIEL KIRTON Esqre Proprietor of the Foursquare and Brewsters estates | who departed this life on the 4th of March 1859 | Aged 75 years | This tablet was erected by his children and grandchildren.

1134. Sacred to the Memory of JONAS WILKINGSON ESQRE | who departed this life on the | 16th day of August 1843 | In the 70th year of his age | (4 lines; erected by surviving sons) | Also of | FRANCIS ANNE | daughter of the above | who died on the 16th December 1850 | Aged 19 years | And of | CHARLOTTE, his Wife who entered into her rest | 23 August 1864, aged 81 years.

1135. Beneath this stone | lie the remains of | JOHN PITCHER ESQRE | who was born June 8th 1799 | and died September 1st 1855 | Aged 56 years | (7 lines; erected by his widow.)

1136. In Memory | of | JAMES N. NURSE | born July 30 1834 | Died November 17. 1881 | (2 lines; placed by his friends Henrietta Smith and W. H. Smith.)

1137. Beneath this Tomb rest the | Earthly remains of | BRYAN TAYLOR ESQR | a respectable inhabitant of the Parish of Saint Phillip he | departed this for a better life the 4 day of August 1802 | in the 58th year of his Age.

1138. Here lyeth Interred the Body of | DOROTHY HEARNE Wife of | JOHN HEARNE who departed this life | the 8ᵗʰ day of January 1723 | Aged 26 Years.

1139. Skull and hour-glass.   On a lozenge-shaped marble at end of tomb :—

1839 | E B | E B R | S T H.

1141. MARIA LOUISA | GITTENS | Obiit | August 6ᵗʰ 1854 | Aged 21 years | daughter of | Mary S. Gittens.

1142. Ledger.   Jacobean shield and mantling in sunk circle :—

ARMS.—. . . ., *three pears, out of a chief a demi-lion rampant*; impaling, *A fesse and in chief three roses.*

Archer gives crest : *A raven holding a flower.*   The omission may be my error.

Here lyes yᵉ Body of Mʳ John Perratt | who departed this Life June the 7ᵗʰ 1729 | Aged 74 years | Here also lyes the Body of | Mʳˢ ANN PERRATT Wife of yᵉ abovesaid | who departed this Life March yᵉ 16ᵗʰ 172⅝ | Aged 63 Years or thereabouts.

1143. Here lyeth the Body of | HENINGHAM CARRINTON Widow | of PAUL CARRINTON (*sic*) who Died | January the 28 Day 1744 | Aged 69 Years.

Her will was dated 12 Feb. 1744-5.   Her husband was a doctor.

1144. On an inserted lozenge :—

The Vault of | SAMᴸ GRETTON | ESQ. July 30, 1767.

1145. Here lieth Interred the Body of | M. MARY ROGERS Relict of Capᵗ | HENRY ROGERS who departed | this life the 8ᵗʰ day of September | 1753 Aged 57 years.

1146. Against the south wall of the chancel :—

In loving Memory of | Sarah S. Millard | fell asleep 7 January 1897 | Aged 79 | (1 line.   I was told she was the Rev. R. F. Berkeley's wife's sister.)

1147. In loving Memory of | R. Fitzhardinge Berkeley | Priest | Rector of this Parish 1880—1891 | fell asleep 18 July 1893 | Aged 68 | (1 line.)

1148. In loving Memory of LETITIA MARIA | Wife of the Rev. Lisle Smith | fell asleep in Jesus March 30, 1901 | Aged 64.

1149. On a lozenge fixed on a large vault :—

THE VAULT OF | . . . . | GITTENS F . . . . | 1822.

Archer gives the following 21 inscriptions, which I did not see. As most of them were fragmentary, they have no doubt been lost beyond recovery :—

1150. John Best . . . . died 21 Aug. 1758 aged 50.

1151. J. B. died 1743. J. B. died 1745.

1152. A. C. died 1752.

1153. Isaac Gittens d. 1819.

1154. John H . . . dy d. 1790. (Fragment.)

1155. Mary wife of Henry Herne d. 1725. (Fragment.)

1156. John Hall Esq. d. 22 March 1729.

ARMS.—*A fess indented between three griffins segreant.*
CREST.—*On a ducal crown a lion sejant.*

1157. Laetitia Moe d. 1735. James Moe . . . . Samuel Moe . . . . Christian Moe . . . .

1158. A . . . . M . . . . d. 1743. (Fragment.)

1159. J . . . . M . . . . d. 1743. (Fragment.)

1160. James Mapp Esq. d. 1757.

1161. Richard Payne . . . . d. 1769. (Fragment.)

1162. W. P . . . . 1741. (Fragment.)

1163. I. P . . . . 1772. (Fragment.)

1164. R . . . . R . . . . d. 1755. (Fragment.)

1165. Mrs Mary Rogers wife of Henry Rogers Esq. d. Sept. . 1753 aged 57.

1166. Henry Scott d. Feb. 6, 1793.

1167. T . . . . S . . . . 1777.

1168. K . . . . W . . . . 1730. (Fragment.)

1169. C . . . . W . . . . 1757. (Fragment.)

1170. William . . | of the kingdom of . . | this life ye 8th . . . | year of his age . . . | dyed ye 19th of . . | . ear of her age . . . | . . rthers . . | Millesaunt . . . (White?) . . | infancy . . .

There is a Quaker burial-ground in the village, but the Rector said there were no stones in it.

HALTON'S PLANTATION.

1171. In a walled enclosure.   Modern white marble tablet :—

THIS TABLET │ MARKS THE BURIAL PLACE OF │ THE ROUS FAMILY │ FROM
WOOTTON UNDEREDGE, COUNTY OF GLOUCESTER │ IN ENGLAND. │ THE HON.
SAMUEL ROUS, │ PRESIDENT OF THIS ISLAND IN THE REIGN OF │ HIS
MAJESTY GEORGE 3ᴿᴰ │ OF MOST GRACIOUS MEMORY; │ S. ROUS DIED A.D. 1784. │
ELIZABETH ROUS │ WIDOW OF THE ABOVE SAMUEL ROUS │ DIED 19ᵀᴴ NOVᴿ
A.D. 1796 │ THEY WERE THE LAST │ WHOSE REMAINS WERE INTERRED IN THIS
VAULT │ THE GROUND BEING FORMERLY PART OF │ HAUGHTON PLANTATION │ IN
THE PARISH OF Sᵀ PHILIP │ BARBADOES.

John Rous, gent., of Wotton-under-Edge, had two sons, John born 1673, and
Thos. born 1674, died 1737.   ARMS.—*Or, an eagle displayed Azure.*   (Rudder's
" Gloucestershire," 851, and Foster's " Alumni Oxon.")

In 1654 Tho. R. of Barbados, Esq., for £6500 c. sold to Geo. Pasfield of
Redriffe, co. Surrey, Esq., a plantation in St. Philip of 217 acres.   (" Barbados
Deeds," vol. ii., p. 668.)

By Mary dau. of Col. Reynold Alleyne, he had a son John.   Will proved
1695.   (" Geo. Fox's Journal," ii., 94.)

Sam. Rous of Clifton Hall plantation seems to have left four daus. and coh.

RICE'S PLANTATION.

1172. On a grey marble slab cracked and cemented, on the top of a vault
touching the road :—

Hic Requiescunt Oſſa │ NICHOLAI RICE ARMᴳᴵ │ Obiit 21 Septembris
1766, │ Annos Natus LXI │ Menſes IV │ Qualis Vixerat │ Talis erat Moriens │
Fide Integerrimus, │ Strenuus Amicitia; │ Refugium Pauperum, │ Suorum vere
Parens. │ A │ Patria procul, │ L . . g . . A . . . um* │ Sedibus, │ Eandem quam ab
iis accepit │ Virtutem uſque │ Coluit │ Patris optimi Memoriæ │ Filius poſuit
JOANNES RICE │ Manent etiam† depoſitiæ │ ANNÆ & NICHOLAI
Filiorum ejus │ Reliquiæ, │ xx ante Anni Det . . . torum │ Here lie interred the
Remains of │ NICHOLAS RICE Eſqʳ │ Who departed │ Septem │ Aged L │
Th . . . . ars IV Months │ remains likewiſe of │ NICHOLAS his . . . . rer │ . . . .
here depoſited th . . . . Year 1740 (or 1746).

ST. LUCY'S CHURCH.‡

1173. There are eight wall tablets.   South aisle :—

CREST.—*A cubit arm erect couped, in the hand a dagger, point upwards.*
ARMS.—*Argent, a chevron Gules between three fleurs-de-lis.*

This tablet is erected by his Friends │ in memory of │ The Hon. Henry Bishop
Skeete │ Born May 4ᵗʰ 1853. Died October 4ᵗʰ 1912. │ His genial manner and high
sense of duty │ Won for him general Esteem. │ He served his Country for 26
years │ As a Legislator and always worked │ Faithfully for his Parish. │ For 21
years │ He was Organist of this Church.

Son of the late Rev. Henry Brathwaite Skeete.   He mar. a dau. of Isaac
Walrond Skinner of Speightstown.   See his obituary in the W.I. Com. Circular
for 5 Nov. 1912.

* Cracked.   † ? hic.
‡ Mr. E. G. Sinckler very kindly transcribed the M.I. of the interior of this church and
tricked the arms, the Editor having mislaid his notes, which were afterwards found and
checked with the above.

1174. On the east wall of the nave, south side :—

IN MEMORY OF | PHILIP LOVELL PHILLIPS ESQ^{RE} M.D. | OF LAMBERTS AND DURANTS ESTATES, IN THIS ISLAND | SON OF JOHN RANDAL PHILLIPS, ESQ^{RE}, ALSO OF LAMBERTS; | DIED JULY 2ND 1869, AGED 63 YEARS | HE WAS HIGHLY ESTEEMED IN THE ISLAND HAVING DONE MUCH | TO BENEFIT THE PEOPLE, | WHOSE INTERESTS HE EVER HAD AT HEART BOTH FOR TIME AND ETERNITY. | ONE OF HIS LAST ACTS IN GODS SERVICE | WAS THE ERECTION OF THIS CHANCEL 1869 | S^T PHILIPS CHAPEL IN THE PARISH OF S^T PETERS WAS ALSO BUILT BY HIM | IN MEMORY OF HIS ONLY SON, IN THE YEAR 1861.

CREST.—Broken off, part of a ducal coronet and a tail only remaining.
ARMS.—Very indistinct. Quarterly : 1 *and* 4, *Or, a lion rampant ; 2 and 3, Argent, a chevron Gules between three wolves' heads erased* (LOVELL). On an inescutcheon, quarterly : 1 *and* 4, *A chevron between three birds' heads ; 2 and 3, Bendy with some charge on a chief.*
MOTTO.—ADJUVANTE DEO.

1175. Tablet of white marble on black. | (1 line) :—

Sacred | to the Memory of | EDWARD | ONLY CHILD OF | EDWARD AND ELIZABETH HART, | WHO DIED OF SCARLET FEVER | AFTER THE SHORT ILLNESS | OF 28 HOURS | ON THE 14TH OF DECEMBER 1837 | IN THE NINTH YEAR OF HIS AGE | (6 lines.)

1176. South aisle. Black marble ledger :—

SACRED | TO THE MEMORY OF | JOHN WRONG LEACOCK | WHO DEPARTED THIS LIFE | ON THE 26TH MARCH 1850 | AGED 78 YEARS | ALSO | TO THE MEMORY OF | HIS WIFE | REBECCA TOWNSEND LEACOCK | WHO DIED THE 1ST NOVEMBER 1831 | AGED 64 YEARS.

1177. South aisle. A tablet of white marble on black :—

SACRED | TO THE MEMORY OF | THE REVEREND HAMBLE JAMES LEACOCK | WHO DIED, AS THE WEST INDIA CHURCH MISSIONARY | TO THE WESTERN AFRICA, AT SIERRA LEONE AUGUST 20TH 1856 | AGED 61 | (9 lines.)

See a tablet to him in the church of St. Paul, Charlestown, Nevis, whereon he is styled the " Martyr of the Pongas."

1178. South aisle, lower part of church. White marble on grey :—

SACRED | TO THE MEMORY OF | JOHN GRIFFIN, | WHO DIED AT ALLEYNE DALE, OF CHOLERA, | JUNE 27TH 1854 | (6 lines ; erected by the children of Sir Reynold Abel Alleyne, Bart., in recognition of his long and faithful service.)

1179. On the north wall of the nave, east end :—

CREST.—*Out of a ducal coronet a griffin's head.*

TO THE GLORY OF GOD | AND IN LOVING MEMORY OF | ARTHUR HODGSON CADOGAN | OF PICKERINGS S^T LUCY, BARBADOS, | AND BRINKBURN PRIORY, | NORTHUMBERLAND, ENGLAND | WHO DIED 11TH MAY 1896.

There is a pedigree of this family in one of the editions of Burke's " Landed Gentry."

1180. On the east wall of the nave, north side.   Gothic brass in colours on black marble :—

Crest of Alleyne.

Arms of Alleyne.—Quartering : *Argent, two chevronels between three trefoils Azure* (? Gay, but escallops for trefoils) ; impaling, *Gules, a lion rampant Or* (OLTON).

MOTTO.—NON TUA SED PUBLICA VOTA.   Badge of Ulster.

Sacred to the loved | memory of Sir Reynold | Abel Alleyne Bar^t | Born June 10th 1789 | Died Feb^ry 14th 1870 | And Rebecca his wife, | Born Aug^st 23rd 1794 | Died June 5th 1860 | (2 lines.)

1181. Font, white marble.   "Given by SUSANA HAGGATT Widow (Relict of ye Hon. SIMON LAMBERT & OTHNIEL HAGGATT) 1747."

Her 2nd husband the Hon. Othniel H. was a merchant of Bridgetown, M. of C. 1726, Chief Baron of the Court of C. P., and died 27 Nov. 1735.   By her 1st husband she had 2 daus. : Jane, who mar. 1730 Nathl. Haggatt, son of Othniel by a previous wife, and Ruth, who mar. the Rev. Dudley Woodbridge, Rector of St. Philip's.

1182. On the floor of the south porch are two blue marble slabs :—

SACRED TO THE MEMORY OF | THOMAS W. GREAVES | *of Mount Poyer in this Parish* | Born June 11th 1792 | Died June 13th 1823 | *and of* | ELIZABETH ALICE | *his wife* | who died May 29th 1817, | *Also of* | EDWARD AUSTIN | *their son* | Born February 9th 1813 | Died December 23rd 1867.

1183. *TO THE BELOVED MEMORY OF* | ELIZABETH GRACE | *wife of* | HENRY LAWRANCE, | *and daughter of* | THOMAS W. AND ELIZABETH ALICE | GREAVES | Born December 18th 1811, | Died September 16th 1869.

1184. West porch.   Blue marble :—

THOMAS GR(IFFITH).   The wooden floor covers the remainder.   The sexton gave me the surname.

1185. On a step to the south porch.   Blue marble.   Jacobean shield with mantling in sunk oval :—

CREST.—*The sun in splendour over a helmet.*   (Archer adds : thereon *a bear or goat statant.*)

ARMS.—*Argent, three barrulets (in relief), in chief three bucks tongues.*

[Here Lye]th the Body of | [Elizabeth Gidy] Wife of | [Matthew Gidy] who was | [Born Jany ye 6] 16[8]7 | [And departe]d this Life | [The 1st day of Apr]il 1726 | [Had issue by t]he said | [Matthew Gid]dy vi sons | [And v] daughters.

The portions within brackets, no longer legible, are from Archer.

CHURCHYARD.

1186. White marble slab over vault :—

JAMES Son of Capt JAMES GRAHAM dep^{td} this life | December the 20th 1729 Aged 38 Years | Capt JAMES GRAHAM father of the aBove said JAMES | Dep: this Life July ye 12, 1730 Aged 77 Years | ELIZABETH Daughter of said JAMES GRAHAM dep^d | this Life July the 16, 1730 Aged 9 Years | MARY Wife of the abovesaid JAMES GRAHAM dep^{td} | this life May the 22^d 1747 Aged 51 Years.

1187. Sacred | TO THE MEMORY OF | EDWARD ONLY CHILD OF | EDWARD AND ELIZABETH HART | WHO DIED ON THE 14TH OF DEC^R 1837 | IN THE NINTH YEAR OF HIS AGE | ALSO | TO THE MEMORY OF | M^{RS} JANE NIHELL HUNT, | WHO DIED ON THE 25TH OF SEPTEMBER 1842, | AGED 54 YEARS | *LEAVING ONLY TWO DAUGHTERS* | *ELIZABETH HART AND MARY JANE SAINTHILL.*

1188. Enclosed within iron railing :—

In Memory of | *MARGERY*, the Wife | of BENJAMIN BABB, | who departed this Life January 26th | 1811 | *Aged 69 Years.*

1189. Enclosed within iron railing :—

SAMUEL LEACOCK | departed this Life | October 19, 1828 | Aged 64 Years.

1190. White marble headstone :—

DOWDING HOLLINGSWORTH, | SON OF JOHN AND ELIZABETH HOLLINGSWORTH, | OBIIT OCT^R 4TH 1841, | AGED 23 YEARS | (16 lines.)

1191. White marble slab* enclosed by railing :—

WE ALL FADE AS A LEAF | IN SOLEMN REMEMBRANCE | OF | OUR BELOVED MOTHER | MRS. MARY GILL | WHO WAS BORN FEBRUARY 2 . . 1776, | DIED MARCH 14TH 1863 | (9 lines ; erected by her son K. G. GILL.)

1192. SACRED | TO THE MEMORY OF | THOMAS CONNELL | WHO DIED 22ND SEPT^R 1846, | AGED 75 YEARS | AND | ELIZABETH HIS WIFE | WHO DIED 12TH JULY 1827, | AGED 53 YEARS.

1193. Blue marble :—

IN MEMORIAM | M^{RS} ANN ROCK | WIDOW, | BORN 17TH MAY 1783 | DIED 2ND MAY 1870.

1194. White marble :—

This Marble | is erected to perpetuate | the Memory of | SUSANAH BOWEN, | wife of | JOHN BOWEN | and BENJAMIN JOHN BOWEN, | son of the said | JOHN & SUSANAH | The former of whom departed this Life, | in giving Birth to the latter | May 1st 1796. | Aged 41 Y^{RS} 11 Mo^s & 24 Days. | and | the latter December 5th 1820 | (3 lines.)

* This stone required cleaning.

1195. White marble enclosed by iron railing :—

Sacred To The Memory Of | SARAH ELLIOTT | only Child of JOHN & MARY EDWARD | ARCHER who died April 1st 1858 | Aged 24 Years | (4 lines) | ALSO | OF JOHN ARCHER | who died January 19th, 1860 | Aged 49 Years | (6 lines.)

1196. Large mausoleum south side of churchyard. Upright white marble let into east end of vault :—

𝔖𝔞𝔠𝔯𝔢𝔡 | to the Memory of | FRANCIS ANN, | wife of | CHARLES WHITFOOT GREAVES | who departed this Life | September 10ᵗʰ 1823 | Aged 29 Years | (4 lines.)

1197. Another large vault has no name.

1198. White marble :—

SACRED | TO THE MEMORY OF | THOMAS WALTER ESQʀᴱ | WHO DIED NOVᴿ 25ᵀᴴ 1813 | AGED 53 YEARS.

1199. 𝔖𝔞𝔠𝔯𝔢𝔡 | TO THE MEMORY OF | JAMES CRAGG, | THE BELOVED CHILD OF | JOHN AND ALITHEA KELLMAN | OF THE PARISH OF SAINT LUCY, | WHO DEPARTED THIS LIFE | 26 MARCH 1840 | AGED 4 YEARS AND 3 MONTHS | (4 lines.)

1200. 𝔖𝔞𝔠𝔯𝔢𝔡 | TO THE MEMORY OF | JOSEPH CORBIN | WHO DEPARTED THIS LIFE JANᴮʏ 1ˢᵀ 1855, | AGED 66 YEARS | (40 years clerk of Sᵗ Peter's parish church) | (many lines ; erected by widow.)

1201. White marble headstone :—

𝔖𝔞𝔠𝔯𝔢𝔡 | TO | THE MEMORY OF | JOHN KELLMAN ESQʀᴱ | OF CHANCE HALL IN THIS PARISH | BORN 18ᵀᴴ DECEMBER 1794 | DIED 10ᵀᴴ JULY 1862 | (4 lines.)

1202. White marble headstone :—

𝔖𝔞𝔠𝔯𝔢𝔡 | TO THE MEMORY OF | SHADRACK KELLMAN ESQʀᴱ | OF THIS PARISH | WHO DEPARTED THIS LIFE JULY 8ᵀᴴ 1865 | AGED 69 YEARS | (2 lines.)

1203. Large vault. No name. ? Grannum, according to the Sexton.

1204. Covered up with turf :—

THIS STONE | IS INSCRIBED BY | WILLIAM WATSON | OF THE COTTAGE PLANTATION, | TO THE MEMORY OF HIS FATHER, | WILLIAM | WHO DIED 13ᵀᴴ JULY 1818 | AGED 56 YEARS.

1205. Partly buried :—

This Marble is dedicated | to the *MEMORY* of | THOMAS WHITFOOT Efquire | who died 17ᵗʰ July 1796, | Aged 41 Years | (9 lines.)

1206. A stone ledger in the floor of the north porch :—

Underneath lieth the Body of | GRISSEL MACKAY | who departed this Life the 19ᵗʰ Septʳ | 1787 aged 37 Years.

1207. A large ledger standing against the west side of the interior of the porch :—

This Grave not to be opened | (space where a shield* has been) | Thomas Cadogan Efquire | died Auguft the 2ⁿᵈ 1790 | In the 63 Year of His Age | And was buried here | the next Day | (5 lines.)

See No. 1179.

1208. A large vault :—

SACRED | TO THE MEMORY OF | COLIN HUGH DALRYMPLE | BUCHANAN | WHO DEPARTED THIS LIFE | ON THE 24ᵀᴴ OF JULY 1845 | AT THE EARLY AGE OF 27 YEARS | (3 lines.)

1209. A large grave enclosed by iron railing. On the gate :—
JOHN HENRY LEACOCK.

On a black marble obelisk :—
.. F . . . . | wife of . . H . . . .† | born 1822 departed this life 1891 | . . . . born 1825 departed this life 1884.

On a ledger of white marble :—
Jane A. Leacock, | Widow of John H. Leacock M.D. | born March XIV. MDCCXCIII | departed this life | March XIV. MDCCCXLII. | (3 lines ; placed by her Son John H. Leacock.)

1210. A large tomb :—

SACRED | TO THE MEMORY OF | JOHN P. HART | WHO DIED 14ᵀᴴ DECᴮᴿ 1858 | AGED 60 YEARS | AND | THOMAS P. HART | WHO DIED 5ᵀᴴ MARCH 1859 | AGED 51 YEARS.

1211. On a ledger over vault :—

On a Jacobean mantled shield in sunk oval :—

ARMS.—*Ermine, a lion rampant ducally crowned.*
CREST.—*A lion's paw erect erased over W. and H.*

Here Lyes | COLLONELL JOSEPH PICKRING | Obiit 14 March 1715.

---

* This metal shield was removed by a mason named Rutter to Bridgetown some five or six years ago, and the Rector has not since seen it.
† There are five initials in this line in Old English and illegible.

1212. On an iron Gothic cross surrounded by an iron railing :—

" In Memoriam.   Sarah Howard, 9ᵗʰ Septʳ 1850."

Mrs. Sarah Howard, wife of Wm. Murrell Howard, M.C.P. for St. Philip's, then for St. Lucy's for many years.   She was a sister of Joseph Lyder Briggs, father of the late Sir Graham Briggs, Bart.   She mar. my maternal grandfather in 1822, and died aged 62.   The Rector wrote in the Diocesan Magazine asking persons to have the graves of their forbears renewed, so H. Graham Yearwood and I are having our maternal grandmother's cross and railing repainted and the mason work repaired.   It is in the churchyard on the right going in. [E. G. Sinckler.]

Archer gives in addition eight inscriptions :—

1213. James Butler . . 1696.   (Fragments in wall.)

1214. Several lines of eulogy to a young wife of 18.

1215. Thomas Whitecote, Esq., died 7 July 1796.   (Fragments.)

1216. I. I. Seals . . . .

1217. Michael Boyce Senior died May 9, 1750 aged 63 0. 3.

1218. W. M. Brown.   (Very old stone.)

1219. . . Salmon.   (Fragment.)

1220. R . . . . I . . . . 1750.

1221. On white marble slab set upright against the north face of a large mausoleum in canepiece near St. Swithin's Chapel :—

SACRED | To | THE MEMORY OF | MARY JANE, | WIFE OF SHADRACK KELLMAN ESQ. | WHO DEPARTED THIS LIFE THE 24ᵀᴴ DAY | JUNE 1854, AGED 47 YEARS 2 MONTHS & 9 DAYS | (several lines) | (ANN GRAGG her yˢᵗ chᵈ died of cholera 24 June aged 14 years together with her Mother.)

HOPE PLANTATION.

1222. There is a marble slab here dated 1742 to Capt. Joshua Greaves.   The dining-room has been built over it, so that it can no longer be seen.

BROMEFIELD PLANTATION.

1223. On an oval stone which was formerly part of the arch of the old windmill at Forster's :—

F. | W. M. | DECᴿ 12 | 1745.

The old tomb which formerly stood in the wood has disappeared, with the exception of a fragment of elaborate carving of white marble lying outside the entrance of the house.

ST. THOMAS' CHURCH.

The floor being new, probably the old ledgers have been removed.

1224. White marble. West wall of nave, south side :—

Sacred to the Memory of | *ELIZABETH MARTHA SMITTEN* Daughter | of *RICHARD & KATH^E SMITTEN* who died | Auguſt 31ˢᵗ 1808 Aged 20 Months | (10 lines.)

1225. White marble, north side :—

SACRED | TO THE MEMORY OF | REYNOLD ALLEYNE ELLCOCK ESQᴿᴱ | WHO DIED ON THE 2ᴺᴰ OCTOBER 1821, | AGED 32 YEARS | (2 lines ; erected by widow.)

He mar. Oct. 1811 Miss Applewhaite of Bentleys, and their only child Mary mar. 6 Oct. 1834 T. Noel Harris.

1226. North wall of nave :—

THIS TABLET IS ERECTED BY | THOMAS ELLIS | IN AFFECTIONATE REMEMBRANCE OF | HIS BELOVED SON | JOHN BRYANTE | WHO DIED AUGUST 3ᴿᴰ 1869 | AT THE EARLY AGE OF 24 | (1 line.)

1227. North wall of nave :—

THIS TABLET IS ERECTED BY | THOMAS ELLIS, AS A TOKEN OF DEEP | REGRET FOR THE LOSS OF HIS AFFECTIONATE WIFE | MARY JANE, WHO DIED IN LONDON SEPᴿ 11ᵀᴴ 1856, | AGED 45 YEARS | ALSO FOR THEIR ONLY DAUGHTER MARY ANNE, | WHO DIED AT PORTSMOUTH MAY 29ᵀᴴ 1851, | AT THE EARLY AGE OF 12 YEARS | (6 lines.)

1228. Marble mosaic tablet north wall of chancel :—

𝔗𝔬 𝔱𝔥𝔢 𝔰𝔞𝔠𝔯𝔢𝔡 𝔪𝔢𝔪𝔬𝔯𝔶 𝔬𝔣 | Thomas Ellis of Canefield | plantation in this parish who | died in London on the XIV | Day of November A.D. MDCCCLXX | Aged LXV Years also of Mary | Jane his wife, who died in | London on the XI day of Sepᵗ | A.D. MDCCCLVI Aged XXXV years | and were both buried in the | cemetery Kensal Green this | monument is dedicated by | their sons William and Thomas.

1229. South wall of nave :—

SACRED TO THE MEMORY OF | ARABELLA CHAVASSE, | THE BELOVED AND AFFECTIONATE WIFE OF | NATHANIEL FORTE ESQᴿ | BORN 4 APRIL 1816 | DIED 3ᴿᴰ APRIL 1851 | (4 lines.)

1230. Ditto :—

SACRED TO THE MEMORY OF | SAMUEL MAYNARD ALLEYNE | OF RIDGWAY ESTATE, | IN THIS PARISH ; | BORN 25ᵀᴴ AUGUST 1809 | (3 lines ; a husband and father) | WHO WAS DROWNED, | WHILST BATHING AT BATHSHEBA, | 20ᵀᴴ MAY 1847 | (5 lines.)   H. Wood, BRISTOL.

Bathsheba on the Windward Coast is a cool retreat much frequented by persons desiring change of air. The currents there are dangerous and cases of drowning occasionally occur.

1231. Floor of west porch :—

W. R. | Ian^r 4 | 1715 | S. R.

CHURCHYARD.

1232. Large mausoleum :—

EYARE KING Eſq | MAY .. | 18 ..

1233. Ditto :—

SACRED | TO THE MEMORY OF | WILLIAM GRANT ELLIS ESQUIRE | WHO DEPARTED THIS LIFE | JANUARY 10TH 1841 | AGED 69 YEARS.

1234. Ditto : North of chancel. No inscription.

1235. Fixed on iron railing :—

THE BURIAL GROUND | OF | RICHARD GRANNUM | ERECTED BY HIS DAUGHTER AMELIA G. GRANNUM.

On the ledger :—

SACRED TO THE MEMORY | OF | WILLIAM BRIAN GRANNUM | HUSBAND OF | SARAH ELIZABETH GRANNUM | AND BROTHER OF | SARAH MARGARET ELLIS | AMELIA G. GRANNUM | AND MARY GRANNUM | HE DEPARTED THIS LIFE | AUGUST THE 13TH 1820 | AGED 23 YEARS | ALSO | TO THE MEMORY OF | RICHARD GRANNUM | THEIR FATHER | WHO DIED OCTOBER 6TH 1820 | AGED 52 YEARS | AND TO THEIR MOTHER | AMELIA GRANT GRANNUM | WHO DIED NOV^R THE 22, 1821 | AGED 56 YEARS.

1236. Headstone :—

IN LOVING MEMORY | OF | JOHN KELLY YEARWOOD | DIED 1ST JANUARY 1895 | AGED 30 YEARS | (1 line.)

1237. Altar-tomb :—

SACRED | TO THE MEMORY OF | RICHARD RODERICK HALL | WHO DEPARTED THIS LIFE JULY 29TH 1843, AGED 40 YEARS | (6 lines, 4 of them Latin.)

1238. Close by :—

SACRED | TO THE MEMORY OF | FRANCES J. HALL | WHO DEPARTED THIS LIFE | ON THE 24TH SEPT^R 1838 | AGED 26 MONTHS.

1239. Fine old blue marble ledger. Below is a Jacobean shield with mantling in an oval :—

CREST.—*A tree on W. and H.*
ARMS.—*. . . . two bars gemelles . . . ., a bend, on a chief . . . . a tower.*

Here lyes interred the boddy (*sic*) | of major Gennerall Timothy | Thornehill who died the | first of August 1681 as likewise | the boddyes of his two wifes | boeth named Sussana & his | Eldest sonn Timothy & his Daug | hter Elizabeth & his two bro- | thers John & Isaac Thornehill.

1240. Blue marble next to it :—

Here lies Interr'd the Body of M^{RS} | IEAN WOOD (wife of MR THOMAS | WOOD and Daughter of MR ROGER | and IEAN PIGGOTT) who departed | this life the 21st Day of April 1733 | and in the 45th Year | of her Age.

1733, April 22. Mrs. Jean Wood wife of Mr Thos. Wood. (Burial Register.)

1241. Ledger :—

Died February 14th 1820 | WILL^M MARSHALL | Aged 14 Y^{rs} & 10 Months | Sacred to the Memory | of | Margaret Kedslie, and Lucy Hol- | len (twin sisters) | daughters of Geo^e | T. and Anna W. Shepherd, the for- | mer of which died Febr^y 5th 1849 | Aged 5¼ Mon^s & the latter June | 3rd Aged 9½ Mon^s | (4 lines.)

1242. Blue marble ledger :—

Here lyeth interred the body of | M^r william allamby aged about | 72 years who departed this life | upon the 4th day of october 1678.

1243. Blue marble ledger, very perfect, one crack across left bottom corner. Jacobean shield and mantling at top :—

Crest.—*A wyvern over W. and H.*
Arms.—*A lion guardant passant.*

Here lieth the bodies of Capt. | Edward Thompson Esq. who depart (*sic*) | this life the 6th day of April 1659. | And of Capt. Samvell Thompson | his Brother who departed this | life the 18th of March An^o 1655.

The preceding two old ledgers look as though they had been formerly in the church.

1244. White marble ? headstone lying loose and broken on top of a mausoleum, a portion missing. The top part is blackened. There are several lines of eulogy :—

. . . . eminent Stations | in this Island, | expired 16 Auguft 1765 | Aged 63 Years. | Mrs SARAH DUKE | who lived and died worthy fuch a Confort | is buried with Him.

"1765, Aug. 16. William Duke Esq. buried." The Rev. Wm. Duke was inducted 28 Aug. 1758. He copied the old Registers damaged by the hurricane of 10 Oct. 1780. Humphry Duke had a patent for 60 acres in St. Peter's in 1630. My copy of the "Early Settlement of Barbados" was presented by Mr. Wm. Duke, Clerk of the Assembly in 1756, to Gov. Pinfold.

1245. Ledger :—

In memory of | JOHN DRAYTON Esqr | of mollineux plantation | who departed this life | on the 11th day of Jany 1849 | aged 55 years | (3 lines ; placed by widow rebecca jane drayton.)

A A

1246. Two ledgers inside railing :—

𝕾𝖆𝖈𝖗𝖊𝖉 | TO THE MEMORY OF | GRIFFIN BASCOM ESQUIRE | LATE OF
DEMERARA | WHO DIED IN THIS ISLAND | THE 9TH JUNE 1852* | AGED 62 YEARS.

1247. Letters mossy :—

SACRED | To the Memory of | MRS MARY BASCOM | Wife of
MR JAMES BASCOM | who departed this Life | October the 30th 1789 | Aged
42 Years | (4 lines.)

1248. Ledger :—

IN MEMORY OF | WILLIAM BRIAN ELLIS | ELDEST SON OF | JOHN
THOMAS ELLIS ESQUIRE, | BORN JANUARY FIRST 1821, | DIED DECEMBER SECOND
1854, | AGED 33 | (4 lines ; erected by widow.)

1249. Alongside :—

SACRED TO THE MEMORY | OF | JOHN ELLIS | FATHER OF | JOHN THOMAS
ELLIS | AND | SARAH ELIZABETH GRANNUM | HE DEPARTED THIS LIFE | MARCH
24TH 1801 | AGED 32 YEARS | ALSO TO | REBECCA ELLIS | THEIR MOTHER | WHO
DIED | OCTOBER THE 24 TH1842 | AGED 73 YEARS.

1250. On iron railing :—

THE BURIAL PLACE | OF | WILLIAM R. GILLS | FAMILY.

1251. White marble headstone to JOHN R. G. GILL DIED 21ST MAR.
1891 AGED 28 Yrs. | (erected by widow.)

1252. White marble headstone :—

IN MEMORIAM | GEO. THOS. SHEPHERD | DIED 28 MARCH 1892 | AGED 78
YEARS | AND OF HIS WIFE | ANNA WILLIAM | DIED 6 JUNE 1897 | AGED 73 YEARS.

1253. White marble headstone enclosed by railing :—

𝕾𝖆𝖈𝖗𝖊𝖉 𝖙𝖔 𝖙𝖍𝖊 𝕸𝖊𝖒𝖔𝖗𝖞 | 𝖔𝖋 | THE HON. | JAMES WILLIAM PARRIS C.M.G. |
OF AYSHFORD | BORN 18TH NOVR 1815 | DIED 20TH JULY 1908 | (1 line) | ALSO OF |
SUSANNA HIS WIFE | BORN 7TH JAN. 1816 | DIED 20TH FEBY 1883 | (1 line.)

Paul Carrington Parris, s. of David of B., esq., matric. from Xt Ch., Oxf.,
21 Oct. 1808, a. 19. (Foster.)

1812, May 13. At Pimlico, Paul Carrington Paris, esq. of B. ("G.M.," 597.)

John Parris, Esq., will dated 1660 (161, May), seems to have been the
founder of the family.

Some modern headstones to Payne, Williams, Packer, Inniss, and Worm I did
not copy.

The four following inscriptions given by Archer are not now visible. He does
not state if they were in the church or churchyard :—

1254. William Briant Esq. & Mary his wife a native of this island, after an
exemplary discharge of ye domestic virtues, with temper & with health, by

* The 1852 doubtful. It might be 1862.

diligence with prosperity, during a most tender union of fifty-eight years, were by death separated 4 months & 11 days only, she dying Nov. 6, 1756, aged 74, he the 16th March 1757, aged 78.

To whose blameless memory this stone was deposited by their grateful & affectionate grandson J. Worrell.

ARMS.—*A chevron between three escallops.*
CREST.—*A dexter arm in armour brandishing a sword.*

They and their three children, Wm., Ann and Mary, were living here in 1715. Leigh Hunt's grandfather, the Rev. Dr. Hunt, was related to the family.

1255. A vault of the Osbornes of Springhead. No tablet.

1256. On a lead coffin :—

Here lies C. Skeet ob. Feb. 3, 1758.

1257. M. S. Sub hoc marmore positæ sunt reliquæ Ephraim Smith de agro Lincolniensi orundi matheseos scientia celebris mensurandi artis æq. professione ac usi longe primarii. Gubernante Radulpho Dom. Greio Barone de Work illustri chiliarcha et Francisco Russello precessori Barbadis facilitate perquam benefici. Ex hac vita spe beatoris excelsit Oct. 27, 1701. Pariter vitam cum sanguine fudit posuit G. Lillingtonus in hac insula regiæ majestatis consiliis.

Lord Grey was Gov. in 1701.

STURGES PLANTATION.

1258. In a cane piece near Welshman Hall gully is the old family burial-ground enclosed by a wall now broken down. It contains but a single memorial, a black marble slab, on the upper part of which, on a sunk oval, is a Jacobean shield with mantling :—

ARMS.—*Three covered cups, on a chief two lions passant.*
CREST.—*A lion's jamb erased, holding a covered cup, over W. and H.*

To | the Memory of | Doctor IONATHAN WORRELL | who clofed an ufeful Life | 21 September 1753 | Aged 56 Years | this Stone is depofited by his | affectionate and only Son.

The Manager told me that Dr. Carrington was also buried here.

CANE GARDEN PLANTATION.

1259. This slab, which was covered with earth, lies in a garden behind the village :—

HERE LYES yᶜ BODY OF | LIFᵀ COLᵒ HUMPHRY HOOK | WHO DEPARTED THIS LIFE | MARCH yᶜ 24ᵀᴴ 166⅞ | ALSO | THE BODY OF JONE HOOK HIS WIFE | WHO DEPARTED THIS LIFE 8ᴮᴱᴿ | yᶜ 22ᴰ 1673 | ALSO | THE BODY OF CAPᵀ JOHN RIDᴱʀ (*sic*) | WHO DEPARTED THIS LIFE MAY | yᶜ 18, 1675 | ALSO | THE BODY OF MARGᵀ WIFE TO | CAPᵀ GEORGE LILLINGTON WHO | DEPARTED THIS LIFE JUNE yᶜ 3ᴰ | 1680.

Capt. Geo. L. was M. of C. and aged 60 in 1708, and his will was proved in 1712 (116, Barnes).

RUGBY PLANTATION.

1260. This slab, consisting only of the upper half, was lying loose in the yard :—

Here lieth Inter'd the Body of | SARAH MASCOLL HOLLOWAY Daughter | of EDWARD & ELIZABETH HOLLOWAY | who departed this Life Auguſt 15th 1760 | Aged 9 Months 15 days | Alſo the Body of EDWARD HOLLOWAY Esqr | Father of the above Said SARAH MASCOLL | HOLLOWAY who depar (rest broken away and lost).

AYSHFORD PLANTATION.

1261. In the old burial place under trees, quite close to the house, is a slab cracked in several places :—

SACRED TO THE MEMORY OF | GEORGE HENRY TYLER | TO WHOSE PIOUS REMEMBRANCE THIS | MEMORIAL IS PLACED BY HIS | DISCONSOLATE WIDOW AS A POOR AND | LAST TRIBUTE OF HER AFFECTIONS | FOR HIS BELOVED REMAINS | WHO DEPARTED THIS LIFE FEBY 22ND 1832 | AGED 28 YEARS | (11 lines.)

1737-8, Jan. 2.   Mercy the d. of Edward Holloway Esqr & Mary his wife bap.

1832.   John Henry Tyler in the private burial ground of the Foderingham family (abode), Bridge Town, 23rd February 26 (sic).   (Parish Register.)

1262. This slab, which was formerly a step to the kitchen door, has been removed to the yard, where it is fixed near the water tank :—

Here lies Interr'd the Body of | MARY ANN the Loving and beloved | Wife of ROBERT AYSHFORD Eſqr | who after an Exemplary diſcharge of | the Several relative duties of Wife | Parent Daughter and Friend was to the | great grief of her afflicted family | . . . . lated from this Earthly abode | on . . of March 1772 Aged 37 Years | (4 lines.)

1728, Nov. 4.   Anthony the S. of Robert & Damaris Ayshford bap.

1731-2, Jan. 24.   Captain Robert A. buried.

1739, Nov. 12.   Mr Robert A. buried in a Vault in his Garden.

1772, March.   Mrs Mary Ann Ashford buried the 8th.   (Parish Register.)

STRONG HOPE.

1263. In a gully is a vault cut out of the rock with a square of marble fixed in the wall :—

WITHIN THIS VAULT | ARE DEPOSITED THE REMAINS OF | WILLIAM WILKINSON ESQ. | PROPRIETOR OF STRONG HOPE ESTATE | 1828 | . . . . | DOROTHY WILKINSON | HIS WIFE | WHO DIED OCTOBER . . . 1829 | AGED 74 YEARS.

1829. Dorothy Wilkinson Relict of the late Wm Wilkinson, Strong Hope Plantn. 4th Oct. 74.

1828. William Wilkinson, Strong Hope Plantn in this Parish. 30th Nov. 69 Years. (Burial Register.)

VAUCLUSE PLANTATION.

1264. On a blue slab in the grassland :—

HENRY PETER SIMMONS | BORN 17 MAY 1776 | DIED 19 FEBRUARY 1843.

ST. JOSEPH'S CHURCH.

The ancient parish church which formerly stood in the valley was blown down by the hurricane in 1831, and a small mortuary chapel occupies its site. This old Church is shewn in " A Prospect of Hackelton's Cliff" in Hughes' " Natural History of the Island" of 1750. The Hon. Percy Haynes of Bissex Hill kindly accompanied me on my visits to this district, and pointed out all objects of interest.

OLD CHURCHYARD.

In the floor of the mortuary chapel are four slabs.

1265. Blue marble :—

In Memory | of | DANIEL McCLOUD | Who died June 13 | 1759 | Aged 50 Years.

Gap in Burial Register from 20 Nov. 1758 to 26 Aug. 1760.

1266. CREST.—*A demi-lion couped rampant over W. and H.*
ARMS.—*A lion rampant.*

Here lieth Interred the Body | of Live : (*sic*) Coll: *JOSEPH SHENE* | Merchant in Bridgtown of | Barbadoes who departed this | Life the 20ᵗʰ of Auguſt 1709 | Aged 44 Years.

1267. Blue marble :—

Here Lyes Interred the Body of | EDWARD BENNEY Esqʳ who was | born in the Town of Shrewsbury | the 24ᵗʰ day of Iune 1619 and | departed this life the 16ᵗʰ day of | September 1701 He was an Inhabitant | of this parish Since the yeare 1647 & | Served in the Aſsembly as one of the | Repreſentatives of the Sᵈ parish | severall yeares | (8 lines.)

1686, Nov. 4. Capᵗ James Benney & Alice Lassels. (St. John's.)

1268. White marble :—

Sacred | to the Memory of | MARY JUDITH, | wife of | JOHN ELLIOTT HEWITT: | who departed this Life | April 9ᵗʰ 1824. | Aged 36 Years | (4 lines.)

The new parish church of St. Joseph stands close to the high road leading to Joes River, and was built soon after 1831.

1269. South wall of nave :—

SACRED | TO THE MEMORY OF | JAMES BENJAMIN MAYERS | WHO DEPARTED THIS LIFE | 13ᵀᴴ OCTOBER 1854 | AGED 62 YEARS | ALSO | DOROTHY HIS WIFE | WHO DEPARTED THIS LIFE | 18ᵀᴴ NOVEMBER 1853 | AGED 59 YEARS | (7 lines.)

1270. On a brass on the north wall of nave :—

Sacred | to the memory of | Rachel Frances Walcott | who died 24 Feb. 1894 | Aged 71 Years | et | Robert Bowie Walcott M.D. | who died 6 April 1894 | Aged 73 Years | (5 lines.)

1271. White marble on south wall of the chancel :—

In Memory | OF | ROBERT | *INFANT SON OF* | COL. ROSS R.E. | AND OF | ALETHEA EMMA | *HIS WIFE* | Born May 5, 1864 | Died October 17, 1864.

CHURCHYARD.

1272. On a marble headstone :—

In | **Memory of** | **Samuell Maynard Alleyne** | **eldest son of S. M.** **and S. A. Alleyne** | **he was born August 25th 1809** | **and drowned while** **bathing** | **at Bathsheba May 20th 1847** | (5 lines.)

1273. Cross :—

REV. JOHN BRADSHAW M.A. B.M. T.C.D. | (FOR 17 YEARS RECTOR OF THIS PARISH) | AND | MARY JANE BRADSHAW | (4 lines ; erected by children.)

ANDREW'S PLANTATION.

The private burial-ground here is fairly large, and contains three old ledgers, besides a few small headstones.

1274. On a marble slab :—

ARMS.—*A chevron between three boars' heads couped, on a chief three roundles.* CAP^T ROBERT WARDALL AGED 22 YEERS | DEPARTED THIS LIFE THE 14TH OF IVNE | 1667.

1275. On a second large marble ledger with very large lettering :—

Here lieth ye Body of Jacob | de Hem Deceased ye first of | March 1677.

Tobias de Hem of Norwich (s. of Jaques de Hem) mar. 1611 Susanna Corsellis, and his will was proved in 1629 (75, Ridley). Adm'on of the estate of Susanna de Hem was granted Feb. 1658-9, her sons James and Tobias her Ex'ors, now both deceased.

1276. Large marble ledger between the preceding :—

In Memory of | Capt *WILLIAM MORRIS* | of the City of Briftol who died | the firft day of April 1772 | Aged 47 and lies Interred | underneath | He left in England a difconfolate | Widow and three Children | to lament the lofs | of an affectionate Hufband | a tender Parent | and | an Honeft Man. | He Married *MARY* Eldeft | Daughter of | *JOHN* and *ELIZABETH WINTER* | of Watchet in the County | of Somerfet who Placed this | Monument | of her Grief and Affection.

JOES RIVER PLANTATION.

1277. In a cane piece above the works is a tomb of the Holders, but I saw no inscription on it. It is supposed to be the grave of Brigadier-Gen. the Hon. Henry Evans Holder, who died in 1771.

MALVERN PLANTATION.

1278. On Hackleton Cliff is a tomb with three compartments belonging to the Stuarts, Mayers and Harpers. I saw no name on it. On a wall of the works is carved the crest of a demi-lion rampant.

ST. ANDREW'S CHURCH.

1279. On a grey marble slab in the floor of tower :—

Here Lyeth Interr'd yᵉ Body of | Mʳˢ MARY MORRIS yᵉ Daughter |
of Majʳ ROBERT MORRIS born | yᵉ 14ᵗʰ Day of March 1694 Married |
to JAMES DO . . . N ESQᴿ the 7ᵗʰ | of February 1713 Departed this | life
yᵉ 12 Day of Iuly 1720.

Archer gives James " Dothie," but Dottin would be more likely.

1280. Ditto :—

To the Memory of | *ELIZABETH MARY* | Daughter of *SAMUEL
MAVERICK Efquire* | and | Wife of *ANTHONY GREGG M.D.* |
(8 lines ; erected by husband) | (died) on the 23 Day of Octʳ 1790, | Aged
49 Years (? 4).

There were also Mavericks in New England. See New England Register for
Oct. 1913.

1281. In the chancel floor near the communion rail :—

Here Lyes Interred the Body of | TVRPIN WILLOUGHBY | Who
Departed This Life March | The 2, 1741 Aged 61 years.

1282. Partly under the steps to the pulpit :—

To the . . . . | JACOB HINDS and . . . . | who departed this | the
former | in September 18 . . . | Aged 68 Years | the Latter | July the 10ᵗʰ
1806 | Aged 58 Years | *Their affectionate Son* | *JACOB HINDS* | *has* |
caused to be erected | *this Marble* | *as a lasting tribute* | *to his affectionate
and tender Parents.*

1283. Floor of north-east of nave :—

Here lies : the Body of | ANN POOLE | Who departed this Life The . . . |
day of Ianuary 1740 Aged 56 | Years.

1284. East window :—

IN MEMORIAM | COLERIDGE HUDSON | (no date.)

1285. Under south gallery of nave. Blue marble, cracked, a fragment in
the floor :—

. . ere lieth the Body | of the | . . . *WILLIAM THOMAS* | Rector of this
Parifh | who died Decʳ 20ᵗʰ | Aged 46 Years | (5 lines.)

1286. On two halves of grey marble in the floor. On the upper half :—

Here lieth the Body of | MARGARET RUDD . . . | (several worn away
lines*) | . . . . 52. | Here alfo . . . . Body of | . . . . DAVID RUDDER Efq. |
. . . . Elizabeth Rudder | Who departed this life | (the second half has poetry.)

* Archer gives " Daughter of David & Elizabeth Rudder, died June 16, 1752 . . . . Also
David Rudder her father died April 17, 1753."

1287. Blue marble, skull and crossbones (cracked) in the floor:—

Here lyeth the body of | M^{RS} Lᴠᴄʏ Iᴏʜɴsᴛᴏᴠ . | late Wife of Capt Aʀᴄʜ : | Jᴏʜɴsᴛᴏᴠɴ who departed this | . . fe y^e . .th of 9^{br} 1680 born (? bein) | about 22 years of Age.

1288. White marble tablet near south door:—

This Tablet | In Memory of | JOHN HENRY ROGER | who died June 16th 18 . . | Aged 9 Years | is here placed | by his much afflicted | Parents | (6 lines.)

CHURCHYARD.

1289. Two vaults enclosed by railing south of chancel:—

Sacred to the Memory | of | ORMOND G. OLTON | Born | December 17th 1850 | Died | July 29th 1873 | (4 lines.)

1290. ꜱᴀᴄʀᴇᴅ ᴛᴏ ᴛʜᴇ ᴍᴇᴍᴏʀʏ | ᴏꜰ | CHARLES M. OLTON | Born | March 14th 1844, | Died | January 14th 1872 | (4 lines.)

1291. G. A. F. | *September 9, . . 76 | aged 69.*

1292. J. T. F. | January 1876 | *Aged 35.*

1293. South of Tower, on a white marble cross enclosed by railing. There are three vaults:—

Iɴ ᴍᴇᴍᴏʀɪᴀᴍ | ʀᴇᴠ. ᴊᴏʜɴ ʜᴜᴛꜱᴏɴ | ᴛᴡᴇɴᴛʏ-ꜰɪᴠᴇ ʏᴇᴀʀꜱ ʀᴇᴄᴛᴏʀ | ᴅɪᴇᴅ 18ᵀᴴ ɴᴏᴠᴇᴍʙᴇʀ 1865, ᴀɢᴇᴅ 59 | ᴀɴᴅ | ꜱᴜꜱᴀɴɴᴀ ᴊᴀɴᴇ, | ʜɪꜱ ᴡɪᴅᴏᴡ, | ᴅɪᴇᴅ 12ᵀᴴ ᴍᴀʏ 1891, ᴀɢᴇᴅ 84 | ᴀʟꜱᴏ | ʜ. ᴀ. ʜᴜᴛꜱᴏɴ | ɢʀᴀɴᴅꜱᴏɴ, | ᴅɪᴇᴅ ᴏᴄᴛᴏʙᴇʀ 1876, ᴀɢᴇᴅ 3 ᴍᴏɴᴛʜꜱ | (2 lines.) He was father of the present Rector of St. Lucy's.

Archer gives four other inscriptions, now lost:—

1294. Here lies the body of ᴊᴏʜɴ ꜰᴏᴏʀᴅ, Gent. who was b . . . ᴏᴠᴛ° (*sic*) ᴛʜᴇ . . . 1617, ᴀɴᴅ ᴅɪᴇᴅ . . . .

1295. ᴇᴅᴡᴀʀᴅ ʟᴀᴍɪɴɢ . . died Jan. 17 . . . . aged 59.

1296. ɴ . . . . ɢ . . . . died . . 1758. (Fragment.)

1297. . . ᴠᴀᴜɢʜᴀɴ, 1733 . . . . (Fragment.)

1298. In the disused burial-ground a short distance from the church are two flat stones, besides numerous grave mounds:—

A Friend | causes this Stone | to be erected to the memory of | JANE ANN THOMPSON | *Free Coloured Woman* | and her three Infant Children | as a mark of Esteem | (3 lines) | who departed this Life | January the 27th 1816 | Aged 35 Years.

1299. On a white marble slab :—

Sacred | to the Memory of | FRANCES BOOTMAN | daughter of | *FRANCIS & REBECCA BOOTMAN* | Born October 29th A.D. 1787 | who departed this Life | July 13th 1819 | Aged 30 Years | (2 lines.)

ST. JOHN'S.

Nave. There are six ledgers, including one in porch.

1300. Blue marble :—

Here lyeth Interr'd the Bo . . . of | TIMOTHY ROBERTS of this Pari . . . | who departed this life ye 1 .th of Octbr 17 . . (cement) | Aged 57 Years.

1301. Blue marble :—

Here lieth Interred the Body of | MR RICHARD HANNIS | Born November the 5th 1667 | died May the 19th 1752. | As alſo of his Daughter | ELIZABETH HANNIS | Born the 17th of January 172⅜ | died the 17th of Auguſt 1733.

1752, May 20. Mr Richard Hannis. (Burial Register.)

1302. Grey marble :—

Here lyeth the Body of ELIZABETH | ESTWICKE the daughter of Mr | CHRISTOPHER ESTWICKE and | SUSANNA ESTWICKE who departed | this life the 17 day of June and in | the seventeenth Year of her Age | Anno : Domi : 1732.

1733, Oct. 28. Susanna Estwick.
1735, June 5. Christopher s. of Christo Estwick. (Burial Register.)
See pedigree in " Caribbeana," iii., 60.
Gap in Burials 24 Nov. 1722 to 21 April 1733.
1641. Richd E. leased his 100 acres in this p. " under the Cliff " for 21 years at the yearly rent of 1000 lbs. of cotton. (Vol. i. of Deeds, p. 926.)
1643. Mr Henry E. owed the Church of St. Geo. 445 lbs. of cotton. (*Ibid.*, 168.)
1647. Richd E. & Francis E., gent., sell 100 a. in St Geo. (Vol. ii., p. 104.)

1303. Blue marble slab fixed against the west wall of nave. Jacobean mantling and shield in a circle :—

Motto above.—SIC NOS SIC SACRA TUI MOR.
CREST.—*A cubit arm couped, holding a short sword over W. and H.*
ARMS.—*In pale three lions passant.*

Here lies Interr'd the Bodies of | Mr MICHAEL MAHON | Of the Kingdom of Ireland and MARGARET | his Wife of Barbadoes with ſeveral | of their Children and Grand-Children | and in Memory of them this Monument | has been erected by Mr JAMES MAHON | Son of the above MICHAEL & MARGARET,

B B

1304. Blue marble, also fixed against west wall of nave. Above is an incised
Jacobean shield with mantling :—

CREST.—*A rook over W. and H.*
ARMS.—*A chevron charged with a mullet between three rooks* (ROKEBY).

VNDER THIS STONE LYES BVRIED Yᴱ BODY OF | KATHERINE LATE WIFE OF
IOHN ROKEBY | MERCHANT DAVGHTER & COHEIRIS OF CHRISTO | PHER THOMPSON
LATE OF THIS PARISH GENT. | & KATHERINE HIS WIFE WHO DEPARTED THIS |
LIFE Yᴱ 15ᵀᴴ OF APRIL 1666 IN Yᴱ 79ᵀᴴ YEARE | OF HER AGE.

Below is a second shield :—

ARMS.—*Three birds*, impaling : *On a fess indented three estoiles, on a canton
the sun in its glory.* (Not in Papworth, 789.)

1305. Ledger in porch :—

This Stone covers two Infants | of IOHN and ELIZABETH WAITH |
And is Sacred to SUSANNAH MOLL | a Daughter | who died December 7,
1779 | Aged . O Years | (4 lines) | Also Eliz. . . . ith their Mother | Who lived
respected & died lamented | on the . . May 17 . . | Aged 22 (? 32) years | (6 lines.)

1779, Dec. 8. Susanah Moll daughtʳ of John Waith. (Burial Register.)

WALL TABLETS.

1306. White marble. On west wall of nave :—

A figure of a woman standing nursing a babe, a small child beside her.

(3 lines) | ELIZABETH CHRISTIAN PINDER | WIFE OF THE HONORABLE FRANCIS
FORD PINDER, | AND DAUGHTER OF JONAS AND CHRISTIAN MERCY MAYNARD, |
(17 lines) | (died) ON THE 9ᵀᴴ OF DECᴿ 1799, | AGED 30 YEARS.

Jonas Maynard mar. Christian Mercy, dau. of . . . . Clarke. Their dau. Eliz.
was born 22 Nov. 1769, and mar. 12 April 1790. Her husband born 31 March
1767; died at Bath 27 Jan. 1843.
See *ante*, No. 105.

1307. North wall of nave. There are five tablets on this wall :—

IN AFFECTIONATE REMEMBRANCE | OF | ROBERT HAYNES, | OF THIM-
BLEBY LODGE, YORKSHIRE, | WHO DEPARTED THIS LIFE | FEBRUARY 17, 1873, |
AGED 78 YEARS | (3 lines.)

He was 2nd son of Gen. Robert H., born 2 Jan. 1795 at Newcastle plantation.
His father gave him Clifton Hall in 1815. He mar. twice and had a large family.
See his pedigree in Burke's " Landed Gentry."

1308. SACRED TO THE MEMORY OF | HENRIETTA PEARCE SHARP | THE
BELOVED WIFE OF WILLIAM SHARP ESQUIRE | OF THIS PARISH | AND MOTHER OF
SIX SURVIVING CHILDREN | SHE DIED JANUARY 28ᵀᴴ 1840 | IN THE COUNTY OF
DEVON ENGLAND | AGED 55 YEARS | HER REMAINS ARE DEPOSITED IN THE CHURCH-
YARD | OF THE PARISH CHURCH OF TOR | (20 lines.)

1309. SACRED TO THE MEMORY | OF | ANN ISABELLA SEALY, | THE BELOVED WIFE OF | JOHN SEALY | ATTORNEY-GENERAL OF THIS ISLAND | SHE DEPARTED THIS LIFE | ON THE 31ST OF MARCH 1859, | AGED 48 YEARS | (7 lines.)

1645, May 14. Ensign Wm. Sealey gent. sells 30 a. in St John's. (Vol. i., p. 654.)

1310. IN THE FAMILY VAULT OF | THIS CHURCH YARD | ARE DEPOSITED THE REMAINS OF | MARY MERCY HOLDER, | WIFE OF | JOHN A. HOLDER, | DIED JULY 16TH 1826, AGED 41 | (4 lines; erected by husband.)

1311. East wall of nave, north side :—

SACRED TO THE MEMORY OF | HENRY HIGGINSON HAYNES | SENT BY HIS FATHER FROM ENGLAND TO THIS, | THE ISLAND OF HIS BIRTH FOR THE | FULFILMENT OF A DUTY ASSIGNED HIM, | HE DIED BY A SUDDEN VISITATION OF DIVINE | PROVIDENCE JANUARY 15TH 1853 | (5 lines) | ÆTATIS SUÆ XXI.

He was 2nd son of Robert H. of Clifton Hall Plantation and Thimbleby Lodge, Yorkshire.

1312. A brass on the east wall of the nave near the pulpit :—

CREST.—*A lion rampant Sable.*
ARMS.—*Argent, a fess Gules, between three lions rampant Sable, a mullet for a difference.*
MOTTO.--PRINCIPIIS OBSTA.

TO THE MEMORY OF | JOHN SHAFE THORNE, | ONLY SURVIVING SON OF | JOHN AND REBECCA ELIZABETH THORNE, | DIED 7TH DECEMBER 1814, | AGED 32 YEARS AND 2 MONTHS, | WHOSE REMAINS LIE INTERRED | WITH THOSE OF HIS KINSMEN IN | THE FOX VAULT IN THE CHURCHYARD. | THIS TABLET | IS ERECTED ACCORDING TO THE WISH OF | THE LATE MAJOR H. A. T. | BY HIS EXECUTOR.

1313. Chancel, north wall. White marble on black :—

IN MEMORIAM | REV. WILLIAM LESLIE | FIRST RECTOR 1653—1676 | GRANDSON OF FIFTH LAIRD OF | KINCRAIGIE | AND | GREAT GREAT GRANDSON BY HIS | GRANDMOTHER OF | JOHN LESLIE | EIGHTH BARON OF BALQUHAIN.

CREST below.—*A griffin's head, the wings addorsed.*
MOTTO.—GRIP FAST.

1314. North wall of chancel. Brass :—

IN MEMORY OF | EVAN McGREGOR SEALY, M.A. | RECTOR OF THIS PARISH 1879—1904 | CANON AND RURAL DEAN. | THIS BRASS IS PLACED BY HIS BROTHER CLERGY | OF THE DIOCESE.

As 3rd s. of John S. of B., esq., he matric. from Trin. Coll., Oxf., 19 Jan. 1861, a. 19; B.A. 1865; M.A. 1867; Chaplain to the Bishop 1882. (Foster.)

1315. Brass near by :—

To THE DEAR MEMORY OF LULU SEALY | WHOSE MUSICAL TALENT WAS A RARE GIFT, ORGANIST OF THIS CHURCH | FROM JULY 1904 UNTIL HER DEATH JANUARY 19, 1909, AGED 23 | (1 line.)

(Dau. of the Rector, who was son of Sir John S.)

———

1316. East window :—

In memoriam Lucretiæ Gittens obiit 14th January 1859 ætatis suæ 67.

At the top of the window is a shield with these arms :—

Argent, on a chevron Or, between three lions rampant Gules (facing sinister), as many bugle horns; impaling: *Gules, on a bend sinister, between six birds (facing sinister), a talbot's head.*

———

1317. West wall of nave, south side of door :—

THIS MONUMENT | IS INSCRIBED | BY CONJUGAL AFFECTION | TO THE MEMORY OF | A BELOVED WIFE | SARAH ANN HAYNES | WHO | (5 lines) | DIED JULY 30TH 1824 | AGED 27 YEARS | (6 lines; leaving three young children.)

———

1318. South wall of nave, west end of it :—

SACRED | TO THE MEMORY | OF THOMAS MILLER ESQR | WHO DEPARTED THIS LIFE | MAY THE 5TH 1801. | IN THE 63RD YEAR OF HIS AGE | (11 lines.)

———

1319. IN MEMORY OF | CHRISTOPHER HENRY MASSIAH, | WHO DIED IN THIS PARISH MARCH 18TH 1872, | AGED 69 YEARS | (4 lines.)

———

1320. M. S. | SIR FRANCIS SOUPER BAYLEY, KNT | OF MALVERN | IN THIS ISLAND | HE DIED IN THE ISLAND OF PENANG | (OF WHICH HE WAS RECORDER) | ON THE 16TH OF OCTR 1824, | IN THE 35TH YEAR OF HIS AGE | (2 lines.)

As s. of Fra. B. of B'os, Esq., matric. from Queen's Coll., Oxf., 20 Oct. 1808, a. 18; B.A. 1812; M.A. 1815. (Foster.) There is a tablet to him on the east wall of the south aisle of St. Mary's, Oxford, which gives his birth in B. 19 Dec. 1789 and death 20 Oct.

———

1321. HENRY CHRICHLOW HAYNES ESQR | Born 1826 Died July 2nd 1854 | Aged 28 years | (4 lines; erected by brother.)

? son of Wm. Clarke H. (4th s. of Genl. Robert H.) by Margaret Crichlow his wife.

———

1322. IN MEMORY | OF | FRANCIS SHORLEY BAYLEY, | OF MALVERN ESTATE, ESQRE | WHO DIED MARCH THE 9TH 1808, | AGED 51 YEARS | AND OF | SARAH BAYLEY, HIS WIFE, | WHO DIED JUNE THE 6TH 1812, | AGED 63 YEARS.

———

1323. Sacred to the memory of | **HENRY HUSBANDS HAYNES** **Esqre** | **sixth Son of Robert and Ann Thomasine Haynes ;** | **of this Island.** | **who died August 14th** 1852 **aged** 51 **years** | (4 lines; erected by widow and children.)

B. 10 Sept. 1801. On 8 May 1814 he was entered as a Mid. on board H.M.S. Venerable. His father gave him the Bath plantation on 10 Feb. 1835.

1324. CREST.—*A heron, wings expanded over W. and H.*
ARMS.—Quarterly : 1 and 4, *Three crescents ;* 2 and 3, *Two billets in pale.*
MOTTO.—VELIS ET REMIS.

SACRED TO THE MEMORY OF | ROBERT HAYNES LATE OF THIS PARISH ESQUIRE, | LIEUT. GENERAL OF MILITIA | AND SOMETIME SPEAKER OF THE HOUSE OF ASSEMBLY, BARBADOES | (5 lines) | BORN 27TH SEPT 1769, DIED 18TH APRIL 1851 | (3 lines.)

He left an interesting journal which was privately published in 1910 by the Haynes family. He owned Newcastle, Clifton Hall and the Bath.

1325. SACRED TO THE MEMORY OF | GEORGE A. DEAN, ESQUIRE, | WHO DIED SEPTEMBER 10TH 1842, | AGED 54 YEARS | (4 lines; erected by widow.)

1326. At east end of nave :—

This tablet | is erected to the memory of | EDMUND HAYNES, ESQUIRE, | late of Haynes-field, in this parish | who died at Cheltenham, | in the Kingdom of Great Britain, | in the 66th year of his age | It is designed to commemorate | his christian exertions and munificent contributions, | in the erection of this sanctuary | after the destruction of the former one | in the hurricane of 1831 | (9 lines; erected by the Rector and Vestry of his native parish.)

He was the youngest brother of Genl. Robert H., born 9 Feb. 1781; mar. in 1805 Sarah, dau. of Fra. Bell. She died s.p. in North America. He remar. 11 April 1822 Lucy, dau. of Geo. Reed of Bath, and died 2 May 1846.

1327. **In Memoriam** | HENRY FRANCIS HART, M.D. | OF ASHFORD ESTATE IN THIS PARISH ; | BORN 30TH NOVR 1794, | DIED 9TH NOVR 1876 | AND | MARY PARRIS HART, | WIFE OF THE ABOVE ; | BORN 14TH DECR 1800. | DIED 4TH AUGST 1877.

CHURCHYARD.

1328. Mausoleum :—

THE FAMILY BURYING-PLACE OF | JOSEPH BRIGGS MAYERS | A NATIVE OF THIS ISLAND, AND | FOR MORE THAN FORTY YEARS A RESIDENT | IN THE COLONY OF BRITISH GUIANA | (2 lines.)

On its south side are two panels :—

SACRED TO THE MEMORY OF | GLADYS | (DAUGHTER OF J. B. MAYERS) | WHO DIED IN THIS ISLAND 28TH JANUARY 1900 | AGED 16 YEARS.

SACRED TO THE MEMORY OF | JOSEPH BRIGGS MAYERS | WHO DIED IN LONDON 22ND DECR 1906 | AGED 68 YEARS.

1329. THO^s | ESTWICK | Died D^{ec} 12, 1860 | aged 80 | YEARS.

He was a coloured millwright. (Sexton.)

1330. On north wall of church :—

IN | MEMORY | OF | W. GILKES | DIED 1864.

1331. Ledger :—

𝕾acred to the 𝕸emory | of | WILLIAM FRS. (*sic*) FENTY | BORN
11TH NOV^R 1821 | DIED 30TH AUGST 1879 | (2 lines; erected by widow.)

1332. To perpetuate the Memory | of two ever to be lamented Parents |
FRANCIS and JANE BAYLEY | The former died October 21st 1777 | Aged
52 Years | The latter November 10th 1803 | Aged 68 Years | This Marble is
inscribed | by their Son FRANCIS SOUPER BAYLEY | As a Mark of Filial
Affection | Sacred to the Memory of | ELIZABETH S. | the Wife of
IN^O L. TOPPIN | (5 lines) | (died) on the 26th Day of July 1820 | Aged 22 |
(10 lines.)

1333. SACRED To The Memory | of | HARRIET | *The Beloved Wife of* |
ALEXANDER CARRINGTON | *Who Died 2nd October 1847* | *Aged 27 Years* |
ALSO | *To the Memory of Their Daughter* | ALEXANDRA | *Who Died
15th October 1847* | *Aged 21 Days.*

1334. Mausoleum :—

GALL . . . 1823.

1335. Large vault :—

TO THE MEMORY OF | *AGNES ROUS ALLDER* | WHO DEPARTED THIS LIFE
APRIL 13TH 1849 | IN THE 38TH YEAR OF HER AGE | (12 lines.)

1336. Here lyeth THOMAS FOX Senr | and his two Wife's | PRUDENCE
& RACHAEL FOX | two Sons JOHN & WILLIAM two | Daughters SARAH
& ESTHER four | Grand Children THOMAS, JOSEPH | WILLIAM &
MARY, WILLIAM | being ye last Aged 27 Years dyed | Sep^{br} 14th 1754 | Here
lyes Interr'd ye Remains of | Captⁿ WILLIAM FOX | Who chang'd this
Mortal Life for | Immortality | on ye 14th day of Sep^{br} 1754 | ÆTATIS
SUÆ 27 | (9 lines.)

1754, Sept. 15. Willm Fox Esqr Capt. (Burial Register.)

On another stone at the bottom :—

HEREIN | WITH THOSE OF HIS KINSMEN | LIE THE REMAINS OF | JOHN
SHAFE THORNE | ONLY SURVIVING SON OF | JOHN AND REBECCA
ELIZABETH THORNE | DIED 7TH DECR. 1814 | AGED 32 YRS. AND 2 MO^s.

1337. White marble :—

BENEATH THIS MARBLE | LIES THE BODY OF | JOHN LEWIS, | SON OF THE | REV^D JAMES LEWIS, | AND REBECCA HIS WIFE ; | WHO DEPARTED THIS LIFE, | ON THE TWENTY-SEVENTH OF APRIL | EIGHTEEN HUNDRED & FORTY-THREE | AGED SEVENTY-SEVEN YEARS.

1338. SACRED | TO THE MEMORY OF | JOHN HOTHERSALL ESQUIRE | WHO DIED NOVEMBER 22ND | A.D. 1796. | ALSO | WILLIAM PINDER ESQUIRE | WHO DIED 16TH DECEMBER 1806 | AND | ANNE ISABELLA | HIS WIFE | ELDEST DAUGHTER | OF THE ABOVE MENTIONED | JOHN HOTHERSALL | WHO DIED IN APRIL 1807 | ALSO | FRANCIS FORD | THE INFANT SON OF THE | REV^D JOHN HOTHERSALL PINDER | M.A. | AND ANNE BRATHWAITE | HIS WIFE | WHO DIED AUGUST THE 14TH | A.D. 1824.

Wm. P. was Chief Justice.   See pedigree of Pinder in Jewers' "Wells Cathedral M.I.," p. 278.

1796, Nov. 1.   John Hothersall.   Aged 80 y^rs.   (Burial Register.)

1339. Enclosed by iron railing :—

IN MEMORY OF | GEORGE A. DEAN *ESQ^RE* | WHO DIED SEPT^R 10TH 1842 | AGED 54 YEARS.

1340. Upright grey marble slab set in masonry :—

SACRED TO THE MEMORY OF | the Revd WILLIAM LAKE PINDER A.M. | Rector of the Parish of St George, | Who died of fever at Rowans, | on the 4th July 1841 in the | 60th Year of his Age. | And of | HARRIET WILSON his Wife, | who departed this life | at Easington Rectory, in the County of York, | on the 24th of February 1836. | Aged 52 Years | SACRED | also to the Memory of their Second Son, | CHARLES WILLIAM, Lieu^t in H.M. 55th Reg^t | who died of fever in Fort William Calcutta, | on the 18th February 1841, | in the 26th Year of his Age | And to that of | ELIZABETH MARGARET | their only Daughter | Wife of Captn JOHN WILSON | late of H.M. 93^d or Sutherland Highlanders | Who died of fever at Rowans, | on the 26th of October 1841 | in the 32^d Year of his Age | (4 lines.)

The Rector was 3rd son of the Hon. Wm. P.   His wife, mar. 8 June 1808, was a dau. of Dr. Chas. Wilson.

1341. White marble :—

Here lieth the Body of JAMES PRAT (*sic*) Son of Doctor | HENRY PRATT & DOROTHY his Wife who Dep^ed | This Life April 23, 1738 Aged 2 Years & 7 days | also the Body of HENRY PRATT son of the aforesaid | HENRY & DOROTHY who Dep^ed this Life September | the 16, 1740 Aged 8 Years | Also the Body of Sarah their Daughte^r who Dep^ed | this life Nove^br 14, 1740 Aged 5 hours | Also the Body of DOROTHY Wife to the said | HENRY PRATT who Departed this . . . . June | the 19th 1749.

1342. Modern upright stone :—

HERE LYETH YE BODY OF | FERDINANDO PALEOLOGUS | DESCENDED FROM YE IMPERIAL | LYNE OF YE LAST CHRISTIAN | EMPERORS OF GREECE | CHURCHWARDEN OF THIS PARISH | 1655 1656. | VESTRYMAN TWENTYE YEARS | DIED OCTOBER 3, 1678.

There is a gap in the Burial Register 1669—84, but Schomburgk in 1847 gave this entry: "October 3ʳᵈ 1678, Lieut. Ferdinando Paleologus." Also a copy of his will, and of the brass in Llandulph in Cornwall to his father Theodore, who died 21 Jan. 1636. There is also an account in the "Gent. Mag." for 1843, p. 17, and 1847, p. 208.

1343. CROSS :—

IN MEMORY OF | SIR JOHN SEALY | K.C.M.G. | 28 YEARS ATTʸ GENˡ OF BARBADOS, | DIED 13ᵀᴴ FEBʸ 1899 AT THE CLIFF | AGED 91 | (1 line.)

1344. *IN MEMORY OF | FRANCES ANN, | THE BELOVED WIFE OF | THOMAS KERR, | WHO DIED 28 SEPTEMBER 1854 | AGED 32 YEARS.

IN MEMORY OF | MARY ELVIRA, | THE BELOVED WIFE OF | FRANCIS POLLARD CARTER | WHO DIED 23ᴰ JANUARY 1880 | AGED 55 YEARS.

1345. A. G. D. REED. | AND | M. E. NICCOLLS | 1886.

1346. WILLIAM H. LEWIS | AND | ROLAND C. TAYLOR | 1838.

1347. CHRISTOPHER MASSIAH, | 1818.

1348. Sacred to the Memory of | ANN HAYNES born March 14ᵗʰ 1746 | married to *Col°* RICHARD HAYNES | January 21ˢᵗ 1768 | and died February 25ᵗʰ 1781 | (7 lines.)

She was his first wife, dau. of Grant Elcock.

1349. Mausoleum :—

Here lies inter . . . . Body of SARAH BELL Daugᵉʳ | of FRANCIS & SARAH BELL who departed this | Life the 23ᵈ of Augˢᵗ 1736 Aged 26 Months | Alſo the Body of Col. FRANCIS BELL Eſq. who | departed this Life the 6ᵗʰ day of April 1739 Aged | 57 Years | Alſo the Body of FRANCIS ſon of the above ſaid | FRANCIS & SARAH who departed this Life the | 16ᵗʰ of Augˢᵗ 1747 Aged 14 Years | Alſo the Body of SARAH Wife of FRANCIS BELL | who departed this Life the 14ᵗʰ of February 1747 | Aged 38 Years | Here also lies the remains | OF | The Honᵇˡᵉ Franciſ Bell Eſqʳ chief Baron of the | Exchequer Obᵗ Augˢᵗ 1760 Aged 56 Years | Mary, hiſ Widow afterward Mary Clark | Obᵗ Augˢᵗ 1780 Aged 63 Years | Anna Maria their daughter Obᵗ 1760 Aged 22 Months | Sarah Henty Obᵗ Oct. 1781 | Mary Elizaᵇᵉᵗʰ A Daughter of Francis Bell | Franciſ A Son | Franceſ A Daughter | Ann Grant Ob. 178 . Aged 67 | Franciſ Grant Ob. 1790 Aged 36 | Chriſtian Ann Grant Obᵗ 1783 Aged 49 | Rebecca Sainthill Obᵗ 1789 Aged 63.

1843, Aug. 15. At the residence of his mother, Bedminster, aged 26, Edmund Haynes, 3d s. of the late Francis Bell of B. ("G.M.," 442.)

---

* Owing to the rocky nature of the soil, most of the tombs are built high out of the ground.

1350. Broken column, enclosed by railing:—

HERE LIES | THE MORTAL REMAINS | OF | THOMAS JO⁸ KNIGHT | Who departed this life | NOVEMBER 9ᵀᴴ 1863 | AGED 30 YEARS.

1351. In wall of chancel. Blue marble fragment:—

Here lies the Body of | .. ARY MARGARET HUSBANDS | .. e wife of JOHN HUSBANDS | .. after of a London Ship & the | .. aughter of FRANCIS and ANN,

1352. White marble tablet outside south wall of nave:—

In Memoriam | ALFRED HOTHERSALL | BISHOP, M.A. | BORN SEPTEMBER 5ᵀᴴ 1822 | DIED AUGUST 1ˢᵀ 1879 | FOR THE LAST SIXTEEN YEARS OF HIS LIFE | RECTOR OF THIS PARISH | (1 line.)

He was not at Oxford.

1353. Ditto:—

WILKINSON HART | BORN | NOVEMBER 8ᵀᴴ 1829 | DIED | JULY 3ᴿᴰ 1870.

1354. Ditto:—

RICHARD HENRY SMITH | BORN AUGUST 31ˢᵀ 1805 | DIED AUGUST 21ˢᵀ 1871.

1355. Ditto:—

HOWARD YOUNG SMITH | BORN DECEMBER 29ᵀᴴ 1847 | DIED SEPTEMBER 187 . (creeper in way.)

1356. Headstone:—

SACRED | to the memory of | MARY ELIZABETH | Infant Daughter of | William Francis and Mary Elizabeth | GRONEY. | Born 3ʳᵈ August 1857 | Died 9ᵗʰ November 1858 | (3 lines.)

BURIALS.

1669   Aug.   7   Lᵗ Coll. Conset.*

Gap from 27 Feb. 1669-70 to 7 Sept. 1684, 1700—16, 1722—33, and 1800—25.

1685-6 Jan. 16   Robert Mead Esqʳᵉ.
1691   Sept. 27   Honˡ Henry Quintyne Esqʳ.
1710-11   Mar. 8   Col. John Leslie Esqʳ.

The families of Bromley, Colleton, Estwick, Hacket, Hothersall, Pemberton, Prideaux, Rous, Sealy, Vaughan and Walrond are often mentioned.

* He died suddenly, after supping with Col. Chr. Codrington, under suspicious circumstances, some people suggesting poison. Consets plantation passed to the latter. Consets Point is close to the College estate.

MARRIAGES.

1657	Dec. 25	Lt Col. Bayley and Eliza Foster.
1659	July 28	Mr John Lewes and Ann Hothersall.
1663	Apr. 28	Henry Quintyn and Mary Pilgrim.
1667-8	Feb. 3	Capt Robert Benson and Mary Cheesewright.
1669	July 25	Sr Tobias Bridge and Rebecca Hothersall.
1670	Nov. 12	Capt Arch^d Henderson and Elizabeth Yeamans.

Gap from 16 Oct. 1672 to 15 Oct. 1682.

1687-8   Mar. 22   Capt Henry Gollop & Mary Baldrick.

Gap from 1672—82, 1700 to 1716.

1763	Sep. 23	Benj^a Mellows Esqr to Mrs Sarah Estwick Widd.
1766	Jan. 30	Mr William Pindah to Miss Ann Issabella Hothersall.

HAYNES HILL PLANTATION.

There is here an ancient tomb cut out of the rock, in the face of which has been fixed a modern white marble tablet:—

1357. WITHIN THIS VAULT | ARE INTERRED THE REMAINS OF | SAMUEL FORTE GENTLEMAN | OBIT 1711 | AND HIS WIFE URSULA, | OBIT 1700 | AND MANY MEMBERS OF | THE FORTE FAMILY.

1700, Sept. . . (between 17 and 26).   Ursula wife of Mr Saml Forte.
1712, April 27.   Mr Samuel Forte.

EASY HALL PLANTATION.

1358. Here is a family burial-ground walled in and entered by iron gates. In the enclosure is a large vault without name, also a grave railed in. On a square of marble is cut: "J. B. M. 1854." On a white marble slab on the top of another vault is:—

Under this Marble is depofited | the remains of ELIZABETH wife | of ABEL ALLEYNE CULPEPPER | who when that contagious diftemper | the small Pox was spreading itself | thro' the Island &c. | (26 lines follow). | De . . t efse mortalis Dec. 25th | An Atatis 33 Salvtio nostra | 1793.

ST. JAMES'.

1703   8^{ber} 16   Mr Alleyne Culpeper at St Philips.   (Burial.)

ST. JOHN'S.

1748	Mar. 14	Mr Alleyne Culpeper. (Burial.)
1667	Nov. 10	Reynold Skeete and Marg^t Culpepper.
1772	Aug. 30	John Alleyne Culpeper to Hester Robinson.
1781	June 21	Abel Alleyne Culpeper to Miss Eliz^a Pollard.

Richd. Alleyne, D.D., in his will dated 21 April 1650, says: "£100 to Margaret my dau., wife of Wm. Culpeper, to be paid to Sr Cheney C. & Dr Steed.

£200 I have secured by lands to them." Sir Cheney C., Knt., son of Sir Thos. of Hollingborne, co. Kent, is entered in the Visitation of Sussex in 1633. He was knighted at Farnham 8 Sept. 1628.

Reynold Alleyn of St. Philip's, Barbados (grandson of the above Richard). Will dated 25 Oct. 1675. Mʳ Alleyn Culpepper and Fra. C.

THE SOCIETY'S CHAPEL.

1359. In the churchyard is a stone cairn surmounted by a granite cross over the grave of:—

RICHARD RAWLE, BISHOP | PRINCIPAL | OF | CODRINGTON COLLEGE | BORN 1811 | DIED 1889.

1851, Jan. 14. At Cheadle, Staff. the Rev. Rich. Rawle, Principal of Codrington coll. in B,, to Susan-Anne, the eldest dau. of J. M. Blagg, esq. of Cheadle. ("G.M.," 421.)

There are a few graves about, one dated 1838.

CODRINGTON COLLEGE CHAPEL.

1360. There is a modern (1888) brass to "Sir* Chr. Codrington" the Founder. The person who wrote the inscription has knighted him without authority.

1710, April 8. Collᵒ: Christopʳ Codrington Esqʳ: late Genˡ: of yᵉ Leward Islands in Church. (Burial Register of St. Michael's.)

1361. A brass :—

IN MEMORY OF | THE REVᴰ MARK NICHOLSON | FORMERLY A FELLOW OF | QUEENS COLLEGE OXFORD | A PRINCIPAL OF THIS COLLEGE | FROM THE YEAR 1801 | TO THE YEAR 1821 | WHO DIED | ON THE 16ᵀᴴ DAY OF JUNE | 1838.

1838, June 16. At Clifton, aged 68, the Rev. Mark Nicholson, for 25 years President of Codrington coll., B. He was the s. of Mr. John N. of Barton in Westmorland; was matriculated of Queens coll. Oxf. in 1790 & graduated B.A. 1795, M.A. 1797. ("G.M.," 223.) Archdeacon Bindley states that Principal is an error, and that he was President of the Grammar School 1798—1821.

There are three brasses against the screen :—

1362. TO THE MEMORY OF | REV. WILLIAM THOMAS WEBB, M.A. | HEADMASTER OF THE COLLEGIATE SCHOOL 1850—1864 PRINCIPAL 1864—1884 | ARCHDEACON OF GRENADA 1878—1884, RURAL DEAN OF Sᵀ JOHNS 1879—1884 | BORN MARCH 15, 1825, DIED MAY 6, 1896.

Placed in 1897 by past and present students.

* Archdeacon Bindley has corrected this error in his "Annals." Mr. N. Darnell Davis also drew attention to it, but no steps have been taken to erase the "Sir" and substitute "Col."

1363. TO THE MEMORY OF | THE RIGHT REVEREND RICHARD RAWLE, D.D. | PRINCIPAL 1847—1864 | BISHOP OF TRINIDAD 1872—1888 | PRINCIPAL OCT. 1888—MAY 1889.

Placed in 1891 by public subscription.

1364. IN MEMORY OF | REV. JOHN HOTHERSAL PINDER, M.A. | PRINCIPAL 1829—1835 | AFTERWARDS FIRST PRINCIPAL OF | WELLS THEOLOGICAL COLLEGE | AND CANON OF WELLS CATHEDRAL. | BORN 1794 DIED 1868.

Given by his nephew the Rev. North Pinder, R. of Rotherfield Greys. (Bindley.)

1365. On the brass chandelier :—

THE GIFT OF Mᴿ HENRY PRATT | AND Sᵀ JOHNS PARISH.

1366. TO THE MEMORY OF | REV. EDWARD PARRIS SMITH, M.A. | PEMBROKE COLLEGE OXFORD | ACTING ASSISTANT MASTER 1822 | TUTOR & BURSAR 1828 TO 1852 | CURATE OF Sᵀ MARKS AND Sᵀ CATHERINES 1837 TO 1840 | BORN DEC. 15ᵀᴴ 1803, DIED MARCH 12ᵀᴴ 1878.

As eldest s. of Richard Henry S. of B., esq., matric. from Pemb. Coll. 2 June 1824, a. 20; B.A. 1828, M.A. 1840. (Foster.)
This brass was given by his sons in 1891.

1367. TO THE MEMORY OF | THE RIGHT REV. HENRY HUTTON PARRY, D.D. | BALLIOL COLLEGE OXFORD | TUTOR OF CODRINGTON COLLEGE 1855 TO 1860 | ARCHDEACON OF BARBADOS 1861 TO 1868 | BISHOP COADJUTOR OF BARBADOS 1868 TO 1876 | BISHOP OF PERTH W.A. 1876 TO 1893.

As 2d s. of Thos. P., Bishop of Antigua, matric. from Ball. Coll. 29 May 1846, a. 19; B.A. 1851, M.A. 1859; Chaplain to the Forces 1860-1; D.D. by diploma Durham 1876. (Foster.)
This brass was fixed in 1894 by Principal Bindley and friends.

1368. On a lozenge :—

R. N. ob. Dec. 29, 1810.

1369. On the front of altar :—

General Sir WILLIAM JOHN CODRINGTON. Born 26 Nov. 1804 Died 6 Aug. 1884.

There is also a tablet on the wall with inaccurate inscription.
See "Annals of Codrington College, 1710—1910," by Archdeacon Bindley for much relating to past worthies.

St. Ann's Chapel.

1370. On a tablet:—

IN MEMORY OF | NATHANIEL T. W. CARRINGTON | A RESIDENT PROPRIETOR OF THIS PARISH | WHO DEVOTED MUCH TIME | TO SUPERINTENDING THE BUILDING OF THE CHAPEL | BORN IN 1801 ; DIED IN 1855 | ALSO IN MEMORY OF | CHRISTIAN W. CARRINGTON | HIS WIDOW | BORN IN 1815 ; DIED IN 1883 | THIS TABLET IS ERECTED IN 1890 | BY THEIR SIX SURVIVING CHILDREN | IN AFFECTIONATE REMEMBRANCE.

1371. Under the east window of the chancel :—

In affectionate remembrance of Susan and Emme Josephine | the beloved wives of WM. T. Armstrong of Little Island St Joseph, 1891.

Modern graves and vaults in churchyard.

There are several other Chapels belonging to the Church, as well as to various congregations of Dissenters, but they all date from modern times.

JEWISH BURIAL-GROUND, BRIDGETOWN.

This is situated in a central though isolated part of the town around the Synagogue. There are hardly any Jews now in the Island, and services, I believe, are rarely if ever held, but the Synagogue is in good order, and there is a man in charge of the place. Mr. Baeza, a Member of the Assembly, is of the Portuguese Jewish faith and one of the Trustees. There were no memorials in the Synagogue.

I commenced copying the inscriptions in the oldest ground, but had not time to do more than 100, leaving off at the line of the caretaker's house. There were about 160 more in that portion. In the S. and E. divisions, walled off and divided by a path, there appeared to be quite another 100. In White's Alley is a later ground, opened in the year 1828, which I did not visit. It was a matter for regret having to leave the Island with this portion undone, but the various parish churches and churchyards occupied most of my time, and it was only towards the termination of my visit that I came across the Synagogue. The Secretary of the American Jewish Historical Society in New York wrote me on 17 July 1914 : "There was a considerable migration from the British W.I. to this country, which may explain why the Barbados community has dwindled away almost to the vanishing point."

Mr. T. Colyer-Fergusson has kindly read my MS. and added some notes.

I have omitted " S⁴," which heads most of the inscriptions, and " SUA ALMA GOZE DA GLORIA," the last line of many of them. Some of the stones have Hebrew verses, but as a rule Portuguese is the language used.

North Portion.

1372. HERE LYETH Yᴱ BODY OF | DAVID RAPHAEL DE MERCADO | MERCHANT WHO DEPARTED | THIS WORLD Yᴱ 14ᵀᴴ OF AUGUST | 1685.

There are also Portuguese and Jewish inscriptions, all three languages being probably used for the same inscription.

1685. Will of David Ralph or Raphael Mercado, " my bodie to be interred in the burying place with my brethren at the beginning of the row," directs that a

white marble stone be placed on his grave; mentions his wife Grace and appoints
her ex'trix; nephew David de Isaac de Mercado and his nephew and adopted sonne
David son of Moses H. de Mercado. In Barbados 21 July 1685. Appeared
personally 28 Aug. 1685 Aaron Baruh and Isaac Gomes, who were sworn on the
five books of Moses. Translated from the "Portingall tonge" 31 Aug. 1685.
Proved 9 Dec. 1685 by Antonio Louzada of London, merchant, att' to Grace de
Mercado of Barbados. (P.C.C., 153, Cann.) [T. C.-F.]

1373. DA BEM . AUENTURADA | ESTER GAON QU . . . . | RECOLLYDA . AS . . . . |
POUOS . EM . 21 . DE . . . . Y. | ANO . 5427 . SUA . ALMA | GOZE . DA GLORYA.

1374. To ZELA . . . . | (5 lines, very worn.)

1375. DO BEM AVENTVRA | DO VARAÕ SELOMOI | TINOCO QVE FOY | APANHADO
ASEVS | POVOS EM 24 DE | KISLEVA 5448.

1376. DA YNCURTADA DONZELA | RAHEL ESTER HENRIQUES QVE | FALECV EM
11 DE SEBAT | ANNO 5448.

1377. DE . . . . NICOLAV | . . . . . FALECV | . . . . 48.

1378. Broken across, much worn.

1379. DO BEM . AVENTVRADO | VARAÕ DAVID YSRAEL Q̃ | FALECEV EM 21 DE
TAMVS | ANNO 5449.

1380. DO YLVSTRE | VARAÕ HONRADO | & SVBLYME Dᴺ | EPHAIM YESVRVN |
HENRRIQUES | FALECEO EM 19 | E TISRY DO ANO | 5450 DA GRIACA | DO MUNDO.

1381. Do yncurrado Eynsigne | mancebo Abraham de | medina que Rendeu
A alma | A seu Criadon em 11 de | Nisan anno 5452.

1382. DE RIBCAH FILHA D | AB & JAEL VALVERDE | FALECEO EM 22 D |
MENAID 11 Aº 5447.

1383. DE MOSE Fº DE IOSEPH | MENDES FALESEV | EM 12 (flaked) NAHEM |
Aº . . . .

1384. DE MOSEH HAMIS FALESEO | EM 10 DE NISAN 5440.

1385. D ABRAHAM YDANA Fº | D YACOB YDANA QVE | PARTYV DESTE MVNDO |
EN 21 D HESVAN 5439.

1386. DA INCURTADAD ESTEP | MENDES FILHAD IOSEPH | MENDES QUE N . . . . FOI | SERVIDO RECOL HEP EM | 12 D TAMUS . D 5440.

1387. D SARAH ESTER PER^A | D LEAO M^R DE MOSEH | PER^A D LEAO QVE FALECEO | EM 16 D ELVL 5438.

1388. DA BEM AVENTVRADA | SARAH SIMIIA . ISRAEL | DE PIZA QVE FOYAPA- | -NHADO . ASEOS POVOS | EM . 7 DE . TAMVS . A° : 5438.

1389. Flaked and illegible.

1390. DE YOSIVAHV REPHAEL | FILHO DE DAVID CASTE | LLO . QVE FOY DEVS SER | VIDO LEVALO PERA SI | EM 16 DE VEADAR ANO | 5459 | (3 Hebrew lines.)

1391. DE YACOB FILLO DE | JOSEPH . EIAEL . YSVRVN | MENDES FALESEV | EN 27 DE TAMVZ 5436.

1392. DE SARAH GABAY | RISSON FALECEV EM | 13 DE NESAN 5432.

1393. DO BEN . AVENTVRADO | ENCURTADO DEDIAS | ISHAK GABAY RISSON | QVE FALECEO EM 15 | DE NISAN ANNO 54 . . | (flaked.)

Three smaller stones to children, inscription left on only one :—

1394. DE MOSEH F . . HO DE | AB & JAEL VALVERD . . | FALECEO EM . . . . | TISRY A° 5 . . .

1395. DE HANAH . . . IOSEPH | SENIOR FALESEO EM | DE TEBET 5440.

1396. DO . EMCVRTADO . ARON | DE MERCADO . . QVE | FAIE . SEO . EM . 9 . DE . ADAR | 5420.

The 3rd row commences here, and consists of sixteen stones.

1397. DO BEM AVENTVRADO | DE YACOB ABRAHAM | LEVEREZIO | QVE FOY APANHADO | SEVS POVOS EM | 21 DE ADAR SENI | ANNO 5421.

1398. DO BEM . AVENTVRADO | DE YSHACK | LEVY | REZIO | FALECEV | EM 16 DE ADAR 5427.

1399. DO YNCVRTADO VIRTVOZO | EMANSO CORDEIRO | ABRAHAM LOPES PEREIRA | QVE FOY APANHADO ASEVS POVOS | EM 19 DESEBAT | ANNO 5431 | (and long Hebrew inscription.)

1400. DO BEM . AVENTVRADO | DE MOSSEH HAYM | NAHAMYAS QVE FOY | DEOS SERVIDO | RECOLLEIO ASEOS | POVOS EM 28 DE ELVL | 5432.

1401. DO BEM . AVENTVRADO | DOVTOR ABRAHAM | HENRIQVEZ FLO RES | QVE FOI APANHADO | ASEVS POVOS EM 3 | DE SEBAT ANNO | 5433.

1402. Broken slab.   Around the edge framewise :—

. . . . N & ESTER LOUZADA WHO DIED JAN^Y . . 21.

And in the centre :—

. . . . Israel | . . . . Filho | . . 5502.

1681, Aug. 9. Petition of Aaron Baruch Lanzade (*sic*) and others on behalf of the Jews as to the use of the Courts for their protection as traders.   Minutes of Council of Barbadoes.   (Col. Cal. of State Papers, p. 99.)

Some of the Lousadas migrated to Jamaica.   Aron Louzada of L., merchant. Will dated 28 April 1768.   (321, Secker.)   "To my cousin Aron Baruch Louzada of Barbados & his brother Jeremy Baruch Louzada £50 apiece, & to the children of their late brother David Baruch Louzada £50."   The family vault was in the burial-ground of the Portuguese Jews at Mile End.   The late J. B. Lousada of Ascot told me that his family at one time owned much property in Jamaica.   He died at Worthing in 190 ., aged about 92.   His wife Sarah, dau. of Isaac, Duke de Losada, died at Ascot about 1909, aged 90 or more.   A younger brother, Capt. S. C. Lousada, died at Cheltenham, and a sister, Mrs. Bacon, died June 1913, aged 102.

1403. Broken in two pieces :—

. . . . (missing) VRADO . D | MOSEH . . . . DELEON | FALECEV EM 26 DE ADAR | ANNO 5 (flaked) 35.

1404. DO BEM . AVENTVRADO E | VIRTUOSO VARAO DAVID | IESURUN MENDES QUE FOI | APANHADO ASEUS POVOS | DE HIDADE DE 90 ANNOS | EM 5 DE NISAN ANNO 5435.

1405. Very worn :—

DO BEM AVENTVRADO | DAVID Y^S DIAS | FALESEV . . . . | 2 NIS . . | 5436.

1406. Inscription worn away.

1407. DE MOSEH BARVH | LOIZADA FALECEV | EM 9 ELVL | A 5437.

1408. DO BEM . AVENTVRADO | YEHOSVAH HAYAYAF° | EM . 7 DE . ELVL . A° 5438.

1409. DA . BEM . AVENTVRADA | SARAH . MVLHER . DE | YEHOSVAH . HAYAYA . F° | EM . 27 . DE TAMVZ A° | 5439.

1410. Broken across:—

DA . BEM AVENTVRADA | RI . A PACHEGO QVE | FALECEV . EM . 10 DE AB | Aº 5441.

1411. DO BEM AVENTVRADO DE | YACOB PACHECO QUE FALECEO | EM 28 DE ADAR RISON 5442.

1412. In wall:—

DO BEM . AVENTVRADA | HANAH ALVARES | FALECEO EM 17 YEAR | 546 .

1413. DE RACHEL FILHA DE | IOSEPH EJAEL YESVRVM | MENDES FALECEV EM 28 | . . VIAR Aº 5446.

1414. Small stone:—

De Yshac Filho | Jacob E Ribcah Ba- | -ruh Louzada que | faleceo em 2 DEADAR | Aº 5446.

1415. Small stone:—

De Eliau filho de | Jacob E Ribcah | Baruh Louzada | que faleceo em | 21 DE SEBAT 5451.

1416. DE ABRAHAM FILHO | DE IOSEPH EJAEL | IESVRUM MENDES | FALESEO EM 22 DE | HESUAN 5445.

1417. DE MOSE FILHO | DE IOSEPH EJAEL | IESVRVM MENDES | FALESEO EM 5 DE | KISLEY 5442.

1418. DE DAVID FILLO DE | JOSEPH EJAEL Y*VRVN | MENDES QVE FOY | RECOLLIDO A SEV | GRIADOR OVLTIMO | DIADEPESAH DO ANNO | 5440.

1419. DO YNCVRTADO | E VIRTVOSO MANCEBO | SELOMOH RODRIGVES | SOAREZ QVE FOY | RECOLLIDO AMILLOR | MVNDO EM 2 DE SIVAN | ANNº 5440.

1420. DA BEM AVENTVRADA | DE DYNAH PACHECO | QVE FOY APANHADA | ASEVS POVOS EM 14 | DE NISAN DE 5441.

1421. DO BEM AVENTVRADO | DE AARON NAVARRO | QVE FALECEO EM 23 | DE YLVE Aº 5445.

1422. Very large and deep lettering:—

Da Bem aven- | turada vertu- | oza mulher de | Fonſado Rahael | namia qvo foy | deſcanſ . r aſeos | Povos Em 22 de | Roſhodes yhill | Anno 5444.

1423. DA BEM AVE . . . . | TVRADA HA . . . . (or RA) | CARDOSO QVE . . . . | F . . ECEV . . . . | DE HESVAN 5449 (? year).

* Hole in stone.

D D

1424. DO ENCVRTADO DE ABRAHAM | DE YSHAC YSRAEL DE PIZA | FALECEV EM 23 DE NISAN | Anno 5466.

A fifth row commences here:—

1425. DE YSHAC DO | VALE FA° EM | 20 ADAR 5452.

1426. Flaked away.

1427. DE ESTER . ODRI | QVE FALECEV | EM 11 TAN . VS . . | 5451. (Indistinct.)

1428. Flaked away.

1429. DEL BIEN AVIENTVRADO | E VIRTVOZO ISHAG DE | DAVID DA SILVA Q^a | RECOLLEO DEVS PARA SVA | GLORIA EM 17 DE TANZ | 5452 QVI | CONRESPONDE A 26 DE | IVLHO.

Below in a sunk square is an arm chopping a tree through the trunk. This occurs frequently later.

1430. Very large lettering:—

ESTER DE | CASERES 2 | AB 45.

1431. DA BEM AVENTVRADA | JUDICA ISRAEL DIAS F | EM 3 DE TEBET | A° 5451.

1432. DO ENCURTADO DE ABRAHAM | ARON F° DE JOSEPH MENDES | QVE FOY DS SERVIDO RECOLHER | ASEOS POVOS EM 8 DE TISRY A° | 5452.

1433. Lettering raised instead of incised:—

(6 Hebrew lines above) | DO BEM AVENTVRADO | PAGDIEL ABUDIENTE* | QVE FALESEO EM 27 DE | AB 5451 EM BARBADAS | (skull and crossbones below).

1434. DO BEM AVENTVRADO SELO | MOH E MEDINA 9 FOI DS | SERVIDO RECOLHER ASEOS | QVOS EM 24 DE HESVAN | A° 5452.

1435. Eleven Hebrew lines above:—

Do Bem aventurado & Temerozo | De Dos^{or} Abraham Abudente* que | De 84 annos palsoudesta Vida a | Da gloria Etterna Em 4 Tamuz | 5457 | Conrresponde a Conta | Vulgar com 3 Julho | 1697.

1436. DA VERTVOZA & HONESTA | RACHEL MOTHER QVI FOY | DE ABRAHAM ABVDIENTE* | Q FALLECEV EM 22 HESVAN | A° 5456 | Q CONRESPONDE COM 21 | 8^{bro} 1695.

* The Hebrew name of Gideon. See under Baron Eardley in Burke's "Extinct Peerage." (T. C.-F.)

1437. Only two lines, but worn :—

JUD .. H ....

1438. Much worn. A° . 452 is legible.

1439. DA BEM AVENTVRADA | ABIGAIL DA FONSECA | MEZA F° EM 19 YYAR | A° 5452.

1440. DO BEM AVENTVRADO | S°R JAHACOB MASSIAH | FALLECEV | EM 11 DE IEBE (crack) A° 5453.

1441. DA BEM AVENTVRADA | S^ra DEBORAH MASSIAH | FALLECEV | EM 6 DE ADARDO A° 5453.

1442. Several cracks :—

Da Bem aventurada | Virtuoza Donã Rachel | Idanha Que foy Ds | servido Recolher aseos | Povos em 7 de Sivan | de 5453 ã Que Cor- | -responde a Pr°: de Junio | de 1693 ã.

1443. Hebrew inscription in wall.

A sixth row commences here.

1444. Cracked :—

D . PEM AVENTVRADO DE | JOSEPH SENIOR SARAIVA | QVE FOI APANHADO ASEOS | POVOS EM . 26 DE | MENAHEM A° | 5454.

1445. DABEM AVENTVRADO | YAEL SERANA . FALLECEV | EM 7 DE TISRI A° 5455.

1446. Do Bem aventurado de | Abraham de Leao fillio | de Mosseh Perreira de Leao^s | q foy Ds Servido Recol- | -ler a Seos Povos em 6 de | Hesvan ano 5453 q Cor- | -responde a 6 de Octubro | 1692.

1447. Do bem aventurado de Isaque | Mendez fillo de Josseph Mendez | que foy D^s servido recoller naffor | de sua Idade p^a Plantarlo em . an (crack) | Eden Lugar dos J .... Evir- | -tuosos adonde su . muita | Gloria supra a .. alta de sua | Idade fallesco em 7 de Tebet | 5456 que corresponde a 3 de | Dec^bro 1696 ã.

Around the sides and top runs :—

HERE LYETH INTERRED THE BODY OF ISAAC MENDEZ SON OF | JOSEPH MENDEZ WHO DEPARTED THIS LIFE ON THE 30 DECEMBER AGED XXI YEARES.

1448. Do BEM AVENTURADO | YSHAK DE MEZA QUE | FALECEO EM 21 DE HESUAN | 5457.

1449. De DANIEL Filho | De SIMHON E SARA | MASSIAH q faleceo | EM 29 de Tebet | 5466.

———

1450. Skull and crossbones below :—

DO BEM . AVENTVRA- | DO DAVID CHILLAO | QVE FALECEV EM 14 | DE TEBET Aº 5458.

———

1451. DA VIRTVOZA DONZELA | SARAH FILHA DE MANVEL | ISRAEL DIAS FALECEO EM | 5 DE ADAR RISON 5464.

———

1452. Much flaked :—

. . . . Burgos | . . . . | 5467.

———

1453. Under a tree, much flaked.

———

1454. Da Sʳᵃ Rachell de Meza | Que falleceu Sendo VV | dosᵒʳ: Ishak de Meza em | 17 Nissan 5459.

———

1455. Da bem Aventurada Evertuosa | Mulher de fonsado A Sᵗᵃ Ribca | Letob Aqual Recolheu osʳ | Deus para millor Mundo | faleseu EM 22 de Sivan 5463 | que Comresponde a 27 de | Mayo Anno 1703 Que sua | Bendita alma goze da devina | gloria.

1456. Flaked away.

———

1457. Da bem Aventurada de | Sarah Mulher de Danell J . osuah | de Leao que foy D. S . . . . | Recolh . . seos Povos em . . . . | Tebet 5456 que Conresponde | a 19 Decemᵇʳᵒ 1695 Emais ascos | pez . . . . Enterada huma sua | C . . ca (p nome Rahell que faleseu | Em 30 de Sebar 5456 Seos | Seija perda de | Se pacado.

———

1458. DA . BEM . AVENTRADA | JVENERABLE VELLA Sᴴᴬ | RIBCA MVLLER qᶜ FOY DOSᴴ | DAVID VLLOA qᶜ Dˢ TEMq FOY | Dˢ SERVIDO RECOLLER DESTᴴ | MAV MVNDO Pᴬ OVTRO | MELLOR EM 23 DE ROSHODES | NISAN 5470-qᶜ CONRES PONDE | EM 11 DE-ABRILL 1709.

———

1459. Skull and crossbones below :—

Do bem aventurado MoSseh | Haim Coutinho que faleceo em 10 | de Sivan 5466 que Corresponde, a 12 | Mayo 1706, Sv.

———

1460. Below is an arm out of clouds chopping down a tree :—

Da Bem Aventurada Honesta | Devota E Caritativa Donha Sarah | Abigail Mendes Mulher que foy | da Mosseh de Selomoh Mendes | que foy arrebatada desta para | melhor vida na flor de sua idade | Em 27 Adar 5474 que Corresponde | a 3 Marco 17¹³⁄₁₄ | (7 Hebrew lines follow).

———

1461. Flaked away.

JEWISH BURIAL-GROUND, BRIDGETOWN.205

1462. A slab illegible, partly buried, to " SARA."

1463. Do Y . . VRTADO EVIRTVOZO | MANCEBO A . . . . AIM BVRGOS (? Aaron Haim) | 2 FOIAPANA . . . . VOS | EM DIA DE BVOTO DE . . . . AN | Aº 5 . 6 .

1464. Da bem aventurada de | bem Venida Gomes Hen- | -riques Vinua de Isaque | GOMES Henriques que | faleceo Em 31 de Agosto | 1701 que Corresponde | a 6 de Elul 5461.

1465. De bem Aventurada onesta | Evertuoza Ester Antunes que | faleseu de ydade de 84 annos | em 16 de Sebat do Anno 5463 | da Criacao do mundo que Com- (*sic*) | -responde em 22 Janeiro 170⅘.

1466. DO BEM . AVENTURADO & TEMEROZO | DE Dˢ OSᴼᴿ JOSEPH JESSURUN MENDEZ | QUE FALLECEV DE 83 ANNOS FUNDOU A | EZNOGA DE NIDHE ISRAEL A DEFENDEU | & PROTEJEU ATE SUA JAZIDA COM SEUS | PAES QUE FOY EM 15 TEBETT 5460 | Here is Buried the body of | Mᴿ LEWIS DIAS who was beloved | Respected by all men in his time | he died on the 27ᵗʰ of December Aº | 1699 Being 83 yeares of age.

1467. Above is a cupid's head :—

DAMALLOGRADA VIRTVOZA | ETEMEROZA mulher asʳᵃ Efter | mulher de Mofeh Efpinoza | que for nolo fenhor Servido | chamar para Si em 24 de | tamus 5470 que correfpondᵈᵉ | a 8 de Iullio 1710.

1468. Da Bem Aventurada | Yvirtuoza de Lüna Mulher | De JACOB FRANCO NUNES | que foy deos Servido | Recolher para Sy em 6 | De Yiar 5466 | que Comresponde A 9 | De Abril 1706.

1469. Do Bem . aventurado & | Caritatvo IAIIACOB | FRANCO NUNES que foy | Deos fer vido recolher para | fua Santa Gloria em Sabat | 8 Hefvan 5487 de Annos | 80.

Around the sides and top runs :—

Here Lyeth Interred the Body of the Pious and Charitable | Mᴿ JACOB FRANCO NUNES, of Barbadoes Merchᵗ | who departed this life on the 8ᵗʰ of Hefvan 5487 of yᵉ Creation | of yᵉ WORLD, which is yᵉ 22ᵈ of October 1726 Aged | 80 Years.

1470. Da bem aventurada Evirtuoza | Ribcah Mulher de Jacob Baruh | LOUZADA que foy Deos servida | Recolher a Milhor Mundo | flor de sua Ydade em 24 | Menahem Anno 5457 que | Corresponde a primeiro de | Agosto 1697.

To the south of this are six stones to VALVERDE, and several to MASSIAH, touching the house.

1471. Do B. A. De AARON BARUH | LOUZADA que foy Dˢ Servido | Recolher pᵃ sy em 5ᵃ: fᵃ: 6 de | Nifan 5528 que Correfponde | 24 Marco 1768 de Idade de | 64 Annos 11 Mezes and 20 Dias.

1472. *Da Bemaventurada y | Virtuoza Pia y Devota | Ester Sarah Mulher que | Foy de Aharon Baruh | Louzada Fº em 26 Hes- | -van Aº 5505, Coresponde | a 20 de Outubre 1744 da | Ydade de 36 Anos y 1 | Mezes.*

Around the sides and top runs :—

HERE LYETH INTERRD Yᴱ BODY OF Yᴱ CHARITABLE | ESTER SARAH LATE WIFE OF AARON BARUH LOUZADA | WHO DEPARTED THIS LIFE THE 20 OF OCTᴿ 1744 AGED 36 Y. & 7 MONˢ.

Aaron and Ester Baruh-Louzada. They are the progenitors of the Lousada family now settled in England. Francis Clifford Duke de Losada y Lousada, Comm. R.N., represents the senior branch. Ester Baruh Lousada was the daughter of Aaron Lamego (died 1747) of Jamaica, who late in life came to England, and lies buried in the old Portuguese Jewish Cemetery at Mile End behind the Beth Holim.

The Lousadas married into the principal families of the Sephardi community such as the Lopes, Ximenes, Francois, Aguilars, Lopes Pereiras, Barrows, Mocattas, Mendes da Costas, etc., and played a prominent part in communal affairs, but now there are very few of the family left in the community.

I cannot recall Barbados being mentioned on the stones at Mile End (I have only worked at the more modern burial-ground the Beth Haim, a short distance from the ancient ground at the Beth Holim), excepting one to Judith Montefiore, wife of Eleazar Montefiore. She is described as a "Native of Barbadoes," and died 13 May 1836. She was a dau. of Jacob Joseph Levi, he an uncle of Sir Moses Montefiore. She was a connection of the Barrows, another Barbados family.   [T. C.-F.]

STEPNEY, CO. MIDDLESEX.

In the burial-ground of the Portuguese Jews on the north side of Mile End Road :—

Abraham Hisquian Gabay Isidro, Rabbi of the congregation at Barbadoes, 1755. (Lysons' "Environs of London," iii., 478.)

Aº 1680. LIST OF THE JEWS IN ST. MICHAEL'S TOWN.
(Hotten, 449.)

	P'sons.	Slaves.		P'sons.	Slaves.
Isack Abof	2	1	Abraham Costauio	2	6
Gabriell Antunes	2	4	Samuell Dechavis	2	4
Abraham Burges Aron	2	2	Mʳˢ Leah Decompas	3	1
Moses Arrobas	4	2	David Ralph Demereado	3	11
Sarah Atkins	1	–	Moses Desavido	5	3
Abraham Barruch	3	3	Paul Devrede	2	3
Aron Barruch	5	5	Lewis Dias	6	8
Rebecah Barruch	1	1	Isaac Gomez	3	2
Daniell Boyna	3	11	Moses Hamias*	2	1
Rachell Burges	6	2	David Israell	5	3
Soloman Cordoza	3	2	Judith Israell	2	–

* Perhaps this should be "Namias."

	P'sons.	Slaves		P'sons.	Slaves.
Abraham Lopes	2	1	Mordecah Palache	1	–
Eliah Lopez	5	2	Isaac Perera	6	3
Rachell Lopez	4	1	Isaac Perera	2	4
Leah Medinah	7	–	Jacob Preet	1	1
Moses Mercado	5	2	Abraham Qay	2	2
Isack Meza	3	4	Judith Risson	4	2
David Namias	9	5	Anthony Rodrigus	3	10
Samuell Navarro	4	1	Mordecah Sarah	4	1
Aron Navaro	7	11	Joseph Senior	3	4
Judith Navaro	2	1	Jaell Serano	1	5
Hester Noy	2	–	Hester Bar Simon	5	1
Isace Noy	6	2	Abraham Sousa	2	2
Jacob Franco Nunes	4	1	David Swaris	5	2
Abraham Obediente	2	2	Judieah Torez	2	2
Jacob Pacheco	5	4	Jacob Fonseco Vale	5	4
Rebecah Pacheco	2	4	Abr. Valverde	2	4

ADDENDA.

BRIGHTON PLANTATION, ST. GEORGE'S.

Mr. W. H. Trollope writes that when last year (1914) in Barbadoes he was shewn an early tombstone with inscription and coat of arms to a Wiltshire in a summer-house on this estate, Mr. Lawrie Pile's.

The attention of the Editor was not drawn to this during his visit. According to the Report on Historic Sites the date 1652 is on a beam in this house, which was the seat of the Wiltshires, and a tomb near by probably belonged to them. It was not noted in the official list of tombs on plantations.

Ensign Henry Bradshaw of the parish of St. Peter, Barbadoes, gent. Will dated 29 March 1664. To my wife Jane 23½ acres. A silver boule of £5 for the communion table of St. Peter and a sermon to be preached on 10 April. My brother Lieut. Tho. Bradshaw of Rochdale, Lancashire. My father Col. John B. of the said county, Esq. My brother George. My friend Mr John B. of St. Philip 500 lbs. of sugar. Deposition of John Bradshaw, aged 50, 6 Nov. 1665. (Barbados Records, vol. i., 40.)

John Bradshaw, the regicide and former President, died 22 Nov. 1659 (Chester's " Registers of Westminster Abbey "). It has been stated that his son James removed his body to Jamaica, and buried it on a hill near Martha Brae. James had two patents for land of 250 acres and 650 acres surveyed in 1688, but this was 28 years later.

Gent. Mag.

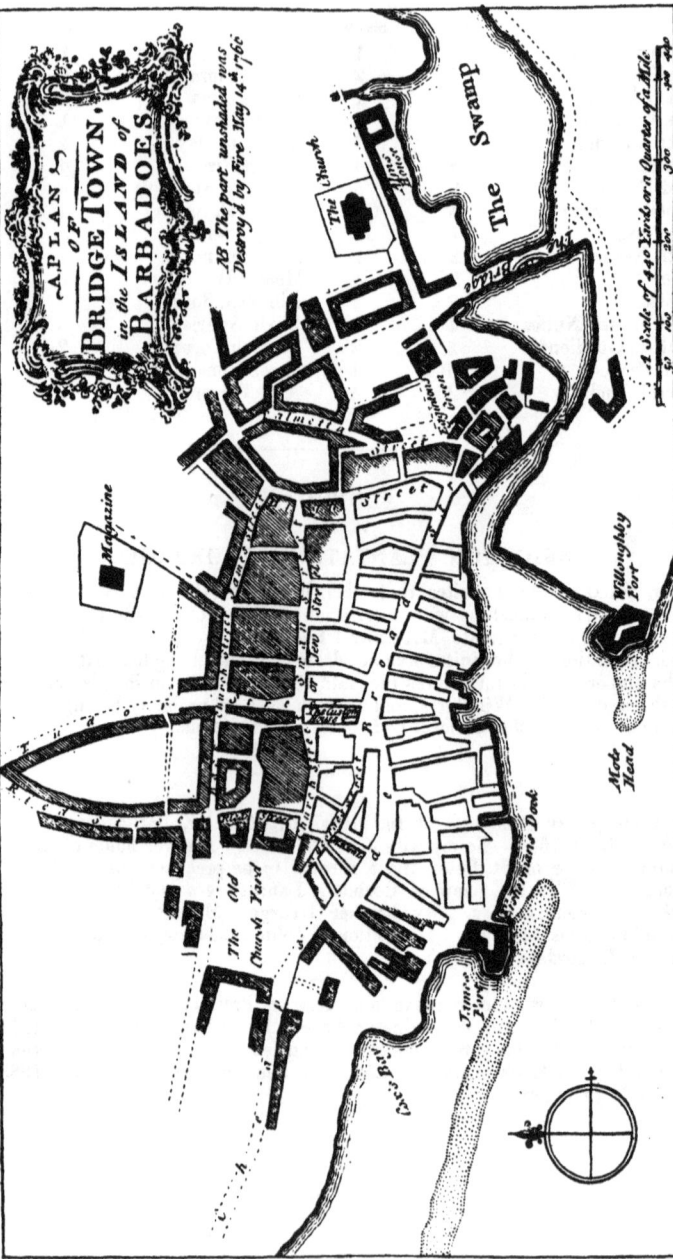

A PLAN of BRIDGE TOWN in the ISLAND of BARBADOES.

NB. The part unshaded was Destroy'd by Fire May 14th 1766.

The Church

Lighthouse

BRIDGE

The Swamp

A Scale of 440 Yards or a Quarter of a Mile.

100 200 300 400

Magazine

Willoughby Fort

Mole Head

The Old Church Yard

Cary's Bay

James Fort

Careenage Dock

J. Gibson del. et sculp

INDEX NOMINUM.

Surnames in *italic* denote the Arms are given.

A

A . . . ., E. M., 80.
A . . . ., J. W., 148.
Abel, Christian, 138 ; Jane, 138.
Abof, Isack, 206.
Abudiente (Abudente, Obediente), Abraham, 202 (2). 207 ; Pagdiel, 202 ; Rachel, 202.
Ackroyd, George, 67.
Adams (Addams), James Elliot, 29 ; John, 14 ; Margaret. 29 (2) ; Mary, 29, 111 (2) ; Samvell, 111 (2) ; Thomas, 29 (2).
Agard, Constance Louise, 151 ; Emma L. M., 151 ; Joseph W., 151.
Aguilar, —, 206.
Aikman, Alex., 75.
Alder (Allder), Agnes Rous, 190 ; Charlotte Eliz., 80 ; C. H., 63 ; I. C., 78 ; John C., 80 ; John Richard, 80 ; Sam. Brock, 92 ; W. H., 78.
Alkins, George, 57 ; John Haynes, 57.
Allamby, Wm., 177.
Allen, Damaris, 10 ; Eliz. Adamson, 41 ; Eliz. Ashby, 41 ; H. T., 18 ; John, 41 ; Phillip, 10 ; Tamasin, 10 ; Wm. Ar., 41.
Alleyne, 113, 127, 136, 137, 170.
Alleyne, Anne Walrond, 163 ; Benjamin, 91, 106 ; Charles Thomas, 136 (2) ; Christian, 21, 127, 136, 137 ; Eliz., 113 ; Eliz. Gibbes, 142 (2) ; Eliz. Reynolds, 123 ; Forster M., 38 ; Georgeana, 91, 92 ; Geo. Henry, 160 ; Henry, 136 (2), 141 ; Jane, 38 ; John, 91, 92, 163 ; John Forster, 136, 142 (2) ; John Gay, 142 ; Sir John Gay, 113, 136, 138 ; John Gay Newton, 38 ; Judith, 113 ; Kate Annie, 163 ; Margaret, 194 ; Mary, 21, 142, 168 ; Mercy, 137 ; Rebecca, 170 ; Reynold, 21, 113, 127, 168, 194 ; Sir Reynold Abel, 169, 170 ; Richard, 194 ; S. A., 182 ; S. M., 182 ; Sam. Maynard, 79, 175, 182 ; Sarah Ann, 79 ; Sarah Martindale, 92 ; Tho., 113 ; Timothy, 21 ; Wm. Gibbes, 137 ; —, 113, 136.
Allinson, Frances Eliz., 158 ; Rev. Thos., 158.
Almy, Bridget, 40 (2) ; Job, 40 (2) ; Major, 40 ; Peleg, 40 (2).
Alvares, Hanah, 201.
Ames, Sam. Brewster, 116.
Amwyl, Lt.-Col., 12 ; Senhouse, 12.
Amy, Adelaide Montgomery, 98.
Anderson, Alexander, 129 (2).
Andrews, Thomazin, 27 ; Wardall, 27.
Anton, Mary Sarah Lake, 46.
Antunes, Ester, 205 ; Gabriell, 206.
Applewhaite, Eliz., 125, 130 ; John, 125, 130 ; Miss, 175 ; Mrs., 130 ; Susanna, 130 ; Thomas, 125, 130 (2).
Applewhite, Frances, 126.

Archdall, J., 93.
Archer, Ann, 163 ; John, 163, 172 ; Joseph A., 49 ; Mary, 73 ; Mary Edward, 172 ; Sarah Elliott, 172 ; William, 151 ; Wm. A., 75.
Armstrong, Eliz. Leslie, 80 ; Eliz. Martindale, 80 ; Emme Josephine, 197 ; George, 67 ; Prudence A., 65 ; Susan, 197 ; Thos. Gent., 148 ; W. T., 197.
Arnold, Wm., 156.
Aron, Abraham Burges, 206.
Arrobas, Moses, 206.
Arthur, Joseph Inniss, 77 ; Sam. Brandford, 77.
Ashby, Alexander, 129 (2) ; Eliz., 39 ; Geo. Jonothan, 39 ; John, 39 ; Mary, 129 ; Mary Louise, 129 ; Sarah Eliz., 129.
Ashehurst, 115.
Ashehurst, Benjamin, 115 ; John, 115 ; Magdalen, 115.
Ashmead, C., 25.
Astley (Astle), Francis Wm., 95, 105.
Atkins, Frances, 7, 8 ; J. W., 85 ; Sir Jonathan, 7, 8 ; Sarah, 206.
Attor, Nathan Iiddon, 87.
Atwell, Ambrose, 116.
Atwood, Hen. Sacheveral Smith, 80 ; John, 80.
Austin, Brucie Inniss, 90 ; Helen J., 90 ; James D., 90 ; John, 19 ; Lætitia, 19.
Aynsworth, 162.
Aynsworth, Eliz., 162 ; James, 162.
Ayshford, Anthony, 180 ; Damaris, 180 ; Mary Ann, 180 (2) ; Robert, 180 (3).

B

B . . . ., E., 166.
B . . . ., J., 167 (2).
B . . . ., R., 66.
B . . . ., Richard, 86.
B . . . ., W., 76.
Babb, Benjamin, 171 ; Margery, 171.
Baber, James, 165 (2) ; Mary Anne, 165 ; Walter, 85.
Bacon, Mrs., 200.
Badcock, George, 38 (2).
Baeza, Mr., 197.
Bailey, Mary, 81.
Baker, F. B., 15 ; John, 161.
Baldrick, Mary, 194.
Ball, Mary, 21 ; —, 21.
Balquhain, John Leslie, Baron of, 180 ; *see also* Leslie.
Balston, *see* Ralston.
Bamfield, Elizabeth, 63.
Bannis, Eliz. Dove, 37 ; Wm. Gaskin, 37.
Barbados, 23.

E E

83 ; Wm., 11 ; Wm. Coleridge, 83 ; Wm. E.,
68 ; Wm. Phillips, 118 ; —, 116, 186.
Claypool, Alice, 131 ; Alice Sarah, 131 ; Ed-
ward, 131 (2) ; Eliz., 131 ; Sarah, 131.
Cleland, A. B., 18, 121 ; Alexander B., 120 ;
Fanny Kemp, 121.
Clement, John, 66.
Clinckett, Abell, 16, 78 (2) ; Rev. G. M., 78 ;
Jane, 78 ; Mary Abell, 16 ; Mary Judith, 78.
Clinton, Eliz. Grazett, 57.
Clune, Margaret, 102 ; Patrick, 102.
Clutterbuck, Lieut., 25 ; Wm., 14.
Cobb, Thomas, 40.
Cobham, John, 13 ; Lucy, 13.
Cock, John, 62 (2) ; Richard, 62.
Codd, W. T., 61.
Coddington, Mary, 40.
Codrington, Chr., 193, 195 ; Rich. Gibson, 59 ;
Sir Wm. John, 196.
Cole, Alex. A., 84 ; Eliza, 26 ; Eliz., 26 ; Julia
Amanda, 84.
Colebrooke, Emma Sophia, 53, 91 ; Mary Har-
riet, 53 ; Sir Wm., 53 ; Sir Wm. M. G., 120.
Coleridge, 23, 113.
Coleridge, Sarah Eliz., 23 ; Wm. Hart, Bishop
of Barbados, 23, 105, 113 ; Wm. Rennell, 23.
Colleton, —, 193.
Collier, Abel, 43 ; Eliz., 43 ; James K., 43 ;
Jane, 43 (2) ; Samuel, 43 (2) ; Wm., 43 (2).
Collins, 118.
Collins (Collyns), Ann, 141 (3) ; Benjamin, 150 ;
Charles, 118 ; John, 141 (2) ; J. C., 131.
Collymore, Charlotte, 61 (2) ; Henry, 61 (2) ;
John, 61 ; Katherine, 132 ; Robert, 132.
Colyer-Fergusson, T., 197.
Combermer, Lord, 34.
Connell, Eliz., 171 ; Thomas, 171.
Connolly, James, 14.
Consett, Lieut. Coll., 193.
Cooke, J. T., 92.
Cooper, Mary, 31 ; Simon, 31.
Copley, P. G., 109.
Coppell, I. L. J., 55.
Corbin, Charles, 151 (2) ; Cordelia Violet, 94 ;
James, 151 ; John T., 150 ; Joseph, 172 ;
Mary Amelia, 150 ; Mary E., 151 ; —, 151.
Cordoza (Cardoso), Ha .... (Ra ....), 201 ;
Soloman, 206.
Corsellis, Susanna, 182.
Corstorphan, George, 77.
Costanio (Coutinho), Abraham, 206 ; Mosseh
Haim, 204.
Cotton, Daniel, 71 ; Dudley Page, 71 (2), 89 ;
Mary Rebecca, 71 ; R. E., 15 ; Rebecca Jane,
71.
Coulsten, James, 58 ; John, 58.
Coulthurst, Eliz., 7 ; Matthew, 7, 21.
Couper, Arthur C., 120 (2) ; Sir Geo., 120.
Cousins, Herbert T., 109.
Cowse, James, 87.
Cox, A., 100 ; G. H. Richardson, 94 ; Howard
Plestow, 101 ; H. T., 66 ; R. Albert, 66 ; Wm.,
162.
Cozier, John, 49 (2) ; Sarah Ann, 49 ; Susanna,
49.
Crane, Henry Thomas, 65 ; Margaret Ann, 65 ;
Martha, 65 ; Sarah Nattali, 65 ; Wm., 16.
Crichlow, Charlotte, 13 ; Henry, 13 (2) ; Lucy,
13 ; Margaret, 188 ; Wm., 13.
Crick, Eliz. Leslie, 80 ; Eliz. Nicolls, 80 ; Eliz.
Thomas, 107 ; John S., 69 ; Martha, 107.

Crisp, 3.
Crisp, Edward, 4 ; Jane, 4 ; John, 4 (3) ; Jo-
seph, 4 ; Margt., 4 ; Mary, 4 ; Nich., 4 ;
Samuel, 4 ; Sarah, 4 (2), 87 ; Sybella, 4 ;
Tho., 4.
Crispin, Joseph, 120.
Crofton, Thomas, 100 ; Wm., 100.
Cromartle, Martha, 61 ; Robert, 61 (2) ; Robt.
Thomas, 61.
Crompton (Crumpton), Ernest, 119 ; Henry,
119 (2) ; Sarah Henry, 119.
Croney, I. W., 85.
Crosby, Rev. John, 77.
Crosse, Robt. Noble, 93, 104.
Crouch, Charlie, 104 ; Chas. E. Y., 81 ; Clemen-
tina, 81 ; Eliz., 6.
Crowe, James, 9 (2).
Crumpton, *see* Crompton.
Culpeper (Culpepper), Abel Alleyne, 194 (2) ;
Alleyne, 194 (2), 195 ; Sir Cheney, 194, 195 ;
Eliz., 194 (2) ; Fra., 195 ; Hester, 194 ; John
Alleyne, 194 ; Margt., 194 ; Sir Thos., 195 ;
Wm., 194.
Cumming, Henry, 76.
Cummins, Ann, 53 ; Eliz., 129 ; George, 53 ;
Henry S., 53 ; James, 53 ; John, 129 ; Mary
Ann, 106 ; Norman J. D., 13, 84 ; Thomas
Joshua, 106 ; —, 108.
Cunard, Abraham, 66 ; Margaret, 66.
Cunningham, 44.
Cunningham, Alex., 44 ; Anne, 44 ; Chas.
Thornton, 76 ; J., 15 ; John, 44 (2) ; Rebecca
Anne, 76 ; Zebulon, 44.
Curtis, Bezin K., 45 ; James A., 45.
Cutting, Dr., 70 ; Emmeline P., 84 ; Rev. Ernest
A., 84 ; John Hen., 133 ; Sarah Margaret,
133 ; —, 70.

D

D .... , J. D. D., 55.
Da Costa, Mendes, 206 ; —, 108.
Da Fonseca, Abigail, 203.
Dalzell, Allen, 128 ; Anne Wilhelmina, 128.
Dampier, Julia Sophia, 91 ; Rev. R., 91.
Daniel, John Thos., 56 ; Maria Anne, 25 ; Sarah
Eliz., 56 ; Thomas, 25.
Darby, Christopher T., 60 ; Mary, 60.
Darling, Anne Wilhelmina, 128 ; Chas. Henry,
128 ; Chas. Hen. Hay, 128 ; Ellen, 14 ; Henry
Chas., 128 ; —, 128.
Da Silva, David, 202 ; Isbac, 202.
Davidson, John, 90.
Davis, G. E. J., 120 ; John, 120 ; N. Darnell,
195 ; St. George G. S., 120 (2).
Dayrell, Edmund, 130 ; Francis, 41.
Dean (Deane), Anne Walrond, 163 (2) ; Arnold
Evans, 154 ; Dorothy, 154 ; George A., 189,
191 ; George Henry, 163 ; John, 154 ; J. W.,
62 ; Sarah Martindale, 92.
Dear, Eliz., 61 ; Geo. Edward, 61 ; John, 61 ;
S. E. A., 138.
Death, Edwin, 120.
Dechavis, Samuel, 206.
Decompas, Leah, 206.
de Hem, Jacob, 182 ; James, 182 ; Jaques, 182 ;
Susanna, 182 ; Tobias, 182.
De la Roche, Henry Ant., 87.
Deleon, Moseh, 200.
Demercado, *see* Mercado.

Denny, William, 120.
Desavido, Moses, 206.
Desse, Dorothy, 67.
Devenish, Keturah Shepherd, 26 ; Lieut., 26.
De Vins, Cath. Henriette, 159 ; Count Richard, 159.
Devrede, Paul, 206.
De Wend, Edward Michael, 66.
De Winton, R., 93.
De Witt, Cornelius, 87 ; Mr., 87.
Dias, David Ys, 200 ; Israel, 202 ; Lewis, 205, 206 ; Manvel Israel, 204 ; Sarah, 204.
Dilkes, Richard, 98.
Divles (?), John, 27 ; Philippa, 27.
Dixon, John, 63.
Dodsworth, Hannah, 38 ; Henry, 38.
D'Olier, Theophilus, 61.
Dolman, John, 33.
Donovan, Danl., 66 ; Martha Jane Frances, 53 ; Thomas, 53 ; Thomasin William, 66.
Doran, B., 15.
Dorington, C. R., 18 ; Chas. Rich., 101 ; John Edward, 101 ; Sir John Edw., 101 ; Susan, 101.
Dottin, 137.
Dottin (Dotin), Anne, 134 (2), 137 (2) ; Christian, 136 ; Edward Jordan, 134 (2), 135 (2) ; James, 137, 183 ; John, 137 ; Joseph, 134, 136, 137 ; Mary, 183 ; Mercy, 137.
Dowding, Eliz., 7 ; John, 7 ; Mary, 7 ; Rebecca, 7 ; Sam., 7 ; Rev. Wm., 7.
Drake, C. C., 75 ; Ellen, 75.
Drakes, Edward, 140.
Draper, Robert, 33.
Drax, Eliz., 124 ; Henry, 124 (2) ; Sir James, 124.
Drayton, Jas. Culpepper, 84 ; John, 177 ; Mercy, 126 ; Rebecca Jane, 177 ; Samuel, 126 ; Wm., 126.
Dreiduiz, —, 151.
Duck, Benjamin, 67.
Dudman, Robert, 19 ; Rr., 99.
Duesbury, Eliz., 62 (2) ; Rebecca, 62 (2).
Duffey, Jane, 31.
Duke, 24.
Duke, Henry, 24 ; Humphry, 24, 177 ; Rev. John, 29 ; Sarah, 177 ; Thomas, 24 ; Wm., 24, 29, 177.
Dummett, Edw. James, 54.
Dunn, Margaret Ann, 22.
Durant, Alice, 83 ; Fred., 83 ; John, 115 ; Mary, 115 ; Thos., 115.
Duthy, J., 15.

E

E . . . ., A. H., 75, 76.
Eardley, Baron, 202.
Eckel, Rev. E. A., 151 ; Susan E., 151 ; Rev. Theodore, 151 ; —, 151.
Edgill (Edgell, Edghill), Caroline, 81 ; Chas. James, 15, 57 ; Christian Gay, 36 ; J., 15 ; James Young, 81 ; Samuel, 36.
Edwards, 6.
Edwards, Jane, 6.
Eginton (Egginton), Jeremiah, 11 (2) ; John, 11.
Elcock (Ellcock), Ann, 192 ; Grace, 130 ; Grant, 130, 192 ; Mary, 175 ; Reynold Alleyne, 175 ; —, 21, 175.
Elder, Annie, 45 ; Augusta Matilda, 74 ; James,

74 ; J. W. E., 59 ; Robert, 45, 74 ; Roderick, 64.
Ellery, William, 88.
Ellicott, Judith, 30 ; Susannah, 30 (2) ; Thomas, 30.
Elliot, 112.
Elliot. Eliz., 112 ; James, 112 ; Richard, 112 ; —, 115.
Ellis, Edw., 87 ; John, 15 (2), 178 ; John Bryante, 175 ; John Thos., 178 ; Mary Anne, 175 ; Mary Jane, 175 (2) ; Rebecca, 178 ; Sarah Eliz., 178 ; Thomas, 175 (4) ; Wm., 175 ; Wm. Brian, 178 ; Wm. Grant, 176.
Elvie, E. C. T., 85.
Emerton, Mary R., 42.
Engren, Edouard, 30.
Enright, Alexander Hunter, 75.
Esdaile, Sam. John, 54.
Espinoza, Ester, 205 ; Moseh, 205.
Estwick, Christopher, 185 (2) ; Eliz., 128, 185 ; Eliz. Susanna, 128 ; Francis, 185 ; Henry, 185 ; Richard, 185 (2) ; Samuel, 128 ; Sarah, 194 ; Susanna, 185 ; Tho., 190 ; —, 193.
Evans, Francis Henry, 85 ; Johanna Walrond, 85 ; Nicholas, 85 ; Susannah, 85.
Evelyn, Susan Frances, 132 ; Wilhelmina Ann Stanton, 114 ; —, 116.
Eversley, Eliz., 10, 113 ; Eliz. Anne, 10 ; Mary, 10 ; Rebecca, 10 ; Sarah, 10 ; Wm., 10 (3), 113.
Ewing, Eliz. Ford, 148 ; Mary, 148 (2), 151 ; Robert, 148, 151.

F

F . . . ., G. A., 184 ; J. T., 184.
Fairchild, Hamlet, 88.
Fairman (Pairman), Harriet, 108 ; James, 108.
Falcon, Michael, 123 ; Thomas, 123.
Farley, Eleanor, 6 ; Isaac, 6.
Farmer, Christian, 9 ; Jane, 79 ; Kath., 9 ; Rich., 79.
Farnum, Edwin, 59 ; P. J., 54 ; P. R., 54 (2) ; Sarah E., 59.
Farrar (Farrer), Hannah, 26 ; Robert, 26 (2), 112 ; Thomas, 26.
Farrell, Eliz., 114 ; John Richard, 114 ; Sidney Baynton, 109.
Faulkner, Eliz., 103.
Felton, John, 27.
Fenty, Samuel James, 154 ; Wm. Frs., 190.
Fercharson (Ferchardson), Bowden, 143 (3) ; Eliz., 32 (2) ; Honour, 143 ; Kath., 32 ; Mary, 32 ; Tho., 32, 143.
Field, Ada H., 83 ; James E., 83 (3) ; James O., 83 ; Sarah Massiah, 83.
Fitchatt, Rev. Francis, 137, 138.
Fitzpatrick, James Evelyn, 115 (2) ; Mary E., 148 ; Sarah Eliz., 115 ; Wm., 76 ; —, 76.
Fitzthomas, Maria E., 22 ; Mary Worrell, 22, 84 ; Versepuy, 84 ; Wm. Versepuy, 22, 84 ; —, 22, 84.
Fletcher, J. W., 15 ; John Wynne, 11.
Floud, Ross Moore, 120 (2) ; Tho., 120.
Foderingham, N., 155.
Follett, Hannah, 107 (2) ; John, 107 ; Sarah, 107 (3).
Foord, John, 184.
Forbes, Mary, 161 ; Wm., 161.

Hooper, Mary, 21 ; Reyland, 1 ; Robert, 1 (2), 12 ; Tho., 1 ; —, 21.
Hope, Sir John H., 95 ; John Thomas, 95 ; Nich., 88.
Hopson, Peregrine Tho., 88.
Hordle, Agnes Downes, 34 ; Ann, 44 ; Honor, 44 ; John Dapwell, 44 ; Margaret, 34 ; Mary, 44 (2) ; Sarah, 34 ; Thomas, 34, 44 (2).
Horsham, Dr., 70 ; William, 70.
Hothersall, Ann, 194 ; Anne Isabella, 191, 194 ; Eliz., 47 ; John, 9, 191 ; Meliora, 9 ; Rebecca, 194 ; —, 193.
Hovell, Eliz., 69 ; Richard, 69 (2).
Howard, Ann Bell, 145 ; Anthony, 57 (3), 132 ; John Robt., 145 ; Mary, 2 ; Michael, 145 ; Michael Skeete, 145 ; Ruth Johnson, 57 (2) ; Sarah, 174 ; Thomas, 57 ; Wm. Henry, 132 ; Wm. Murrell, 174.
Howell, Annie Bruce, 24 ; Benj. Carlton, 154 ; Conrade Adams, 65 ; Conrad Goodridge, 65 ; Hinds, 65 ; Jane Carleton, 65 ; John Rous, 65 ; John Simpson, 24, 83 ; Mary Jane, 154 ; Thomas Walrond, 65.
Hoyle, Mr., 26 ; Rob., 26.
Hudson, Coleridge, 183.
Hughes, Rev. John S., 119.
Humpleby, John, 1.
Hunt (Hunte), Rev. Dr., 179 ; Eliz., 171 ; E. F., 83 ; F., 165 ; Jane Nihell, 171 ; Leigh, 179 ; Mary Jane, 171 ; Mary Thomas, 159 ; R., 165.
Hunter, Eliz., 76 ; Euphemia, 102 ; John, 102.
Husbands, Harriet, 108 (2) ; John, 193 ; Mary Margaret, 193.
Hustler, Charlotte, 123 ; Wm., 123.
Hutchinson, Eliz. Ann, 163 ; Emanuel John Cock, 163 ; Horace E. B., 100 (2) ; Sir Wm., 100.
Hutson, H. A., 184 ; Rev. John, 184 ; Susanna Jane, 184.
Hutton, Anne Mary, 121 ; Richard Holt, 121.

I

I . . . ., R., 174.
Idanha, Rachel, 203 ; *see also* Ydana.
Ifill, Benjamin, 14 ; Susan, 14.
Ifman, John, 62.
Ince, George, 117 ; Henry Jemott, 65 ; John, 117 (2) ; Margaret, 117 (2).
Incledon, Mary H., 71 ; Robt. J., 71.
Inniss, Ann, 64 ; B., 83 ; John, 6 ; Joseph Wm., 72 ; Mercy Ann, 64 (2) ; Richard, 132 ; Rose Walrond, 72 ; Sarah Ann, 64 (2) ; Sarah Jane, 64 (2) ; Thomasin Ann, 72 ; Wm., 64 (2) ; —, 71, 178.
Irvine, 46.
Irvine, Alexander, 46.
Irwin, Montgomery, 95, 104.
Isidro, Abraham Hisquian Gabay, 206.
Israel, David, 198, 206 ; Judith, 206.

J

J . . . ., C., 65.
J . . . ., Edmund, 10.
J . . . ., W. H., 148.
Jackman, Eliz., 154 ; John Abel, 154.
Jackson (Jacson), Charlotte Louisa, 102 ; Christopher, 3 (2) ; Eliz., 3 ; John, 3 ; Mary Shepherd, 102 ; Thomas, 3 ; Rev. Wm., 120 ; Wm. Walrond, 102.
James, 136.

James, Henry, 96 ; Jemima, 96 ; Mary Harriet, 31 ; . . . eva . . John, 96.
Jekyl, Jos., 88.
Jemott, Crichlow, 65.
Jenkins, Ann, 36 ; William, 36 (2).
Jezzeph, James, 34.
Johnson, Eliz. G., 56 ; John, 87 (2) ; Joseph, 148 ; Judith, 87 ; Louisa, 54 ; Richard, 56 ; Rich. Payne, 56 ; Sam. Daniel, 56 ; Walter Thos., 56.
Johnston, Archibald, 25 ; James, 36.
Johnstoun, Archibald, 184 ; Eliz., 123 ; Lucy, 184.
Jones, 33.
Jones, Ann, 33 ; Anne Isabel, 72 ; Anne K., 48 ; Benjamin, 77 ; Benj. Howell, 77 ; Dorothy, 128 ; Eleanor, 77 ; Eliz. Susanna, 128 ; Ernest Henry, 77 ; F. Brandon, 48 ; F. F., 85 ; H., 78 ; James, 33 ; Jane, 124 ; John Foster Drake, 72 ; John Weekes, 79 ; Maria Farre, 72 ; Mary Jane, 78 ; Rebecca, 7 ; Robt. Burnet, 128 ; Wm., 81.
Jordan, 137.
Jordan (Jordain), Ann, 10, 134 (2), 135, 137 (2) ; Edward, 5, 122, 134 (2), 135, 137 (2) ; Eliz., 5, 122 ; Frances, 134 ; Joseph, 122 ; Mary, 34 (2) ; Sybella, 4 ; Thomas, 134 ; Wm., 34 (2) ; Wm. Walker, 122.
Joycelin, Robt., 88.

K

K . . . ., S., 147.
Keane, 19.
Keane, Esther, 20 ; Fra., 20 ; Hugh Perry, 20 ; Michael, 19, 20 ; Susanna, 20.
Kellman, Alithea, 172 ; Ann Gragg, 174 ; James Cragg, 127, 132, 172 ; John, 172 (2) ; John Eyare, 132 ; Mary Jane, 174 ; Sarah Payne, 127 ; Shadrack, 172, 174.
Kelly, Charlotte Caroline, 150 ; E., 15 ; Sir John, 150.
Kelto, Ann, 33 ; Wm., 33.
Kemp, John, 73.
Kendrick (Keanrick), Eliz., 155 ; J., 14 ; Rev. Scawen, 155, 156.
Kent, Chas., 120 (3) ; W., 94.
Kerr, Frances Ann, 192 ; Robt. Elder, 86 ; Thomas, 192.
Keysar, Edmund, 126 ; Eliz. Ann, 126.
Killikelly, Wm., 94.
King, Alexander, 59 ; Ann, 82 ; Eliz. Augusta, 30 ; Eyare, 176 ; George Laurance, 138 ; Henry Peter, 124 ; Ida, 82 ; James W., 30 ; John E., 159 ; Joseph R., 138 ; Rebecca Frances, 138 ; Samuel, 22 ; S. W., 82 ; Thomas, 22, 134 ; Wm. J., 82 ; Wm. John, 94 ; —, 114.
Kingsland, Nathaniel, 153.
Kirton, Ann, 111 (3) ; John, 34, 111 (2) ; Nathaniel, 165 ; Richard, 116 ; —, 111.
Knight, Edmund, 16, 65 ; Eliz., 149 ; Mary Eliza, 16 ; Thomas Jos., 193 ; —, 149.
Kopkee (Koplee), Jacob, 2.

L

L . . . ., C. I., 144.
L . . . ., H., 76.
Lambert, Jane, 170 ; Ruth, 170 ; Simon, 170 ; Susana, 170.
Lambly, Patrick Nelson, 48.
Lamego, Aaron, 206 ; Ester, 206.

Laming, Edward, 184.
Lamont, Bessie, 84 ; James D., 84.
Lamplee, Alexander, 107 ; Robt., 107 ; Ruth, 107.
Lang, Edward, 151 ; Kath., 151 ; Joseph, 151.
Langlands, Alexander, 120.
Lascelles (Lassels), Alice, 181 ; Dorothy, 49 ;
  Edward, 49 (2) ; Francis, 49 ; Mary, 49 (3) ;
  Sarah, 49 ; Thos., 49.
Laurie, —, 91.
Law, Peter, 48.
Lawless, E., 109 ; John, 99.
Lawrence (Lawrance), Eliz. Grace, 170 ; Eliza
  Wells, 99 ; Henry, 170 ; John Henry, 79 ;
  Lydia, 140.
Lawson, Anna Maria, 63 ; Frances Ann, 139 ;
  James Francis, 63.
Leach, Henry P., 71.
Leacock, Rev. Hamble James, 90, 169 ; Jane A.,
  173 ; John H., 173 ; John Henry, 173 (2) ;
  John Wrong, 169 ; Joseph, 48, 89 ; Rebecca
  Townsend, 169 ; Sam., 171 ; Wm. Parker, 89.
Leao, Abraham de, 203 ; Danell Josuah, 204 ;
  Moseh Pereira, 199, 203 ; Sarah, 204 ; Sarah
  Ester Pereira, 199.
Lear, 110.
Lear, Alice, 110 ; Sir Peter, 110 ; Sir Thomas,
  110 (2).
Leard, Charles, 144.
Leary, John, 34 ; Matthew, 34 (2).
Le Blanc, T. E., 15, 109.
Lee, Andrew Calvert, 74 ; Andrew Crichton,
  74 ; George, 47 ; Thomas, 47.
Le Gay, Benjamin, 30 ; Eliz., 30 ; Jacob, 30 ;
  John, 30 ; Kath., 30.
Legg, Edward, 88.
Le Hunt, Alex., 88.
Le Neve, —, 117.
Lenoir, Isaac, 87 ; John, 87.
Lernouet, Adrian Lernouet, 32.
Leslie, 187.
Leslie, John, 193 ; John, Baron of Balquhain,
  187 ; Rev. Wm., 187.
L'Espinasse, Editha, 39 ; John, 39.
Letob, Fonsada A. St. Ribca, 204.
Leverezio, Jacob Abraham, 199.
Levi, Jacob Joseph, 206.
Lewes, Ann, 194 ; John, 194.
Lewis, Isabella, 79 ; Rev. James, 191 ; John, 79,
  191 ; Maria Anne, 25 ; Rebecca, 191 ; Thomas,
  25 ; Wm. H., 192 ; .... durd, 134 ; *see also*
  Louis.
Lightbourn, Paul, 63.
Lillingston, G., 179 ; George, 179 ; Margt., 179.
Lindall, Abigail, 47.
Lindsay, John, 95, 105.
Littleton, Adam, 141 ; Sir Adam, 141 ; Edward,
  141 ; Thomas, 141 ; Sir Thomas, 141 (2).
Lopes (Lopez), Abraham, 207 ; Eliah, 207 ;
  Rachell, 207 ; —, 206.
Loraine, Sir Charles, 10 ; Henry James, 10 ; J.,
  15 ; Sir Wm., 10.
Lord, Gabriel, 135 ; Sam. Hall, 164.
Louis, 17.
Louis, Elliot Grasett, 89, 91 ; Marion Crawford,
  91 ; Mrs., 17 ; Thomas, 17, 89 ; Sir Thomas,
  17, 89 ; —, 164 ; *see also* Lewis.
Lousada (Loizada, Louzada), Aaron, 200 ; Aaron
  Baruh, 200 (2), 205, 206 ; Antonio, 198 ;
  David Baruch, 200 ; Eliau, 201 ; Ester, 200 ;
  Ester Sarah, 206 ; Francis Clifford, Duke de,
  206 ; Frederick Baruh, 107 ; Isaac, 201 ;

Isaac, Duke de, 200 ; Jacob, 201 (2) ; Jacob
  Baruh, 205 ; J. B., 200 ; Jeremy Baruch, 200 ;
  Moseh Baruh, 200 ; Ribcah, 205 ; Ribcah
  Baruh, 201 (2) ; Sarah, 200 ; S. C., 200.
Love, Clementina, 70 ; Nathaniel, 70.
Lovell, 169.
Lovell, Eliza, 87 ; Eliz. Went, 12 ; Phillip, 12
  (2) ; Robert, 12 ; Roger, 87 (2).
Lowe, Joseph, 19 ; Sarah Scott, 19.
Lowle (?), 136.
Lowther, Gov., 10.
Lucomb, Rosa, 54.
Lyde, Allan, 26 ; Francis, 26 ; Jane, 26.
Lydford, J., 15.
Lynch, Anthony, 88 ; Hellenor, 87 ; James, 22 ;
  James Alsop, 23, 106 ; James Challoner, 22 ;
  Rowena, 22, 106 ; Sarah Eliz., 106 ; Susannah,
  90 ; Walter Herbert, 24.
Lyte, 124.
Lyte, Bessie, 139 ; Jane, 124 ; John, 124, 128 ;
  Paul, 124 (2) ; —, 128, 139.

M

M ...., A., 167.
M ...., F. W., 174.
M ...., G., 129.
M ...., J., 167.
M ...., J. B., 194.
M ...., S. R., 86.
M ...., Wm., 31.
McAlpin, Charles, 62 ; Isabella St. Hill, 62 ;
  John, 62 (2) ; Marian, 62 ; Wm., 62.
Macbreedy, John King, 93.
McCabe, J., 15 ; Mary, 15.
MacCann, Robert, 67.
MacKay, Grissel, 173.
MacKenzie, Harriet, 108 ; Sinclair, 108.
McClean, Julian Wilkinson, 73 ; Marcus Byron,
  73 ; Maude Byron Chenery, 73 ; Wallace, 73.
Maclear, John, 98.
McClenahan, David, 46 (2) ; Eliz., 46 ; Na-
  thaniel, 46.
McCloud, Daniel, 181.
McClure, Francis, 71 ; Samuel, 71.
McCollin, E., 41.
McConney, Sarah Eliz., 48.
MacDermott, Geo., 35 ; Grace, 35.
McDonald, Sarah, 58.
McDougall, Duncan, 14 ; Lieut., 25.
McGeachy, Forster, 136.
McGlean, Geo. Mills, 68 ; Geo. Wilkinson, 68
  (3) ; Robert Arnott, 68.
McIntosh, Ann, 37 ; Thomas, 16, 37 ; —, 37.
McKenzie, John Bissett, 68 ; Lieut., 68.
McLaurin, Isabella, 50.
M'Nemara, Mary, 29 ; Michael, 29.
McNicol, Dugald C. F., 100 ; Jessie Maria, 100 ;
  Jessie Maria Bone, 95, 100 ; Mary E., 100.
McOhlery, David, 79 ; John, 78.
Macpherson, Hugh Fraser, 160.
McQueen, Jas., 76 ; Wm., 76.
McSwiney, Cath. Mary, 75 ; John, 75.
McWilliam, John, 54 (2) ; Martha E., 54.
Mahon, 157, 185.
Mahon, James, 157, 185 ; Margaret, 157, 185 ;
  Michael, 157, 185.
Maitland, Frederick, 123 ; Kath. Worsam, 123 ;
  Louisa, 123.
Mallins, J., 15.

F F

Surtees, V. A., 93, 104.
Swain, Comy.-Genl., 77 ; Marg. Ann, 77.
Swaris, David, 207.
Symons, John, 109.

T

Taggart, —, 121.
Tancock, Eliz. A., 75.
Taylor, Bryan, 165 ; Roland C., 192 ; Samuel, 37.
Terrill, Edward Brace, 50.
Tho . . . ., Charles, 43 ; Susannah, 43.
Thom, Aunt, 69.
Thomas, 38.
Thomas, Ann, 45, 63 ; Anthy. Henry, 124 ; Eliz., 149 ; Hannah, 38 (2) ; John, 45 (2), 101 ; John Pilaro . t, 34 ; Lynch, 63 ; Mary, 45, 149 ; Sarah, 39 ; Stephen, 38 (3) ; Wm., 4, 45, 183 ; —, 108.
Thompson, 177, 186.
Thompson, Christopher, 157, 186 ; Edward, 177 ; Jane Anne, 184 ; Katherine, 157 (2), 186 ; Samvell, 177.
Thornborough, Dr., 6 ; Geo., 87 ; Helen, 6.
Thorne, 89, 187.
Thorne, Benjamin, 58 ; Caroline, 105 ; Eliza S., 85 ; Eliz. Jemmett, 38 ; Elvira Cox, 85 ; Emma Louise Jane, 89 ; Henry Albert, 89 ; Hen. Edward, 89 ; H. A., 187 ; John, 38, 187, 190 ; John Shafe, 187, 190 ; Joseph, 28, 105 ; Rebecca Eliz., 187, 190 ; Sarah Jane, 38 ; . . . . en J. Harris, 38 ; —, 91.
Thornhill, 176.
Thornhill (Thornehill), Eliz., 176 ; Eliz. S., 124 ; Isaac, 176 ; John, 176 ; Lady, 9 ; Philippa, 27 ; Susanna, 176 (2) ; Thomas, 27 ; Sir Thomas, 9 ; Thomazin, 27 ; Timothy, 124, 176 (2) ; —, 142.
Thorpe, Alice, 144.
Thurbarne, Eliz. Anne, 91.
Tierney, John, 67.
Tinoco, Selomoi, 198.
Todd, S. K., 62.
Toosey, Frances, 12 ; Mary, 12 ; Wm., 12.
Toppin, Eliz. S., 190 ; Ino L., 190 ; Mehetable Morris, 160 ; Miles, 160 ; Robert Pilgrim, 160.
Torres, Ann Worrell, 60 ; Mr., 60.
Torez, Judicah, 207.
Tovey, Margaret, 4.
Trant, Maurice, 87 ; Richard, 87.
Trench, Le P., 93.
Trent, Auco, 141 ; Fra. Onslow, 145 ; Judith, 145.
Trent-Stoughton, Harrison Walke John, 145 (2) ; Rose, 145.
Trimingham, John Francis, 67 (2) ; Sarah Ann, 67 ; Warwick George, 67.
Trollope, F. C., 164 ; W. H., 206.
Trot, Samuel, 63.
Trotman, B., 46 ; Eliz., 127 ; Eliz. Ann, 133 ; Eliz. P. W., 133 ; Henry, 127 (2), 133 (3) ; John Warren, 133 ; Joseph, 133 (2) ; Simon Lee, 133 ; Susannah, 133 ; Tho., 127, 133 ; Tho. Clarke, 127 (2), 133 ; Wm., 118.
Trusler, Ann, 131 ; Jacob, 131 ; Mercy, 131.
Tryon, Rowland, 87 ; Susannah, 87.
Tudor, Tho., 44.
Tull, S. E., 96.
Tunckes, Thomas, 88.

Tur . . . ., —, 34.
Turner, Edwd. L. Disney, 121 ; Eliz. Augusta, 122 ; Fredk. Morse, 121 ; H. A., 121 (3) ; Hen. John, 95 ; R. Mathilda S., 121 ; Wilton Geo., 122.
Turpin, Sarah, 116.
Turton, Hen. Thos., 76.
Turney, John, 56 ; Lucretia, 56 ; Wm. M., 56.
Tynes, Aunt Thom., 69 ; J. N., 69 ; Jno. W., 24.
Tyler, 96.
Tyler, Geo. Henry, 180 ; John, 96, 102.
Tyley, J., 127.

U

Umphrey, Edward, 65 ; Eliz. Ann, 65 ; George, 65.

V

Vale, Ishac do, 202 ; Jacob Fonseco, 207.
Valpy, Dr., 54.
Valverde, Ab., 198, 199, 207 ; Jael, 198, 199 ; Moseh, 199 ; Riscah, 198 ; —, 205.
Vaughan, Robert, 87 ; —, 184, 193.
Venables, James, 120.
Verfenstein, Caroline, 97 ; Joseph, 97.
Veren, Nath., 47.
Vines, Richard, 87.
Vinor, Samuel, 87.
Vulliamy, Colwyn, 132 ; Lilian, 132 ; Lilian Isabel Dydogu Mary, 132.

W

W . . . ., C., 167.
W . . . ., K., 167.
Wade, —, 149.
Wadeson, 40.
Wadeson, Eliz., 40 (3) ; Samuel, 40 (5).
Wadlow, John, 87.
Wadsworth (Wadworth), Jane, 28 ; John, 28.
Waite, Edward, 85 ; Sarah, 85.
Waith, Eliz., 186 (2) ; John, 186 (2) ; Susannah Moll, 186.
Walcott (Walcot), Agnes D., 118, 119 ; Frances Caroline, 48 ; Margaret, 58 ; Rachel Frances, 181 ; Robert Bowie, 181.
Waldron, 107.
Waldron, Anthony, 107.
Walke, Tho., 145.
Walker, Eliz. Ann, 103 ; James, 103 ; Wm., 151.
Walley, George, 93, 98 ; Julia, 93, 98 ; Kat., 93, 98.
Walrond, 112.
Walrond, Ann, 38 ; Anthony, 38 ; Caroline Frances, 48 (2) ; Eliz., 112 ; Frances Caroline, 48 ; Francis Henry, 85 ; H., 46 ; Mabell, 38 (2) ; Nathaniel, 38 (2) ; Tho., 8, 112 ; W., 65 ; Wm., 48 ; . . . . ascom, 47 ; . . . . m, 47 ; —, 115, 133, 193.
Walter, Eliz. Christian, 148 ; Malinda, 148 ; Richard, 136 (2) ; Thomas, 148, 172.
Walters (Watters), John, 47.
Walton, Thomas, 80.
Walwyn, 143.
Walwyn, Jacob, 143.
Wanton, 28.

Wanton. Edward, 28 ; Ruth, 28 ; Wm., 28.
Ward, 4.
Ward, Agnes, 4 ; Espine, 109 ; Sir Henry, 11 ;
Henry T., 4 ; Joseph 4 ; Maria, 14 (2) ; Maria
Jane, 14 ; Tho., 4 ; Wm., 14 ; —, 109.
Wardall, 182.
Wardall, Robert, 182.
Warnep, J. J., 109.
Warner, Aucher, 91 ; Sir Thomas, 87.
Warren, 43.
Warren. Robert, 43 (2) ; Susannah, 43 ; Thomas,
43 ; Wm., Lucien, 131.
Waterman, Joseph, 157 ; —, 116.
Watson, Benj. L., 70 ; John, 70 ; Mary, 20 (2) ;
Mary G., 70 ; Sarah Christian, 20 ; Thomas,
55 ; Wm., 20, 172 (2).
Watts, Francis, 36.
Wayles, William, 45.
Webb, Rev. Wm. Thos., 195.
Webster, Frances R., 53 ; Rowland, 53.
Weekes, Frances Maynard, 49 ; Nath., 49 (2),
160 ; Nath. Sims, 160 ; Ralph, 49.
Welby, Sir W. Earle, 50 ; Lady Wilhelmina,
50.
Wellington, Duke of, 25.
Welman, William, 120.
Welsh, Eliz., 55 ; John, 55 ; Mary, 55 ; Thos.,
55.
West, Ann, 32 ; Sir Benjamin, 128 ; Edward,
32 ; Eliz. Ann, 32 ; Kath., 32.
Wharton, Rev. Thos., 37.
Wheeler, Thos. Honer, 104 ; Wm., 87.
Whetstone, John, 87.
White, Eliz., 29 ; Henry, 33 (2) ; Margaret, 33
(2) ; Millicent, 163, 167 ; William, 167.
Whitecote, Thomas, 174.
Whitelock, Bulstrode, 29 ; John, 29 ; Mary
Lewis, 29.
Whitfield, John F., 74 ; John Freer, 74.
Whitfoot, Thomas, 173.
Whitla, George, 73 ; Wm. John, 73.
Whitney, Margaret, 72 ; Samuel, 70, 72.
Wildey, Eliz., 46 ; Mary Sarah Lake, 46 ; Rich-
ard, 46.
Wilee, Ann, 131 ; Robert, 131 ; Valentine,
131 (2).
Wilkey, Wm. Henry, 60.
Wilkinson (Wilkingson), Charlotte, 165 ; Doro-
thy, 180 ; Francis Anne, 165 ; Jonas, 165 ;
Wm., 180.
William, King of England, 136.
Williams, Ann Gaskin, 31 ; Frances, 62 ; Henry,
96, 101, 121 ; James Thomas, 133 (3) ; Mar-
garet, 140 ; Margaret Eliz., 133 ; Margaret
Smith, 133 ; Robert, 121 ; Thomas, 92 ; —,
178.
Willing, Charles, 142 ; Eliz. Hannah, 142.
Willoughby, Cholmeley, 1 ; Dorothy Frere, 1 ;
Eliz., 42 ; Henry, 87 ; John, 15, 55 ; Lord,
153 ; Mary Ann, 15 ; Mary Clarke, 55 ; Tur-
pin, 183.
Willy, Roland, 140.
Wilson, Charles, 191 ; Eliz. Margaret, 191 ;
Fleetwood Thomas Hugh, 57 ; Harriet, 191 ;
Henry, 35 ; James Thos., 98 ; John, 98, 191 ;
Lieut.-Col., 98 ; Mark, 97 ; Wm., 82.
Wiltshire, Mary, 26 ; Garet, 26 ; Ri., 26 ; —,
206.
Winter, Eliz., 182 ; George, 72 ; John, 182 ;
Leouard, 72 ; Mary, 182 ; Sophia Mary Julia,
72 ; Wm. Bassell, 65.

Winterbottom, J., 93 ; John, 103, 104 ; Pene-
lope, 93, 104.
Winton, R. de, 93.
Wintour, Edward, 161 ; Jane, 161.
Withers, Mary, 5 ; Tho., 5.
Wood, H., 175 ; Jean, 177 ; Judith, 42 ; Samson,
42 (2) ; Sarah, 42 ; Thomas, 177 ; W., 15 ;
Wm., 120 ; —, 14, 16, 115.
Woodbridge, 137.
Woodbridge, Ann, 134 (2), 135, 137 (2) ; Rev.
Dudley, 134, 135, 137, 170 ; Ruth, 170.
Woodin, John, 31 ; Mary, 31 ; Samuel, 31 (2).
Woodward, —, 140.
Woolcott, John Rowden, 13.
Woolford, Ann, 36 (4) ; Dorothy, 36 ; Eliz., 36 ;
Rebecca, 36 ; Robert, 36 ; Thomas, 36 (3) ;
Walter Hyde, 36.
Worm, R. J., 39, 85 ; R. M., 39 ; Sydney, 39 ;
—, 178.
Wornum, Catherine, 24.
Worrell, 179.
Worrell, J., 178 ; Jonathan, 179.
Worsam, Kath., 123 ; Rich., 123.
Wrong, John, 47.
Wyatville, Ann, 12 ; Geo. Geoffrey, 12 ; Jeffrey,
12.

X

Ximenes, —, 206.

Y

Ydana, Abraham, 198 ; Jacob, 198 ; *see also*
Idanha.
Yeamans, Eliz., 194 ; Frances, 117 ; Sir John,
117 ; Mary, 32 ; Robert, 32.
Yearwood, Chas. Edward, 90 ; Mrs. Graham,
91 ; H. Graham, 174 ; John, 90 (2) ; John
Davidson Dalrymple, 90 ; John Kelly, 176 ;
John Washington, 81 ; Mary Olive, 90 ;
Muriel Olive Rose, 90 ; Sam. Thomas, 80 ;
Susannah, 90 ; Wm. Rich., 90.
Yeats (Yate), Margaret, 4 ; Mary, 4 (2) ; Rich-
ard, 4 ; Robert, 4 ; Thomas, 4 (2).
Yellings, 38.
Yellings, Eliz., 38 (2) ; John, 38 ; Mary, 38.
Young, Astley Ann Cooper, 160, 161 ; Bryan
Taylor, 22, 63 ; Charles Edwin, 94 ; Charles
Lewis, 94 ; Eliz., 159 ; Eliz. Ann, 22 ; Joseph,
42 ; Lewis, 159, 161 ; Marianne Charlotte,
160, 161 (2) ; Mary, 159, 161 ; Mary Edith,
94 ; Mary Eliz., 161 ; Nathan, 159, 161 ;
Nathan Lewis, 159, 160 (2), 161.

No Surname.

—, Alexr., 41.
—, Ann, 193.
—, Christr., 62.
—, Elspe., 41.
—, Francis, 193.
—, Garrett, 86.
—, Hester, 7.
—, John, 86.
—, John Thomas, 101.
—, Josephine. 82.
—, Judah, 203.
—, Ma., 45.
—, Sara, 205.
—, Sir Thomas, 7.
—, Zela, 198.
. . . . mew, E., 29 ; Hen-
ry, 29.
. . . . odri, Ester, 202.
. . . . okeley, Ag., 97 ;
Thomas, 97 ; —, 97.
. . . . pster, Cap., 129.
. . . . ton, Elinore, 35.

Arms without name, 150 (2), 186.

ABBREVIATIONS.

A.   " History of Antigua," by the Editor.

Archer.   " Monumental Inscriptions of the British West Indies," by Capt.
            Lawrence Archer.

C.   " Caribbeana," by the Editor.

Col. Cal.   Calendar of State Papers, Colonial Series, America and West Indies.

D.N.B.   " Dictionary of National Biography."

Foster.   " Alumni Oxonienses," by Joseph Foster.

Fothergill. " Emigrant Ministers to America 1690—1811," by Gerald Fothergill.

Hotten.   " The Original Lists of Emigrants to the American Plantations," by
            J. C. Hotten [with transcripts of some Barbadian Registers of
            1678—80].